DUBLIN CITY UNIVERSITY, 1980–2020

Dublin City University, 1980–2020

DESIGNED TO BE DIFFERENT

Eoin Kinsella

FOUR COURTS PRESS

Typeset in 10.5pt on 13pt Ehrhardt by
Carrigboy Typesetting Services for
FOUR COURTS PRESS LTD
7 Malpas Street, Dublin 8, Ireland
www.fourcourtspress.ie
and in North America for
FOUR COURTS PRESS
c/o IPG, 814 N Franklin St, Chicago, IL 60610

A catalogue record for this title is available
from the British Library.

ISBN 978-1-84682-808-9 (hardback)
ISBN 978-1-84682-809-6 (paperback)

Printed in England
by TJ International, Padstow, Cornwall

For Kate

Contents

Foreword

The year 2020 is very significant for Dublin City University – it marks forty years since the very first intake of students, thirty years since the establishment of our renowned Access programme, and it is the year in which the fourth president of the institution will commence in post. The publication of DCU's first authoritative and rigorous history represents an important milestone in this anniversary year. The motivation for commissioning this history of DCU was not only to mark these significant milestones but also to ensure that the historical record of such a rapidly changing and impactful institution could be captured as accurately as possible, when many of those directly involved in its development could contribute their personal recollections.

After just forty years of development and growth, DCU is not only a well-established and highly regarded institution in the higher education landscape in Ireland, but the university has also developed a significant international reputation based on key aspects of its mission and profile. At the time of writing, DCU is one of only two Irish universities selected by the European Commission to participate in the European Universities initiative, which is exploring innovative models of the 'University of the Future'. DCU is the only university on the island of Ireland that is ranked in the top 100 of the world's young universities (i.e. those established in the last fifty years) in both the QS and *THE* ranking tables, it is ranked twelfth in the world for its commitment to sustainability, and it is positioned in the top twenty globally for its graduate employment rate.

From a personal perspective, having been a member of the staff at DCU since 1986 and having had the privilege of being president of the university for almost a decade, I have developed a deep appreciation of the institution. For me, the key words that characterize DCU are dynamism, innovation, inclusion, and engagement. From the outset, DCU has always been a place of change – in campus landscape, in student population, in curriculum, in footprint, and in so many other areas – but it has never been about change for its own sake. Rather, the emphasis has always been on change with purpose. Much of the change can be linked to the culture of innovation in the university, where problems were always viewed as challenges to be overcome with creative solutions, and new ideas and better models were fostered in an atmosphere of positivity. From the beginning, DCU has been committed to educational opportunity, a commitment derived from a core belief that ability alone should be the determining factor regarding access to higher education. Our 'widening participation' agenda has grown significantly from its original focus on economic disadvantage to now address and overcome many other potential barriers to access, so that DCU is justifiably renowned for its culture of inclusion. We have always been committed to active engagement with our various communities. Indeed, DCU has been the antithesis of the 'ivory tower university' and this feature has resulted in many positive and sustained relationships with a broad range of organizations and communities in our region, stretching along the eastern corridor from Dublin city to the border.

Although Universities are complex, multi-faceted institutions, their role can be distilled into two core elements: the creation of knowledge and the development of rounded talent. From its establishment, these two elements have been central to DCU's strategic development and the university is now a highly regarded, research-intensive institution with an international reputation for the quality and impact of its graduates. From humble beginnings in the early 1980s, where research was carried out primarily by individual researchers and small groups in modest laboratories in prefabricated buildings, DCU now has a strong research profile across all of its five faculties, and boasts a number of major research centres of international repute hosted in impressive facilities. Academic excellence and scholarship are highly valued and hardly a year passes without at least one DCU staff member being admitted to the Royal Irish Academy, the highest tier of academic recognition in Ireland. Similarly, a culture of continuous improvement has permeated the education environment at DCU and the quality of the student learning experience has always been high on the agenda. Significant innovations have been introduced in the area of curriculum reform over the decades and the commitment of staff to such enhancements has been palpable. The positive feedback received on a regular basis from external stakeholders, especially employers, regarding the quality of DCU graduates is a testament to the efficacy and impact of these innovations. With our continued focus on developing rounded individuals, DCU graduates in Ireland and across the globe are contributing significantly to the advancement of society in all its dimensions.

I am delighted with the work carried out by the author of this history, Eoin Kinsella. He has delivered a comprehensive work based on rigorous research and detailed interviews and I want to express my gratitude to him on behalf of the university. DCU's first four decades have been captured in an appropriate and accurate fashion.

The success of organizations and institutions is always about people. DCU is no exception to this. In just four decades, the university has established itself as an important and impactful institution in both the national and international higher education landscape. All of this is rightfully attributed to the quality, commitment, loyalty and support of our staff, students, graduates and friends. For that we are hugely grateful, and I believe that the journey of impressive development captured in this book will bring great satisfaction to all of those who shared our journey. Go raibh maith agaibh!

Prof. Brian MacCraith
President, Dublin City University, 2010–20

Réamhrá

Is bliain shuntasach d'Ollscoil Chathair Bhaile Átha Cliath í an bhliain 2020 – sonraíonn sí dhá scór de bhlianta ón chéad líon iontrála mac agus iníon léinn, tríocha bliain ó chéadbhunaíodh ár gClár Rochtana clúiteach, agus is í an bhliain í ina gcuirfidh an ceathrú huachtarán tús lena ré san ollscoil. Léiríonn foilsiú an chéad chuntas údarásach, glinn de stair DCU sprioc cinniúnach sa bhliain chuimhneacháin seo. Ní amháin chun an chlochmhíle thábhachtach seo i stair na hollscoile a mharcáil a rinneadh an stair seo a choimisiúnú ach chun cuntas beacht, cruinn a thabhairt ar institiúid atá ag athrú go mear agus ag dul i gcion ar an phobal, agus iad siúd atá bainteach leis an fhorbairt seo a éascú lena gcuid machnaimh phearsanta a chur leis an staidéar.

Gan taobh thiar di ach daichead bliain d'fhorbairt agus d'fhás, is amhlaidh go bhfuil dlús curtha lena clú acadúil, chomh maith le rath ar cháil DCU i measc institiúidí tríú leibhéil na hÉireann. Lena chois sin tá urraim léirithe don Ollscoil go hidirnáisiúnta, fréamhaithe ina misean agus ina próifíl. In am seo a scríofa, níl ach dhá ollscoil de chuid na hÉireann roghnaithe ag an Choimisiún Eorpach – agus DCU mar cheann acu – le bheith páirteach i dTionscnamh na nOllscoileanna Eorpacha, tógra a fhiosraíonn múnlaí nuálacha do 'Ollscoil na Todhchaí'. Is í DCU an t-aon ollscoil amháin ar oileán na hÉireann a rangaítear taobh istigh den chéad 100 ollscoil óg barr feabhais (i.e. iad sin a bunaíodh le caoga bliain anuas) sna táblaí rangaithe QS agus *THE*, tá sí sa dara háit déag ar an domhan dá cuid tiomantais don inbhuanaitheacht, agus rangaítear í i measc an scór ollscoil ag barr an oird fheabhais go domhanda do ráta fostaíochta a cuid céimithe.

Ó mo dhearcadh pearsanta, mar bhall d'fhoireann DCU ó 1986 – agus d'onóir agam a bheith i m'Uachtarán le beagnach deich mbliain anuas – tá tuiscint thar na bearta agam ar an institiúid. Domsa, is iad na heochairfhocail a chuireann DCU in iúl ná spleodar, nuálachas, cuimsiú agus rannpháirtíocht. B'institiúid í DCU ariamh ina raibh borradh agus áthrú – ina líon mac/iníon léinn, ina curaclam, sa rian a d'fhág sí, agus i réimsí eile nach iad. Ach níor athrú ar mhaithe le hathrú amháin a bhí i gceist ariamh ach oiread. Leagadh béim i dtólamh ar athrú le cuspóir ar leith in aigne. Thig cuid mhór den athrú a cuireadh i bhfeidhm a cheangal le cultúr an nuálachais san ollscoil, institiúid ina mbreathnaítear ar fhadhbanna mar dhúshláin atá le sárú go cruthaitheach, áit a gcothaítear smaointe nua agus múnlaí nua in atamaisféar deimhnitheach. Ón tús, tá DCU ag tacú go diongbháilte le deis oideachasúil, le tiomantas a eascraíonn as croíchreideamh gurb é cumas an duine agus an cumas sin amháin a ba cheart rochtain ar ArdOideachas a ordú. Tá ár gclár 'leathnú rannpháirtíochta' i ndiaidh fás go suntasach ón bhunfhócas a bhíodh ann ar mhíbhuntáiste eacnamaíoch, leathnaithe amach anois chun freastal ar go leor cúiseanna eile a chuireann bac le dul chun cinn san earnáil, sa dóigh is go bhfuil clú tuillte agus tuillte go maith ag DCU anois as a cultúr cuimsithe. Ariamh anall bhí muid tiomanta do chaidreamh gníomhach agus rannpháirtíoch leis na pobail éagsúla a mbímid ag plé leo. Ar ndóigh, a mhalairt ar fad í DCU ón 'Ollscoil Thúr Eabhair' agus is í an ghné seo den institiúid a ghin an iomad buanchaidrimh dhearfacha le raon leathan eagraíochtaí agus pobail in oirthear na tíre, ag spréadh aneas ó Bhaile Átha Cliath go dtí an teorainn.

Bíodh is gur institiúidí casta, ilghnéitheacha iad ollscoileanna, thig a ról a dhríogadh in dhá bhunghné: cur chun cinn an eolais agus forbairt cumais ar bhonn iomlán. Ó bunaíodh í, tá an dá ghné seo lárnach i bhforbairt stráitéiseach DCU. Seasann an Ollscoil anois i lár an aonaigh mar institiúid cháilúil, dírithe ar thaighde, le clú idirnáisiúnta as siocair cháilíocht agus chaighdeán a cuid céimithe. Ó thosach simplí go luath sna 1980aidí, uair a dhéanadh taighdeoirí indibhidiúla agus grúpaí beaga a gcuid grinnscrúdaithe i saotharlanna bunúsacha i bhfoirgnimh réamhdhéanta, tá DCU anois ag léiriú go bhfuil próifíl láidir taighde aici thar an chúig dhámh ar fad, agus maíonn sí as líon sonrach lárionad taighde de chlú idirnáisiúnta, lonnaithe i saoráidí éachtacha. Tá meas ag an ollscoil ar an fheabhas acadúil agus ar an léann, agus is beag bliain nach nglactar le ball amháin foirne, ar a laghad, in Acadamh Ríoga na hÉireann – an leibhéal is airde scoláireachta in Éirinn. Ar an dul céanna, leathnaíonn cultúr síorfheabhsaithe ar fud thimpeallacht teagaisc DCU; i gcónaí, bhí taithí foghlama na mac/iníonacha léinn chun cinn i ngach beart a bhí againn. Tugadh isteach go leor nithe nuálaíocha thar na blianta in uasdátú an churaclaim, agus is ríléir diongbháilteacht na foirne agus iad ag dul i ngleic leis na feabhsuithe seo. Is teist í ar éifeacht agus ar thionchar na nuálaíochtaí seo an dea-aischothú a fhaigheann DCU mar gheall ar a céimithe ó pháirtithe leasmhara, go háirithe ó fhostaitheoirí. Agus muid ag strócadh linn chun daoine dea-oilte amach is amach a chothú, cuireann céimithe DCU go sonrach, go sainiúil agus go domhanda le cur chun cinn na sochaí i ngach gné ar fad.

Tá lúcháir orm faoin dua a léirigh údar an leabhair seo, Eoin Kinsella. Cuireann sé romhainn saothar cuimsitheach bunaithe ar dhiantaighde agus ar mhionshonrú sna hagallaimh. Thar cheann na hollscoile, ba mhaith liom mo bhuíochas a ghabháil leis. Tá cur síos beacht agus cruinn tugtha leis go hoiriúnach anseo.

Is ar na daoine atá ag feidhmiú iontu a mbraitheann dul chun cinn eagraíochtaí agus institiúidí, Ní eisceacht ar bith í DCU. Taobh istigh d'achar gearr, tá DCU i ndiaidh í féin a lonnú in earnáil oideachais ag an tríú leibhéil go suaitheanta agus go húimléideach. Is mar gheall ar an fhoireann atá ag obair inti gur féidir linn é sin a mhaíomh, agus de thairbhe na diongbháilteachta, na dúthrachta agus na tacaíochta a léiríonn siad don institiúid – gan trácht ar chuibheas agus ar chóiriúlacht ár gcuid mac agus iníonacha léinn, ár gcéimithe agus ár gcairde. Dar liom go mbainfear an-sásamh as an chur síos sa leabhar seo ar aistear forbartha na hinstitiúide i measc na ndaoine sin ar fad a bhí páirteach san imram seo. Go raibh maith agaibh!

An t-Ollamh Brian MacCraith,
Uachtarán, Ollscoil Chathair Bhaile Átha Cliath, 2010–20

Acknowledgments

Writing the history of any institution is a daunting task. This is especially true when the institution in question is relatively young and continues to evolve at a rapid pace. I am grateful to the president of DCU, Brian MacCraith, for entrusting me with this task, for giving an outsider unfettered access to the President's Office Archive, and for placing the university's resources at my disposal. I have been fortunate to receive help, guidance and support from many quarters during this project, particularly from retired and current members of DCU's staff, as well as former students. Thanks to Fina Akintola, Sheila Bridgeman, Martin Clynes, Mary Colgan, Gaye Crowley, Chris Curran, Vikki Doyle, Ciarán Fagan, Alan Floyd, Anthony Glynn, Mark Glynn, Daire Hall, Richard Kelly, Colum Kenny, Colette Keogh, Maeve Long, Ciarán Mac Murchaidh, Gerard McEvoy, Brigid McManus, David Meehan, Danielle Montgomery, Alice O'Byrne, Theresa O'Farrell, Danny O'Hare, Ferdinand von Prondzynski, Adolfo Rey, Anne Scott, Frank Soughley, Joseph Stokes and Deirdre Wynter. Michael Burke, Eugene Kennedy, Pat O'Mahony and Brian Trench generously shared their memories and made personal collections of material relating to NIHED/DCU available to assist my research. Juliette Péchenart kindly provided me with a copy of a history of the School of Applied Languages and Intercultural Studies – a wonderful example of the value of microhistory for capturing institutional memories.

Help with university statistics came from a variety of sources. Aisling McKenna and Karen Johnston of the university's Quality Promotion Office, and Cathy McLoughlin of the Access Service, provided me with highly detailed student statistics. Martin Leavy, Aoife Minahan and Norma Wilkinson of Human Resources provided me with same relating to staff. Phylomena McMorrow, Valerie Cooke and Orna Heuston filled in many gaps in the list of Chancellor's Medal recipients found in appendix 5. Eamonn Cuggy and John Kilcoyne helped assemble financial information, while Plunkett Tormay of DCU Educational Trust kindly clarified several aspects of the Trust's operations. I am very grateful to all for their assistance.

Special mention must go to Yvonne Duff, Susan Folan and David O'Callaghan, who, in the absence of a formal institutional archiving policy, for many years acted as guardians and curators of DCU's visual and written records. Without their efforts to preserve historical papers, photographs and ephemera – particularly for the period 1975 to 2000 – this project would not have been possible. Along with her colleagues Natalie Hooper and Jane Neville, Yvonne also kindly assisted me with several research queries. Susan clarified numerous points, while David provided me with digital copies of the majority of the photographs reproduced in this book – many of which he took himself. DCU owes them a debt of gratitude for ensuring that much of its history has not been irretrievably lost.

The university convened a committee to assist with my research, and I am very grateful to Patricia Barker, Ellen Breen, Susan Folan, Padraig McKeon, Ross Munnelly, Helena Sheehan, Frank Soughley, and Brian Trench for their advice and encouragement. Two other committee members, Mary Canning and John Horgan, read the entire manuscript in draft and provided invaluable feedback. Special thanks to Daire Keogh and Albert Pratt, both for reading and commenting on the manuscript, and for ensuring that I received all of the support and resources I needed to complete my work. The School of History and Geography at the St Patrick's campus in Drumcondra provided a welcome and stimulating home for much of this project. I am particularly grateful to the head of school, James Kelly, both for his advice as a member of the project committee and for providing a home, and to Neville Scarlett for generously sharing his office. Thanks also to Juliana Adelman, Jonathan Cherry, Marnie Hay and William Murphy for their company and advice.

In addition to the help I have received from within DCU, I am grateful to Ciara Kerrigan, assistant keeper at the National Library of Ireland, for her assistance in tracking down material in the Chief Herald's Office. Brigid McManus, former secretary general of the Department of Education and Skills, shared her memories of the Incorporation process. Caroline McGee introduced me to the archivists at Cornell University who have responsibility for the archive of Atlantic Philanthropies. Despite the fact that this material was closed to public access until 2020, Joanne Volpe Florino and Phoebe Kowalewski very generously arranged for me to consult the material relating to DCU during the summer of 2018 and ensured that my visit to Ithaca went smoothly. Thanks also to Michael Kennedy and John Gibney of Documents on Irish Foreign Policy for their encouragement, and to Carole Holohan of Trinity College Dublin, who graciously took the time to read and improve much of the manuscript.

Most importantly, my thanks to my wife, Lily, who not only helped with the conversion of statistics into tables and graphs, but whose support and selflessness after Kate's arrival enabled me to complete this project.

Illustrations

PLATES

(*between pp 140 and 141*)

FIGURES

TABLES

Abbreviations

EDITORIAL NOTE

Dublin City University has had two formal designations. Between 1974 and 1989 it was known as the National Institute for Higher Education, Dublin. The text that follows refers to 'the Institute' or 'NIHE Dublin' when discussing that period. NIHED is used in footnotes. 'Dublin City University', 'DCU' or 'the university' are used for the period after 1989. When discussing topics or themes relevant both before and after 1989, NIHED/DCU is preferred. All references to pounds (£) in the text refer to the Irish punt.

AC	academic council, minutes and papers
AFI	Academic Framework for Innovation
APA	Atlantic Philanthropies Archives #8540, Division of Rare and Manuscript Collections, Cornell University Library
BITE	Ballymun Initiative for Third Level Education
BRL	Ballymun Regeneration Ltd
CAO	Central Applications Office
CDVEC	City of Dublin Vocational Education Committee
CHIU	Conference of Heads of Irish Universities
CICE	Church of Ireland College of Education
CII	Confederation of Irish Industry
DCU	Dublin City University
DCUET	DCU Educational Trust
DCUPO	President's Office Archive, Dublin City University
DCUSU	DCU Students' Union
DIB	James McGuire and James Quinn (eds), *Dictionary of Irish Biography* (Cambridge, 2009) and dib.cambridge.org
DIT	Dublin Institute of Technology
ECTS	European Credit Transfer System
EEC	European Economic Community
GA	governing authority, minutes and papers
GB	governing body, minutes and papers
HEA	Higher Education Authority
HEDAS	Higher Education Direct Access Scheme
ICSTI	The Irish Council for Science, Technology and Innovation
IDA	Industrial Development Authority

IFUT	Irish Federation of University Teachers
ILU	Industrial Liaison Unit
INTRA	INtegrated TRAining scheme
NAI	National Archives of Ireland
NBST	National Board for Science and Technology
NCEA	National Council for Educational Awards
NDEC	National Distance Education Centre
NIHED	National Institute for Higher Education, Dublin
NIHEL	National Institute for Higher Education, Limerick
NUI	National University of Ireland
OECD	Organisation for Economic Co-operation and Development
PRTLI	Programme for Research in Third-Level Institutions
RCSI	Royal College of Surgeons in Ireland
RHA	Royal Hibernian Academy
RIAM	Royal Irish Academy of Music
RTC	regional technical colleges
SFI	Science Foundation Ireland
SIPTU	Services, Industrial, Professional and Technical Union
STEM	science, technology, engineering and mathematics
UCC	University College Cork
UCD	University College Dublin
UCDA	University College Dublin Archives
UL	University of Limerick

Introduction

On 31 July 1981 the minister for education, John Boland, addressed the governors of the National Institute for Higher Education, Dublin.[1] With the Institute's first academic year just completed, Boland highlighted its importance to Ireland's future and welcomed the arrival of a new form of third-level education:

> The National Institute for Higher Education, Dublin is a new higher education institute – equivalent to a technological university – designed for modern times and for the future. The primary role of the Institute is to produce well qualified graduates with a breadth of practical knowledge attuned to a rapidly changing technologically-based society ... NIHE Dublin, while placing a high value on applied studies, also places a heavy emphasis on research and its associated activities. This approach results in staff being fully aware of industry's needs and of current practice in industry. It also ensures that staff make an effective contribution to industrial development and innovation.[2]

Conceived as part of a radical restructuring of Irish higher education, the Institute's opening in November 1980 marked the endpoint of a decade-long expansion of the sector, unprecedented in the history of the state.[3] That expansion largely focused on the areas of technical and technological education, prompted by a series of reports produced during the 1960s and early 1970s that highlighted the state's shortcomings in these areas and the need for a new generation of highly skilled graduates in targeted areas.

This book draws upon the records available to provide an overview of the university's history, outlining the context in which NIHE Dublin was established and subsequently operated, as well as the development and maintenance of educational philosophies, curricula and pedagogical approaches. I have also highlighted pivotal moments in the university's evolution, mapped the physical transformation of the university's campus and infrastructure in a crowded urban

---

1 Boland's address coincided with the first meeting of the Institute's statutory governing body. See chapter 2 for more on legislation for the Institute, enacted in 1980, and governing body's appointment and activities between 1975 and 1981. 2 Speech by John Boland, minister for education, 31 July 1981 (DCUPO, 'NIHE Dublin: general'). 3 The 1970s had seen the opening of the National Institute for Higher Education in Limerick (1972), while regional technical colleges were opened at Athlone (1970), Carlow (1970), Dundalk (1970), Sligo (1970), Waterford (1970),

environment, and provided insights into its pioneering engagement with socially innovative education strategies and community outreach.

Plans for the creation of a new, degree-level educational institution in Dublin had been in gestation since the late 1960s, though the proposal was not formally adopted as government policy until December 1974. The subsequent six-year delay in opening the Institute arose from a multitude of factors, including a bitter dispute over the future of technological education in Dublin, and a lack of clarity in government policy. Less than a decade after opening its doors, however, NIHE Dublin was adjudged to have implemented teaching and research programmes of a standard that matched or exceeded the traditional universities, leading to its inauguration as Dublin City University in September 1989. Over the ensuing thirty years the university has experienced significant growth in every area. Teaching capacity, research expertise, student population and international prestige have all been enhanced despite numerous challenges, both internal and external.

Such growth has been achieved through the lows of the economic crises of the 1980s and 2010s, as well as the highs of major philanthropic support and increased research funding witnessed during the 1990s and early 2000s. NIHE Dublin was designed to be different to any other degree-level institution in Ireland – more technical in its educational focus than the universities or NIHE Limerick, and distinguished from regional technical colleges by the strength of its research programmes. Established as the paradigm of human capital development began to permeate government policy for higher education, the Institute was intended to represent a new era in Irish education and to enhance the connections between the industrial, commercial and higher-education sectors.[4] DCU has subsequently evolved as an occasionally uneasy synthesis of liberal ideals of university education and a vision of higher education as a tool for economic development. While its goal of producing graduates tailor-made for the employment market remains unchanged, recognition of the trans-formational nature of higher education has seen a number of additions to the university's mission, softening its intense focus on serving the national economy. University status was the catalyst for sustained engagement with local communities and concerted efforts to widen access to education, forming the

Letterkenny (1971), Galway (1972), Cork (1974) and Tralee (1977). For an overview of the history of higher-education policy during this period, see John Walsh, *Higher education in Ireland, 1922–2016: politics, policy and power – a history of higher education in the Irish state* (London, 2018) and Tony White, *Investing in people: higher education in Ireland from 1960 to 2000* (Dublin, 2001).
4 NIHED Statement of Mission, 8 June 1983 (NIHED, *Academic procedures* (Dublin, 1987), pp 7–8). For the development of NIHED/DCU's curriculum, see chapter 5. For more on human-capital theory and its impact on Irish higher education, see Walsh, *Higher education in Ireland*, pp 233–46, 387–449; Denis O'Sullivan, *Cultural politics and Irish education since the 1950s: policy, paradigms and power* (Dublin, 2006), pp 100–50.

base of a more recent focus on socially innovative education strategies led by staff and students. The chapters that follow trace the evolution of NIHED/DCU over more than four decades, from the appointment of its first governing body in 1975 up to the aftermath of the Incorporation process, completed in 2016. Chapters 2, 3 and 4 offer a chronological overview of the university's development, while the subsequent three chapters provide thematic analyses, focusing on educational ethos and curriculum, campus development and engagement with the local community.

Chapter 2 provides the context in which NIHE Dublin was conceived and brought into existence. As the government embraced the link between economic prosperity and investment in education, its focus was concentrated on increasing the number of graduates with technical and technological training. Regular changes in government and ministerial tenures ensured a lack of consistency in the formation of policies for the future of higher education in Dublin. As a result of the ensuing 'technological tangle', and despite the evident need for an increase in the number of third-level places in the city, the Institute faced vigorous opposition from within the higher-education sector. This was especially true in the case of the City of Dublin Vocational Education Committee, whose plans to use the Albert College site in Glasnevin were thwarted. This chapter also examines the legislation enacted to place the Institute on a statutory footing, alongside governing body's preparations for the opening of the Institute, including its efforts to locate the Institute on an alternative site in north Dublin.

Between 1975 and 1980, NIHE Dublin's governing body overcame a series of challenges to the existence of the Institute, before its doors had even opened to students. Once that milestone had been achieved, challenges of a different order arose. Chapter 3 examines the nine years between the admission of the Institute's first students and its inauguration as Dublin City University. Relations between the Institute, the Higher Education Authority and the Department of Education were frequently strained, due in no small part to restrictions placed on the Institute's autonomy and the sustained lack of government funding. The ability of NIHED/DCU's staff to overcome chronic underfunding and a paucity of resources to deliver high-quality education and conduct high-quality research provides one of the narrative threads of the institution's history. Their efforts were key to convincing a body of international experts that the Institute was operating at a standard at least equivalent to the universities. It would be another two years after that body presented its recommendations before NIHE Dublin became DCU, the first university to be established in Dublin north of the River Liffey.

Chapter 4 sheds light on several inflection points in the history of DCU that have proven key to its evolution. The arrival of sustained and unprecedented levels of financial support from Atlantic Philanthropies in 1989/90 allowed for major investment in the development of the university's campus, particularly its teaching and research capacities. That funding was augmented by increased government support, including the introduction of the PRTLI and SFI schemes. Those major funding schemes were introduced at the turn of the millennium, shortly after the implementation of the 1997 Universities Act and retirement of the university's founding president, Danny O'Hare. Chapter 4 also explores the linkages between the university and higher-education institutions in its locality, beginning with St Patrick's College, Drumcondra, in 1993. Almost twenty years later the university began the Incorporation process, whereby St Patrick's College, Mater Dei Institute and the Church of Ireland College of Education became fully integrated into the university. That process culminated in a major expansion to the Faculty of Humanities and Social Sciences, along with the creation of the Institute of Education, Ireland's first faculty dedicated to teacher education from primary through to third level.

NIHE Dublin represented a new departure in the provision of degree-level technological education. Its mandate to anticipate and meet the needs of industry was foregrounded in the development of the Institute's educational ethos and curriculum, dominating discussions around academic development for much of the following two decades. Chapter 5 outlines the development of that educational ethos, its embodiment in the design of degree programmes and the importance of academic council to the continued evolution of the curriculum. To devote adequate time to the work each school and faculty within NIHED/DCU invested in enhancing pedagogical techniques and learning experiences would require a multi-volume history. Chapter 5 instead offers case studies of the INTRA programme, distance education and the introduction of academic credits for students' extracurricular work, key components in the delivery of a diverse and innovative education experience.

Arriving on campus in late October 1980 to take up a post with the School of Biotechnology, Richard O'Kennedy found 'incomplete and defective labs and a chronic shortage of everything'.[5] Aerial photographs of the Institute taken in 1981 (see plate 11) illustrate the lack of facilities available on campus; the Institute's physical size was doubled by two buildings newly opened that year. Chapter 6 traces the physical development of NIHED/DCU from a single-campus institution, with just 191 students, into a multi-campus university that serves more than 17,000 students each year. The institution that exists today differs greatly from the vision set out by NIHE Dublin's planners in the late 1970s. The analysis presented in this chapter augments chapter 3 in outlining the debilitating effects of a lack of finance and investment in NIHE Dublin during the 1980s. Particular attention is paid to the development master plans drafted by renowned architect Arthur Gibney during the 1980s. The first plan was visionary in its conception of a unified campus connected by glazed 'streets', but

5 Richard O'Kennedy, 'Coming of age: 21 years at DCU', *DCU News*, Mar. 2002.

ultimately proved unattainable. Under pressure to adopt a scheme more amenable to a modular development better suited to inconsistent and piecemeal funding, Gibney provided a revised plan that set in place the future arrangement of the campus around a central mall – a design that endures today. The role of Atlantic Philanthropies in the university's development is once again highlighted. Case studies of the planning and construction of the Helix and the sports centre, as well as strategic land purchases, demonstrate the pressures brought to bear on the university's infrastructure as student enrolment steadily increased.

Located less than two kilometres from the centre of Ballymun town, NIHE Dublin opened during a national economic recession. The effects of that recession were felt all the more acutely in Ballymun, and across much of the Institute's immediate locality. Planning for the Institute during the 1970s had emphasized the importance of establishing close ties with the local community, but a distinct lack of resources and consequent inward focus meant that aspiration was largely unmet in the 1980s. The arrival in 1989 of university status, alongside significant philanthropic and European Community funding, provided the catalyst for greater interaction with the university's surroundings. Chapter 7 traces the evolution of the Access programme at DCU – designed to increase participation rates for disadvantaged students – from its beginnings in 1990 as the BITE and Direct Access programme, through to its present incarnation. The policies and programmes introduced by DCU to widen access to education were not only largely unprecedented in Ireland, they proved highly influential in the subsequent development of national policy on the issue. This chapter also examines other initiatives designed to increase the university's engagement with its locality, including the DCU in the Community programme, and its collaboration with community groups and enterprises endeavouring to stimulate the economy of the north Dublin region and regenerate Ballymun town.

A NOTE ON SOURCES

This book is in fact the third official history of DCU, though it is the first to be written in two decades. In seeking to present the most authoritative account of the university's genesis and evolution yet written, I have been fortunate to have the work of John Horgan and Tony Bradley to build upon. Formerly members of the academic and administrative staff at NIHED and DCU, respectively, Horgan and Bradley compiled their histories to mark significant institutional milestones. Horgan's *Dublin City University: context and concept*, published in September 1989, was written to commemorate NIHE Dublin's inauguration as Dublin City University. A decade later, Bradley's pictorial history of DCU was commissioned to mark the retirement of Daniel O'Hare, NIHED/DCU's long-serving president.[6] Both works provided detail of the kind that can no longer be found in written records, and proved invaluable as guides to the major milestones of the 1980s and 1990s. What follows in chapters 2, 3 and 4 amplifies and expands upon some of the details and conclusions presented in both works.

In a memorandum drafted in 1989, Danny O'Hare compiled a list of problems arising from the government's failure to invest in the university's infrastructure. Apart from inadequate teaching and research facilities, one of the more trivial problems related to the keeping of records. There was no central archive for filing important documents: 'No space for it; files are dispersed throughout the Institute in offices and filing cabinets.'[7] Perhaps as a result of this lack of space, NIHED/DCU never implemented a formal archival policy for the preservation and storage of important documents, or of institutional ephemera. In the absence of such a policy, the university's archive consists of records that were generated by or passed through and were retained by the President's Office. Over time, that material has been curated and preserved (in difficult conditions) by the office's administrative staff.

The key collection in the President's Office Archive is a comprehensive set of minutes and papers generated by governance committees, including governing body/authority and academic council. The records are otherwise arranged thematically and stored in box files. Access to these records was unrestricted, and they have provided the bulk of the material used in writing this book. Between 1975 and 1998 NIHED/DCU produced annual reports that constitute a treasure trove of information, featuring reports on individual schools, academic units and staff activities. Publication of such reports ceased between 1999 and 2004 and, though resumed in 2005, thereafter adopted a shorter format with a consequent loss of insight into the university's internal activities.[8] Two informative newsletters, *Nuacht* (first published in June 1983) and *Newslink* (first published in January 1984), ceased publication in 1996 and 1999, respectively. An informal staff newsletter, *By Degrees*, briefly and intermittently appeared in the early 1980s. Surviving copies of similarly or even shorter-lived newsletters, information notices and miscellaneous staff publications have proven elusive. The survival of student publications is even patchier. At the time of writing, government records were only available up to 1988. The evidential deficit is compounded by the fact that the records in the President's Office Archive are

6 John Horgan, *Dublin City University: context and concept* (Dublin, 1989); Tony Bradley, *'Twigs for an eagle's nest': a pictorial history of Dublin City University* (Dublin, 1999).   7 Undated memorandum, *c.*1989 (DCUPO, 'NIHE Dublin physical matters, 1978–86, 2/2').   8 NIHED, *Annual reports, 1978–88*; DCU, *Annual reports, 1989–98*; DCU, *President's reports, 2005–15*. No annual reports exist for the period 1999 to 2004, or from 2015 onwards. The first two 'annual' reports published by NIHE Dublin covered the periods 1975–8 and 1978–82. The reports grew in length each year, culminating in a 500-page report for 1997/8.

richest for the period from 1975 to the end of the millennium. There are a number of reasons for this, not least the increasingly prevalent use of electronic communication between staff from the mid-1990s, as well as between the university and outside bodies. As might be expected given the source and nature of the archive, the records utilized in reconstructing the university's history largely present a top-down picture of the university's affairs, with consequent impact on the topics explored in the narrative that follows. My ability to draw upon the records of Atlantic Philanthropies (housed in Cornell University) has partially mitigated the effects both of the lacunae in the university's archive and its focus on the administration. Atlantic's records also provide an invaluable perspective from beyond the university's cloister, particularly for the 1990s.

While the President's Office Archive contains a number of records generated by each school, faculty and academic unit, I have not drawn deeply upon them for this work. It would not have been possible to do justice to the university's schools and faculties within the space allotted. These records would, however, provide excellent source material for postgraduate work on the development of academic programmes and the intricacies and politics of school and faculty administration. They might also be used by the schools to produce accounts of their individual histories. Published in 2012 to mark its 30th anniversary, the School of Applied Languages and Intercultural Studies has produced a short history that nonetheless serves as an exemplar of the preservation of institutional memory and an ideal template for any school with similar ambitions.[9] Such histories would also serve another purpose. The many academic milestones of NIHED/DCU's staff stretch across four decades and multiple fields of inquiry. They constitute a considerable body of work that stands as a testament to the foresight of NIHE Dublin's planners in integrating research as part of its ethos, and to the quality of academic staff. It is, however, beyond the scope of this book (and the abilities of its author) to assess the achievements of specialists in fields in which I have no training – such assessments are best left to those with the required knowledge, and might well also form the basis of postgraduate inquiry at the university's Institute of Education.

THE EDUCATIONAL LEGACY OF THE GLASNEVIN CAMPUS

Before delving into the history of the university proper, it is worth noting that its location in Glasnevin and the retention of the name Albert College for one of its original buildings continues a tradition that reaches back to the mid-nineteenth century. Many of those present at the turning of the sod ceremony

9 Juliette Péchenart and Jenny Williams (eds), *School of Applied Languages and Intercultural Studies: celebrating 30 years, 1980–2010* (Dublin, 2012).

for NIHE Dublin, held on 1 April 1980, were aware of the long history and educational heritage of the campus. By opening its doors to students seven months later, the Institute ensured the continuation of a tradition of scientific and technical education that began in 1838, encompassing Albert Agricultural College, the Royal College of Science and University College Dublin. One of those in attendance on 1 April, Roger Hussey, afterwards wrote to Danny O'Hare, enclosing a photocopy of his father's history of Albert Agricultural College.[10] An original copy had been discovered by a workman during the renovation of the Albert College building, but, perhaps thinking it might have some value, he could not be persuaded to donate it to the Institute. Hussey's gift was thus all the more appreciated. Registrar Donal Clarke replied to say that he considered it to be of great value: 'We are very interested in preserving the historical associations of the site and before receiving your photocopy I had been planning to try every possible source to see if I could trace a copy.'[11]

Hussey felt compelled to send the book because of the clear parallels between NIHE Dublin's educational mission, and that of Albert Agricultural College: 'It is intriguing to read that the original establishment was set up in the 1830s with the aim of fostering national scientific education – sounds familiar.'[12] In addition to sharing an educational ethos, the Institute's location on the north side of the city was a conscious choice in a city with two universities and a preponderance of higher-education institutions south of the river Liffey. There was nonetheless a long tradition of education and scientific research in north Co. Dublin, stretching back to the late eighteenth century, in which NIHE Dublin would swiftly take its place. Established in 1785, Dunsink Observatory has provided a home to generations of scientists and academics, including the famed mathematician Sir William Rowan Hamilton.[13] The following century saw the foundation of a seminary at All Hallows and St Patrick's teacher-training college in Drumcondra.[14]

Until the arrival of NIHE Dublin in 1980, however, the area was best known for its contribution to the teaching and study of agricultural science. It was at the National Botanic Gardens that David Moore first noticed the potato blight in

10 F.P. Hussey, *Albert Agricultural College: centenary souvenir, 1838–1938* ([Dublin], 1938). Hussey had served as a lecturer at the Glasnevin campus from 1926 to 1961, as a member of UCD's Faculty of Agriculture.   **11** Donal Clarke to R.F. Hussey, 29 Apr. 1980 (DCUPO, 'NIHE Dublin general, 1/2'). Clarke was NIHED's first registrar, and served in the post until 1987, when he joined Bord na Móna as secretary.   **12** R.F. Hussey to Danny O'Hare, 3 Apr. 1980 (DCUPO, 'NIHE Dublin general, 1/2').   **13** David Spearman, 'Hamilton, Sir William Rowan (1805–65)' in *DIB*. Hamilton is best known for his discovery of quaternions in 1843, though he also made important contributions to the study of algebra, optics and the wider field of physics. Following the decision to grant university status to NIHE Dublin in 1989, several names for the new university were considered, including Rowan Hamilton University, Dublin. The university's first major Research and Development building, completed in 1990, was renamed in Hamilton's honour in 2016 (see chapter 6).   **14** St Patrick's signed a linkage agreement with DCU in 1993 before being formally incorporated into the university in 2016. All Hallows closed its doors in 2016, and DCU acquired

1.1 Aerial view of Albert College from the south-east, *c*.1930s. Reproduced by kind permission of UCD Archives (UCDA, AAC1/91).

1845 and predicted its devastating effects.[15] The area's agricultural roots were further strengthened with the opening of Glasnevin Model Farm. Later known as Albert Agricultural College, this teaching and research institution was established by the Board of National Education in 1838; its campus would host agricultural researchers and students for the next 140 years. As was later the case with NIHE Dublin, the model farm's origins lay in a period of transformational educational reform. Seeking to streamline the national school system, during the 1830s the Board of National Education introduced approved textbooks and a standardized curriculum.[16] Reform of the country's agricultural sector was also in the Board's sights. Despite the importance of agriculture to the economy, farming methods were outdated and agricultural education poorly developed. The Board's attempts to rectify this situation saw the introduction of

the campus that year. See chapter 4.   **15** E.C. Nelson, 'David Moore, Miles J. Berkeley and scientific studies of potato blight in Ireland, 1845–7', *Archives of Natural History*, 11:2 (1983), pp 249–61; Patricia M. Byrne, 'Moore, David (1808–79)' in *DIB*. The National Botanic Gardens were established in 1795 following a grant from the Irish parliament to the Dublin Society.   **16** Children were, however, taught religion according to the denomination of their school (John Coolahan, 'The daring first decade of the Board of National Education, 1831–41', *Irish Journal of Education*, 17 (1983), pp 35–54; Tom Walsh, 'The national system of education, 1831–2000' in Brendan Walsh (ed.), *Essays in the history of Irish education* (London, 2016), pp 15–17).

agricultural studies to the national school curriculum and the creation of model schools to train teachers and farmers in the latest farming methods. Glasnevin Model Farm was the first such school established, and its opening in 1838 represented a pivotal moment in agricultural education.[17]

The success of the teaching and experimental-research programmes at Glasnevin Model Farm prompted the Board of National Education to set up a further twenty model schools.[18] In 1858 one of Glasnevin's students won an agricultural essay competition arranged by the Massachusetts Society for Promoting Agriculture, followed by a formal linkage agreement with Pennsylvania State Agriculture College the following year. Glasnevin's international reputation grew further when it was used as a template for agricultural education in eastern Canada.[19]

The growing fame of Glasnevin Model Farm was also noticed across the Irish Sea, leading to an August 1853 visit from Prince Albert, husband to Queen Victoria. Prince Albert's inspection of Glasnevin came during a royal visit intended to show solidarity with a population recovering from the devastating effects of the Famine. More particularly, Albert and Victoria visited to lend their support to the Irish Industrial Exhibition, held on the grounds of Leinster House and sponsored by William Dargan, engineer and railway pioneer.[20] Evidently impressed, Albert sent a member of staff from his own estate in England to be trained at Glasnevin, and consented to the school changing its name to the Albert National Agricultural Training Institution in his honour.[21] The name Albert Agricultural College was first recorded at the end of the nineteenth century, and in 1899 responsibility for the institution was transferred from the Board of National Education to the newly created Department of Agriculture and Technical Instruction.[22] Soon after the transfer the college was incorporated into the Royal College of Science's agriculture faculty, leading to a renewed focus on research and experimental work.[23]

---

17 Hussey, *Albert Agricultural College*, pp 11–20; Mary Daly, *The first department: a history of the Department of Agriculture* (Dublin, 2002), pp 24–5. 18 Daniel Hoctor, *The department's story: a history of the Department of Agriculture* (Dublin, 1971), pp 13–15. 19 Hussey, *Albert Agricultural College*, pp 24–6. See also Richard A. Jarrell, *Educating the neglected majority: the struggle for agricultural and technical education in nineteenth-century Ontario and Quebec* (Toronto, 2016); Juliana Adelman, *Communities of science in nineteenth-century Ireland* (New York, 2009). 20 Dargan was inspired by the Crystal Palace Exhibition, held in London in 1851. Following the template established by that event, Dargan commissioned a lavish, temporary building to house the exhibition (John Sproule, *The Irish Industrial Exhibition of 1853* (Dublin, 1854); Fergus Mulligan, 'Dargan, William (1799–1867)' in *DIB*). 21 Prince Albert later returned to the institution in 1867, and sent a number of his pigs, of the Large White Yorkshire breed, to Glasnevin, where they were cross-bred with the Institute's stock (Hussey, *Albert Agricultural College*, pp 21, 80). 22 The contribution of Albert Agricultural College to Irish agricultural science has not always been appreciated or understood by members of DCU's staff. See Bradley, *'Twigs for an eagle's nest'*, p. 225; cf. Ian Miller, *Reforming food in post-Famine Ireland: medicine, science and improvement, 1845–1922* (Manchester, 2014), pp 48–59. 23 Hussey, *Albert Agricultural College*, p. 93; Daly, *The first*

1.2 Chemistry lab, Albert College (undated). Reproduced by kind permission of UCD Archives (UCDA, AAC1/128r).

Following the extraordinary changes in Irish society wrought by the War of Independence (1919–21), the foundation of the Irish Free State (1922) and the Civil War (1922–3), the Royal College of Science was absorbed into University College Dublin, providing that university with much-needed staff and facilities. Under the provisions of the University Education (Agriculture and Dairy Science) Act of 1926, the premises and functions of Albert Agricultural College were transferred to UCD, forming the basis of its Faculty of General Agriculture.[24] Over the next five decades, courses taught at Albert College under the faculty's aegis adapted to the changing face of the agricultural economy and to keep pace with advances in farming technology.[25] By the 1960s, however, the premises were no longer fit for purpose. Rising student numbers and the increasing urbanization of the surrounding areas placed a strain on facilities, prompting UCD to seek more suitable accommodation. The Lyons Estate near Celbridge, Co. Kildare, was subsequently purchased by the university in 1962; the Albert College site was sold to Dublin Corporation in 1964, which earmarked the majority of its 300 acres for housing and other development.[26] Much to the

department, pp 25, 106–8; Hoctor, *The department's story*, pp 57–9, 65, 139–44. **24** University Education (Agriculture and Dairy Science) Act, 1926 (no. 32 of 1926); Hussey, *Albert Agricultural College*, pp 113–14; Hoctor, *The department's story*, pp 139–41. **25** Hussey, *Albert Agricultural College*, pp 113–26; Hoctor, *The department's story*, pp 103–4, 107, 139–41, 190. **26** *Irish Times*, 21

frustration of the students and faculty of UCD, however, it was not until 1979 that UCD fully extricated its operations from Albert College.[27] Their frustrations were shared by the governors of the National Institute for Higher Education, Dublin, who were waiting impatiently in the wings to begin renovation of their new home.

There are numerous parallels between the educational programmes and experiences of those who studied and taught at Albert Agricultural College (in its various guises) and at NIHED/DCU. Both institutions were established to meet particular educational needs among the Irish population. Both emphasized technical education and combined practical work experience with more traditional pedagogical techniques.[28] The physical legacy of the College remains tangible on DCU's campus, not least in the continued survival of the magnificent nineteenth-century building that bears the College's name. Though some of its grandeur has been obscured through partial demolition and the encroachment of modern development, Albert College's impressive stone-clad facade is the first sight to greet those entering the DCU campus via Ballymun Road. It serves as a reminder that, though Dublin City University is one of Ireland's youngest universities, its campus has served as an educational locus in north Dublin for nearly two centuries.

Sept. 1962, 12 Aug. 1964; Hoctor, *The department's story*, pp 245–6; Daly, *The first department*, p. 407. 27 UCD students staged a march from Albert College to Belfield (*c.*9 miles) in February 1979 in protest at the delay in relocating (*Irish Press*, 20 Feb. 1979; *Irish Times*, 21 Feb. 1979). 28 More specific pedagogical echoes can also be detected. NIHED/DCU's pioneering work in the field of distance education was, for example, foreshadowed in the 1926 radio broadcasts on gardening techniques by G.O. Sherrard, a lecturer in horticulture based at Albert College. The state's first radio station, 2RN, had begun broadcasting on 1 January 1926, with Sherrard's programmes on gardening commissioned by the station and sponsored by the Department of Agriculture (Brian Lynch, 'The first agricultural broadcasts on 2RN', *History Ireland*, 2:7 (1999); *Irish Times*, 19 Feb. 2011; Daly, *The first department*, p. 106).

2

Origins of the National Institute for Higher Education, Dublin, 1968–80

As it evolved during the late 1960s and 1970s, government policy for the provision of technical and technological education was shaped both by international factors and by individual personalities. Conscious of emerging international trends, the Department of Education proved eager to tap into resources made available in the spirit of post-war co-operation. When invited to assess the overall Irish educational landscape during the 1960s, bodies such as the Organisation for Economic Co-operation and Development (OECD) produced landmark reports that heavily influenced the broader formulation of policy. Yet finer policy details were shaped by the changeable priorities of successive ministers for education, along with other individuals with the connections and political nous to influence government to accept or reject competing proposals. Conceived during a radical reshaping of the higher-education sector that ebbed and flowed across the late 1960s and the 1970s, the National Institute for Higher Education, Dublin, was created as part of a push to provide greater opportunities at third level for those seeking technical and technological education. Announced in December 1974, the creation of the Institute was almost entirely unexpected and greeted with a distinct lack of enthusiasm, if not outright opposition. Though the need for a major expansion of Dublin's third-level infrastructure had been recognized from the early 1960s, disagreements over the form such expansion should take delayed the Institute's opening until 1980. The general elections of 1973 and 1977 were also of particular importance, bringing with them reforming ministers who were determined to progress their own distinctive visions for higher education. NIHE Dublin's origins in the rapidly evolving higher-education sector of the late 1960s and early 1970s were crucial in determining its educational remit. Higher education – and in particular the provision of technical and technological training – was seen as increasingly important to economic development, prompting a significant increase in investment in the third-level sector. NIHE Dublin emerged from a proposal by the City of Dublin Vocational Education Committee (CDVEC) to amalgamate its technological colleges in one location – the Ballymun project. Following the announcement of the government's intention to establish NIHE Dublin, an ad hoc governing body was appointed in March 1975. Its work over the ensuing five years was crucial to ensuring that the Institute would in fact welcome its first students on campus in November 1980.

I

The landscape of Irish education, at all levels, was revolutionized during the 1960s. Under the stewardship of Patrick Hillery, minister for education from June 1959 until April 1965, the government commissioned several reviews of the entire sector, resulting in the publication of a number of influential reports and recommendations. Drawing upon international expertise, particularly from within the OECD, these reviews highlighted the consequences of the state's persistent failure to invest in education, illustrating the direct link between slow economic growth and low per-capita education levels. That in turn prompted a number of policy initiatives that would transform Irish society through a dramatic increase in the numbers completing their education at second level. Concurrently, successive governments maintained a programme of targeted investment in the third-level sector, resulting in a rapid expansion of higher-education infrastructure during the 1970s – including the establishment of NIHE Dublin.[1]

Among the most important policy developments was a recognition that the national provision of technical and technological education was utterly inadequate. This was perhaps unsurprising in a country that had largely been bypassed by the industrial revolution, with an economy overwhelmingly reliant on the agricultural sector. Invited to assess the situation in the early 1960s, the OECD's *Training of technicians in Ireland* report highlighted the education system's shortcomings – particularly the lack of bridging courses from the vocational-schools system to university study.[2] Originally intended to provide these bridging courses, a system of regional technical colleges (RTCs) was announced by Hillery in May 1963. Though not properly implemented until several years later, following the recommendations of the government's steering committee on technical education, the creation of the RTC system marked the first step in the state's assumption of responsibility for third-level education outside of the university system.[3]

Training of technicians in Ireland was followed by two further influential reports: *Investment in education* (1965) and the *Commission on higher education*

1 For detailed analyses of the expansion of the higher-education sector during the 1960s and 1970s, on which this section is heavily reliant, see White, *Investing in people*; John Walsh, *The politics of expansion: the transformation of educational policy in the Republic of Ireland, 1957–72* (Manchester, 2009); idem, *Higher education in Ireland*. 2 OECD, *Training of technicians in Ireland* (Paris, 1964); Walsh, *Higher education in Ireland*, pp 259–64; White, *Investing in people*, pp 50–1. 3 The steering committee on technical education was established on 20 September 1966 with a remit to 'advise the Minister [for Education] generally on technical education', with particular reference to the regional technical colleges. Dublin largely lay outside its terms of reference, as the locations for the regional technical colleges had already been decided (*Steering committee on technical education report ... on regional technical colleges* (Dublin, [1969]), p. 5; Walsh, *The politics of expansion*, pp 226–31; White, *Investing in people*, pp 52–60).

(1967).[4] Though focused for the most part on primary and second level, *Investment in education* – also the result of an OECD analysis – marked a watershed moment in Irish educational policy, leading to a fundamental acceptance of the need for the education sector to receive a greater proportion of public finances. It also highlighted the acute problems inherent in the lack of a well-educated workforce, which was increasingly recognized internationally as a requirement for modern economic development. This was not news to the Department of Education. Writing to T.K. Whitaker in November 1961, Tarlach Ó Raifeartaigh had observed that

> the emphasis everywhere at the present time appears to be on investment in education as a necessary prerequisite for economic growth. This was very apparent to the representatives of our Departments who recently attended the policy conference in Washington on Economic Growth and Investment in Education. In a large number of countries long-term scientific planning in regard to education, as related particularly to the economy of each of these countries, has been underway for a number of years.[5]

Most importantly, *Investment in education* convinced a broad spectrum of civil servants of the need for long-term planning in educational policy, and of regular statistical analyses of the system. Hillery would later herald the report's impact, recalling that before *Investment* 'there were no real ideas' in educational policy.[6] It was directly responsible for the introduction of free second-level education, one of the most important changes in Irish society during the 1960s, which would have far-reaching consequences for the higher-education sector.

Even before the introduction of free secondary schooling, there was widespread recognition of the need for reform of the higher-education sector. Appointed in 1960, the Commission on Higher Education undertook a comprehensive review of the sector that spanned seven years. The pace and method of its deliberations has seen the commission described as 'a classic creation of nineteenth-century bureaucracy'.[7] Its conclusions were largely

---

4 For an analysis of these reports, see John Coolahan, 'The Commission on Higher Education, 1967, and third-level policy in contemporary Ireland', *Irish Educational Studies*, 9:1 (1990), pp 1–12; John Walsh, Selina McCoy, Aidan Seery and Paul Conway (eds), *Investment in education and the intractability of inequality*, *Irish Educational Studies* special issue, 33:2 (2014); John Walsh, *The politics of expansion*, pp 120–2, 312–14; idem, *Higher education in Ireland*, pp 141–76; White, *Investing in people*, pp 25–64.   5 Tarlach Ó Raifeartaigh to T.K. Whitaker, 8 Nov. 1961 (NAI, DFA 444/5). Ó Raifeartaigh (1905–84) and Whitaker (1916–2017) were secretaries of, respectively, the Department of Education and the Department of Finance. Ó Raifeartaigh was later appointed as the first chairman of the HEA, a position he held until 1975.   6 John Walsh, Selina McCoy, Aidan Seery and Paul Conway, 'Editorial: *Investment in education* and the intractability of inequality' in Walsh, McCoy, Seery and Conway (eds), *Investment in education*, pp 119–22. Quotation found on p. 119.   7 Horgan, *Dublin City University*, p. 8.

overtaken by rapid developments in educational policy during the 1960s, particularly during the ministerial tenure of Donogh O'Malley (1966–8). It is best known for recommending the creation of a body to oversee the higher-education sector, resulting in the establishment of the Higher Education Authority (HEA).[8]

The Commission also recognized the clear need for new higher-education institutions both in Dublin and Limerick – the future locations for both NIHEs. Addressing the urgent need for the provision of technical education at post-secondary level, the Commission proposed the establishment of 'New Colleges' in Dublin and Limerick, operating at a level slightly below that of universities. Though roundly rejected both within and without the Department of Education and quietly shelved, at least initially, the Commission's recommendation added further credence to arguments in favour of establishing a new higher-education institution in Dublin.[9]

Dublin would, however, have to take its place in the queue behind Limerick. Though Limerick was due to receive a regional technical college, a concerted campaign begun in the late 1950s for the establishment of a university in the region had placed enormous pressure on the government. The concept of a National Institute for Higher Education was new to the education system, first proposed by the HEA in 1969 following a review of the university sector. Their report, also notable for quashing the mooted merger of UCD and TCD, stopped short of recommending a new university for Limerick.[10] Its alternative, based on an identifiable lack of places nationally for third-level technical and technological education, was to create an institution that could deliver continuing education to people already in the workforce, as well as degree-level courses. Under intense political pressure from the Limerick University Project Committee, the HEA's proposal was enthusiastically embraced by the Department of Education. Limerick would have its third-level institution, but not a university. The title National Institute for Higher Education was settled upon by early 1971 and the Institute admitted its first students the following year.[11]

With the successful establishment of NIHE Limerick a template was now available for a similar initiative in Dublin. The need was acute.[12] Unlike the

8 Walsh, *The politics of expansion*, pp 290–2; idem, *Higher education in Ireland*, pp 144–5, 152–3; White, *Investing in people*, pp 99–105; Horgan, *Dublin City University*, p. 8. 9 Commission on Higher Education, *Presentation and summary* (Dublin, 1967), p. 28; *Seanad Debates*, 24 Jan. 1968; Walsh, *The politics of expansion*, p. 243; idem, *Higher education in Ireland*, pp 146, 152; Horgan, *Dublin City University*, p. 10. 10 The idea of merging TCD and UCD had circulated for several years before being adopted as formal government policy in 1967, with Donogh O'Malley as minister for education. See Walsh, *Higher education in Ireland*, pp 147–52; White, *Investing in people*, pp 96–9; Horgan, *Dublin City University*, pp 9–10. 11 For an analysis of the various efforts to establish a university by the Limerick University Project Committee, prior to the opening of NIHEL, see David Fleming, *University of Limerick: a history* (Dublin, 2012), pp 8–49. See also Walsh, *Higher education in Ireland*, p. 262; idem, *The politics of expansion*, pp 294–8; White, *Investing in people*, pp 70–3. 12 Walsh, *Higher education in Ireland*, pp 257–66; White, *Investing in people*, pp 79–92;

situation in Limerick, however, planning for a new Dublin institution would need to be cognisant of pre-existing courses already offered by the CDVEC, which had gradually transformed its curriculum to focus on third-level technical and commercial education.[13] Preoccupied with Limerick and the implementation of the regional technical colleges scheme, the government had neglected to develop a policy for the expansion of technical education in Dublin, creating a gap in planning filled by the CDVEC. The direct antecedents of NIHE Dublin lie in the CDVEC's 'Ballymun project', conceived in the mid-1960s, which called for the creation of a new college of technology and commerce on the site of the old Albert Agricultural College. The idea of replicating developments in Limerick by establishing a National Institute for Higher Education in Dublin was not presented to government until September 1974.[14] Attempts to merge this proposal with the CDVEC's Ballymun project produced a 'technological tangle' during the 1970s, which eventually resulted in the establishment of both Dublin Institute of Technology and NIHE Dublin.[15] The emergence of these two new institutions was not a result of co-operation, but of political indecision, infighting and tensions.

II

For the first four decades after independence the greater Dublin region had been relatively well supplied with third-level institutions, including two universities and various higher-education and teacher-training colleges. Unlike the situation in Limerick, no popular movement emerged in the capital city calling for the establishment of a new university. National demand for higher technical and technological training was rapidly addressed with the opening, between 1970 and 1974, of NIHE Limerick and of regional technical colleges at Athlone, Carlow, Cork, Dundalk, Galway, Letterkenny, Sligo and Waterford.[16] Two such colleges were originally intended for the Dublin region, though that proposal was not advanced until the 1990s. Moreover, technical and vocational education at post-secondary level within the city had traditionally been provided by the CDVEC,

Horgan, *Dublin City University*, pp 9–14.   **13** Thomas Duff, Joe Hegarty and Matthew Hussey, *The story of Dublin Institute of Technology* (Dublin, 2000), pp 13–28; Walsh, *Higher education in Ireland*, pp 265–6.   **14** NAI, 2005/7/352.   **15** The use of the term 'technology tangle' to describe the problems caused by the government's higher-education policy for Dublin can be traced to a lecture by F.S.L. Lyons, provost of TCD, delivered in 1976 (F.S.L. Lyons, *The technology tangle in Dublin* (1976), quoted in Duff, Hegarty and Hussey, *The story of DIT*, p. 57). It also featured as the headline of an incisive piece of journalism by Christina Murphy, education correspondent for the *Irish Times*, published in two parts on 16 and 23 February 1978.   **16** Limerick was also earmarked for a regional technical college, though the subsequent establishment of NIHEL superseded that decision (*Steering committee on technical education report*; F.C. Kintzer, 'The regional technical college system in Ireland', *Higher Education in Europe*, 6 (1981), pp 55–60; Walsh, *The politics of*

which operated colleges of technology at Kevin Street and Bolton Street, and a college of commerce at Rathmines.[17] The quality of the education offered by the colleges had steadily increased to third-level standard, as later recognized by a linkage agreement with TCD.[18]

Enrolments in the CDVEC system rose at a rapid pace in the 1950s and 1960s, increasing the strain on its capacity to accommodate all students.[19] Conscious that the scope for physically expanding its colleges was restricted by their urban setting, the CDVEC created a planning subcommittee to 'advise it on the needs of the city of Dublin in the field of vocational education and to recommend how these needs should be met'.[20] That committee returned the somewhat radical suggestion of relocating the colleges of commerce and technology to a new, single campus on the grounds of the old Albert College. The site had recently been acquired by Dublin Corporation from UCD, which was due to move its Faculty of Agriculture from the premises. The proposal soon became known as the 'Ballymun project'.

The CDVEC's findings were timely, coinciding with the Commission on Higher Education's recommendation for the establishment of a 'New College' in Dublin, as well as the observations of the Steering Committee on Technical Education regarding the shortcomings of higher education in the area. Minister for education Donogh O'Malley was wholly supportive of the idea.[21] While his sudden death in March 1968 is thought to have deprived the proposal of vital momentum, his successor, Brian Lenihan, encouraged the CDVEC's ambitions when he referred to the government's intention to create a new technological institution at Ballymun.[22]

Following consultations with the CDVEC in February 1969, Lenihan referred the Ballymun project to the HEA. Its report – delivered in December 1970 but not published until 1972 – largely endorsed the Committee's findings, including the urgent need for at least 3,300 additional higher-education places in Dublin, largely in the areas of technical and technological education.[23] However, the HEA's report undermined the Ballymun project in one of its most important conclusions: the new institution should have a governing body independent of the CDVEC and be financed by the HEA. This was a bitter disappointment to

expansion, pp 225–8).   **17** The Committee also operated colleges of music (Chatham Row), marketing and design (Parnell Square) and catering (Cathal Brugha Street). For the broader history of the CDVEC and its higher-level colleges, see Duff, Hegarty and Hussey, *The story of DIT*. **18** Duff, Hegarty and Hussey, *The story of DIT*, pp 72–83.   **19** HEA, *Report on the Ballymun project* (Dublin, 1972), p. 10.   **20** Quotation from Duff, Hegarty and Hussey, *The story of DIT*, p. 28. Unless otherwise indicated, all information relating to the CDVEC's Ballymun project is drawn from the detailed accounts provided by Duff, Hegarty and Hussey, in addition to White, *Investing in people*, pp 91–153; and Walsh, *Higher education in Ireland*, pp 265–7.   **21** *Dáil Debates*, 11 July 1968. For O'Malley's support, and the belief that his death was a key moment in the ultimate failure of the CDVEC to relocate to Ballymun, see Paddy Donegan interview, [1 Jan.] 2010.   **22** *Dáil Debates*, 11 July 1968.   **23** HEA, *Report on the Ballymun project* (Dublin, 1972), pp 1, 58–64.

the Committee, whose ability to influence the HEA's deliberations had undoubtedly been reduced by the government's decision to remove all the elected members of Dublin Corporation from office in the summer of 1969, due to its refusal to strike rates. As a consequence, the Corporation's subcommittees, including the CDVEC, were dissolved. While many members of the Corporation soon resumed their functions as specially appointed city commissioners, the situation did not lend itself to pursuit of a bold plan for reimagining higher education in Dublin.[24] From that point the prospect of the CDVEC retaining control of any new higher-education institution established at Albert College became increasingly remote.

By the time the HEA delivered its report, Padraig Faulkner had succeeded Lenihan as minister for education. During his tenure, the first regional technical colleges were opened and the concept firmly entrenched in the higher-education system. In other respects, Faulkner's approach to the third-level sector was more cautious, with plans for higher-education reform in Dublin largely sidelined.[25] Further progress in the capital city was delayed until the aftermath of the general election of 1973, which ushered a Fine Gael-Labour coalition into government. Appointed as Faulkner's successor, Richard Burke established a cabinet subcommittee to report on the reorganization of the higher-education sector.[26] It proved to be the first step in an ambitious attempt at higher-education reform.

Burke presented his plans to cabinet in September 1974, where they were rejected by his ministerial colleagues.[27] Chastened but undeterred, the minister's revised proposals were approved on 13 December and made public three days later, with little advance notice afforded to those working in higher education.[28] Burke's plans represented a radical reimagining of the higher-education landscape, including the separation of UCD from the NUI to form an independent university. Other proposals would see St Patrick's College, Maynooth, become a constituent college of either UCD, TCD or the NUI; the National Council for Educational Awards was to be renamed as the Council for Technological Education; and NIHE Limerick would become a recognized college of the NUI. Quite unexpectedly, Burke also announced the creation of a new higher-education institution in Dublin.

---

24 *Dáil Debates*, 1 May 1969; *Irish Times*, 21 June 1974; Duff, Hegarty and Hussey, *The story of DIT*, p. 31. Dublin Corporation was reinstated for the local elections of June 1974.   **25** Faulkner was, however, also responsible for restructuring the National College of Art and Design (Patrick Maume, 'Faulkner, Padraig (1918–2012)' in *DIB*; Walsh, *The politics of expansion*, p. 289; White, *Investing in people*, pp 80–4).   **26** The committee included several high-profile figures within government, including Garret FitzGerald and Conor Cruise O'Brien ('Note of government meeting', 10 Jan. 1974 (NAI, 2005/7/352); Walsh, *Higher education in Ireland*, p. 284).   **27** In a draft memorandum for government circulated in July 1974, the Department of Education referred to the establishment of 'Ballymun Polytechnic', envisioned as equivalent in status to NIHE Limerick. By September the proposed new institution's name had been changed to NIHE Dublin (NAI, 2005/7/352).   **28** Tony White, then working with the HEA, recalled that there was no

The National Institute for Higher Education, Dublin, was to be a recognized college of either UCD or TCD, 'with the capacity to evolve into a constituent college of one or other of the Dublin universities or to become an autonomous degree-awarding institution'.[29] The majority of its governing body would be appointed directly by the government, with representatives from trade unions, agriculture, business, industry and educational interests. Both NIHEs would also be designated as institutions under the remit of the HEA.[30] It was the government's intention to have NIHE Dublin built by the end of the decade, though no accurate cost analysis had yet been undertaken.[31] A site in Ballymun (i.e. Albert College) was regarded as its most likely location. Its degrees would be validated by the university to which it was attached, while diplomas and certificates would be validated by a new body, the Council for Technological Education.[32] In an apposite illustration of the fluidity of higher-education policy during the 1970s, those accreditation arrangements had been fundamentally altered by the time NIHE Dublin opened its doors less than six years later. Little clarity was offered on the intended nature of NIHE Dublin's curriculum, other than an implied similarity to that offered by Limerick. Some were unhappy with the lack of detail provided. Referring to the intention to link the Institute with one of Dublin's existing universities, F.S.L. Lyons, provost of TCD, complained that the vagueness regarding its potential development as an autonomous institution was likely to introduce confusion and delay to the much-needed expansion of Dublin's higher-education sector.[33]

Given the radical nature of the government's broader plans, it was no surprise to find that they generated considerable opposition. None of the stakeholders in the sector, including the HEA itself, appear to have been consulted. A number of proposals were quietly shelved; crucially, the pressing need for extra third-level places in Dublin ensured that stringent opposition to the new NIHE was ignored.[34] While much of the public opposition to the government's policies

---

consultation with that body, or any of the major stakeholders in higher education, before Burke's announcement of his plans (White, *Investing in people*, pp 113, 132).   **29** Cabinet minute, 13 Dec. 1974 (NAI, 2005/7/352); *Irish Times*, 18 Dec. 1974; Horgan, *Dublin City University*, pp 13–14. **30** Department of Education, memo for government, 13 Dec. 1974 (NAI, 2008/148/523). Burke's proposals represented an attempt to introduce a system of comprehensive higher education to Ireland, in contrast to the binary system that then prevailed in which an autonomous university sector sat alongside other higher-education institutions. For a broad analysis of the comprehensive/binary debate in Ireland, see Walsh, *Higher education in Ireland*, pp 281–97; White, *Investing in people*, pp 113–83; Horgan, *Dublin City University*, pp 11–14.   **31** An analysis by NIHED's governing body, undertaken in 1978, put the cost of providing the Institute with all of its physical infrastructure at £33.5m (NIHED, *Plan for the physical development of the Institute* (Dublin, 1978), p. 38; *Irish Independent*, 14 June 1978).   **32** *Irish Times*, 17 Dec. 1974. Within two months Burke had reversed his decision to form the Council for Technological Education, which was originally to be done simply by renaming the National Council for Educational Awards (Department of Education, memo for government, 21 Feb. 1975 (NAI, 2010/151/491); White, *Investing in people*, pp 120–1).   **33** *Irish Times*, 17 Dec. 1974.   **34** Along with the abandoned plan

came from the university sector, Burke's proposals for the establishment of the Institute also represented a cruel blow to the hopes of the CDVEC. Its intention to consolidate and enlarge its colleges of technology and commerce on a new site in Ballymun had been substantially endorsed by the HEA's 1970 report, though undermined with the important caveat that any new institution would not be under the CDVEC's control. That report formed the basis of Burke's plans for NIHE Dublin. More galling was the fact that, when Burke presented terms of reference to NIHE Dublin's governing body six months later, it emerged that the CDVEC was expected to transfer some of its resources and staff to the new Institute. In doing so, Burke created a 'technological tangle' that would take several years to resolve.

III

The establishment of NIHE Dublin initially progressed swiftly. Appointments to governing body, on an ad hoc basis, were approved by the cabinet on 5 March 1975. Its first meeting was held on 19 June, at which Burke presented members with their terms of reference.[35] It would, however, be another five years before the Institute's first students were admitted, the intervening half decade consumed by territorial disputes with the CDVEC, glacially slow decision-making within the Department of Education, and uncertainty about the exact nature of the courses the Institute would offer.

Governing body's terms of reference covered five major points: 1) to plan the Institute's general and administrative structures, its staffing requirements and its future curriculum; 2) to consult with the Department of Education on the design and construction of the Institute's campus; 3) to enter into discussions over the transfer of certain courses from the CDVEC's colleges to the Institute;

to rename the National Council for Educational Awards, the December 1974 policy document had proposed the fundamental reorganization of the NUI, and that TCD and UCD should streamline their undergraduate programmes by ensuring there was no duplication of courses in several areas, including engineering, architecture, dentistry and agriculture (Department of Education, memo for government, 21 Feb. 1975 (NAI, 2005/151/491); Walsh, *Higher education in Ireland*, p. 286–9; White, *Investing in people*, pp 120–1). **35** NAI, 2005/151/451; NIHED, *Annual report, 1975–8*, pp 1–4. Appendix 2 lists all governors of NIHE Dublin/DCU between 1975 and 2019. It is appropriate, however, to record here the names of the original members, initially appointed for a three-year term that was later extended to 1981: Dr John Barry; Robert Clarke; Patricia Corr; Aleck Crichton; Hugh de Lacy; Francis Plunkett Dillon (resigned 1977); Patrick Donegan (chairman, resigned 1979); Senator Michael Donnelly (appointed 1978); Desmond Fay; Philip Flood (appointed 1977) John Gallagher; Peter Gallagher; Michael Keating, TD; Denis Larkin; Robert Lawlor; Sean Lyons (appointed 1977); Thomas J. Maher; Thomas McCarthy; Prof. Michael MacCormac; Dr Sean McDonagh; Prof. John O'Donnell; Dr Daniel O'Hare (appointed NIHED director, 1977); Dr Liam Ó Maolcatha (acting director, 1975–7); Monsignor John O'Regan (resigned 1976); Patrick Rock; Dr Peter Smyth (appointed 1976); Beatrice Trench; James Tunney,

4) to begin exploratory talks with UCD and TCD regarding the accreditation of the Institute's degree-level courses; and 5) to consult with the National Council for Educational Awards regarding the accreditation of any certificate and diploma courses offered by the Institute.[36]

Implementation of the terms of reference was delegated to two main subcommittees. Chaired by Prof. Michael MacCormac, the management committee assumed responsibility for planning the Institute's location and physical development, as well as its financial affairs. Later tasks delegated to the committee included oversight of the search for a permanent director, staff appointments and the acquisition of interim offices. The principal role of the education and planning committee, chaired by Thomas McCarthy, was to draft discussion papers on the development of the Institute's curriculum. It also guided the Institute's initial engagements with the CDVEC, the HEA and the NCEA.[37]

Liam Ó Maolcatha, a senior official with the Department of Education, was appointed as the Institute's acting director. Governing body's second meeting saw the election of Patrick Donegan as chairman.[38] As national group secretary of the Irish Transport and General Workers' Union and chairman of the CDVEC, Donegan was a passionate advocate for the expansion and improvement of third-level educational facilities in Dublin.[39] Nonetheless, given the government's stated intention to transfer degree-level courses from the CDVEC to NIHE Dublin, and its inclination to locate the new institution at Albert College, his appointment as chairman was particularly problematic and contributed to the lengthy delay in the opening of the Institute. There were warning signs. Donegan had publicly criticized the plans announced in December 1974 and warned that the CDVEC would oppose them as strongly as possible. He also initially refused the invitation to join the Institute's governing body – as did his colleague Jeremiah Sheehan, then chief executive officer of the CDVEC.[40]

It is not clear what changed Donegan's mind. He was present at governing body's first meeting, where he was joined by four other members of the CDVEC.[41] Their appointments were intended to smooth the process of

TD; Prof. Barbara Wright.　**36** DCUPO, GB75/1; DCUPO, 'Governing body – reports and working papers, 1975–9'; memo for government, 27 Feb. 1978 (NAI, 2008/148/523); NIHED, *Annual report, 1975–8*, pp 1–2.　**37** DCUPO, GB75, GB76, GB77 and GB78; DCUPO, 'Governing body – reports and working papers, 1975–9'; NIHED, *Annual report, 1975–8, passim.* Prof. Michael MacCormac was dean of the Faculty of Commerce at UCD. He later served as chairman of NIHED's governing body (1979–82). Thomas McCarthy was education and training officer with the Irish Transport and General Workers' Union.　**38** DCUPO, GB75/1, 2; NIHED, *Annual report, 1975–8*, p. 2.　**39** *Irish Times*, 13 Apr. 2013.　**40** *Irish Independent*, 22 Dec. 1974; Department of Education, memo for government, 3 June 1975 (NAI, 2005/151/491); Paddy Donegan interview, [1 Jan.] 2010; White, *Investing in people*, p. 116.　**41** These were Desmond Fay; Michael Keating, TD; Monsignor John M. O'Regan; and James Tunney, TD. Keating and Tunney

transferring courses from the Committee to the new Institute. Yet Donegan and his colleagues had no intention of facilitating any such transfer, which would have represented a major blow to the excellent work of the Committee, over several decades, in building up a substantial level of expertise in technician education and training. The sluggish pace with which discussions with the CDVEC proceeded over the next three years illustrates the level of resistance to the new Institute. Formal contact was not made until February 1976, when exploratory discussions merely resulted in the appointment of a liaison group to co-ordinate further talks between the two institutions. That group's first meeting was not scheduled until 29 October 1976.[42] Pressed by the Department of Education to engage more urgently with the process, the CDVEC issued an unusual press release that simultaneously welcomed and criticized the creation of NIHE Dublin. While declaring its intention to work closely with the Institute so that each could 'assist the other in the establishment of two viable but complementary education systems', the Committee also made clear its irritation at the potential breakup of its 'remarkably successful system'.[43] Its concerns were shared by the chairman of the HEA, Sean O'Connor, who forcefully rejected the government's policy: 'I cannot for the life of me see the need for an NIHE in Dublin.'[44]

In an effort to resolve these differences, Minister Richard Burke created a working party in November 1976 to consider the future of third-level technological education in Dublin. Its remit was to plan for the creation of a new CDVEC college, which would complement NIHE Dublin, and to oversee the transfer of appropriate CDVEC courses, facilities and staff to the Institute. Burke expected swift results and anticipated that NIHE Dublin would admit its first students at the commencement of the 1977/8 academic year.[45] While the latter expectation proved overly optimistic, the working party presented its report to the minister on 20 December 1976. Its recommendations were, however, effectively buried by the CDVEC's refusal to endorse its findings.[46]

were infrequent attendees at governing body meetings, and Monsignor O'Regan resigned his position in 1976 (NAI, 2005/151/451; NIHED, *Annual report, 1975–8*, pp 2–3, 25).   **42** DCUPO, GB76/2–6; NIHED, *Annual report, 1975–8*, pp 8–9.   **43** Quotations from *Irish Times*, 30 Oct. 1976. See also Paddy Donegan interview, [1 Jan.] 2010; Danny O'Hare interview, 28 May 2018; *Irish Times*, 16 Feb. 1978; NIHED, *Annual report, 1975–8*, p. 9; Horgan, *Dublin City University*, p. 16; White, *Investing in people*, pp 149–50; Walsh, *Higher education in Ireland*, pp 264–6. The CDVEC's Society of College Lecturers had, in July 1975, submitted a detailed policy document to NIHE Dublin's governing body outlining a more positive vision for future co-operation between the two institutions (DCUPO, GB75/3).   **44** *Irish Times*, 23 Oct. 1976. O'Connor was later profiled by Christina Murphy, following his retirement as chairman of the HEA. She recalled that at a conference, held *c.*1975, O'Connor referred to the proposal to establish NIHED as 'the greatest load of rubbish I ever heard in my life' (*Irish Times*, 22 Nov. 1979).   **45** *Irish Times*, 26 Nov. 1976. **46** 'Report of the working party on higher technological education in the Dublin area', 20 Dec. 1976 (Brian Trench Papers); DCUPO, GB77/3–6; NIHED, *Annual report, 1975–8*, pp 10–11, 15–16; Duff, Hegarty and Hussey, *The story of DIT*, pp 32–3; Walsh, *Higher education in Ireland*, p. 264–6;

Prof. Michael MacCormac, one of NIHE Dublin's representatives on the working party, later observed that 'dust-covered copies of that report, I am sure, would now fetch a high price in an auction room amongst other memorabilia. No action was taken, possibly for very good reasons, and the governing body of the Institute was left with a broken engagement and the ring returned.'[47]

Apart from the lack of progress with the CDVEC, governing body experienced several other difficulties, particularly in securing suitable office accommodation and administrative staff.[48] On the other hand, its education and planning committee established fruitful working relationships with the HEA and the NCEA, two key bodies that would play an important role in the development of the Institute during the 1980s. Those relationships were formed as part of the diligent preparations carried out by governing body as a whole. By the end of 1978, the Institute's governors had met on 59 occasions, which was indicative both of the challenges involved in creating a new higher-education institution, and of their commitment to their task. Their endeavours produced thirteen separate reports and discussion papers. Among the topics covered were the Institute's academic structures and educational philosophies, as well as its organizational structure and approach to staff recruitment. Perhaps most important were two reports that formed the core of the Institute's strategic planning: *Plan for the future of the Institute* (November 1977) and *Plan for the physical development of the Institute* (May 1978).[49]

Publication of these reports followed the resolution of one of the more intractable problems encountered by governing body throughout 1976: the appointment of a permanent director to replace Ó Maolcatha. Obtaining permission from the Department of Education merely to advertise the position took almost six months, with sharp disagreements emerging over salary levels and the conditions of employment. Candidates were eventually interviewed in September 1976 and, in one of his last acts as minister for education, Richard Burke sanctioned the appointment of Danny O'Hare.[50] Discussions between the CDVEC and the Institute were then at a critical point, with Burke under intense pressure to delay approving O'Hare's appointment. It has been argued that, had he not done so before departing for Brussels as Ireland's European Commissioner, NIHE Dublin might never have come into existence.[51]

O'Hare took up his position on 21 March 1977, the beginning of an extraordinary twenty-two year term.[52] One of the original appointees to

White, *Investing in people*, pp 150–1.   **47** Speech by Michael MacCormac at the turning of the sod ceremony at Albert College, 1 Apr. 1980 (DCUPO, 'NIHE Dublin: general, 1/2'). NIHE Dublin's other representatives on the working party were Patrick Donegan, James Tunney, TD (both also representing the CDVEC) and Liam Ó Maolcatha.   **48** NIHED, *Annual report, 1975–8*, pp 12–13.   **49** DCUPO, GB75–8; DCUPO, 'Governing body – reports and working papers, 1975–9'; NIHED, *Annual report, 1975–8*, pp 5–6, 24.   **50** DCUPO, GB76, GB77/1, 2; DCUPO, 'Governing body – reports and working papers, 1975–9'; NIHED, *Annual report, 1975–8*, p. 12; White, *Investing in people*, p. 150.   **51** White, *Investing in people*, p. 150.   **52** Department of Education, memo for

2.1 Danny O'Hare, pictured following his appointment as director of NIHED in March 1977 (DCU Collection).

governing body, O'Hare's distinguished career up to that point ensured that he was well acquainted with the higher-education sector. Born in Dundalk and educated at Dundalk CBS, O'Hare obtained an MSc in chemistry from NUI Galway before pursuing his doctoral studies at the University of St Andrews, where he received his PhD in 1968. Following two years of postdoctoral research at Michigan State University and the University of Southampton, O'Hare returned to Ireland in 1971 to become the first principal of Letterkenny Regional Technical College (1971–4). This was followed by three years as principal of Waterford Regional Technical College (1974–7).[53] His appointment as director of NIHE Dublin imbued governing body with renewed energy and provided fresh impetus to planning for the Institute's future. By the end of the year five reports and discussion papers had been submitted to the Department, compared to three in the preceding two years.[54]

Fianna Fáil returned to power in the June 1977 general election, with John Wilson assuming office as minister for education. Wilson swiftly implemented a programme to streamline elements of the higher-education sector, in the process

government, 29 Apr. 1977 (NAI, 2007/116/359); NIHED, *Annual report, 1975–8*, p. 12.
53 Danny O'Hare interviews, 12 Oct. 2005 and 28 May 2018; Bradley, *'Twigs for an eagle's nest'*, p. 223.   **54** DCUPO, 'Governing body – reports and working papers, 1975–9'.

providing much-needed clarity on the Institute's future. A month after his appointment Wilson reversed Burke's decision to strip the National Council for Educational Awards of its degree-awarding functions. Four months later the NCEA was designated the accreditation body for degrees awarded by NIHE Dublin, thus removing the potentially awkward hurdle of negotiating a linkage agreement with either UCD or TCD.[55]

O'Hare carefully cultivated his relationship with Wilson – a prudent policy he continued with the thirteen other ministers for education that held office during his tenure.[56] O'Hare's approach soon paid dividends, with Wilson according the *Plan for the future of the Institute* a positive reception despite attempts to persuade him otherwise. Following publication of this major strategic planning document in November 1977, governing body arranged for a presentation outlining its findings to Wilson the following month. Responsibility for that presentation fell to Donegan, who reportedly delivered it to the minister with such a distinct lack of enthusiasm that other governing body members present feared the meeting had fatally damaged the prospect of NIHE Dublin ever opening its doors.[57] The meeting in fact proved pivotal in the formation of Wilson's thinking regarding the Institute, garnering his full support. Drawing in part upon the proposals contained in the document, in February 1978 the Department of Education reiterated its intention to establish NIHE Dublin as a 'third-level educational institution offering degree, diploma and certificate courses with a mainly technological bias'.[58] However, the thorny issue of which CDVEC courses and staff would be transferred to the Institute still remained unresolved.[59]

Despite a meeting between O'Hare and senior officials of the CDVEC the following month, discussions remained at an impasse. The Committee remained unmoved by its teaching staff's broad support for transfer. O'Hare's public

55 Daniel O'Hare, 'The role of the National Institute for Higher Education Dublin in national development', *Science and Technology* (June–July 1981), pp 13–16. The NCEA would also serve as the accreditation body for NIHEL, Thomond College of Education (established in 1973 and integrated into the University of Limerick in 1991) and the regional technical colleges (NAI, 2008/148/523).   56 Three of these ministers held office during the extraordinary events of 1982, a year that saw two general elections: Dr Martin O'Donoghue (9 Mar. 1982–6 Oct. 1982); Charles Haughey (6–27 Oct. 1982); and Gerard Brady (27 Oct.–14 Dec. 1982).   57 DCUPO, GB78/1; Paddy Donegan interview, [1 Jan.] 2010; Danny O'Hare interview, 28 May 2018; Horgan, *Dublin City University*, p. 17.   58 Department of Education, memo for government, 27 Feb. 1978 (NAI, 2008/148/523). At this stage in proceedings, the Department was also considering locating the National College of Art and Design on the Albert College site. Housed at Kildare Street for most of its history, the NCAD eventually moved to premises on Thomas Street at the end of the 1970s. 59 While the Committee's governors remained largely opposed to the transfer of courses and staff, as well as to the concept of NIHE Dublin, its lecturing staff were of a somewhat different opinion. The Society of College Lecturers issued a response welcoming the Institute's *Plan for the future* – with some quibbles – and stated its support for the transfer of all third-level courses and staff to the Institute. Following an invitation from the Society, Danny O'Hare discussed the *Plan* with its

attempts at conciliation, highlighting the potential for the CDVEC and NIHE Dublin to complement each other rather than compete, similarly had no effect.[60] Yet after more than two years of stilted and inconclusive talks, matters soon progressed with remarkable pace. On 8 May the CDVEC wrote to O'Hare, deflecting his latest request for an agreed agenda for talks. Just two days later, the Department of Education sought cabinet approval to draft statutory legislation for NIHE Dublin, and for the commencement of works on the Albert College site in order to accommodate the Institute.[61] The timing was hardly accidental and also coincided with a letter from O'Hare to Taoiseach Jack Lynch, in which O'Hare argued for the urgent need for NIHE Dublin:

> The *Plan* [*for the future of the Institute*] describes the ambitions of a National Technological Institute which will provide programmes of higher education and training on a national as well as on a local scale ... [Y]ou will recognise its critical importance to the school leaver ... [It] is in keeping with the government's intention to increase the number of higher education student places by 12,000 by 1981/2.[62]

Objections to Education's proposals were lodged by the Taoiseach's Department, which frowned upon the lack of consultation with the HEA.[63] The Department of Finance also raised concerns that, in the absence of an 'unqualified agreement' about the transfer of CDVEC courses to the Institute, the start of construction at Albert College could give rise to 'controversy and costly delay'.[64] It is tempting to view Finance's objection as supportive of the CDVEC's rearguard action against the loss of its courses. However, Finance's main concern was the potential for unforeseen costs and the possibility that public resources would be wasted on an unnecessary duplication of facilities. Officials were equally wary of public opposition to any diminution of the CDVEC's position, a fear shared by those within the Taoiseach's Department who wished to delay a decision: 'Since educational developments frequently give rise to lively public controversy ... it is unfair to consider these issues on very short notice.'[65]

Finance was also sceptical of Wilson's contention that by drafting the establishing legislation for NIHE Dublin, pressure could be brought to bear on the CDVEC: 'It is naive of Education to assume, apparently, that the introduction or indeed the passing of legislation will quell any controversy; in fact the opposite effect would seem more likely.'[66] The crux of Wilson's

members at a public meeting, held on 19 April 1978 (Neil Gillespie to Daniel O'Hare, 20 Mar. 1978 (Brian Trench Papers)).   **60** *Irish Times*, 23 Feb., 8 Mar. 1978.   **61** Department of Education, memo for government, 10 May 1978 (NAI, 2008/148/523).   **62** Danny O'Hare to Jack Lynch, [3] May 1978 (NAI, 2008/148/523).   **63** W. Kirwan to D. Nally, 11 May 1978 (NAI, 2008/148/523).   **64** Department of Education, memo for government, 10 May 1978 (NAI, 2008/148/523).   **65** W. Kirwan to D. Nally, 11 May 1978 (NAI, 2008/148/523).   **66** C.K. McGrath to George

argument was that the CDVEC could not be compelled to transfer courses to NIHE Dublin. Under the provisions of the Vocational Education Act of 1930, a transfer of functions could only be effected by legislative means. As the Department of Education observed when defending its position: 'Voluntary undertakings [by the CDVEC] ... could not be relied upon as serving any useful purpose.'[67] There can be little doubt that Wilson was attempting to force the Committee's hand.

On 19 May the government approved Wilson's proposals and formally authorized negotiations with Dublin Corporation for the purchase of the Albert College site, as well as the seeking of tenders for the construction of Phase 1.[68] The eventual opening of NIHE Dublin, uncertain up to this point, was now an inevitability. Facing defeat, and the continued belief within government that it must transfer courses to the new institution, the CDVEC countered with a bold, yet carefully planned move. Just one week after the government's decision of 19 May, the Committee announced its intention to merge its higher-education colleges into a single entity, to be known as the Dublin Institute of Technology (DIT). It had, at a stroke, not only forged a new path for itself, but had radically altered the development of NIHE Dublin's curriculum.[69]

While Wilson remained committed to the transfer of courses and staff from DIT to the Institute, and attempted to establish yet another advisory committee to oversee the process, the CDVEC simply refused to engage.[70] At a meeting with the minister on 18 January 1979, the CDVEC presented a document that queried the need for NIHE Dublin and bluntly stated that it would not be engaging in further discussions.[71] The creation of DIT effectively killed off the prospect of any further collaboration between NIHE Dublin and the CDVEC. All sides emerged from the process somewhat bruised. Even before the irrevocable collapse of negotiations, the Institute's governing body had made no attempt to hide its frustrations. Its first annual report to the minister for education (which covered the period June 1975 to May 1978) was unsparing in its criticisms of the Department of Education and the CDVEC. Drafted and printed before the swift turn of events of May 1978, the report adopted a tone and honesty of detail that is unimaginable in the corporate-communications environment of the twenty-first century. Commenting on the lack of progress with the CDVEC, the report noted that this was inevitable 'given the lack of demonstration of will on the part of Ministers of Education. It is unlikely, therefore, that significant progress will

Colley, 11 May 1978 (NAI, 2008/148/523).   **67** Department of Education, memo for government, 10 May 1978 (NAI, 2008/148/523); Vocational Education Act, 1930 (no. 29 of 1930).   **68** Cabinet minutes, 19 May 1978 (NAI, 2008/148/523); *Dáil Debates*, 12 Dec. 1978. See also chapter 6. **69** Paddy Donegan interview, [1 Jan.] 2010; Duff, Hegarty and Hussey, *The story of DIT*, pp 36–43; White, *Investing in people*, pp 266, 292–3; Walsh, *Higher education in Ireland*, pp 169–70. **70** DCUPO, GB79/1; *Dáil Debates*, 7 Dec. 1978; *Irish Times*, 21 Dec. 1978; White, *Investing in people*, pp 149–53.   **71** DCUPO, GB79/2; *Irish Independent*, 19 Jan. 1979.

be recorded in this regard until such time as the Ministerial will is made known to both parties.'[72]

Wilson's will had been made known during May and the second half of 1978, but effectively rendered immaterial by the emergence of DIT. It was no surprise when Patrick Donegan resigned as chairman of NIHE Dublin's governing body in January 1979, just days after the CDVEC met the minister to reaffirm its continued opposition to the Institute.[73] The impossibility of Donegan's position, following his appointment as chairman, had not been lost on observers of the education sector. Christina Murphy, long-serving education correspondent with the *Irish Times*, had summarized the issue succinctly:

> We now have Mr Donegan chairing a governing body of a non-existent NIHE, whose only real chance of existing is to steal away the colleges Mr Donegan chairs in his other capacity of VEC chairman. 'Any day now Paddy Donegan will have to have an eyeball to eyeball confrontation with himself', was the current joke. To which some people replied: 'And he'll end up crosseyed'.[74]

As O'Hare later recalled, the failure of the two institutions to come to an agreement was entirely predictable:

> They expected him in a sense to preside over the emasculation of the CDVEC ... so it was really very tense. When I was appointed Director of NIHE Dublin I had a chairman who didn't want NIHE Dublin to happen because of his commitment – understandably – to the CDVEC. Really it was a strange situation.[75]

With the prospect of no courses transferring from the CDVEC, the way was in fact cleared for NIHE Dublin's governors and staff to create a curriculum from scratch, a process begun in earnest in late 1978 (see chapter 5). Alongside curriculum development, the most pressing matters facing governing body were determining the best location for the Institute and ensuring that the legislation required to give NIHE Dublin statutory footing was enacted.

IV

Working from figures supplied by Dublin Corporation, and augmented by its own analyses, governing body anticipated that, by the mid-1980s, the Dublin

---

72 NIHED, *Annual report, 1975–8*, p. 11.   73 During the meeting with Wilson on 18 January, the CDVEC reiterated the view that it saw 'no educational reason for the creation of an NIHED' (John McKay to John Wilson, 24 Jan. 1979 (NAI, 2007/50/72)). See also DCUPO, GB79/1, 2; *Irish Independent*, 19 Jan. 1979. Donegan was replaced as chairman of NIHED by Prof. Michael MacCormac.   74 *Irish Times*, 16 Feb. 1978.   75 Danny O'Hare interview, 28 May 2018.

2.2 The John Barry building, which originally housed NIHED's library and later provided laboratory space, was demolished in 2000 (DCU Collection).

area would require space for an additional 9,300 students at higher-education level. According to governing body's estimates, no more than half of that need could be met without seriously undermining both academic standards and the physical environment of the Institute. A student population of 5,000 (with $c.$1,000 staff), to be achieved over a decade of carefully phased physical and faculty growth, was identified as the maximum desirable in order to maintain 'overall institutional unity of community and purpose'. Further demand for third-level education would have to be met by an expansion in the capacity of the CDVEC colleges, and the establishment of regional technical colleges in the greater Dublin area.[76]

The CDVEC's Ballymun project had identified the Albert College site as an ideal location for a new technological college in the late 1960s. Though clearly earmarked for NIHE Dublin from late 1974, the location of the Institute was not finalized until 1978. Influenced by the size of the campus on which NIHE Limerick was located (which grew from an initial 73 acres to more than 120 in a few short years), governing body was concerned that Albert College would not be large enough for the Institute's needs. Assisted by Dublin Corporation and the HEA, the Institute's management committee surveyed several sites.[77] Each

76 DCUPO, 'Governing body – reports and working papers, 1975–9'; DCUPO, 'NIHE Dublin general, 2/2'; NIHED, *Plan for the physical development of the Institute* (Dublin, 1978), pp 9–19; NIHED, *Plan for the future of the Institute* (Dublin, 1977), pp 12–36; NIHED, *Annual report, 1975–8*, pp 18–19.   77 The Institute's management committee was convened on 3 October 1975. Its

had to be located on the north side of the city and be large enough to accommodate the planned expansion of the Institute to a student body of *c*.5,000.

Reporting in 1977, Dublin Corporation's deputy planning officer identified six potential alternatives, each approximately 100 acres in size: Santry Demesne, Abbotstown, Luttrellstown Castle, Nangor, Corkagh Demesne and Brownsbarn.[78] Acquisition costs for each site were estimated at between £400,000 and £600,000, to which servicing costs (site clearance, connection to the electricity grid, drainage, etc.) would also need to be added. Nangor, Corkagh and Brownsbarn were deemed largely unsuitable, due to the amount of noise nuisance from nearby Baldonnell Aerodrome. Moreover, the construction of any building in excess of thirty-five feet in height would need to be sanctioned by the minister for defence, adding a potential obstacle to the future expansion of the Institute. Corkagh and Brownsbarn were also considered to be oriented too far towards south Dublin, which ran counter to the preference for a northside location. The Abbotstown site (which also housed part of UCD's veterinary college) was on undrained land and was otherwise unsuitable due to its relative isolation.

The remaining two sites were more promising. Santry Demesne was easily accessible, but development was likely to be complicated by several restrictive covenants on the land, as well as the fact that ownership was shared by a number of parties, including TCD. Luttrellstown was the most attractive site. Owned by the Guinness family, the trustees responsible for its maintenance were known to be open to offers for the land. Despite the need for some investment to provide adequate services and transport links, the estate was considered the best possible location for a single-campus institution: 'It is a northern location but between two western towns … This is a very fine area overlooking the Liffey Valley and a top-class institution such as NIHE could be a decided asset here.' The report concluded by noting that, if Luttrellstown was rejected, the best alternative was a multi-site campus, with satellite locations at Ronanstown, Blanchardstown or Tallaght complementing the core site at Albert College.[79]

A multi-site campus was, however, at odds with governing body's wishes. The principle of unity of purpose ran throughout the Institute's initial planning process, particularly in the development of interdisciplinary programmes:

membership consisted of Michael MacCormac (chairman); John Barry; Robert G. Clarke; Desmond Fay; Philip Flood; John J. Gallagher; Michael Keating, TD; Denis Larkin; Robert Lawlor; Thomas J. Maher; Patrick Rock; and James Tunney, TD. As governing body chairman and acting director, respectively, Patrick Donegan and Liam Ó Maolcatha were *ex officio* members. Ó Maolcatha was replaced by Danny O'Hare in March 1977, following the latter's appointment as director. Donegan resigned his post in January 1979 (DCUPO, 'Governing body – reports and working papers, 1975–9'; NIHED, *Annual report, 1975–8*, pp 5, 26).   **78** Memorandum by L.P. O'Reilly, [1977] (DCUPO, 'NIHE Dublin: general, 1/2', 'Governing body – reports and working papers, 1975–9').   **79** Ibid.

It is the view of the Institute that the dispersed institution generates a wasteful duplication of certain facilities ... that it causes unnecessary problems for students and staff and hinders the development of unity and flexibility ... The Institute is not impressed by arguments in favour of multi-site development – for example, that dispersed institutions integrate more with the community than their single-site counterparts ... [I]t can be stated with confidence that dispersal will lead to fragmentation and unnecessary duplication and that it will severely limit the options of the Institute in respect of the development of as yet unexpected new course types.

In addition to arguing for a single-site campus, the Institute's governors also made the case for one that was future-proofed in terms of the Institute's physical development: 'Much will be lost if an inadequate site is provided initially which would result in the Institute having to acquire another site or sites should it need to expand in the future.'[80] Such words would prove prophetic, with DCU required to spend tens of millions acquiring additional land during the 1990s. Governing body's preference was for Luttrellstown, not least because of its proximity to the burgeoning towns of Blanchardstown, Lucan and Palmerstown. Following his appointment as director of the Institute, Danny O'Hare opened discussions with the trustees of Luttrellstown for the purchase of 100 acres on the eastern side of the estate. By the summer of 1977 negotiations had progressed to a relatively advanced stage.[81]

These efforts to identify alternative sites for the Institute were, however, ultimately redundant. Discussions between the Institute and Luttrellstown were cut short when a final decision was made by the Department of Education, without consultation with O'Hare or governing body, to locate the Institute at Albert College. It was not until early 1978 that the Department informed the Institute of its own analysis of potential sites in the Dublin region. Focusing on the city centre, the Department's buildings unit considered a number of locations on both sides of the Liffey, including the former Williams and Woods factory on King's Inns Street, Portobello barracks, and UCD's premises on Earlsfort Terrace. More pertinently, as early as 1976 the unit's senior architect had drawn up a detailed development plan for the Albert College site, incorporating multiple four-storey buildings linked to Albert College by a covered arcade.[82] Failure to inform the Institute's planners of this scheme was symptomatic of the dysfunctional nature of communications between the

80 NIHED, *Plan for the future of the Institute*, pp 56–7.   81 Danny O'Hare to G.B. Slater, 15 July 1977; Peter Stonebridge to Danny O'Hare, 18 Aug. 1977 (DCUPO, 'NIHE Dublin: general, 1/2'). See also DCUPO, GB77/5–8; DCUPO, 'Governing body – reports and working papers, 1975–9'). 82 Department of Education, memo for government, 27 Feb. 1978 (NAI, 2008/148/523); Department of Education, 'NIHE Dublin draft development plan', June 1976 (Brian Trench

2.3 The cover of NIHED's first prospectus, distributed in April 1980 (DCU Collection).

Department and governing body, particularly during the lifetime of the Fine Gael-Labour coalition government.[83] Transmission of key information was routinely delayed, often for months on end. It was, for example, not until eighteen months after governing body received its terms of reference that it was made aware of a loan of £400,000 from the World Bank, intended to assist with the development of the Institute's campus.[84]

The Department's buildings unit expressed major concern with the level of work required to develop the necessary infrastructure at Luttrellstown, including sewerage works, road construction and the implementation of three-phase electricity supply. The fact that the purchase money for Albert College would accrue to Dublin Corporation, rather than to a private entity – such as the Luttrellstown trust – was also a factor in the Department's decision. In a memorandum to cabinet, delivered in May 1978, the Department justified the selection of Albert College by noting that its buildings unit had investigated

Papers). See chapter 6.   **83** Fine Gael and Labour formed a coalition government following the general election of February 1973 and remained in power until June 1977.   **84** The World Bank loan was due to mature in 1978, with building works thus originally required to start in January 1979. Following delays in beginning the construction process, including the slow transfer of UCD's agriculture faculty from the site, the maturation date was later renegotiated to 30 June 1979 (NAI, 2007/50/72, 2008/148/523, 2010/53/413, 2010/16/175; NIHED, *Annual report, 1975–8*, p. 14;

numerous city-centre sites, but had ruled each one out for various reasons. Moreover, the Department declared that the Institute's governing body were entirely satisfied with the Glasnevin site. Governing body offered an alternative perspective when it observed that it had been left with 'no alternative but to concur' with a decision that would, in time, place restrictions on the expansion of the Institute.[85] Remarkably, the Department pressed ahead with Albert College despite acknowledging that it was 'not ideal, nor sufficiently big to accommodate adequately a student population of 5,000'.[86]

Negotiations for the purchase of the 50-acre site from Dublin Corporation, at a cost of £1,518,900 (£30,000 per acre) were completed in March 1979.[87] Renovations to Albert College began during the winter of 1979/80, led by Sisk building contractors under the supervision of architects Robinson, Keefe & Devane. The traditional turning of the sod ceremony, marking the official opening of NIHE Dublin and its building programme, was performed in front of Albert College by John Wilson on 1 April 1980. Speaking in front of approximately 200 guests, Wilson declared:

> It is a real pleasure for me as Minister for Education to be here today to cut the first sod for a building project which will have a great impact on the educational scene in this country, and make a valuable contribution to filling a gap which the best projections we can make see developing, not only in the general area of third-level education but more specifically in the area of electronics, computer studies and applied science.[88]

At the time of Wilson's speech, legislation for establishing both national institutes for higher education had yet to be finalized. The legal status of the NIHEs had, however, been confirmed in late 1976 when both were designated as higher-education institutions under the aegis of the HEA.[89] This had been an

---

Walsh, *Higher education in Ireland*, pp 265–6). See chapter 6.　**85** Department of Education, memo for government, 5 May 1978 (NAI, 2008/148/523); DCUPO, 'Governing body – reports and working papers, 1975–9'; NIHED, *Annual report, 1975–8*, p. 14.　**86** Department of Education, memo for government, 27 Feb. 1978 (NAI, 2008/148/523).　**87** Department of Education, memo for government, July 1979 (NAI, 2010/53/413); *Dáil Debates*, 12 Dec. 1978. Dublin Corporation made a substantial profit on the sale, having originally purchased the site from UCD for £1,211 per acre in 1962 (NAI, 2008/148/523). Speaking in the Dáil, the minister for education, John Wilson, commented: 'In my innocence I thought I would get the site cheaper from Dublin Corporation but they must have had a reasonable profit on it' (*Dáil Debates*, 29 Oct. 1980). For Dublin Corporation's decision not to include An Grianán in the sale of Albert College, see chapter 6.　**88** In what could equally be construed as an ominous sign for the Institute's future funding prospects, or a positive one for its ability to secure alternative sources of funding, both the building contractors and the architects contributed £300 towards the costs of the opening ceremony (speech by John Wilson, 1 Apr. 1980; N.J. O'Gorman to Reg Hannon, 19 Mar. 1980; Robinson, Keefe & Devane to same, 20 Mar. 1980 (DCUPO, 'NIHE Dublin: general, 1/2')). Quotation from Wilson speech.　**89** Higher Education Authority Act, 1971 (no. 22 of 1971); S.I. 295/1976.

2.4 Pictured at the turning of the sod ceremony at Albert College, 1 April 1980, are (l–r): Michael Woods (minister for health and social welfare); Michael MacCormac (chairman, NIHED governing body); Liam Ó Laidhin (Department of Education); John Wilson (minister for education); George Sisk; Joe O'Gorman; and Danny O'Hare (director, NIHED) (DCU Collection).

important milestone, elevating the NIHEs to a select group that enjoyed greater autonomy from the Department of Education than was the case with the regional technical colleges. The limits of that autonomy, however, became apparent when establishing legislation was introduced to the Oireachtas.

The process of drafting legislation did not begin until the end of 1979. From Limerick's perspective the matter was of some urgency, with members of its governing body threatening to resign if the government did not address the problems caused by the collapse of the relationship between the NUI and NIHE Limerick.[90] The Limerick legislation was thus drafted first, on the under-standing that the NIHE Dublin equivalent would be identical in all practical respects. Much of the debate on the autonomy and governance structures of the NIHEs thus occurred on the Limerick bill, introduced to the Oireachtas several months ahead of the Dublin bill.[91] Discussions and disagreements ranged across a wide variety of related topics, with opposition TDs reviving old arguments about the role of the HEA, the limits of academic freedom and the need for reform of the universities.

90 NAI, 2010/16/1 and 2010/16/175; *Irish Times*, 20 Dec. 1979; Fleming, *University of Limerick*, pp 73–4.   91 See *Dáil Debates*, 17 Apr., 21, 27, and 28 May, 18, 24 and 26 June 1980; *Seanad*

While these ancillary discussions revealed fundamental philosophical differences between the main political parties regarding the future of the higher-education sector, there were specific elements of the government's policy for the NIHEs that also proved troublesome. Most of the Limerick bill was unremarkable, its provisions largely focused on ensuring the NIHEs were capable of delivering degree, diploma and certificate level courses. Governance structures generally mirrored the traditional universities, with a governing body responsible for overall management of the affairs and property of the Institute. Governing body was also vested with the power to appoint subcommittees as deemed necessary for the running of the Institute and to appoint a director – subject to the approval of the minister for education. Subject to the authority of governing body, academic council would lead planning, co-ordination, development and oversight of the Institute's educational and research work.[92]

Though most TDs and senators welcomed the establishment of the NIHEs, there were sharp exchanges in the Oireachtas relating to the intended level of governmental oversight of the new institutions. The bill's most controversial elements related to the minister for education's influence over the composition of governing body, the appointment of staff and the future development of the Institute. In relation to governing body, the minister for education reserved the right to nominate up to thirteen (sixteen in the case of NIHE Dublin) of the twenty-five members. Both the minister for finance and the minister for education were also required to sanction all staff appointments and capital expenditure.[93]

Criticism from the opposition benches was led by Edward Collins, Fine Gael TD for Waterford, and John Horgan, Labour Party TD for Dublin County South; each was their party's spokesperson on education.[94] Their concerns were shared with (and indeed informed by) the Irish Federation of University Teachers, the Union of Students of Ireland and the Association of Scientific, Technical and Managerial Staffs.[95] Collins pulled no punches in his assessment of the bill. Describing it as a 'monstrosity', he contrasted its restrictive governance provisions with the greater freedoms afforded by the NUI university charters, and accused Wilson of setting up the NIHEs as mere subordinate

Debates, 2 and 3 July 1980.   92 National Institute for Higher Education, Limerick, Act, 1980 (no. 25 of 1980); National Institute for Higher Education, Dublin, Act, 1980 (no. 30 of 1980).   93 For the drafting of the National Institute for Higher Education, Limerick, Act, 1980, see NAI, 2009/135/491, 2010/16/1, 2010/27/306, 2010/27/423, 2010/53/462. See also Fleming, *University of Limerick*, pp 73–6.   94 Edward Collins (1941–2019) served as TD for Waterford from 1969 until 1987, and served as a minister of state from 1981 until 1986. John Horgan served as Labour Party senator for the National University of Ireland (1969–77) and as TD for Dublin County South (1977–81). He was appointed as a member of the European Parliament in 1981, before resigning in 1983 to take up a post as lecturer at NIHE Dublin. Horgan later became the first professor of journalism appointed in Ireland (March 1999) and, following his retirement in 2006, Ireland's first press ombudsman (2008–14).   95 *Sunday Press*, 20 Apr. 1980; *Irish Times*, 8 May 1980; Fleming, *University of Limerick*, p. 76.

2.5 Some senior members of staff on 1 April 1980. Back row (l–r): Barry Kehoe; B. Geraghty; Frank Soughley; Eugene Kennedy; Anthony Walsh; Brian Nettlefold; Alexander Spowart. Front row (l–r): Reg Hannon; Donal Clarke; Liam Ó Laidhin (Department of Education); Michael MacCormac (chairman, governing body); John Wilson (minister for education); Danny O'Hare; Tim Wheeler. (DCU Collection)

branches of the Department of Education.[96] University representatives in the Seanad feared the proposed legislation would set a precedent for increased government oversight of the university sector. Senator John A. Murphy of UCC echoed Collins' assessment: 'What I object to throughout the bill, and it is in virtually every clause, is the overwhelming and intrusive role of the Minister at every hand's turn.'[97]

Wilson's response to these criticisms exposed the tensions inherent in a system under which the state provided (or intended to provide) the bulk of funding. Arguing that comparisons with outdated university charters were irrelevant, Wilson insisted that more appropriate parallels were found in the governance structures of modern European institutions, specifically citing those in place at the Technological University of Eindhoven. More importantly, the bills were intentionally drafted to restrict the NIHEs' ability to introduce courses and adjust research objectives independently. Referring to his speech at NIHE

96 *Dáil Debates*, 17 Apr. 1980.   **97** *Seanad Debates*, 2 July 1980. Murphy was professor of Irish history at UCC.

Dublin's campus on 1 April, Wilson was unequivocal on the need for close control of the NIHEs:

> At Ballymun I referred to the dangers of academic drift, of institutions moving away from the primary objectives for which they were established. I repeat that this is a luxury we cannot afford, that the regional technical colleges and the NIHEs are firmly grounded in the technological and business areas ... and that any drift away from that will not necessarily be for the benefit of education in Ireland or the institutions themselves ... They must not be allowed to divert to a role for which they had not been intended.[98]

Both houses of the Oireachtas combined to present almost 100 amendments to the Limerick bill at committee and report stage. The majority of the opposition amendments were rejected by Wilson, though he did prove amenable to alterations to the composition and functions of academic council.[99] Observations on various iterations of the legislation were also submitted by both NIHE governing bodies throughout the drafting of the Limerick bill, which proved influential in reducing – to a very limited degree – the scope of the intended governmental oversight.[100]

Oireachtas approval for the Limerick legislation ensured that when the bill for NIHE Dublin – a near verbatim copy – was presented to the Dáil on 29 October, debate on its provisions was short. It passed all stages that day, taking just two days to progress through the Seanad.[101] While its speedy passage through both houses was certainly helped by cross-party consensus regarding the need for the Institute, there were dissenting voices on the opposition benches on specific points. Collins and Horgan once more took the lead, seeking clarification on the intended relationship between the CDVEC and NIHE Dublin, as well as the regional technical colleges planned for Dublin.[102] In the Seanad, criticism of the bill once more focused on the prominent role of the government in the Institute's governance. T.K. Whitaker, eminent economist and chancellor of the NUI, observed that 'The staffing provision in the ... Dublin Bill requires the approval of two Ministers for appointments, even though the financial case for staff has

---

98 *Dáil Debates*, 17 Apr. 1980. As approved, the legislation did not require governing body to seek ministerial sanction for the direction of its teaching and research programmes, which would seem to be at odds with the views expressed here by Wilson. However, given that the minister's approval was required for all staff appointments, the minister could have blocked development of curriculum and research programmes by refusing to sanction required appointments.   99 *Dáil Debates*, 21 and 27 May, 18 and 24 June 1980; *Seanad Debates*, 2 and 3 July 1980.   100 DCUPO, 'Governing body, reports and working papers, 1975–9' and GB80/1–5; NAI, 2010/16/175; Fleming, *University of Limerick*, p. 75; Horgan, *Dublin City University*, pp 18–19.   101 *Dáil Debates*, 29 Oct. 1980; *Seanad Debates*, 19 and 26 Nov. 1980.   102 *Dáil Debates*, 29 Oct. 1980. Collins also sought to revive recommendations contained in the report of the 1976 working party on technological education in

to be made to the Higher Education Authority. This seems an unnecessarily restrictive provision.'[103] His colleague, Prof. John A. Murphy, made another plea for reducing the government's influence by noting that nobody from the higher-education sector 'would dispute the need for public accountability, but that is not the same as ministerial suffocation ... There is failure here to trust the institutes and their staff and to trust their academic responsibility.'[104] Such objections were in vain, however, as it was simply not practical for the government to make amendments that would result in different governance structures for the NIHEs. Approved by the Seanad on 26 November, the National Institute for Higher Education Dublin Act was signed into law by President Patrick Hillery on 3 December.[105]

V

The CDVEC's self-contained and well-planned proposal to consolidate its operations at Ballymun ultimately led to the creation of two new higher-education institutions – NIHE Dublin and Dublin Institute of Technology. It was an unintended result of the incoherence of government policy for higher technical and technological education, a consequence of the various stakeholders in higher education navigating their way through the technological tangle of the 1970s. At several points along the way NIHE Dublin might well have simply faded away, a victim of variable government policy and squabbling over course allocation. While reflecting on proposals to bring the DIT colleges together on a single campus in Dublin, thirty years after the collapse of the Ballymun project, Fianna Fáil TD Pat Carey pondered what might have been:

> Those of us who have been for many years associated with the VEC, the DIT and other agencies might be tempted to ask 'what if?' in regard to the former Albert College grounds. When the late Jim Tunney was Leas-Cheann Comhairle and vice-chairman of the VEC and Paddy Donegan was chairman, they wanted to move the DIT onto what is now the DCU site. DCU has grown from humble beginnings to be a significant academic institution. In some respects, it is a pity the opportunity was not available to allow the City of Dublin VEC to locate that part of its development on the Albert College site.[106]

Tempting though it might be to engage in counterfactual speculation, what can be said for certain is that the need for a new higher-education institution in

Dublin.   **103** *Seanad Debates*, 19 Nov. 1980.   **104** Ibid., 26 Nov. 1980.   **105** NAI, 2010/66/72 and 2010/27/843.   **106** *Dáil Debates*, 2 Nov. 2004. Carey was commenting on the proposed relocation of DIT to the Grangegorman campus in Dublin city centre.

2.6 Two students on campus on 11 November 1980, the day that NIHED opened its doors (DCU Collection).

Dublin during the 1970s was acute. The successful establishment of NIHE Dublin was a landmark moment that changed the face of higher education, at both national and local level.

The Institute's governing body was pivotal to that success, despite the presence of internal tensions between the chairman and the majority of its members. Collectively, governing body and its subcommittees met on more than 100 occasions between June 1975 and the formal opening of the Institute in April 1980.[107] In addition to opposition to the Institute from within the higher-education sector, governing body also overcame a variety of logistical challenges. Prior to moving to Albert College in 1980, office accommodation was eventually provided in the McInerney building on Lower Grand Canal Street. It was here that interviews for the first staff appointments were held, and preparations for the opening of the Institute were made in the early months of 1980.[108] Operating its own admissions process, separate to the Central Applications Office, the Institute received more than 2,000 applications in advance of its opening – far exceeding expectations. As late as June 1980 the Institute expected to enrol 400 students. These expectations were, however, gradually reduced as construction

107 DCUPO, GB75–80; DCUPO, 'NIHE Dublin: general, 1/2'.   **108** NIHED, *Annual report, 1978–82*, pp 12–13; Eugene Kennedy to author, 18 Oct. 2017; Patricia Barker interview, 20 Sept. 2018. Designed by well-known architect Sam Stephenson (1933–2006), the McInerney building was refurbished and reopened as The One building in 2018.

delays pushed back the Institute's opening date to November, while many applicants received offers from other institutions. Enrolment estimates had been revised to 240 by the end of October.[109] By the time President Hillery signed its establishing act in December, 191 students were in the fourth week of their studies at the Institute. Their orientation had been held on 11 November 1980 – six years almost to the day after Minister Richard Burke surprised the higher-education sector by announcing the creation of a National Institute for Higher Education in Dublin.[110]

109 *Dáil Debates*, 29 Oct. 1980.   **110** *Irish Independent*, 12 June 1980; NIHED, *Annual report, 1978–82*, pp 10–11.

3

From NIHED to DCU: the making of a university, 1980–9

Writing in advance of the 1982/3 academic year, Michael MacCormac noted with some satisfaction the steady increase in the Institute's student enrolment and the addition of new degree programmes, as well as its burgeoning research profile and positive interactions with industry and business.[1] MacCormac's observations were presented in the Institute's second report to the minister for education, which covered the years 1978 to 1982. Its content marked a dramatic change in tone and substance from the barely suppressed anger and frustration that characterized the Institute's first report. Rather than demands for ministerial and departmental action to enable the Institute to open, this second report thanked both for their assistance and anticipated further years of mutually beneficial co-operation. Looking to the future, the report declared that the Institute would consider itself successful when it had proved to be 'an influential factor in providing a new technological and entrepreneurial generation of graduates who will be central to the future dynamism and wellbeing of this nation'.[2] The Institute faced a number of major challenges in the nine years between the arrival of its first students in November 1980 and its inauguration as Dublin City University in September 1989. Relations with the Department of Education and other government bodies were soon strained as the Institute's leadership chafed against restrictions on its autonomy. Staff recollections vividly convey the paucity of financial and material support available for their educational and research work, as they attempted to create a successful institution of higher education. This lack of resources also impacted the Institute's student body, whose attempts to form vibrant clubs and societies and agitation for improved facilities caused tensions with senior staff and leadership. In spite of these difficulties, the immediate success of the Institute was apparent from the rapidly increasing number of students, the development of innovative degree programmes and the strength of the connections created with industrial and commercial partners. Within a few years NIHE Dublin was on course to attain university status, a stunning achievement for such a young institution, due in large part to the emphasis placed on producing applied and pure research of an internationally recognized standard – a crucial factor in convincing a body of

---

1 NIHED, *Annual report, 1978–82*, p. 5. Having been appointed to governing body in 1975, MacCormac served as its chairman from 1979 to 1982.   2 Ibid., p. 32.

international experts that NIHE Dublin's operations were, at the very least, equal to those of the traditional universities.

I

Though the Institute did not enrol its first students until November 1980, hiring of staff had begun at the start of the year. As Dr Tony Coulson would later recall, 'it was strange being interviewed for a job at a university that didn't really exist yet'. Arriving on campus shortly in advance of the beginning of first term proved to be an eye-opening experience:

> Leslie Davis [head of the School of Applied Languages] gave me the warmest of welcomes in a bare and dusty room in a very dilapidated An Grianán ... I am not sure if we were sitting on cardboard boxes, but if there were two chairs there was not much else. It was not until next year, I believe, that temporary prefabs [the Hamstead building], that wobbled as you walked along the corridor, arrived to serve as offices, situated on what are now the front lawns. It only took one or two of those to house the then Faculty – and we were a literally inter-disciplinary enterprise, all Schools thrown in together: I was sharing with Tony Foley of the Business School, which was quite a stimulating experience.[3]

Patricia Barker took up her role as lecturer in the School of Accounting and Finance in September 1980. Preparations for the arrival of students was then still underway:

> Our first weeks were a frenetic whirl of putting together syllabi for the degrees in Accounting and Finance and Business Studies ... [We] defended a panel visit from the NCEA and spoke confidently and authoritatively about material that we had only just read about, assuring the panel brazenly that we were fully competent to teach it.[4]

Advice and assistance came from a number of quarters, including higher-education institutions at home and abroad. Following his appointment as head of the School of Chemical Sciences in July 1980, Albert Pratt received vital support from Duncan Thorburn Burns of Queen's University, Belfast, and Tony Finan of University College Galway:

3 Tony Coulson, 'The early years' in Péchenart and Williams (eds), *School of Applied Languages and Intercultural Studies*, pp 5–6. The Hamstead building was actually opened in 1980 – see chapter 6.
4 Patricia Barker, 'Years a'growing', *DCU Times*, 2005.

N.I.H.E DIARY

vol. 2   *Friday 13-3-81*

3.1 The cover of the second issue of the NIHED staff newsletter (later renamed *By Degrees*) poked fun at remarks made by the newly elected provost of Trinity College Dublin (DCU Collection).

THIS TOWN AIN'T BIG ENOUGH FOR BOTH OF US!

Duncan and Tony … were members of the interview board that appointed me in 1980 and both were very supportive during the early years. Indeed they had been advising Danny [O'Hare] prior to my appointment and, even before I formally took up the post, I was presented with a thick booklet which they had prepared, and which I still have, and which was a comprehensive list of the equipment required for setting up new chemistry labs. This was invaluable as a starting point and, as you can imagine, saved a huge amount of time in ordering in the equipment in such a short time prior to the first student intake in November 1980.[5]

O'Hare could also count on assistance from Prof. Douglas Wright, president of the University of Waterloo in Ontario, Canada. Several NIHE Dublin initiatives were influenced by systems established at Waterloo, including the model for the Institute's Industrial Advisory Council (which met for the first time in October 1985), and the university hosted fact-finding missions by members of the Institute's governing body and staff.[6]

---

5 Quotation taken from Albert Pratt to author, 28 Aug. 2018.   6 Danny O'Hare to D.T. Wright, 17 Oct. 1985 (DCUPO, 'Correspondence: general, 1980–5').

For all the support received during its early years, some elements within Irish higher education continued to regard the Institute with suspicion or outright hostility. In March 1981, following his election as provost of TCD, Prof. William A. Watts made the extraordinary complaint that his university had been pushed into the background by recent developments in higher education:

> This is something I will have to fight. All the emphasis is on RTCs and NIHEs. Yet the universities are still the largest producers of techno-logically trained people in the State. I suppose there is more political mileage in new institutions, but the government should realise that it is still cheaper to provide additional technological places in the established institutions.[7]

Watts' comments were the latest attempt to undermine the Institute, in public and in private, from senior figures within higher education. Yet O'Hare and his staff also found allies and supporters within the Department of Education and across the sector willing to offer advice and assistance. Those who interacted with the Institute were quick to observe that its standards were impressive. Prof. Jim Larkin of University College Galway served as one of the external examiners for NIHE Dublin's first exams, and later gave O'Hare his impressions:

> I would like to express my congratulations to you on the performance of both your staff and students during 1980–81 in the particular areas I was involved in. The performance of Dr [Alexander] Spowart and Drs [Martin] Henry and [Eugene] Kennedy is to [be] paid a very great tribute … I would also like to note my appreciation of Dr [Albert] Pratt and of course the heavy load carried by the Maths Department.

Larkin noted that the Physics and Basic Computing courses were particularly well structured, and signed off with an observation that no doubt resonated with O'Hare and his staff: 'One of the most obvious needs in the physics area is that of good technical personnel and facilities.'[8]

The benefits of such advice and assistance were, nonetheless, diluted by the Institute's poor relations with the HEA and Department of Education in the key area of staff recruitment. Its ability to hire good personnel was hampered throughout the 1980s by both a lack of finance and the stringent recruitment controls imposed by the Department.[9] Over the course of the decade, both NIHEs repeatedly clashed with the Department and the HEA over the issue of staff appointments.[10] Initial disputes centred on the terms of employment for

7 *Irish Times*, 6 Mar. 1981. 8 J.P. Larkin to Danny O'Hare, 22 Sept. 1981 (DCUPO, 'Correspondence: general, 1980–1'). 9 See pp 36–9 above for concerns relating to government control of recruitment. 10 For NIHE Limerick's difficulties with the HEA and Department of

heads of school, and particularly salary levels.[11] At the end of its first academic year, the Institute employed 48 staff on permanent contracts, 29 staff on temporary full-time contracts, 16 temporary staff and 4 temporary support staff (97 total). These details were requested by the minister prior to issuing the commencement order for the Institute's establishment act, and the Department reacted with surprise to what it perceived as a higher-than-necessary number of staff.[12] This perception, perhaps inevitable, failed to take into account that a low staff/student ratio was not only necessary for the successful launch of the Institute, but also a very temporary situation.

The Department's inability to appreciate these factors was soon made clear. Under Section 9 of the NIHE Dublin Act of 1980, the Institute was obliged to seek the approval both of the minister for education and the minister for finance before employing additional staff, and advance approval was also required before publication of employment terms and conditions. Prior to the act's commencement order (issued on 17 June 1981), the Department clarified these conditions:[13]

> The specific approval of the Minister is, therefore, necessary for the creation of any additional posts at the Institute, whether permanent, temporary, or part time, and the Institute should not in future make any further appointments without such approval. The Minister's approval is also required for the appointment of any applicant proposed for a particular post.

Any proposal concerning the creation of new staff positions at all levels, and the subsequent filling of those posts, was to be submitted via the HEA for approval by the ministers for education and finance.[14] Effectively, the Institute was required to get approval from three separate bodies before it could appoint staff, let alone plan for the creation of new departments or the expansion of existing courses, which would, naturally, entail the employment of additional instructors.[15] As Danny O'Hare later recalled, the end result was a stifling of ambitions:

Education regarding employment of staff, see Fleming, *University of Limerick*, pp 55–7, 163–4; Ed Walsh with Kieran Fagan, *Upstart: friends, foes and founding a university* (Cork, 2011), pp 199–200. **11** DCUPO, 'NIHE Dublin: general, 2/2'; DCUPO, GB 82/A3/8. **12** M. Nic Uidhir to Danny O'Hare, 28 May 1981 (DCUPO, 'NIHE Dublin: general, 1/2'). Staff numbers had increased to 106 by the end of the 1981/2 academic year (NIHED, *Annual report, 1978–82*, pp 38–42). **13** National Institute for Higher Education, Dublin, Act, 1980 (no. 30 of 1980), s. 9; S.I. 213/1981. **14** According to a later note by Danny O'Hare, insistence on ministerial oversight for all new appointments was largely driven by the Department of Finance (M. Nic Uidhir to Danny O'Hare, 14 Jan. 1981; Danny O'Hare to Michael [MacCormac], 15 Apr. 1981 (DCUPO, 'NIHE Dublin: general, 1/2')). Quotation from Nic Uidhir letter. **15** J.F. Dukes to Danny O'Hare, 13 Nov. 1980 (DCUPO, 'NIHE Dublin: general, 1/2'). These restrictions were also to be placed on NIHE

3.2 Members of the first statutory governing body of NIHED, appointed 19 June 1981 (l–r): Danny O'Hare; Susan Folan; Barbara Wright; Ann Saunders; Cathal Brugha; Paul Quigley; John McKay; Terence Larkin; James Glynn; Edward Harney; Anton Carroll; Sean McDonagh; Carol Moffett; Thomas Ambrose; Michael O'Donnell; Robert Nichol; Peter Gallagher; Robert Clarke; Thomas McCarthy; Donal Clarke; Patricia Jo Corr; Michael MacCormac. Missing: Otto Glaser; Patrick Kehoe; John Kelly; Pierce Ryan (DCU Collection).

> [The civil service] controlled absolutely the staff allocations we got, and to the silly extent that they required us to send the names and the CVs and application forms of people we were proposing to appoint to lectureships … to the HEA, who would send it to the Department of Education, who would send it then on to the Department of Finance. And months later you might get a reply. We got fed up of that very quickly.

The Institute's governing body and senior leadership resented such close control of staffing, and in 1981 decided to test the limits of the arrangement by placing several ads in national papers advertising for contract staff, on the basis that the requirement for government-approved hiring only applied to permanent, pensionable posts. O'Hare then left for a holiday in France, thus ensuring he was uncontactable and that the advertisement could not be rescinded.[16]

Limerick, Thomond College and the National Council for Educational Awards. For an example of an advertisement for technical positions at NIHED, which included the disclaimer 'Appointments will be made subject to the approval of the Minister for Education', see *Irish Times*, 5 June 1981. **16** Danny O'Hare interview, 28 May 2018. NIHED advertised a number of positions in the summer of 1981 – see *Irish Times*, 5, 18, 19, 26 June and 10 July 1981.

The Department of Education's reaction was as expected, with Ed Walsh and O'Hare later called into a meeting with the minister, John Boland.[17] Both men were, however, well prepared and came armed with legal advice supporting their positions.[18] Intensive negotiations between all parties over the following eighteen months proved inconclusive.[19] NIHE Dublin later found itself instructed to terminate several contracts, awarded at administrative and support-staff levels, following labour court proceedings that revealed the extent to which the Institute had ignored the Department's specified appointments procedure.[20] Relations between the Institute and the government on this issue remained tense for the remainder of the decade, exacerbated by the government's failure to proceed with the planned Phase 2 campus development.[21]

During her tenure as minister for education, Gemma Hussey identified Phase 2 as one of her top priorities, in light of its potential to provide a further 1,000 student places.[22] Yet with the public finances under enormous pressure, the Department of Finance consistently refused to allow it to proceed, unable to underwrite the projected cost of £23m.[23] Her successor as minister, Mary O'Rouke, faced an equally prohibitive financial climate. As minister for finance, Ray MacSharry famously earned the nickname 'Mack the Knife' following the introduction of the budget for 1987, which implemented drastic cuts to public expenditure. Higher education did not escape MacSharry's knife, with virtually all planned capital investment in third-level infrastructure postponed. MacSharry's cuts also included an embargo on new appointments in the public sector. More damagingly, third-level institutions were required to reduce pay costs by 1 per cent in 1987, and 3 per cent in 1988, while also reducing staff numbers by 3 per cent in both years. Externally funded posts were also included in the embargo on employment, which was a blow to the Institute's ambitions to attract significant research funds from industry. Consulting the legal profession once more, the Institute was advised that sponsorship from the private sector could not be used to develop new projects or appoint staff. Frustrations were soon made clear: 'This appears to us to be an extremely anti-developmental

17 John Boland served as minister for education from June 1981 until March 1982. His tenure was notable for the abolition of corporal punishment in schools (Lawrence W. White, 'Boland, John James (1944–2000)' in *DIB*). 18 Danny O'Hare to Liam Ó Laidhin, 1 Dec. 1981 (DCUPO, 'NIHE Dublin: general, 1/2'); Walsh, *Upstart*, pp 199–200. The legal advice was supplied by Niall McCarthy, the pre-eminent barrister of his day. He was appointed to the Supreme Court in November 1982 (Adrian Hardiman, 'McCarthy, Niall St John (1925–92)' in *DIB*). 19 M. Nic Uidhir to HEA, 22 Dec. 1982 (DCUPO, 'Department of Education, 1981–6'). 20 M. Nic Uidhir to Danny O'Hare, 26 July 1983; 'Note of meeting in the Department of Education', 22 Nov. 1983 (DCUPO, 'Department of Education, 1981–6'). 21 For an overview of the development of the NIHED/DCU campus at Glasnevin, see chapter 6. 22 Walsh, *Higher education in Ireland*, pp 331–2. Hussey held the education portfolio from December 1982 until February 1986. 23 See, for example, Department of Education memo for government, 24 May 1985 (UCDA, P179/158). Phase 2 had been identified as a government priority both in Department of Education's *Programme for action in education, 1984–7* (1984), and the national economic and social development plan,

aspect of the embargo, one which will kill initiative and not save money. It will turn money away from the colleges.'[24] Contracts and research funds from industry sources would thus have to be turned down, and the introduction of several new degree programmes delayed. Arguing for an exemption from the embargo, the Institute pointedly observed that the restriction on external funding contradicted 'stated government policy of making us interact with industry and of encouraging colleges to diversify their sources of funds'. The unilateral application of the new financial dispensation across the sector was also regarded as unfair to a new institution. If funding cuts and recruitment embargoes were to be applied evenly across the board at third level, 'the fatter institutions [will] remain relatively fat and the lean institutions are cut to the bone. Indeed, it seems we are paying a special penalty because we are lean or more cost-effective.'[25]

NIHE Dublin's ambitions during the 1980s were thus restricted in a variety of ways. Employment was closely controlled by the HEA and the Department of Education. The Institute was allocated posts on a stricter basis than any of the 'traditional' universities, and stricter even than NIHE Limerick. While the HEA stipulated that the ratio of students to teaching staff should be 17:1, as the 1980s drew to a close the ratio at NIHE Dublin stood at 19:1. Equally problematic was the fact that the ratio of senior to junior faculty at the Institute was worse than at Limerick and the universities. This put the Institute at a serious disadvantage when attempting to recruit staff to its core research areas, including electronics, computing and biotechnology.

While the Institute's leadership quietly grappled with the implications of government policy and attempted to paper over the cracks evident in the facilities at Glasnevin, teaching and support staff concentrated on providing the best possible learning experience for their students. The Institute's financial woes were seen as a challenge to be overcome. For John Horgan, who joined the School of Communications in 1983, the 'huge energy, optimism [and] sense of adventure' on campus were 'more than sufficient to compensate for the occasional material deficiencies'.[26] Indeed, the Institute's small size was a decided advantage 'in terms of getting all the important players moving in the same direction at the same time. Most of us, myself included, knew little about Danny's past, his private negotiating skills, or his links with those in administrative or political circles, but just got dug in to our work and enjoyed his support.'[27]

Department of the Taoiseach/Government of Ireland, *Building on reality* (Dublin, 1984). 24 'NIHED Factsfile', Jan. 1986 (DCUPO, 'NIHE Dublin: general'). 25 'General points in regard to inflexibilities in the embargo system', July 1987 (DCUPO, 'NIHE Dublin: general'). The Institute also noted that its students paid fees equal to or higher than any other university-level institution in Ireland yet made do with poor facilities, and that its state grant per student and expenditure per student were both the lowest of any university-level institution. 26 John Horgan to author, 13 May 2019. 27 John Horgan to author, 1 May 2019.

3.3 Students and staff at the library issue desk in the Henry Grattan building
(DCU Collection).

Produced intermittently between March 1981 and the end of 1984, the
Institute's staff newsletter, *By Degrees*, illustrates the development and
cultivation of the close-knit community that existed on campus.[28] Initially edited
by Marian Jordan, and later by Leslie Davis, the newsletter printed essays,
poems and editorials, with Richard O'Kennedy of the School of Biological
Sciences one of the most frequent contributors. The intimacy of the Institute in
its early days was evident in a number of ways, including the hosting of a dinner
dance for staff and students at the Gresham Hotel on 5 June 1981.[29] Just two
days earlier the Institute's first staff-vs-students sports day had proved to be an
enormous success. Students ended the day with the Albert College Memorial
Shield – made from a piece of wood scavenged from the old plant pathology
labs.[30]

The bond and camaraderie between staff was strengthened by the shared
experience of enduring the spartan nature of the Institute's facilities, which made
a lasting impression. Library books occasionally made useful, if unsteady,

28 Several issues of *By Degrees* are available in the President's Office Archive. In a nod to the
Institute's name, the first two issues were called *NIHE Diary*. A subsequent competition to select a
more permanent name produced suggestions including The Albert ChroNIHEcle, NIHEWS
and Not Another Memo. The winning entry was suggested by Maeve McCarthy (*By Degrees (NIHE
Diary)*, 13 Mar. and 14 Apr. 1981). **29** *By Degrees*, 21 May 1981. **30** Ibid., 18 June 1981.
Publication of *By Degrees* ceased by the end of 1984, no doubt rendered somewhat obsolete by more
formal institutional newsletters, *Nuacht* and *Newslink*, which began publication in 1983 and 1984,

substitutes for chairs in the early days. The chronic shortage of space in the library proved a perennial problem until the opening of the O'Reilly Library in 2000.[31] The Hamstead building, so unsatisfactory for housing both offices and teaching space, was subject to vandalism of an unusual kind when a badger chewed its way into the building to make a temporary home. There was also no money for the installation of a telephone system before the Institute opened, and for some time afterwards there was just one generally accessible phone on campus – and even that was supplied by the ingenuity of a staff member using methods that were not strictly legal. As a result, while calls out could be made, nobody knew the Institute's phone number until Sandy Spowart happened to be sitting in front of the phone when it rang, picked it up and quickly asked the caller what number they had dialled. Some members of staff avoided queues for the phone by waiting until the end of the day and then using the pay phone in The Slipper, a pub located on Ballymun Avenue. Unsurprisingly, it soon became an unofficial common room, for both staff and students.[32]

Creating a new third-level institution in the midst of an economic recession was no easy task. Richard O'Kennedy recalled arriving to start his new position just days ahead of the first student enrolments in November 1980: 'There was no option but to pitch in and get the show on the road, despite incomplete and defective labs [and] a chronic shortage of everything, but with huge enthusiasm, good humour and co-operation.'[33] Having been present at the opening of a new higher-education institution, many staff felt a sense of ownership that created a personal interest in seeing NIHE Dublin succeed in spite of the difficult economic climate:

> We were living in an environment where everything was tough … and we realised the constraints under which we were operating … Because it was new and we all knew each other – I knew every lecturer in every department around the place – we were hugely enthusiastic about the place, and it's no exaggeration to say that we really wanted to make a success of this.[34]

respectively. *Newslink* was produced by the Industrial Liaison Unit and proved to be a key element in NIHED/DCU's interactions with private industry. *Nuacht* was published on a near monthly basis from the summer of 1983 until the early 1990s, when publication became increasingly erratic. Neither *Newslink* nor *Nuacht* survived the turn of the millennium, as the university increasingly moved towards the electronic dissemination of news. **31** In 1990 there were just 393 seats in the library for a student population of more than 3,000 (*DCU Bull Sheet*, Nov. 1990). See also Paul Sheehan, 'Dublin City University new library – a library for the information age', *Liber Quarterly*, 10:2 (2000), pp 84–93. **32** Richard O'Kennedy, 'Coming of age: 21 years at DCU' (*DCU News*, Mar. 2002); Eugene Kennedy to author, 18 Oct. 2017; Danny O'Hare interview, 28 May 2018; Patricia Barker interview, 20 Sept. 2018; Albert Pratt interview, 19 Oct. 2018. Dr Alexander Spowart was head of the School of Physical Sciences. **33** O'Kennedy, 'Coming of age: 21 years at DCU'. **34** Patricia Barker interview, 20 Sept. 2018.

Staff were forced to rely on their creativity and initiative to develop innovative learning experiences throughout the first two decades, as the facilities available on the Glasnevin campus slowly caught up to the institution's ambitions. As director of the Institute from 1977 until 1999, Danny O'Hare was uniquely positioned to observe the key role played by academic, administrative and support staff in shaping the Institute and driving its successful development:

> We were lucky to get so many good people. They were young, ambitious, dynamic people who, if they joined one of the established universities would be very much junior, and they would have to deal with a lot of bureaucracy. Whereas they walked into NIHE Dublin and they were heads of departments straight away, so they had a lot of influence in what happened, and a lot of ownership.[35]

The Institute's small size also permitted the development of an organizational structure that encouraged individual schools to direct institutional development. Schools and academic units were arranged in a flat, flexible structure that remained largely untouched until the early 2000s.[36] While schools were grouped within faculties headed by deans, each school and academic support unit served as its own cost centre, simultaneously allowing autonomy and direct access to the institution's leadership. Nor was easy access to leadership – initially at least – restricted to heads of school. Somewhat paradoxically, the chronic lack of government investment in the Glasnevin campus served to create a more egalitarian environment, particularly prior to the mid-1990s. Facilities for staff were so spartan that all levels mingled in the same space: the simple act of going for coffee created opportunities for interacting with leadership, offering opinions and influencing decisions.[37] As Helena Sheehan recalled, the staff common room 'could not have been more different from either TCD or UCD. Professors and porters mixed together there and at staff socials and all were in the same trade union.'[38]

Faculties, schools and academic units individually reported to academic council, which in turn reported to governing body. The net result was that the Institute's director, Danny O'Hare, wielded greater executive authority than his university counterparts. With the director appointed as an *ex officio* member of both governing body and academic council, every decision regarding the

---

35 Danny O'Hare interview, 28 May 2018. In a letter written on 28 July 1987 to Liam Ó Laidhin, chairman of the HEA, O'Hare noted that NIHED had developed 'by virtue of obtaining an extraordinary commitment from young, dedicated academics and staff' (DCUPO, 'NIHE Dublin: physical matters, 1978–86, 2/2').   36 Charts illustrating the organizational structure of the Institute (which remained largely unchanged until 2004) are available in the Institute's *Annual report* for 1978–82, p. 35, and NIHED, *Institutional review, 1980–6* (Dublin, 1986).   37 Brian Trench interview, 9 May 2019.   38 Helena Sheehan, *Navigating the zeitgeist: a story of the Cold War, the new left, Irish republicanism, and international communism* (New York, 2019), p. 288.

3.4, 3.5 Inadvertently highlighting the inadequacy of NIHED's facilities, this badger caused significant damage when it attempted to make a home in the prefabs that housed research labs. Reproduced by kind permission of Michael Burke.

Institute's future flowed through O'Hare's office.[39] Between 1981 and the end of 1985, heads of school met on a weekly basis, with O'Hare as chairman. In January 1986 O'Hare established the executive group, which met weekly to oversee day-to-day administration, with meetings of all heads of school taking place on a monthly basis thereafter.[40] Read cumulatively, the minutes of all three bodies indicate that without O'Hare's imprimatur, policy proposals had little chance of adoption. While the clarity of O'Hare's vision and his commitment to the implementation of that vision were vital to the success and growth of NIHED/DCU, the level of oversight maintained by his office was not always welcomed by some of the Institute's more senior academics.[41]

II

Travelling to the Glasnevin campus on the 17A bus on the morning of 11 November 1980, Michael Patton arrived late for his first day as a third-level student. Making his way to the lecture theatre where Danny O'Hare was in the midst of welcoming Patton's classmates, Patton realized that the only entrance was beside the podium where O'Hare was speaking. Unwilling to disturb the Institute's Director in full flow, Patton instead made his way to registration, thus becoming the first student ever to enrol at NIHE Dublin.[42]

Admission to the Institute in 1980 was governed by a mix of points accrued during the Leaving Certificate examination, and performance in aptitude tests and personal interviews. In utilizing this system, the Institute sought a more rounded and comprehensive picture of applicants' abilities than was measured by the Leaving Cert. From 1981 the Institute also participated in the third-level applications system administered by the Central Applications Office. That year more than 6,000 applications for places were received, with room available for only a fraction. To cope with such a large number, aptitude tests were administered in Sligo, Galway, Cork and a number of Dublin locations.[43] The

---

39 National Institute for Higher Education, Dublin, Act, 1980 (no. 30 of 1980), second schedule, s. 7. The position of director was formally renamed president by the Dublin City University Act of 1989, though O'Hare had adopted the title by the end of 1985. 40 DCUPO, GB86/1, 2; NIHED, *Institutional review, 1980–6*, s. 10. Membership of the executive originally consisted of the president, registrar, four deans, the director of Industrial Liaison, the personnel officer and the finance officer. Current membership consists of the president, deputy president, executive deans, director of communications and marketing, two elected staff representatives, president of the Students' Union, the vice president of external affairs, and the university's senior officers. 41 Martin Clynes, 'DCU: the movie' (*DCU Times*, 2005); Michael Townson, 'A very personal memoir' in Péchenart and Williams (eds), *School of Applied Languages and Intercultural Studies*, pp 35–7. 42 Michael Patton, 'Unique claims and holy hour drinks' (*DCU Times*, 2005). 43 NIHED, *Annual report, 1978–82*, p. 11; *Irish Independent*, 5 Nov. 1981. A thorough evaluation of the aptitude-testing programme was completed during the 1983/4 academic year, in conjunction

Institute's popularity with students grew at an impressive rate, with the CAO reporting that demand for places at both NIHEs increased from 17,000 in 1980 to more than 19,000 the following year, a 12.5 per cent increase facilitated by the provision of new buildings on each campus.[44] Figures available for the period 1982–7 demonstrate that the Institute received the third highest number of CAO applications, behind only UCD and TCD, when all preferences were taken into account. Proportionally, however, NIHE Dublin attracted the highest ratio of applications per available first-year place of any institution.[45] Table 3.1 illustrates the growth in CAO applications during the 1980s. While its location within the country's largest population centre was a natural advantage, the necessity of holding aptitude tests at various centres in Connacht, Munster and Leinster demonstrates that students applied for reasons other than ease of access. The number of applicants sitting the aptitude test increased steadily during the 1980s (table 3.2), indicating the Institute's success in increasing national awareness of the nature and quality of its undergraduate programmes. Indeed, by 1982 the Institute had students from every county in the Republic of Ireland, and a student from Northern Ireland. As O'Hare observed in his annual report for 1982/3: 'It is pleasing to note that the "National" in the Institute's title continues to be relevant, in that 50 per cent of the students hail from outside the Greater Dublin Region.' Equally important was the fact that two-thirds of the students from Dublin were from the north of the county.[46]

Table 3.1. **Applications to NIHE Dublin via CAO, 1981–7**

Year	First preferences	All preferences	Direct applications
1981	1,263	6,201	N/A
1982	1,569	8,198	N/A
1983	1,846	9,345	N/A
1984	2,105	9,980	628
1985	2,571	11,133	823
1986	2,538	11,293	680
1987	3,076	12,890	1,029

Source: NIHED, *Annual report, 1986/7*, pp 68–9.

with the Educational Research Centre at St Patrick's College, Drumcondra (DCUPO, GB84/2–4; *Nuacht*, Mar. 1984). **44** *Irish Times*, 20 Aug. 1981. **45** Danny O'Hare to John Hayden, 15 Apr. 1985 (DCUPO, 'NIHE Dublin: physical matters, 1978–86, 2/2'); NIHED, *Annual report, 1986/7*, pp 68–9; *Irish Independent*, 25 July 1987. **46** NIHED, *Annual report, 1978–82*, p. 10; NIHED, *Annual report, 1982/3*, p. 8; Horgan, *Dublin City University*, pp 22–5. Quote from 1982/3 report.

Table 3.2. Number of aptitude tests administered, 1980–7

Year	Number	Year	Number	Year	Number
1980	1,571	1983	6,414	1986	8,301
1981	4,371	1984	7,015	1987	9,513
1982	5,420	1985	8,508		

Source: NIHED, *Annual report, 1986/7*, p. 69.

In addition to the work of the Institute's staff in creating high-quality academic programmes, the cultivation of a vibrant student culture was also necessary for the institution to prosper. There were no clubs or societies waiting to welcome students in 1980, and the campus location offered little in the way of local facilities and amenities. Student Services distributed a comprehensive information pack to new students, outlining the range of supports available.[47] Included within was a survey seeking expressions of interest in the kinds of clubs and societies that students would like to see formed.[48] Based on that survey, Student Services assisted enterprising undergraduates in the establishment of a students' union in 1981, as well as debating and film societies, photography and electronics hobby clubs and a social-action group. Several of the more well-known DCU student societies trace their roots to the 1980s, including the Media Production Society, the university's oldest continually running society. Originally founded to produce *NIcHE*, a student newspaper/magazine known for its creative covers, one of the society's co-founders, John Paul Coakley, later revealed its true origins as 'a shadow funding scheme for a news sheet by a bunch of [Communications] students with, in so far as they had any ideology, an anarchist and republican bag of thoughts, and formed in that crucible of left wing thought – The Slipper.'[49]

Sports clubs for Gaelic football, rugby, basketball, hockey, swimming, badminton and karate were also formed in that first year.[50] The first Gaelic

47 Upon opening, the Institute's Student Services Unit consisted of Barry Kehoe (head of unit), Annette McGee (counsellor), Margo Bellew (accommodation officer), Dr Thomas Coghlan and Dr Mary Coghlan (medical doctors), Fr Patrick McManus (Roman Catholic chaplain), Revd Desmond Harman (Church of Ireland chaplain), Revd K. Lindsay (Methodist chaplain) and Revd Alan Martin (Presbyterian chaplain). They were soon joined by Des Broderick (sport and recreation officer) and Elsie Lawrence (nurse). Broderick was replaced by John Kerrane in 1981.   48 Barry Kehoe to all staff, 17 Nov. 1980 (DCUPO, 'Student Services, 1980–7'). The professionalism of the Student Services Unit was influential in the creation of a similar service at Carlow Regional Technical College in 1984. John Gallagher, principal of the RTC, was a member of NIHED's governing body from 1975 until 1981, and again from 1987 until 1992 (Norman McMillan and Martin Nevin (eds), 'Practical, business and physical education: perspectives from the early years – part 2 of a history of the RTC and IT Carlow', *Carloviana*, 53 (2004) p. 80).   49 Quoted in 'Celebrating 30 years of media production, 1985–2015' (DCU MPS, 2015), p. 5. Coakley's co-founders were Enda Scott and Declan Tracey.   50 Student Services Unit report, Aug. 1981

football team is believed to have assembled on 12 November 1980 and to have played its first match the following day.[51] While that story may well be apocryphal, the Institute certainly fielded a fresher's football team on 19 November, and played Carysfort College in division three of the higher-education league just two days later.[52] The appointment in 1981 of John Kerrane as sport and recreation officer was an important moment in the development of NIHED/DCU's sporting culture, adding further impetus to the creation of sports clubs and the later drive to improve the sports facilities available on campus. Also formed in 1980, the Institute's rugby team – coached by Kieran Molloy – rounded out its inaugural season with a thumping victory over St Patrick's College, Drumcondra.[53]

Athletics was sufficiently well established by March 1985 to allow for the hosting of the Cross Country Intervarsity Championships at Glasnevin. In addition to competing in formal, national competitions, the NIHEs of Dublin and Limerick combined to create the unique 35's Trophy. Held annually, the first competition was hosted by Limerick on 14 May 1981. Sponsored by Bank of Ireland, on that occasion fifty NIHE Dublin students competed against their Limerick counterparts in basketball, Gaelic football, badminton and volleyball. Limerick were victorious in each of the competitions. NIHE Dublin's Fr Pat McManus took the opportunity to praise the excellent sporting facilities on the Limerick campus, lamenting the fact that NIHE Dublin had only just managed to open temporary shower and dressing room facilities.[54]

Precisely three years after the enrolment of its first students, the Institute reached another milestone when it made its first academic awards. Fifty-one students were conferred with primary degrees in communications studies or accounting and finance, while thirty-two students also graduated with diplomas in either journalism or accounting.[55] To mark the occasion, Seóirse Bodley was commissioned to compose an original piece of music for performance at this first and all subsequent graduations.[56] Titled 'Celebration music' and scored for three trumpets and a string quartet, the piece was well received when performed at convocation by the Testore Ensemble.[57]

William Guidera, a senior porter at the Institute until his retirement in the 1990s, composed an essay to mark the occasion. Remembered by those who knew him as a 'true gentleman of the old stock', Guidera noted that this historic

(DCUPO, 'Student Services, 1980–7'); *Irish Independent*, 5 Nov. 1981.   51 *DCU Bull Sheet*, May/June 1991.   52 *Irish Times*, 19 Nov. 1980.   53 *By Degrees*, 5 Apr. 1981.   54 *By Degrees*, 21 May 1981. Speaking in 1999, UL's special events manager, Ben Angley, claimed that the longevity of the 35's Trophy competition and continued good relationship between the UL and DCU student bodies was down to the fact that DCU was 'a hell of a lot less pretentious' than the other Dublin universities (*College View*, Dec. 1999). The competition is no longer extant and was last held *c*.2005.   55 DCUPO, 'Conferring 1983'; NIHED, *Annual report, 1982/3*, pp 118–19; Horgan, *Dublin City University*, p. 23.   56 Danny O'Hare to Seóirse Bodley, 23 Apr. 1983 (DCUPO, 'Conferring 1983').   57 DCUPO, 'Conferring 1983'; *Irish Independent*, 12 Nov. 1983; *Irish Times*, 18 Nov. 1983; Gareth

moment in the Institute's evolution was an apposite continuation of the educational legacy of its campus, begun almost 150 years earlier with the opening of the Albert Agricultural College:

> The National Institute for Higher Education in Dublin is to be found in the grounds, and incorporated into the buildings, of the old Albert College. This was itself a celebrated seat of learning devoted to the teaching of agricultural and horticultural science. The fusion of old and new blends happily here. A broad avenue entered through massive stone gate piers and lined by graceful and ancient lime trees leads directly from Ballymun Avenue to the Albert College. This latter building is typical of Victorian architecture in its solidity. Great blocks of cut limestone set fair to last timelessly in durable masonry form the outer shell of the building, which is designed along strictly utilitarian lines. The giant beech and elm trees which surround the south and west side of this building soften its harshest lines. A more simple functional entrance from Collins Avenue with a smooth driveway, flanked with a pedestrian path, winds through undulating parkland. A vista of glass and russet brown brickwork greets the eye as the entirely new laboratories, classrooms, canteen and reception area come into view. Imaginatively and artistically landscaped grounds with groups of standard trees and massed shrub borders help to bring together old and new and unify both into a very pleasing and acceptable oneness.
>
> That oneness of unity is borne out again when one reflects on the origins of the two establishments: the old Albert College and the new NIHE. Way back in 1838, the first was set up to supply a great need … [A]t its inception, its aim was no different from that of the authorities of the NIHE today. To train the eager young people of now in the technology and skill which will enable them to make a living in our modern world. Then, as now, success depends to a great degree in being right up to date in knowledge and skill.
>
> Our present day young people should consider themselves fortunate, for here at Glasnevin the environs in which they conduct their studies must be as near ideal as is possible. The aspect is open and airy. Between gaps in the trees are glimpses of mountain vistas. As Shakespeare said of a lesser place: 'The Heaven's breath smells wooingly here.'[58] The lightness and grace of well-designed glass and brickwork structures have an uplifting effect on the spirits. The elegant lawns, colourful shrubberies, sparkling fountains and amplitude of luxuriant, leafy shade should embrace within their range all the ideals which the ancients summed up for the ideal place of study: 'The Groves of Academe'.

Cox, *Seóirse Bodley*, Field Day Music 4 (Dublin, 2010), p. 119.   **58** The quotation is taken from Macbeth, Act 1, Scene 6.

In the past, at the heyday of its achievements, the Albert College brought lustre to the name of Glasnevin. Its work in plant breeding brought into being new varieties of wheat and oats infinitely better suited to Irish climatic conditions than any which had previously existed. Names like Glasnevin Success and Glasnevin Supreme spring to mind.[59] Work like this was to stand us in good stead in the 1939–1945 war years when we were forced to be self supporting or starve. Old residents remember De Valera presiding at functions held on the lawn of the Albert to celebrate the successful breeding of a new plant at Glasnevin. No doubt again, and before very long, the fruits of the dedication and labour of some of today's students will again immortalize the name of Glasnevin.

Thus hand in hand go the old and the new. So much of what we have today depends on the labour of the past. Inside the entrance gate of the Botanic Gardens,[60] down the road, stands a rose bush which was grown from a cutting of the original 'last rose of summer' immortalised by Thomas Moore. In a shrub border on the south side of the Albert College building are three roses salvaged by the porters here at the NIHE from the depredations of the builders. The porters planted them here and they have taken on new life. Their old world appearance and their lingering, exquisite and nostalgic aroma of 'what roses used to smell like' is heart-stirring. All very simple and artless you may say, but it symbolises in a very important way the marriage of old and new. Old efforts, dreams and hopes are welded with the new and are ready, poised to take advantage of the exciting and challenging days of the future.[61]

Addressing the graduation ceremony, Danny O'Hare acknowledged the faith displayed by the students in choosing to attend an institution that had no prior academic tradition to act as a calling card:

This is a very special day for all of us; for you because you have succeeded in achieving your goal and for us because we have assisted you in this. You will remain especially in our thoughts, as the trailblazing, adventurous young people who believed us in 1980, that we could, together, achieve so

59 Glasnevin Success was a variety of oat produced at Albert College. Other varieties of oat pioneered at the College were known as Glasnevin Sonas, Glasnevin Ardri, and Glasnevin Triumph (Jim Burke, John Spink and Richie Hackett, 'Wheat in the Republic of Ireland' in Alain Bonjean, William Angus and Maarten van Ginkel (eds), *The world wheat book: a history of wheat breeding* (London, 2011), ii, p. 116). **60** The National Botanic Gardens of Ireland, located in Glasnevin, close to the campus of NIHED/DCU, were established by the Royal Dublin Society in 1795. **61** William Guidera (1920–2010). My thanks to Sheila Bridgeman for sending me a copy of the essay and for sharing her memories of Guidera. The essay was first published in the September 1983 issue of *By Degrees*. A photocopy of the essay's original handwritten manuscript, written in June 1983, is found at DCUPO, 'Conferring (1st) 1983'. It is reproduced here with some silent

much. When I think of that year, your entrepreneurial spirit and belief in the aims of the Institute, I can only think that you have many of the essential qualities which the Industrial Development Authority, the Confederation of Irish Industry, and government have encouraged us to develop in our graduates. You were adventurous in believing our promises.[62]

Over the ensuing four decades, more than 60,000 students have followed in the footsteps of these first graduates.[63]

The close-knit community that developed at the Institute during the 1980s was not limited to members of staff. The relatively small number of students ensured that close ties developed between the academic and student bodies: 'We knew when our students did well, or got promoted, out in the real world. You kind of tracked them, you knew them. Of course the numbers allowed us to do that … [I]t's easy when the organisation is small.'[64] The Institute's personal-tutor system played a key role in fostering such close relationships. Formally implemented in 1982, the system was designed to acknowledge the different ways in which students required help and support. Implemented with pastoral rather than academic guidance in mind, tutors were expected to maintain contact with their tutees throughout the duration of their undergraduate degree. Staff were encouraged to involve the Institute's counselling service when thought necessary, to meet their tutees at least twice in their first year, and once a year thereafter at a minimum.[65]

Early in the 1983/4 academic year, Student Services brought academic council's attention to the growing problem of student stress. Contact with similar services in other third-level institutions indicated that the Institute's students were subjected to more pressure and heavier workloads than their counterparts in any other degree-level college: 'Our conviction from our day-to-day work is that [stress levels] are sufficiently high to merit concern, and we feel that this conviction is shared by many of our academic colleagues.' Student Services had documented extreme cases where students were leaving home before 7am and not returning until after 11pm, and students were regularly seen working on campus past 3am during the week. A considerable portion of the student body was observed on campus at weekends, making use of library and computer facilities. The schedule that students worked to was certainly demanding, with lunch hour viewed as the only time they had available for socializing.[66] Following consideration at academic council, the majority of Student Services'

editorial corrections. **62** DCUPO, 'Conferring 1983'. **63** Statistics provided by DCU Quality Promotion Office. **64** Patricia Barker interview, 20 Sept. 2018. **65** DCUPO, AC82/5, 6; *Nuacht*, Apr. 1984. **66** *NIcHE*, 5 Oct. 1983. Wednesday afternoons were also largely left free of teaching in an attempt to allow students some time for study and extra-curricular activities, though growing student numbers and increased pressures on teaching space ensured that custom had fallen away

recommendations for the alleviation of student stress were adopted. Course boards were instructed to examine ways of reducing formal contact hours on each course, alongside a wider review of the Institute's educational model with a view to increasing the use of active-learning techniques. The purpose, frequency and timing of assignments were also to be reviewed. Academic council did, however, note that for each of these aspirations to be met, the Institute would need to greatly improve its library facilities and related infrastructure.[67] Despite ever-growing student numbers, the personal tutor-system has remained a core feature of the DCU undergraduate experience.

Even with such concerted efforts to provide students with as much support as possible, frustration with the Institute's inadequate facilities was inevitable. As the student population steadily increased, problems of overcrowding became more acute. The issue was repeatedly highlighted in student publications during the 1980s (and indeed beyond). The 1984/5 Students' Union handbook was highly critical of the Institute's leadership for its dismissive attitude towards the student representatives on governing body, and described the Institute's facilities as 'appalling'. In response, Danny O'Hare and Registrar Donal Clarke agreed to participate in a videotaped discussion with two SU representatives, despite the fact that it was likely to prove an uncomfortable experience.[68]

During the 1985/6 academic year, while in the final year of his business-studies degree, Colm Ó Raghallaigh sought to draw O'Hare's attention to how overcrowding had led to a deterioration in the services provided for students and the severe overloading of the Institute's recreational facilities:

> I very often spend my entire day on campus, as do many others. We all need somewhere to relax and get away from the charged atmosphere, somewhere to unwind for some short amount of time. I urge you to consider the space allocated to students in square footage terms, for recreational purposes. There is quite simply nowhere to go to relax from study … I would like to say that I have nothing but good will for the Institute, and so this letter is not a complaint, rather a request for action … [A]s a fourth year student I have seen the number of students almost double, without a corresponding increase in facilities. Secondly, I have just returned from my INTRA placement after five months in industry. This brought home strongly to me that people are not machines; they need certain conditions in order to operate to maximum efficiency.[69]

by the end of the 1980s. **67** 'Student stress discussion paper', June 1984 (DCUPO, 'Student Services, 1980–7'); DCUPO, AC84/A3/5. Minor revisions to the tutor system were introduced in 1987, and again in 1991. Among the 1991 revisions was the capping at fifteen of the number of students assigned to each tutor. Implementation of the system has varied; in 2008 the School of Mechanical and Manufacturing Engineering's practice acknowledged the importance of the system by requiring its academic staff to spend one hour per week on personal-tutor activities in lieu of teaching (DCUPO, AC2008/3, 4). **68** DCUPO, 'NIHE Dublin: general, 2/2'. **69** Colm Ó

3.6 Membership card for Film Soc, 1985/6 academic year. Reproduced by kind permission of Pat O'Mahony.

Film Soc, which had quickly established itself as one of the most popular student societies, was not immune to the pressures of space. A reshuffling of room allocations at the end of the 1986/7 academic year threatened the society's activities by forcing a move from their traditional screening venue to the canteen – a venue rejected as unsuitable for the society's purposes. O'Hare's response promised that every effort would be made by the Institute to minimize disruption to the society's plans, but finished with the observation that the Institute was in the 'invidious position of having to decide between the educational needs of our evening students and the needs of the Film Society. And it is not at all clear to me which need might be deemed more pressing.'[70]

Interactions between the Institute and its student body were not always so polite. One of the earliest known student protests took place on campus on 1 June 1982 when a group picketed the formal opening of the Henry Grattan building, attended by Martin O'Donoghue, minister for education, and other local dignitaries. Primarily driven by a 25 per cent rise in the Institute's academic fees, protestors also highlighted the inadequate student facilities on campus.[71] The following year the Department of Education advised the universities and the

Raghallaigh to Danny O'Hare, 15 Oct. 1985 (DCUPO, 'Correspondence: general, 1980–5'). **70** Film Soc memo, Apr. 1987; Danny O'Hare to Bary Kehoe, 11 May 1987 (DCUPO, 'Student Services, 1980–7'). **71** *Irish Independent*, 2 June 1982; Patton, 'Unique claims and holy hour drinks'.

NIHEs to once more raise their fees by 25 per cent for the 1983/4 academic year, prompting strong protests from SU representatives at governing body. If fees were to increase by 25 per cent, they noted, the cost of attending the Institute would range from £700 (accounting and finance degree) to £1,560 (postgraduate diploma in journalism). Sympathetic to student concerns on this occasion, governing body referred the issue to a committee, a decision welcomed by SU President Mick O'Donnell:

> Fees cannot be seen in isolation from grants and this fact has now been recognised ... There was some concern on the Governing Body that students are already paying exorbitant fees. What we have to do is translate this sympathy with the student view into opposition to fee increases.[72]

O'Donnell's concern that the increase in fees was not matched by an increase in government and local-authority grants reflected the difficult financial circumstances of many of the Institute's students during the 1980s. The number in receipt of financial aid increased from 38 in 1980/1 to 1,044 by the end of the decade, a rise from 19 per cent to 38 per cent of the total student population.[73]

Student activities on campus, particularly after hours, also created conflict between the SU and the Institute's governors and administrators. A decision in 1985 to begin charging the SU £150 for every disco it hosted in the restaurant prompted a furious response. Permission had originally been granted to the SU to host discos the previous year as part of efforts to establish an Ents (Entertainments) Office. The charge of £150 was portrayed as a necessary student contribution towards essential renovations. The incoming SU executive for the 1986/7 academic year declared themselves 'vehemently opposed' to any levy on student use of the Institute's facilities:

> While currently paying one of the highest fees in the country, *you*, via the SU are now being asked to fork out money for a floor which was needed anyway. To say that the HEA would not have given the money without a guarantee that the SU would have made this contribution sounds dubious to say the least. Soon students will be contributing to the new library, new playing fields, new gym ... [W]here will it all end?[74]

---

72 *Broadsheet: Organ of the SUNIHE*, 5 Apr. 1983.   73 Approximately 80% of these students were in receipt of a Higher Education Grant or Vocational Educational Committee Scholarship, with *c*.5% in receipt of direct assistance from the Institute (HEA, *Accounts and student statistics, 1980–92*).   74 *The Sun: Student Union Newsletter*, 20 Oct. 1986. The latter point proved prescient, as within a few years DCU students voted in favour of levies to help fund new sports and student centres. See chapter 4.

The SU also opposed the disco levy on the grounds that it reduced the Union's profit-making capability and that of individual clubs and societies, which would in turn reduce the number of student social events and extracurricular activities. In its defence, Student Services noted that the Institute covered all disco insurance costs, alleviating a considerable financial strain on the SU's finances. Intense negotiations saw a revised arrangement implemented whereby the SU would contribute £130 per disco, which would be used by the Institute to promote extracurricular activities.[75] It proved to be a brief reprieve, with the university eventually taking the radical step of banning student discos on campus. The response from the Students' Union was scathing, as it accused the Institute of focusing on external relations at the expense of the on-campus student experience:

> This is a small school. It's terribly well run and not often disrupted. The equipment and facilities sometimes fail to match the administration's slick style. Yet I also can't help feeling that the college is full of career students, professional trainees, hard workers with limited vision. There is no great interaction of loaded minds here, no sparks. The college permits minimal personal development in order to output highly trained, well paid workers for industry and commerce. This is evidenced by the high level of industrial sponsorship here.[76]

As momentum gathered behind the Institute's efforts to attain university status, the Students' Union grew increasingly frustrated with slow progress on the construction of a dedicated student centre. Mandated by members to prepare a submission for governing body outlining long-standing concerns relating to student facilities, the SU executive delivered its findings in January 1986. O'Hare strongly resisted the presentation of the paper, arguing that it was highly unusual for governing body to consider material that originated from outside of formal channels and subcommittees. His hesitancy was understandable. While it was certainly the case that the Institute had consistently pressed the HEA and the Department of Education for funding to improve the student experience on campus, the fact remained that NIHE Dublin's students were poorly served. The SU document pulled no punches in arguing that university status should also bring facilities approaching the standard found on university campuses across the country, as well as those enjoyed by students at NIHE Limerick.[77]

Further protests were held on campus in November 1988, once again focused on the issues of overcrowding and the failure to build a dedicated student centre.

---

75 Barry Kehoe to Kevin Gildea, 30 Oct. 1986; discos in Institute restaurant contract, 26 Nov. 1986 (DCUPO, 'Student Services, 1980–7').   76 *DCU Bull Sheet*, Nov. 1990. The ban on late-night student events was lifted soon afterwards.   77 'Improvements in student affairs required by the Institute to prepare for university status', [1986] (DCUPO, GB86/1).

3.7 Danny O'Hare, Mary O'Rourke and Terence Larkin at the announcement of university status for NIHE Dublin on 12 January 1989 (DCU Collection).

Clare Daly, president of the SU, also aired the students' grievances at governing body meetings, criticizing the Institute's failure to engage fully with the SU's proposals for the management of the student centre.[78]

Protests are an integral part of student life on any campus. A veteran of the protest that greeted Martin O'Donoghue's visit to Glasnevin in June 1982, Michael Patton recalled that O'Donoghue was met with a 'welcome wall of wailing students'. Yet Patton's recollections of his time at NIHE Dublin (1980–3) were similar to those of the Institute's staff – students were engaged in the process of building a viable institution: 'My memories of the nascent NIHE Dublin in its formative years are vivid and positive. We were a very small community then, crammed into the Albert College building … It meant that we had a real opportunity to in some ways shape the future of the college.'[79] For Padraig McKeon, a communications studies student (1983–6) and future member of DCU's governing authority, the Institute's small size was a virtue:

> This place always wanted to be different from other colleges. In the mid-1980s it had no difficulty doing so. Aside from having strange courses like

78 DCUPO, GB89/1. Though the student centre had yet to open, discussions between Student Services and the Students' Union about its future management structures had proven particularly difficult.   79 Patton, 'Unique claims and holy hour drinks'.

Biotechnology, Analytical Science and Communications Studies, it was also a college with limited social or sporting facilities and no heritage – not that that stopped us … People of course made the day, as they always do, and by virtue of its size, you were only one mad haircut or one mad outfit away from college-wide notoriety.[80]

III

On 12 January 1989 Mary O'Rourke, minister for education, announced that NIHE Dublin was to receive university status. By the end of the year, the Institute was no longer in existence, its place taken by Dublin City University. In practical terms, the new status had little impact, with day-to-day life on campus largely unchanged: 'There was no clear dividing line before and after. It was always a work in progress.'[81] From a broader perspective, however, the decision to grant university status had a profound impact on future development, and arguably stands as the most important event in the history of NIHED/DCU.

The prospect of the NIHEs evolving into 'technological universities' had been signposted during Dáil debates in 1980.[82] In the decade that followed, both Danny O'Hare and his Limerick counterpart, Ed Walsh, pursued it with vigour. Relentless in their lobbying of government ministers and officials, the project might never have come to fruition without the ambition and drive demonstrated by both men. The government of the time was characterized by ministers who 'lacked the scope and inclination to promote new policy initiatives involving institutional or structural innovation'.[83] While O'Hare shared Walsh's ambitions, it was Walsh who proved to be the more provocative and vocal lobbyist during the 1980s, with O'Hare more often to be found working the back channels of the Department of Education and eliciting support within the higher-education sector.[84]

The first fruits of Walsh and O'Hare's efforts arrived in October 1985. Speaking at the opening of a major extension to the teaching and laboratory space on NIHE Limerick's campus, Gemma Hussey, minister for education, signalled her willingness to consider university status for the NIHEs: 'I told them in my speech that I was going to set about investigating giving University status to NIHE Limerick and NIHE Dublin and of course they were all over the moon about that.'[85] Hussey envisaged the creation of a federal National Technological University, with the two NIHEs as constituent colleges.

80 Padraig McKeon, 'DCU, 1983–6', *DCU Times*, 2005.   81 John Horgan to author, 13 May 2019. 82 *Dáil Debates*, 17 Apr. and 12 Nov. 1980; White, *Investing in people*, pp 212–13.   83 Walsh, *Higher education in Ireland*, p. 339.   84 Ibid.; Danny O'Hare interview, 28 May 2018.   85 Gemma Hussey, *At the cutting edge: cabinet diaries, 1982–7* (Dublin, 1990), p. 174, diary entry for 4 Oct. 1985. See

The response from both institutions was extremely positive.[86] Welcoming the decision, O'Hare referred to the benefits that university status would bring not just to the Institute, but also its surrounding environs: 'We should not forget that we are located in north Dublin, an area that has not received the attention in developmental terms that it merits. The emergence of a Technological University in North Dublin must be seen as a boost to the north and, perhaps, most importantly as of considerable assistance to North Dublin's industrial development.'[87] Within days of Hussey's speech, O'Hare and Walsh met to discuss a joint strategy, which included the bringing together of both governing bodies in joint session and the issuance of a joint statement welcoming the proposal. Both NIHEs collaborated in the drafting of guiding principles for the development of a national technological university, based on principles of equality and parity of esteem for both institutions, as well as the maintenance of their autonomy as constituent colleges.[88]

The first step, however, was the appointment of an international study group to advise the government on the proposal and the overall future of technological education in Ireland.[89] Ten days after Hussey's announcement, O'Hare and Walsh met with the minister's adviser, John Harris, to discuss the general composition of the group and to agree on the appointment as chair of Tom Hardiman, then chairman of the National Board for Science and Technology.[90] Both men maintained good relations with Harris throughout the process, allowing O'Hare also to suggest that Douglas Wright, president of Waterloo University, be appointed a member of the group – Wright had offered invaluable guidance to O'Hare during the early 1980s, and was well disposed towards NIHE Dublin.[91] More difficult meetings were held with the Conference of Heads of Irish Universities (CHIU) and the NCEA, with both bodies determined to resist the creation of new universities.[92] Early meetings with the CHIU were particularly tense.[93]

Shortly after Hussey's announcement, O'Hare quietly shed the title of director and assumed the more traditional university title of president. Though this was, technically speaking, a breach of the legislation establishing the

also *Irish Times*, 5 Oct. 1985; *Nuacht*, Dec. 1985; Fleming, *University of Limerick*, pp 80–1. 86 Much of the preparatory work from NIHED's perspective is documented in DCUPO, 'University status for NIHE Dublin: preparation (1985–9)'. 87 DCUPO, GB85/9; *Nuacht*, Nov. 1985. 88 DCUPO, 'Department of Education, 1981–6'; DCUPO, 'University status announcement, 12 Jan. 1989 and follow-up'; *Nuacht*, Dec. 1985; Fleming, *University of Limerick*, p. 81. 89 Speech by Gemma Hussey, 4 Oct. 1985 (DCUPO, 'Department of Education, 1981–7'); Horgan, *Dublin City University*, pp 23–6; Bradley, '*Twigs for an eagle's nest*', pp 58–60. 90 Walsh, *Upstart*, pp 218–20. 91 Danny O'Hare to John Harris, 16 Oct. 1985 (DCUPO, 'Department of Education, 1981–6'). 92 As discussed by White, the NCEA's decision to exclude Walsh and O'Hare from its most important decision-making committees during the 1980s was a strategic mistake, particularly in light of their stated ambitions to attain complete autonomy for their institutions (White, *Investing in people*, p. 213). 93 Walsh, *Upstart*, p. 219.

Institute, it was not a surprise.[94] O'Hare's counterpart in Limerick had adopted the title of president as early as 1982.[95] As a more cautious operator, O'Hare waited until after Hussey's speech before seeking legal advice on following Walsh's lead. Assured that it would bring no legal difficulties, governing body agreed to the change on the grounds that it would help the perception of the Institute in the industrial and commercial sectors, as well as within the international academic community. An equally important consideration was the need to ensure that O'Hare and the Institute's staff retained parity with Limerick in the eyes of any future review of the higher-education sector.[96]

Sustaining the momentum created by Hussey's announcement required concerted pressure on the government. Political will to effect change in the higher-education sector was lacking beyond the halls of the Department of Education, and Hussey was frustrated by Taoiseach Garret FitzGerald's indecision: '[Garret] wants to revolutionise the universities but not to talk about the immediate problems.'[97]

Registrar Donal Clarke kept a close eye on progress throughout 1986. In August he informed Terence Larkin, chairman of the Institute's governing body, of the likely composition of the international study group:

> I was informed yesterday of 'rumours' that the Commission has been appointed and that it 'might' consist of Professor Michael MacCormac, Mr Tom Hardiman, one Canadian, and one British, and two continental European members. The Secretary is Mr Michael Gleeson of the HEA ... I was told that constituent college status in the NUI was not a likely option. I was warned that NCEA lobbying against the [National Technological University] was very strong and that we should deploy every argument against and document every unfavourable experience we have had with that body.[98]

Patrick Cooney, appointed minister for education in Hussey's place following a cabinet reshuffle in February 1986, formally established the international study group the following November.[99] The group's specific remit was to examine third-level technological education in Ireland, and to assess the case for a technological university. The considered approach adopted by the NIHEs in their interactions with the Department of Education, and their ability to

94 Section 7 of the National Institute for Higher Education, Dublin, 1980 Act referred specifically to the chief officer of the Institute as the director.   95 Fleming, *University of Limerick*, p. 79; White, *Investing in people*, p. 212.   96 DCUPO, GB86/1.   97 Hussey, *At the cutting edge*, p. 178, diary entry for 5 Nov. 1985.   98 Donal Clarke to Terence Larkin, 21 Aug. 1986 (DCUPO, 'NIHE Dublin: general, 1/2').   99 The Department submitted a memorandum to government on 15 April 1986 proposing the establishment of the study group, with an estimated cost of £30,000. Membership of the group had already largely been decided by that point. Formal government

influence the study group's membership, was evident in the group's composition. Two of NIHE Dublin's preferred candidates were appointed. Hardiman was confirmed as chairman, and Douglas Wright (of Waterloo University) was also appointed. There was an added bonus in the appointment as deputy chairman of Michael MacCormac, chairman of NIHE Dublin's governing body from 1979 to 1982. It is also worth noting that Michael Gleeson, seconded from the HEA to serve as the study group's secretary, was later appointed as secretary of DCU.[100] The two remaining members were R.E.D. Bishop, vice chancellor of Brunel University, and O.H.G. Mahrenholtz, of Hamburg's University of Technology.[101] The decision to appoint the study group was a pivotal moment in the NIHEs' progression towards university status. Though convened by Cooney, the importance of the role played by Gemma Hussey was gratefully acknowledged by O'Hare: 'I remember clearly your fundamental and important initiation of the idea … and I feel sure that you must have continued to indicate your positive support. It is now up to Ed Walsh and I and our staff to convince the Study Group.'[102]

Anticipating a number of campus visits from the group during 1987, preparation of the Institute's case for university status was led by a small team, including Donal Clarke, John Pratschke, David Owens, Owen Ward and Anthony Glynn.[103] Displaying full confidence in the high calibre of its teaching and the quality of its undergraduate and postgraduate programmes, the Institute also placed a heavy emphasis on its research capabilities and track record. Despite the government's ambivalence towards the necessity for the NIHEs to develop research capacities comparable to the universities, the development of applied and pure-research programmes had formed a central part of the Institute's plans from the very beginning, with the ambition of matching (or surpassing) university standards.[104] As one of the first subcommittees constituted by academic council, the research and postgraduate studies committee was convened in July 1981. In addition to its oversight of postgraduate studies, the committee was responsible for encouraging and promoting research within the Institute, as well as the formulation of an overall research policy.[105] The Institute's mission statement, adopted in 1983, linked its research ambitions with the acceleration of the country's social and economic development.[106]

approval was granted on 3 July (NAI, 2017/11/317). **100** The position of university secretary has since been renamed chief operations officer. **101** NAI, 2017/11/317. **102** Danny O'Hare to Gemma Hussey, 16 Dec. 1986 (DCUPO, 'Correspondence: general, 1986–8'). During the cabinet reshuffle of February 1986, Hussey was appointed minister for social welfare. **103** DCUPO, GB85/9; DCUPO, 'University status for NIHE Dublin – preparation (1985–9)'; *Nuacht*, Dec. 1985. **104** Danny O'Hare interview, 28 May 2018. See also Walsh, *Higher education in Ireland*, pp 293–5. **105** DCUPO, AC81/6, 7; NIHED, *Institutional review, 1980–6* (1986), s. 4. The RPSC was renamed the Research Committee in 1997, coinciding with the creation of the post of dean of research (DCU, *Annual report, 1996/7*, p. 50; Bradley, *'Twigs for an eagle's nest'*, p. 184). **106** NIHED, *Academic procedures* (1987), p. 7.

The desirability of maintaining an active research profile was regularly imparted to staff. Writing in 1982, Richard O'Kennedy emphasized the importance of research for the enhancement of the Institute's reputation, and for the academic development of staff:

> Each and every one of us must have a research frame of mind. We must not be deflected from doing research – we must make some time every week which is free from memos and meetings. If we do not do this now, we may stagnate academically.[107]

In its submission to the study group, the Institute could point to research collaborations with a number of Irish and international universities and research laboratories. Agencies funding research at the Institute included An Post, the World Bank, the Irish Cancer Society, the Industrial Development Authority, and the Organisation for Economic Co-operation and Development. Applied and contract research was also being provided for companies such as Guinness, the Irish Sugar Co., Westinghouse Electronics, Loctite, Bausch & Lomb and Varta Batteries.[108]

The Institute had earned its first research grant in October 1980, from the National Board for Science and Technology, before it had even begun teaching.[109] By 1989 more than £12m in research funding had been received, a remarkable achievement for such a young institution.[110] Supplied by private and government sources, in addition to significant investment from the European Community, these funds allowed for the establishment on campus of several specialist research centres, including the National Centre for Cell and Tissue Culture; the National Bioprocessing Centre; the Centre for New Technologies in Education; the Chemical Services Centre; the Optronics Centre; and the Translation and Interpreting Consultancy Service.[111]

Interactions with private industry and potential research partners had emphasized the problems associated with the Institute's name and quasi-university status, a factor that O'Hare and his staff were anxious to convey to the study group. While a seemingly trivial matter, experience had shown that the appellation NIHE often gave rise to confusion, even within Ireland. Upon taking a phone call, one staff member was asked if the caller had been connected to the Ballymun branch of NIHE Limerick.[112] In May 1984 John Pratschke received a letter that was several weeks late in arriving, because the letter was addressed

---

107 *By Degrees*, 15 Mar. 1982. O'Kennedy was then chairman of the Research and Postgraduate Studies Committee.   **108** *Institutional Review, 1980–6* (1986), s. 4.   **109** O'Hare, 'The role of the National Institute for Higher Education Dublin, p. 15.   **110** *Newslink*, Feb. 1989.   **111** The Institute was particularly successful in attracting research funding from the European Community, and participated in a variety of European and International research projects, including Brite, Esprit, Euromath, Eurotra and Docdel.   **112** O'Kennedy, 'Coming of age: 21 years at DCU'.

using the Irish version of the Institute's name: An Foras Náisiúnta um Ardoideachais. The confusion this created in the post office was apparent from the multiple notes written on the envelope, advising postmen to try the HEA, the Church of Ireland College of Education and Rathmines School of Management, before its intended destination was eventually divined.[113]

The incident serves as a useful way to highlight overall public confusion as to the exact nature and status of the Institute. As O'Hare noted in a memorandum for governing body, the internal organizational structure of schools with heads (rather than departments, as in traditional universities) was also problematic: 'When being introduced to others the title "Head of School of ..." is quite long and raises the question as to what a School is and what a Head is. This often produces embarrassment and lack of clarity for senior staff in meeting with other academics and industrialists. I have encountered similar problems in explaining what NIHE is, particularly to foreigners.'[114]

O'Hare's preference was for the Institute to be described as equivalent to a Technological University. Reacting to an article in the *Irish Times*, O'Hare rejected comparisons made between the NIHEs and the polytechnic colleges in the United Kingdom.[115] By invoking the UK's controversial binary divide between universities and polytechnics, O'Hare felt that the article implicitly downgraded the status and quality of the NIHEs. In a letter to the newspaper's education correspondent, Christina Murphy, O'Hare wondered why the NIHEs could not be referred to as 'universities or technological universities':

> The government funds us on the same basis as the older Universities, our academics are as well qualified and publish as much and Universities abroad have signed exchange agreements with us – in teaching and research! Sure, we do not have the University title – yet! – but, in all respects, we are Universities.[116]

Murphy's article is likely to have prompted an advisory memo circulated to the Institute's executive, which lamented the tendency of staff to refer to the Institute in various ways. A universal method of reference was proposed, in the hope that the preferred nomenclature would trickle down and convince others to adopt the same terminology. 'The University' and 'this University' were to be used in place of 'the Institute' and 'this institute'. Formal replies to any query as to what NIHE Dublin was should be along the lines of 'a non-traditional university' or, better yet, 'a technological university'.[117] These suggestions were

113 John Pratschke to various, 7 May 1984 (DCUPO, 'NIHE Dublin: general, 2/2'). 114 'Titles for heads of schools and heads of units', Apr. 1982 (DCUPO, GB 82/A3/8). 115 *Irish Times*, 26 Nov. 1987. For the UK's binary system of universities and polytechnics, see John Pratt, *The polytechnic experiment, 1965–92* (Buckingham, 1997). 116 Danny O'Hare to Christina Murphy, 16 Dec. 1987 (DCUPO, 'Correspondence: general, 1986–8'). 117 Danny O'Hare memo, 16 Dec.

an extension of an informal policy that had been in existence for some time. An information leaflet outlining the full-time primary degree courses available at the Institute, prepared in early 1987, explained that NIHE Dublin's international equivalents were known as technological universities.[118]

The expectation of the eventual acquisition of university status had been boosted following the delivery of the international study group's report in September 1987. Its recommendations, while certainly a relief to both NIHEs, were largely expected. Its most significant finding was that both institutions were already operating at the required standard:

> [The] standards of scholarship are as high as one would associate with universities ... No serious deficiency or second-rate work was found. The NIHEs have plainly done well and the Group believes that they have reached a stage of development and achievement where they should be self-accrediting.[119]

Rather than the creation of a federal university, with constituent colleges in Dublin and Limerick, the group urged the establishment of two independent, self-accrediting universities.[120] During visits to the NIHEs in early 1988, Mary O'Rourke was assured that both were happy with the proposal for independent university status.[121] Even so, there was still no guarantee that the study group's report would lead to action. The public finances remained in a parlous condition. As O'Rourke later noted, after she took office as minister for education in March 1987 the elevation of the NIHEs to university status 'did not loom large on my horizon, because there were all these huge, horrendous cuts to be made everywhere'.[122] Nonetheless, Walsh and O'Hare continued 'mercilessly' lobbying for the implementation of the study group's report.[123] Members of both NIHE governing bodies were well positioned to augment their efforts. The influential Confederation of Irish Industry proved ardent supporters of the campaign – its submission to the study group had repeated, almost verbatim, several of the arguments advanced by the NIHEs.[124] This was not a surprise. Aside from the

1987 (DCUPO, 'NIHE Dublin: general, 2/2'). NIHE Limerick's formal newsletter, *NIHE News*, had begun carrying the description 'Limerick's Technological University' in its masthead in September 1984.   **118** 'Summary of full-time primary degree courses', *c*.Apr. 1987 (DCUPO, 'NIHE Dublin: general, 2/2').   **119** Department of Education and Skills, *Technological education: report of the international study group to the minister for education* (Dublin, 1987), p. 30.   **120** Ibid., pp 31–2.   **121** DCUPO, GB88/2–4; *Newslink*, June 1988; Fleming, *University of Limerick*, p. 81. **122** Mary O'Rourke, *Just Mary: a memoir* (Dublin, 2012), pp 62–4. See also Walsh, *Higher education in Ireland*, p. 340.   **123** O'Rourke, *Just Mary*, p. 63.   **124** Don Power, director of economic policy at the CII, later wrote to congratulate O'Hare on the announcement of university status for NIHED, and noted that the next stage was to ensure that the required legislation was speedily introduced: 'In this context I have already fired the first shots in our continuing campaign' (Don Power to Danny O'Hare, 24 Jan. 1989 (DCUPO, 'University status announcement, 12 Jan. 1989

close links created by both institutes with Irish industrial and commercial entities, the president of the CII, Dermot Whelan, served as deputy chairman of NIHE Limerick's governing body. One of his predecessors at CII, Terence Larkin, was in the middle of his first term as chairman of NIHE Dublin's governing body.

The incessant pressure paid off, aided by a slight recovery in the state's financial position in 1988 that created much-needed fiscal space. On 12 January 1989 O'Rourke appeared in both Limerick and Dublin, where she announced the creation of the first new universities since the foundation of the state in 1922. O'Hare welcomed the minister's decision as one of historical significance, and a practical recognition of the efforts of those who had supported the Institute throughout the decade: 'This decision will enhance NIHE's ability to develop research links with other European and international universities, it will increase our prospects of attracting contract research and development work from international business and it will greatly improve our fund raising activities nationally and internationally.'[125] O'Hare and Walsh issued a joint statement of appreciation to Irish industry and business, marking the announcement.[126]

Dozens of letters and messages of congratulations arrived in the following days and weeks. The Federated Workers' Union of Ireland, with whom the Institute's administration had clashed on a number of occasions, welcomed the prospect of a university in north Dublin with the caveat that it hoped the new university would not become a 'bastion of the rich and privileged'.[127] The university presidents and governing bodies, despite their initial reluctance to see the NIHEs elevated to university status, uniformly expressed a warm welcome for the development. So too did various government ministers and TDs, including former minister for education, John Wilson, who wrote that it was a matter 'of some pride to me that this decision has been taken because of my initial involvement in establishing the Institute'.[128] Of possibly greater satisfaction to O'Hare and his senior staff were the multitude of messages received from the industrial and commercial sector. Some, such as Daithí Ó Brollacháin of Procyon Informatics, were pleased at the boost the announcement would bring to north Dublin:

> Without wishing to be parochial about what is a national body, I do believe that you and your colleagues in Glasnevin play a critical role in the revitalisation of North Dublin ... In a way, you continue a tradition of know-how, craft and skill (based on science) evident from older North

and follow-up'); White, *Investing in people*, p. 214).   **125** DCUPO, GB89/1; *Nuacht*, special edition, Jan. 1989; *Newslink*, Feb. 1989.   **126** DCUPO, GB89/1; Walsh, *Upstart*, pp 218–20. **127** Federated Workers' Union of Ireland press release, Jan. 1989 (DCUPO, 'University status announcement, 12 Jan. 1989 and follow-up').   **128** John Wilson to Danny O'Hare, 18 Jan. 1989 (DCUPO, 'University status announcement, 12 Jan. 1989 and follow-up').

Dublin institutions, e.g. Albert College, Dunsink Observatory, Botanic
Gardens, etc.[129]

With university status now secured, the Institute was presented with a fresh
challenge – selecting a new name. The international study group recommended
either the University of Leinster or Dublin City University. With the incentive
of a case of 'tolerably good' wine on offer for the winning entry, staff were also
encouraged to suggest names, with a reminder to beware the acronyms that
might arise (e.g. Millennium University Dublin – MUD).[130] Numerous entries
were received, many of which drew upon the city's heritage, including Rowan
Hamilton University Dublin, Henry Grattan University Dublin, University of
North Dublin, University of Dublin North, City of Dublin University and
Dublin European University. With eighteen different possibilities put to a vote,
Dublin City University emerged as the most popular choice. It was, however, a
very close contest, with DCU only narrowly emerging as favourite ahead of City
of Dublin University.[131]

Preparation of the legislation necessary to implement O'Rourke's decision
proceeded at a much quicker pace than had been the case in 1980.[132] Minimal
changes were made to the statutory basis on which the new universities would
operate. The necessary bills were presented to the Dáil on 25 May 1989; both
managed the rare feat of being introduced and approved in a single day. Some
drama attended their passage through the Oireachtas, which took place on the
same day as the dissolution of the Dáil following a government defeat earlier that
month. More than twenty other pieces of legislation fell as a result of that
dissolution, leading to rising anxieties in the Dáil gallery, where senior figures
from both NIHEs had gathered to witness history being made. Even with cross-
party support, there were some who expressed reservations about the contents
of the legislation, and more broadly at the direction of higher-education policy.
Every minute that the debate continued increased the chances that the legislation
would fall. Garret FitzGerald, taoiseach at the time of the appointment of the
international study group, pleaded for the adequate provision of resources to the
new universities. Recognizing that the public finances continued to be limited,
however, he devoted most of his attention to the minimalist nature of the
legislation and pointed out the need for structural reform of both NIHEs. As
FitzGerald noted, the chairperson and all members of governing body would
continue to be appointed by the minister for education, and staff appointments
also remained – at least nominally – subject to government approval. This was in

129 D. Ó Brollacháin to Danny O'Hare, 16 Jan. 1989 (DCUPO, 'University status announcement,
12 Jan. 1989 and follow up').   **130** *Nuacht*, special edition, Jan. 1989.   **131** DCUPO, 'University
status announcement, 12 Jan. 1989 and follow-up'; *Nuacht*, June 1989. The winner of the case of
wine was the Institute's finance director, Frank Soughley.   **132** For the drafting of the NIHE
Dublin Act, 1980, see chapter 2.

contrast to the traditional universities, which enjoyed far greater autonomy.[133] Yet FitzGerald ultimately welcomed the legislation, and the debate in the chamber concluded at three minutes to 7pm. Taoiseach Charles Haughey entered the chamber for the final vote: 'The bill was approved and the Taoiseach remained standing and with his next breath announced the dissolution of the Dáil.'[134] Four weeks later, Mary O'Rourke issued Statutory Instrument no. 148 of 1989, which decreed that the Dublin City University Act of 1989 would come into effect the following day. NIHE Dublin had ceased to exist.

IV

Speaking in the National Concert Hall during the formal inauguration of Dublin City University on 29 September 1989, Taoiseach Charles Haughey declared that the university stood:

> at the threshold of a new era which will give scientific effort, research and innovation a new status and prominence in Irish academic life ... We need scientific education, applied research ... [and] institutions in which originality, inventiveness and skills can be applied with imagination to the industrial, commercial and national advancement of our society.[135]

Less than a month later the new university held its first convocation, at which 564 graduates received the first primary degrees, masters' and doctorates to be awarded by DCU.[136] In total, 2,366 students had graduated from NIHED/DCU since the beginning of the decade.[137] Aerial photographs of the Glasnevin campus at the end of the 1980s, which portray the cramped nature of its facilities, demonstrate the singular achievement of the Institute's staff in providing a university-standard education to its students, as well as in attracting research funding in a competitive international environment. The Institute's progression during the 1980s was rapid. If the underlying theme of the decade was a scarcity of resources, both financial and material, the energy and drive of the staff ensured that numerous milestones were reached on or ahead of schedule. Innovative degree courses were introduced in the STEM fields and the applied humanities; the Distance Education Unit steadily expanded its

133 *Dáil Debates*, 25 May 1989; Dublin City University Act, 1989 (no. 15 of 1989); *Irish Times*, 26 May 1989; White, *Investing in people*, pp 214–15; Walsh, *Higher education in Ireland*, p. 340. **134** Walsh, *Upstart*, pp 259–60; Eugene Kennedy to author, 18 Oct. 2017; Danny O'Hare interview, 28 May 2018. Quotation from Walsh, *Upstart*. **135** DCUPO, 'University status: ceremonial inauguration, 29 Sept. 1989'; *Newslink*, Nov. 1989. See also *Irish Times*, 30 Sept. 1989. **136** *Newslink*, Nov. 1989. The ceremony took place on 20 October, with each of DCU's first graduates having the unusual distinction of having begun their studies – and indeed their final academic year – as a student of NIHE Dublin. **137** Statistics supplied by DCU Quality Promotion

3.8 Pictured at a function in the National Concert Hall to mark the formal inauguration of DCU on 29 September 1989 are (l–r): Sheelagh O'Hare, Mary O'Rourke (minister for education), Anthony Glynn, Mary Glynn, Charles Haughey (taoiseach), Des Byrne and Danny O'Hare. (DCU Collection)

operations; and the Industrial Liaison Unit and the INTRA programme had steadily raised NIHE Dublin's profile within Ireland's established and emerging industries.[138] Achievements of a smaller scale were no less important in establishing the Institute's reputation. Industry sponsorship enabled the creation of professorial chairs in applied physics, applied mathematics and applied languages.[139] Gerard Byrne and Dermott Pearson were awarded doctorates in November 1985, a year ahead of the first such degree to be awarded by NIHE Limerick. Siobhán Bergin, a member of the first class to graduate with a BSc in biotechnology in November 1986 and recipient of the Chairman's Medal, became the first female trainee brewer at Guinness.[140] On 26 April 1988 the

Office. See appendix 6.   138 See chapter 5 for the establishment of the Distance Education Unit, the Industrial Liaison Unit and the broader development of the curriculum at NIHED/DCU. 139 The chairs were sponsored by Landis and Gyr (applied physics), Wescan (applied mathematics) and Irish Shell (applied languages). For details, see 'An outline of research priorities at DCU', Nov. 1989 (DCUPO, 'DCUET proposals/approaches, 1989–94').   140 *Newslink*, Dec. 1986; 'An outline of research priorities at DCU', Nov. 1989 (DCUPO, 'DCUET Proposals/Approaches, 1989–94'). See appendix 5 for Chairman's/Chancellor's Medal recipients.

Institute welcomed Prof. Klaus von Klitzing, 1985 Nobel laureate in physics, to its campus for a seminar – a ringing endorsement of its School of Physical Sciences.[141]

University status marked a crowning achievement in the short life of NIHE Dublin, a testament to the astute leadership of the Institute's governors and executive, as well as staff's ability to rise above inadequate facilities and funding. The work of developing the university was, however, only just beginning. Just one month after the celebrations in the National Concert Hall, O'Hare warned that DCU was suffering from a 'crippling lack of space … [W]e have lost research projects because of lack of facilities, while staff and students have been asked to achieve standards with resources significantly less than in any other university.'[142] The challenge facing the new university was to translate any momentum generated during the 1980s into sustained growth in research and teaching capacity.

---

141 The seminar and associated dinner were attended by Sean McCarthy TD, minister of state for science and technology, as well as the most eminent academics in the field of physics then working in Ireland (Eugene Kennedy to author, 15 May 2018; Eugene Kennedy Papers; *Newslink*, June 1988; Bradley, *'Twigs for an eagle's nest'*, pp 77–8).   **142** *Irish Times*, 21 Oct. 1989; *Newslink*, Nov. 1989.

4

Inflection points: the evolution of a university, 1989–2019

In September 1989, the beginning of its first full academic year, Dublin City University welcomed 3,500 students to its campus. Within a decade the student population had jumped to more than 8,000, a period of rapid expansion enabled by significant philanthropic investment, increased exchequer funding for capital projects, and a consequent increase in the number and diversity of available undergraduate and postgraduate programmes. Student numbers continued to climb in the new millennium, rising to more than 14,000 by 2016 – three times the population envisaged by NIHE Dublin's planners in the late 1970s. Such rapid growth brought with it a fundamental change in the character of the university as it transitioned from a small, start-up institution, to one in which differing visions for the future could produce collaboration and tension in equal measure. Many of the major inflection points in DCU's evolution were readily apparent to outside observers, effecting major changes in financial health, research objectives and governance structures, as well as the absorption of other third-level institutions. Others had significant impact yet were more subtle, including improvements to staff and student facilities and the implementation of measures to combat employment inequality. Whether through its relative abundance or scarcity, funding provides the underlying thread to much of the university's history. The 1990s witnessed a sea change in the financial resources available, driven by a combination of increased government funding, the creation of alternative revenue streams and – most importantly – the support of Atlantic Philanthropies. Within the space of fifteen years, teaching and research capacities were transformed at the university. The relationship between DCU and Atlantic Philanthropies, which started in 1990 as Atlantic began a programme of substantial investment in the future of Irish higher education, was of profound importance to the university. Over the next two decades Atlantic's philanthropic donations to DCU allowed the university to accelerate its growth in a manner that would not otherwise have been possible – as did DCU's success in attracting major research funding under the PRTLI and SFI schemes introduced by the government in the late 1990s and early 2000s. The turn of the millennium witnessed a changing of the guard in the leadership of DCU, following the retirement of long-serving president Danny O'Hare and appointment of Ferdinand von Prondzynski as his successor. New leadership brought significant alterations to the university's governance structures and its strategic objectives.

The cultivation of formal links with other third-level institutions in DCU's hinterland were a hallmark of the O'Hare and von Prondzynski presidencies, a strategic objective continued by the university's third president, Brian MacCraith. The completion of the Incorporation process in 2016, whereby St Patrick's College, the Mater Dei Institute and the Church of Ireland College of Education were amalgamated into DCU, was the signature development of MacCraith's tenure.

I

The importance of sourcing revenue streams for the university that would provide independence from government funding had been recognized from an early stage. In 1985 the finance office observed that 'because of the tightness of state finances it is increasingly important to maximize "other income", that is, income other than student fees'.[1] Reliance on the government would in fact later increase following the abolition, in 1995, of tuition fees for students registered for full-time undergraduate studies.[2] However, beginning in earnest in 1990, the university's governors focused on augmentation of its revenue through two distinct channels – commercial activity and philanthropic donations. Under the terms of the Dublin City University Act of 1989, the university was permitted to create limited liability companies 'for the purpose of exploiting the results of research and development work undertaken by the university'.[3] On 5 July 1990 governing body approved the establishment of City Research and Development Ltd, a holding company wholly owned by the university. The decision marked the first step in the creation of a portfolio of companies, and the development of commercial activities as a steady and increasingly important source of revenue.[4] These were largely uncharted waters, as there was little precedent within the university system for generating large-scale revenues from non-government sources.

City Research and Development was set up as a non-trading research company, limited by share capital, with the power to establish subsidiary companies to cater for specific activities, such as the management of student residences and other university property. There were several advantages to this structure for taxation purposes. Profits arising from one subsidiary could be

---

1 Just 3% of the university's income in 1984 derived from sources other than student fees and government grants (NIHED, *Annual report, 1984/5*, pp 48–9, 152–3. Quotation on p. 48).   2 The abolition of tuition fees was a key policy tool intended to widen access to higher education. Students paid half-fees in 1995/6, and none from 1996/7 onwards. The policy was strongly opposed by university presidents, who feared that universities would be reliant on the government for at least 80% of their funding (*Irish Times*, 7 Feb. and 29 Dec. 1995; Walsh, *Higher education in Ireland*, pp 351–2).   3 Dublin City University Act, 1989, s. 3.   4 Memo, 'Company formations under DCU Act 1989', 25 June 1991 (DCUPO, 'Industrial liaison, 1980–92'; GB90/1, 6 and 7). See fig. A6.4

4.1 A wheelbarrow race during the 1984 staff sports day. Background (l–r): Bernie Creeven, Keith Moloney, Mike Aughey, Monica McGorman, unknown, Imelda Shanahan, Jim Doyle, Valerie McManus, unknown, unknown, unknown, Lynda Dignam, Ann Malone, Cora Cooney, Fidelma Atkinson, Maureen McNamara, Mary Meaney, unknown. Foreground: unknown pushing Peig Ward on the left, with Catherine Roche pushing Eileen Buckley on the right (DCU Collection).

grouped with losses arising from another in a corresponding tax period, and assets could be transferred between subsidiaries without incurring any capital gains tax liability. The holding company could complete transactions that were commercial rather than academic, carry out functions that benefitted from non-university management and acquire the added protection of limited liability. It would also allow DCU to sidestep certain policies it (along with the other universities) regarded as restrictive, including the employment of staff on salary scales that were not dictated by HEA/public-sector policy.

Physical assets could now be exploited for their commercial potential, as demonstrated following the decision to construct campus student accommodation. In the early 1990s dedicated student accommodation on university campuses was virtually non-existent.[5] Uncertain of its economic viability,

below, in appendix 6.   **5** HEA statistics reveal the near complete dearth of campus accommodation across the higher-education sector prior to the mid-1990s. In the 1986/7 academic year, just 699 out of 33,031 students (2.1%) were living in campus accommodation, the majority of these at TCD. Three years later the national figure had risen to 2,041 (4%) following the opening of campus accommodation in UL, University College Galway and DCU (HEA, *Report, accounts and student statistics, 1987/88*, p. 64; HEA, *Report, accounts and statistics, 1990/91 and 1991/92*, p. 70; HEA,

governing body was reluctant to green-light development and was persuaded only after receiving assurances that there was no financial risk to the university. Plans to have 260 students in residence on campus by the autumn of 1991 were subsequently unveiled, with an expected rent of £33 per week.[6] The economic benefits were quickly apparent, with a dramatic increase in the university's alternative operating income – from €149,000 in 1990 to €2.186m in 1992 – significantly boosted by student rent.[7] In 1996 DCU commenced construction on a second block of campus accommodation, consisting of 299 student rooms and six penthouse apartments for visiting faculty and guests.[8] Further student accommodation was added in 2000 and 2004 (see table 6.1).

Development of the commercial potential of the university's academic research was largely overseen by the Industrial Liaison Unit, a function absorbed by DCU Invent following its establishment in 2001. Between 2001 and 2014, Invent played a pivotal role in the translation of academic research into commercial success with the spin-out of 30 companies and negotiation of 120 licences, options and assignments to industry.[9] The benefits of its activities were recognized during successive quality-review processes as not merely economic, but also essential to providing the university's undergraduate and postgraduate students with valuable opportunities for educational opportunities and work experience.[10]

Philanthropy

Large-scale philanthropic donations (often in the form of major endowments) are an integral feature of the funding landscape in the American and – to a lesser extent – United Kingdom higher-education systems.[11] In Ireland, where the funding of education at all levels is primarily seen as the responsibility of government, the concept was practically unknown prior to the 1990s. It is, however, now difficult to overstate the importance of philanthropy to Irish higher education. Between 2005 and 2008 almost half of total capital expenditure in the

Report, accounts and statistics, 1992/93 and 1993/94, p. 178).   6 DCUPO, GB90/2, 3 and 6. 7 Campus Residences, Ltd, was set up as a subsidiary of City Research and Development to manage the university's residences. The university's current companies are DCU Commercial DAC, Campus Residences DAC, DCU Language Services DAC, Campus Property DAC, Trispace DAC and UAC Management DAC.   8 Construction cost £6.426m, with £2.28m provided by Atlantic Philanthropies and the remainder borrowed by Campus Residences Ltd. Half of the rooms came on stream by the end of 1997, with full completion by March 1998 (APA, Grant #7405).   9 DCU, *Capturing the economic and social value of higher education: a pilot study of Dublin City University* (Dublin, 2014), p. 11.   10 DCUPO, 'Invent'; EUA, *Institutional quality review of Dublin City University* (2005), p. 12; Irish Universities Quality Board, *IRIU report: institutional review of Dublin City University* (2010), p. 21; QQI, *Institutional review report 2019: DCU* (2019), p. 7.   11 John Thelin and Richard Trollinger, *Philanthropy and American higher education* (New York, 2014); *Times*

4.2 Pictured at the formal launch of DCU Educational Trust in Dublin Castle on 2 April 1992 are (l–r): Danny O'Hare, Patrick Lynch (Irish Shell); Paddy Marron (Nestlé Ireland); Pat O'Neill (Avonmore and chairman, DCUET); Bertie Ahern (minister for finance); Bernard Dillon (Amdahl); George McCullagh (Brown Thomas); N. Dowling; B.S. Ryan (Woodstream Estates) (DCU Collection).

sector was provided by private sources, with approximately €50m raised per annum in philanthropic donations.[12]

Small levels of philanthropy and corporate support for NIHE Dublin were received during the 1980s, which was vital for an institution starved of resources. Conscious of the ongoing delays in improving the Institute's infrastructure, governing body appointed a subcommittee to identify ways to exploit the potential for donations and assistance from industrial and private sources. Acting on the advice of this committee, governing body established the NIHE Dublin Educational Trust on 18 October 1988.[13] Renamed DCU Educational Trust in

Higher Education, 28 July 2015.   **12** Department of Education and Skills, *National Strategy for Higher Education to 2030* (Dublin, 2011), p. 115; Department of Education and Skills, *Investing in national ambition: a strategy for funding higher education* (Dublin, 2016) p. 48. The Cassels Report (2016) does not specify when the peak of €50m was reached.   **13** NIHE (Dublin) Educational

October 1989, it set an ambitious target of £5m in fundraising by the end of May 1992.[14] In addition to easing the university's immediate need for investment in buildings, equipment and people, the Trust also hoped to provide 20 per cent of the university's annual budget through its activities, thus further reducing the university's reliance on government grants.[15] A reward system was proposed for high-value contributors. Presidential Partner status would be accorded to those who donated £25,000 or more, while contributions between £10,000 and £25,000 would confer Presidential Associate status. A range of rewards accompanied the proposed system, including commemorative plaques on campus.[16]

Inexperience and inertia ensured that initial progress was slow. Just over 30 per cent of the £5m target had been achieved by February 1991. The vast majority of that had come from one source – Atlantic Philanthropies.[17] Writing in February 1990, Danny O'Hare thanked John R. Healy for his assistance in securing a major donation of £700,000 towards the construction of DCU's R&D building:

> I wish to acknowledge the extraordinarily generous contribution to which your letter of 18 January 1990 refers. This news was received with delight by our senior staff; it constitutes a magnificent boost to morale and, most importantly, to our research capability … It is rather difficult – even impossible – to convey to you in writing the great delight which your generosity has generated on campus.[18]

The investment was timely, following a decade characterized by repeated postponement of the planned Phase 2 campus development. Coming so soon after the award of university status, such a substantial private investment enhanced a sense of growing momentum. The identity of the university's benefactor was known only to a handful of people, due to the strict anonymity

Trust, deed of trust, 18 Oct. 1988 (APA, Folder 'Dublin City University: DCU Educational Trust, 1/2'). See also DCUPO, 'DCUET proposals/approaches, 1989–94'. Bernard Dillon (Amdahl Ireland) and John Withrington (Irish Shell) were the original signatories to the deed of trust, later joined by Patrick O'Neill (Avonmore Creameries) and Danny O'Hare.   14 Of that £5m, £800,000 was earmarked for an arts centre, £1.6m for a sports centre, £125,000 for a chaplaincy building and £2.5m for a research-and-development excellence fund (DCUPO, 'DCUET: general, 1994–5').   15 That ambition was quickly scaled back to 5% of the annual budget ('DCU: vision of the university in 2002', c.Aug. 1992 (DCUPO, 'DCUET: general, 1994–5')).   16 DCUPO, 'DCUET: general, 1994–5'.   17 As of June 1991 Atlantic had approved funding for four different projects at DCU: construction of a research and development building and a business-education centre, seed funding for DCUET's fundraising campaign, and for the establishment of the Centre for Talented Youth, Ireland (APA, Grants #7018, #7031, #7032, #7060).   18 Danny O'Hare to John Healy, 13 Feb. 1990 (APA, Grant #7018). Healy's letter of 18 January had confirmed a donation of £700,000 towards the R&D building, which was later renamed the Hamilton building (see table 6.1). Formerly director general of the Irish American Partnership, in 1990 Healy was appointed managing director of Tara Consultants, a company established that year to manage Atlantic Philanthropies' activities

clause attached to the donation. It was, in fact, the first of sixty-nine donations to the university over the following two decades by the American billionaire Chuck Feeney, who distributed his wealth anonymously through Atlantic Philanthropies.[19] The cumulative impact of Atlantic's involvement with DCU during the 1990s and 2000s was profound, extending far beyond the provision of financial support. The net effect was to transform the university's campus, its research and teaching capacities and its ability to plan strategically for future development.

Atlantic's first involvement in Irish higher education followed a chance encounter between Feeney and Ed Walsh, president of UL.[20] The success of their subsequent relationship convinced Feeney of the need to create a knowledge economy in Ireland, resourced by philanthropic donations. Feeney's engagement with the other Irish universities began with DCU, the relationship initiated by a carefully orchestrated meeting with Danny O'Hare in early 1989.[21] O'Hare was unaware that the unassuming American seated beside him at a dinner function had such lofty ambitions in mind:

> We were chatting and were getting on quite well … And of course anybody that sat down with me for dinner in those years or any other time, what did I speak about? Only my nearest and dearest NIHE Dublin. I was not in fundraising mode. I was just sharing with a chap who seemed to be interested in higher education, what the problems were. And the problems were we were successful, but we had terrible problems with accommodation … He said, 'What's your latest project that you're looking for funding for?' I said it was a research and development building … And he said, 'What kind of money are you talking about?' I said, 'It's very expensive' – if I had only known who I was talking to – 'it's about a million pounds'. 'Would you mind', he says, 'writing up a little piece for me on it and let me have it?'[22]

in Ireland.   **19** Over the course of three decades, AP eventually distributed €1.1bn across the island of Ireland. For more on Feeney and Atlantic Philanthropies, see Conor O'Clery, *The billionaire who wasn't: how Chuck Feeney secretly made and gave away a fortune* (New York, 2007); Liam Collins, *The Atlantic Philanthropies: Republic of Ireland* (New York, 2017); Atlantic Philanthropies, *Laying foundations for change: capital investments of the Atlantic Philanthropies* (2014), pp 49–146; Atlantic Philanthropies, *The Atlantic Philanthropies in the Republic of Ireland (1987–2014)* (http://www.atlanticphilanthropies.org/wp-content/uploads/2015/11/The-Atlantic-Philanthropies-Republic-of-Ireland.pdf, accessed 11 Apr. 2017).   **20** Fleming, *University of Limerick*, pp 233–4; O'Clery, *The billionaire who wasn't*, pp 137–8; Walsh, *Upstart*, pp 234–5.   **21** O'Clery, *The billionaire who wasn't*, pp 176–7; Atlantic Philanthropies, *Laying foundations for change*, p. 56.   **22** Danny O'Hare interview, 13 Oct. 2005. The dinner was organized by Co-operation North, a charity founded in 1979 by Dr Brendan O'Regan with the aim of improving economic links and co-operation between Northern Ireland and the Republic of Ireland.

It was on the basis of this conversation, and the outline submitted in response to Feeney's request, that Atlantic committed its initial £700,000.[23] DCU undertook to raise the remaining costs, a target exceeded when the university leveraged Atlantic's support to secure a further £750,000 from European Community Structural Funds.[24] That success allowed DCU to complete two separate projects: the R&D (Hamilton) building, and the Computer Applications (McNulty) building.[25] It was a salutary lesson in the power of philanthropic support in leveraging exchequer and European Community funding. Atlantic typically required its donors to use the promise of their funding to leverage matching donations from alternative sources, whether government or other philanthropists, thus potentially doubling the impact of Atlantic's contribution. While the philosophy that underpinned Feeney's desire for anonymity was informed by several considerations, perhaps none was as important as the concept of leveraging matching funding. If Feeney remained in the shadows, 'some other individual might contribute to get the naming rights' to a building or other initiative.[26]

Given the eventual extent of Atlantic's investment in the Irish higher-education sector, it might be argued that its support for DCU was inevitable. There is, however, little doubt that the personalities involved on both sides, and the connections they cultivated, were crucial to the eventual scale of that support. Of particular importance were the relationships developed by Danny O'Hare with Chuck Feeney and, especially, John Healy. As the principal conduit between Atlantic's board and funding applicants in Ireland, Healy was a pivotal figure in DCU's history.[27] Between 1990 and 2013 Atlantic invested €116m in DCU, making it the third largest recipient of funding in Ireland, after UL and TCD.[28] As many of these donations imposed an obligation to secure matching funding, the true value of Atlantic's support for DCU was significantly higher. All but two of Atlantic's sixty-nine donations were made between 1990 and 2003. Just over €107m of the total donated was invested in 'bricks and mortar' projects, rapidly accelerating the physical development of the Glasnevin campus during the 1990s. Its largest single donation to the university of €20.5m enabled the purchase of strategically important land adjacent to the campus.[29] Atlantic also

23 Atlantic's commitment eventually totalled £725,000, with a further £125,000 provided by Joe Lyons via the Irish American Partnership. A senior figure at Duty Free Shoppers, Lyons was encouraged to make his donation following a conversation with Feeney and a visit to DCU's campus (John Healy to Joe Lyons, 24 Jan. 1990 (APA, Grant #7018)). 24 APA, Grant #7018. 25 For a timeline of building completions at DCU, see table 6.1. 26 *New York Times*, 5 Jan. 2017. This was a strategy used to great effect in DCU, where buildings were occasionally named for donors whose contribution, while very significant, was sometimes less than that of Atlantic. 27 As Atlantic's operations in Ireland grew, Healy was joined at Tara Consultants by numerous other people, including Ruth Barror, John A. Healy, Angela Mahon, Colin McCrea and Ray Murphy. Healy was later appointed chief executive officer of Atlantic Philanthropies in 2001, a role he fulfilled until 2007. 28 Atlantic Philanthropies, *The Atlantic Philanthropies in the Republic of Ireland*, p. 1. 29 However,

4.3 The mall during Rag Week, 1998 (DCU Collection).

wholly funded the purchase and development of the St Clare's sports campus, providing a total of €10.7m, and other capital projects to receive significant funding included the Helix performing-arts centre (€22.1m), the John and Aileen O'Reilly Library (€5.825m) and the Lonsdale building (€6.1m).[30]

As a regular visitor to the university, Feeney took an interest in developments on campus. Of all the buildings constructed using Atlantic's funds, Feeney displayed the most interest in what seemed like the least interesting – the multi-storey car park.[31] His interest in seeing architectural plans and being guided through designs could occasionally prove tricky, particularly while he insisted on retaining anonymity. Viewing plans for the indoor sports centre in the company of Danny O'Hare and Barry Kehoe in 1991, Feeney made some casual suggestions for alterations to the design. Unaware that Feeney's organization was contributing more than half the cost of the centre, Kehoe rejected them out of hand. Horrified, O'Hare kicked his colleague under the table until he took the hint and became more amenable to Feeney's comments. When pressed afterwards to explain himself, O'Hare recalled Kehoe's previous training for the priesthood and decided to trust his discretion: 'This is the man … through whom the money is coming. Do give him a little bit more of your ear than you normally give to people, including myself!'[32]

difficulties in developing this land led to the decision, in 2019, to put it up for sale. See chapter 6. **30** Figures collated from material in Atlantic Philanthropies Archive, Cornell University. **31** Collins, *The Atlantic Philanthropies*, p. 9. **32** Danny O'Hare interview, 13 Oct. 2005; O'Clery,

Feeney was forced to reveal that he was the source of Atlantic Philanthropies' funding in 1997, yet steadfastly refused to accept recognition in the standard forms associated with major philanthropy.[33] His name is not attached to any building, scholarship or research institute at DCU, and no plaques indicating his transformational contributions to the university are found on the campus. The university has, nonetheless, found other ways to honour his legacy. DCU Educational Trust inaugurated its Medal for Transformation Through Philanthropy in 2017, to honour donors to the university who demonstrate a 'vision, generosity and sustained passion for change that is truly extraordinary'. Feeney was the first recipient, marking one of the few times he has accepted personal recognition for his philanthropy.[34] Danny O'Hare's letter in response to Atlantic's first donation to DCU (quoted above) had spoken of the magnificent boost it gave to the morale of the university's staff. Almost thirty years later Brian MacCraith, third president of DCU, contributed the foreword to the official history of Atlantic's activities in Ireland. He echoed O'Hare's sentiments, highlighting Atlantic's pivotal role in DCU's development:

> Investments by Atlantic Philanthropies in more than 15 buildings have had a major influence on the dramatic development and impact of DCU since its formal establishment as a university in 1989. In the 28 years since, DCU has achieved international recognition for the quality and impact of its research, its focus on the student learning experience, and its emphasis on social inclusion and equity of student access to educational opportunities … None of this would have been possible, at least in this timescale, without the support and investments of Atlantic. The growth and transformation of DCU has benefitted – and will continue to benefit – tens of thousands of students, and Irish society in general.[35]

In September 2012 DCU joined with the eight other universities on the island of Ireland to confer a joint honorary doctorate on Feeney, the only one of its kind ever awarded.[36]

The injection of funding provided by Atlantic Philanthropies during the 1990s and early 2000s was channelled through DCU Educational Trust. Outside

The billionaire who wasn't, p. 177. Quote from O'Hare interview.   **33** When the anonymity of the source of Atlantic Philanthropies' funding was threatened by a lawsuit arising from the sale of Duty Free Shoppers, the company Feeney had co-founded and made his fortune from, Feeney arranged an interview with the *New York Times* in which he revealed the scale of his philanthropic activities (*New York Times*, 23 Jan. 1997).   **34** DCU, *DCU Educational Trust supporter impact report* (Dublin, 2017), pp 36–7. In a rare break with tradition, Feeney accepted the award at the Ireland Funds Gala in San Francisco, in March 2018.   **35** Brian MacCraith, 'Foreword' in Collins, *The Atlantic Philanthropies*, p. 8.   **36** *DCU News*, 9 Aug. 2012; *Irish Times*, 7 Sept. 2012; *Irish Independent*, 7 Sept. 2012; Brian MacCraith interview, 1 Oct. 2018.

of its relationship with Atlantic, however, the Trust was struggling to cultivate other high-value donors. Atlantic's staff in Ireland were conscious of the paradoxical effect of its strong support for DCU: 'It wouldn't be unfair to say that if it was not for one anonymous donor the office and the board of DCUET would not be seen as being successful. If it continues as before, the situation will not improve.'[37] In an effort to increase the Trust's success in raising donations from alternative sources, Atlantic invested in the Trust itself, providing logistical support and training, as well as seed funding to cover operational costs and strategic planning in the early 1990s.[38] Discreet assistance was also offered in negotiations with major donors during the 1990s, including Tim Mahony and Anthony O'Reilly.[39] Following Atlantic's withdrawal from higher-education funding – particularly with respect to capital projects – the Trust has adapted its fundraising strategies. By the end of 2011 the 'quiet phase' of the current campaign had begun, with a focus on raising funds for campus infrastructure, student initiatives and community engagement.[40] Four years later the Trust publicly launched this initiative as the 'Shaping the Future' campaign, with a target of raising €100m by 2021.[41] Its continued importance to the university was demonstrated by its ability to maintain and even expand the Access programme for disadvantaged students during the 2010s, despite plummeting government investment in higher education.[42] Student philanthropy has also played an important role in financing the university's development, a point acknowledged by Brian MacCraith when the university unveiled its new student centre, the U, in September 2018.[43] The U is the third iteration of student centre to be built on campus, with *c*.€8m of the €15m cost raised by students following an overwhelming vote, in March 2014, in favour of a levy to support construction.[44] Each iteration of the student centre has been part-funded by the student body, with more than £100,000 contributed to the Campus Social Centre (opened Nov. 1990) and *c*.£1.5m to the Hub (opened Sept. 2000). Student levies also contributed to the cost of the sports centre.[45]

37 Colin McCrea memo, 29 Nov. 1996 (APA, Folder 'Grants, strategic planning, 1992–2001, 1/2'). 38 APA, Grants #7032, #7219, #7299, Folder 'Grants, strategic planning, 1992–2001'; DCUPO, 'DCUET: general, 1994'. 39 DCUPO, 'Arts centre – DCU'; APA, Grant #8037. 40 DCUPO, GA2012/1. Patrick McDermott served as the Trust's CEO from 2001 until 2014. 41 The campaign had raised €75m by the end of 2019 (DCUPO, GA2015/6, GA2017/7; *DCU News*, 11 Sept. 2019). 42 See chapter 7 for the Access programme. 43 The U was formally opened by Michael D. Higgins, president of Ireland, on 27 September 2018 (*DCU News*, 27 and 28 Sept. 2018; Brian MacCraith interview, 1 Oct. 2018). 44 The referendum was passed with 92% voting in favour out of a valid poll of 2,325 (APA, Grant #7696; APA, Folder 'DCU policy: background, strategic planning, 1991–2003, 2/3'; *Irish Times*, 10 Nov. 1998; *College View*, 28 Mar. 2014). 45 The initial push for a student centre on campus has been credited to Alan Murphy, SU president in 1987, whose proposal was rejected by the Institute's administration. By 1990 Murphy's successor, Clare Daly, had secured the university's agreement to proceed with a centre. However, such was the dire state of the finances at NIHED/DCU in 1989 that governing body considered imposing a

PRTLI and SFI

Most of Atlantic's direct support for DCU took the form of capital investment intended to improve the university's physical infrastructure. Research and teaching capacity would thus be boosted by the availability of better facilities. Government funding both for capital projects, and to support research activity, also rose from the early 1990s and remained on an upward curve until the end of the following decade. State investment in higher education rose to a high of *c*.€2bn in 2009.[46] While the 1980s had thus been characterized by the government's inability to invest adequately in NIHE Dublin's development, the following two decades witnessed a reversal of fortunes. DCU received a considerable share of the HEA's capital grants programme in 1991, totalling £2.472m of the £7.667m disbursed that year. Half of DCU's allocation came as part of the HEA's undergraduate expansion programme, initiated in March 1990 to increase the number of student places made available for new entrants.[47] In 1991 DCU once again received the largest allocation (£4.653m, or 28 per cent) of the HEA's capital grants. While the university's share of capital funding fluctuated thereafter, at the end of the decade it received the second largest capital grant (€7.426m), more than half of which was provided by European Regional Development funds and the newly launched public-private initiative on capital funding for higher education.[48] The turn of the millennium once more witnessed a notable increase in capital funding for DCU. The HEA's budget for capital investment increased dramatically from €30.2m in 1999 to €61.7m in 2000 and €64.5m in 2001. DCU's share for those three years stood at €7.4m (24.5 per cent), €21.4m (34.6 per cent) and €20.1m (31 per cent), respectively.[49] The surge in funding available from the HEA followed the introduction of the

'development levy' of £10 on all students, with the executive arguing strongly in favour. Countering the proposal, Daly argued that students should not be called upon to fund capital projects (DCUPO, GB89/6–8). Nonetheless, the Students' Union contributed to the construction of the Campus Social Centre, and a student levy was approved by the student body to help fund the Hub. For a report on the opening of the Social Centre, including floor plans, see *DCU Bull Sheet*, Nov. 1990. For a potted history of the planning and construction of the Hub, see *College View*, Oct. 2000. **46** Oireachtas Library and Research Service, *Higher education in Ireland: for economy and society?* (Dublin, 2014), p. 2. See also figs A6.1 and A6.2 in appendix 6, below.   **47** DCU used the money to build a 500 sq.m. extension to the library, then located in the Henry Grattan building. The extension currently houses Information Systems Services (HEA, *Reports, accounts and student statistics, 1990/91 and 1991/92*, pp 24–9). See table 6.1 in appendix 6, below.   **48** The joint public-private initiative on capital funding in the higher-education sector was introduced in 1996 and scheduled to run for four years. Its aim was to provide an additional 6,200 university places, at a total cost of £60m. Universities were required to raise matching funds for state investment. DCU's 1999 capital grant contributed to construction of the Biological Sciences/Chemical Sciences (Lonsdale) building (HEA, *Reports, accounts, 1999, 2000 and 2001*, p. 34).   **49** DCU also received capital equipment and building maintenance grants totalling €317,615 (1999), €736,808 (2000) and €1.4m (2001) (*Reports, accounts, 1999, 2000 and 2001* (HEA, 2003), pp 26–30).

Programme for Research in Third-Level Institutions (PRTLI) scheme. Relative to size, DCU outperformed all other universities in Ireland in its success under the first three rounds of PRTLI, a testament to the quality of the university's academic research.

Between 1995 and 2009 the university's research grants and project income rose quite consistently, with slight yearly decreases in 2001 and 2004. Income peaked in 2009 at €50m, before falling to a ten-year low of €41m in 2017 (fig. A6.2). The PRTLI and SFI programmes accounted for the majority of this funding. Announced in 1998, PRTLI altered the landscape of research funding and had a profound impact on the higher-education sector as a whole. An independent assessment carried out in 2003 labelled the programme a 'remarkable endeavour'.[50] Without the foresight and investment of Atlantic Philanthropies, the programme would never have existed. Following the sale in 1997 of Duty Free Shoppers, Atlantic Philanthropies received an influx of capital.[51] Determined to speed up the development of Ireland's knowledge economy and its universities, Feeney instructed John Healy and Colin McCrea to approach the Irish government with a proposal: Atlantic would donate £60m for research projects at Irish universities, if the Irish government matched the contribution.[52] The proposal proved to be the catalyst for the largest ever sustained investment programme in Irish higher education, consisting of five competitive funding cycles administered between 1999 and 2010. Amounting to €1.2bn in total, approximately 30 per cent was raised from non-exchequer sources, including philanthropic donations, European Union funding and partnerships with private and commercial entities.[53]

Over the course of the five cycles, DCU received a total of €109.5m in PRTLI funding, with €62.783m awarded during the first three cycles, €23m awarded in Cycle IV (2007) and €23.8m in Cycle V (2010).[54] Funding was directed towards a mix of capital projects, equipment purchases and related research project costs. Major research centres established in this manner included the Research Institute in Networks and Communications Engineering (RINCE), the National Centre for Plasma Science and Technology and the National Centre for Sensor Research.[55] Though DCU had undoubted success in attracting PRTLI funding,

50 HEA, *The Programme for Research in Third Level Institutions [PRTLI] impact assessment* (Dublin, 2004), i, p. 12.   **51** Atlantic Philanthropies, *The Atlantic Philanthropies in the Republic of Ireland (1987–2014)*, p. 6.   **52** Atlantic Philanthropies, *Laying foundations for change*, p. 59. See also Walsh, *Higher education in Ireland*, p. 402.   **53** Having provided the impetus for the programme, Atlantic Philanthropies contributed a total of €178m to the first three PRTLI award cycles (Walsh, *Higher education in Ireland*, p. 402; Atlantic Philanthropies, *The Atlantic Philanthropies in the Republic of Ireland (1987–2014)*, p. 6; HEA, *PRTLI impact assessment*, i, p. 24).   **54** HEA, *PRTLI impact assessment*; *DCU News*, 18 Sept. 2007 and 19 July 2010.   **55** Each of these three centres were eventually housed in the Engineering and Research (Stokes) building, completed in 2002 at a cost of *c.*€45m; €25m was provided under PRTLI Cycle I, with a further €16.6m coming from the exchequer in two separate contributions (APA, Grants #7866, #7903; HEA, *Reports, accounts,*

that success was somewhat qualified by the embarrassment of receiving no funding at all under the scheme's second cycle, the results of which were announced in July 2000. The failure of the university's proposals to even make the cycle's shortlist was made all the more acute by the successes of the institutes of technology in Cork and Sligo.[56] Informal feedback received by the university indicated that, while individual funding applications were of high quality, DCU's collective proposal did not indicate an institution-wide strategy for the development of interdisciplinary collaborations.[57]

Determined not to repeat the mistakes of Cycle II, the university took the bold decision to focus all of its attention on a single proposal for Cycle III, to establish a National Institute for Cellular Biotechnology. DCU's reputation in the field had long been recognized, beginning with its designation as a national centre of excellence in biotechnology in 1987.[58] The NICB proposal was also timely, with the sequencing of all genes in human DNA completed and published in 2001. Atlantic Philanthropies identified the proposal as worthy of support in view of the university's 'courageous and strategic [decision] in identifying the development of its international competence in this niche area as an overriding research goal'.[59] This daring strategy was rewarded with the largest single grant (€34.283m) received by the university under the PRTLI scheme.[60]

Under Cycle IV (awarded in 2007) the university concentrated its resources on establishing interdisciplinary and inter-institutional projects. Changes in the HEA's criteria for funding, coupled with a tight deadline for funding proposals, presented considerable challenges for the university's PRTLI project management team, headed by Dr Niamh O'Dowd.[61] Cycle IV marked a significant breakthrough for the university in that funding was also awarded for two humanities- and social sciences-based projects. Announced in July 2010, the fifth (and to date latest) cycle of PRTLI funding concluded in 2015. Each of the DCU-led submissions was successful, including the proposed construction of a Nanobioanalytical Research Facility, which received €16m in capital funding.[62] Inspired by the success of the PRTLI programme, the government established Science Foundation Ireland (SFI) in 2003, initially tasking it with the administration of a fund of £650m for investment in economically strategic areas related to STEM research. DCU also had notable success under the Science Foundation Ireland funding calls. With the announcement in 2010 of €16.8m in

1999, 2000 and 2001, pp 33–4).   **56** *Irish Times*, 23 May 2000; HEA, *PRTLI impact assessment*, ii, pp 47–50.   **57** Ferdinand von Prondzynski to all staff, 19 Oct. 2000 (APA, Folder 'DCU Policy: background, strategic planning, 1/3'); DCU, *Leading change: DCU strategic plan, 2001–5* (Dublin, 2001).   **58** The university had also introduced the first degree programme in biotechnology in 1982 – see chapter 5.   **59** Atlantic Philanthropies grant recommendation, [2001] (APA, Grant #9754).   **60** HEA, *PRTLI impact assessment*, ii, pp 47–50.   **61** DCUPO, GA2007/1, 2 and 4; *DCU News*, 18 Sept. 2007.   **62** DCUPO, GA2010/3, 4; *DCU News*, 19 July 2010.

funding for the Centre for Next Generation Localisation, DCU had achieved the distinction of receiving the two largest awards made under that scheme to that point. Previous major success had led to the funding and construction of the Biomedical Diagnostics Institute (BDI), a proposal led by the university's future president, Prof. Brian MacCraith.[63]

II

PRTLI and SFI funding were implemented in the wake of major reform of the university sector. The need for such reform had been recognized in the 1960s, but, while the overall shape of higher education had been recast with the introduction of the regional technical colleges and NIHEs, the traditional universities had largely remained unchanged. That situation changed during the tenure of Niamh Bhreathnach as minister for education (for the second time) between December 1994 and June 1997. Drafting of the Universities Act of 1997 began in 1995 and produced the first – and to date only – piece of legislation to comprehensively address the university sector in the history of the state. Bhreathnach's department worked closely with the HEA, the Conference of Heads of Irish Universities (CHIU) and other stakeholders throughout the drafting process. As a member of the CHIU, Danny O'Hare and DCU's governing body were well placed to contribute, in the process offering the perspective of the youngest university in the state and one operating under considerably different statutory parameters than its counterparts.[64]

Following multiple revisions in response to stakeholder contributions, the Universities Act was approved by the Oireachtas and came into force on 16 June 1997.[65] Its effects were wide-ranging, including major structural reform of the National University of Ireland.[66] In terms of university administration, standardized structures and a common statutory framework were introduced for all universities, which were, in effect, 'a compromise between traditional academic and managerial understandings of the university'.[67] The net result was legislation that has defined the legal parameters of the university sector for more than two decades, with a particular emphasis on creating coherent and homogenous governance structures.[68] For DCU the legislation marked a

---

63 DCUPO, GA2007/5, 6; GA2008/1; *Irish Times*, 25 June 2010. The BDI attracted a total of €44m in SFI funding between 2003 and 2010. Construction of the Institute was funded by the university.   64 For selected documents recording DCU's contributions to the drafting of the legislation, including O'Hare's correspondence, see CHIU, *Universities Act, 1997, archive* (4 vols, Dublin, 2003), ii, pp 1507–1635. See also DCUPO, 'Legislation' and 'Universities Act 1997'. 65 Universities Act, 1997 (no. 24 of 1997); S.I. 254/1997 – Universities Act, 1997 (Commencement) Order, 1997.   66 For a summary of the literature relating to the 1997 Universities Act, see Walsh, *Higher education in Ireland*, pp 362–74.   67 Ibid., p. 409. See also White, *Investing in people*, pp 224–9. 68 HEA and IUA, *Governance of Irish universities* (Dublin, 2012).

4.4 President of Ireland Mary McAleese during a visit to DCU on 19 March 1998 (DCU collection).

significant moment, placing the university on an equal statutory footing with its older counterparts.[69] The legislation's impact on the older universities was arguably greater, particularly in the subsequent trend experienced by most universities to consolidate power within small leadership groups. While DCU was not immune to this advance towards managerialism, its foundational legislation had already established a governance structure with more power vested in the executive than was the case with the older universities.[70]

Governing body was renamed governing authority. The title of chairperson was changed to chancellor, with Thomas P. Hardiman the first to assume the role. Hardiman was well acquainted with the institution, not least from his chairmanship of the international study group that had recommended university status for NIHE Dublin. Among the many changes implemented to the university's governance structures, one of the most far-reaching concerned membership of the new governing authority. Prior to 1997, the extent of the minister for education's influence on appointments to NIHED/DCU's

---

69 The legislation was also passed just days after DCU won the RTÉ television quiz show *Challenging Times* for the only time in its history, defeating UL in a controversial final. The quiz show ran for eleven years, with UL and TCD the only universities not to emerge victorious at least once (*Irish Times*, 22 Apr., 7 and 21 Oct. 1997). **70** National Institute for Higher Education, Dublin, Act 1980 (no. 30 of 1980). For more on managerialism and the impact of the 1997 Universities Act on the governance of universities, see Hedley, 'Managerialism in Irish universities'; Walsh, *Higher education in Ireland*, pp 408–14.

4.5 Eugene Kennedy (left) and Brian MacCraith (School of Physical Sciences) enjoy a celebratory drink. Reproduced by kind permission of Michael Burke.

governing body had been a continual source of disquiet.[71] Sixteen of the twenty-five members of governing body had previously been appointed either directly by or on the recommendation of the minister. Under the new legislation that number was reduced to three. Staff and students also gained greater representation, with at least six and three representatives, respectively.[72] In an indication of the importance of the Educational Trust to the university's development, it was empowered to nominate at least one member to the authority up to a maximum of three.[73]

Elections for the appointment of staff members to governing authority took place in November 1997, yet by February 1998 no date for the first meeting of the new body had been fixed. In light of unrest among staff at the delay, Gay Mitchell, TD, raised the issue in the Dáil, where he was assured by the minister for education and science that (unspecified) delays in appointing members of the body had been overcome and the body's first meeting was imminent.[74] Five days later governing authority's first meeting was finally confirmed for 24 March.[75]

---

71 See above, chapters 2 & 3.   72 The legislation allowed for the election of a maximum of fourteen staff members and four students to governing authority (Universities Act, 1997 (no. 24 of 1997), s. 16 (2)).   73 Universities Act, 1997 (no. 24 of 1997), s. 16 (5). The legislation also ensured that the Trust's equivalent in Limerick, the University of Limerick Foundation, would be represented on UL's governing authority. No other university was required to have a representative of its philanthropic arm on its governing authority.   74 *Dáil Debates*, 19 Feb. 1998.   75 Ibid., 24 Feb. 1998. DCU was the last of the Irish universities to hold a meeting of its governing authority,

Staff now had a greater say in the university's governance than ever before. The impact of this change was felt the following year, as DCU sought to appoint a new president.

DCU's contributions to the drafting of the Universities Act, and its marked success in attracting a significant share of funding during PRTLI Cycle I, were achieved in the last years of Danny O'Hare's tenure as university president. Having first taken office in March 1977, his intention to step down was publicly announced in November 1998 with a departure date of September the following year.[76] It would prove to be a pivotal moment in the university's evolution. The search for a successor was poorly managed, in part due to a lack of institutional experience in replacing its most senior officer. Overseen by a subcommittee of governing authority, operating under the terms of a hastily drafted university statute, the search was conducted by a recruitment consultancy that had also managed recent searches for new presidents of University College Cork and the University of Limerick.[77] The dangers of this strategy later became apparent, when it was revealed that the first choice for the position at DCU had withdrawn at the last moment. It was also revealed that this same candidate had placed second in UCC's search and had also declined the position at Limerick. No reserve candidate had been recommended.

Faced with the reality that a new president would not be in place by the time of O'Hare's retirement, governing authority considered a proposal for O'Hare to rescind his resignation and remain *ad interim* until a new search could be completed. Chancellor Tom Hardiman urged acceptance of the offer, arguing that the university did not have the appropriate governance structures to allow for an acting president. There was, however, a prominent belief among academic staff that a change in leadership would allow the university to explore new directions. Tensions emerged, with governing authority divided over the best way to proceed. Under pressure from several members of the authority, Hardiman agreed to ascertain the views of heads of schools and staff at professorial level. Though consensus was initially not forthcoming, further consultations confirmed a desire for a fresh perspective in the president's office. Governing authority was mandated to conduct a new search; in the meantime, an interim chief officer would be appointed.[78] Anxious to learn from the poor handling of the first process, Tom Hardiman sought the assistance of John R. Healy and Atlantic Philanthropies to create a more robust search procedure.[79]

though the delay was not altogether anomalous in that only two universities had convened a governing authority before the end of 1997. UCD's first meeting was not held until 10 Mar. 1998. **76** *Irish Times*, 20 Nov. 1998; *Newslink*, Apr. 1999. **77** Statute no. 1 of 1999, DCU (www.dcu.ie/policies/ statutes.shtml). Governing authority was empowered to draft statutes necessary for the governance and regulation of the university by section 33 of the 1997 Universities Act. **78** Information relating to the recruitment of O'Hare's successor provided to the author by private sources. See also DCUPO, GA1999/1–6. **79** Tom Hardiman to John R. Healy, 27 Aug.

While the second search was underway, the role of director general was defined and inscribed in another hastily drafted university statute.[80] As a member of governing authority and one of the university's longest-serving academics (having been appointed head of the School of Chemical Sciences in July 1980), Albert Pratt was nominated and accepted the interim position. His experience and familiarity with the university marked him as an ideal candidate to manage a difficult transitional period: 'All I'm trying to do is move things on, so that the next person can take over and move smoothly into the next stage.'[81] Pratt's most pressing challenge was to prevent any adverse effect on governance during the second search, thus ensuring no further damage to the university's reputation. His assured stewardship from late 1999 until the summer of 2000 allowed the institution to remain on an even keel during the completion of several major projects, including the purchase of strategically important land.[82] Pratt's pragmatic and understated approach to the role enabled a smooth transfer to the incoming president, Ferdinand von Prondzynski, who took up the post in July 2000.[83]

By the time of his retirement, Danny O'Hare had served as director/president of NIHED/DCU for twenty-two years. His stewardship had seen NIHE Dublin evolve from a start-up third-level institution, starved of resources, into a vibrant university. Approaching the new millennium, the university's student population had risen above 6,000, located on a campus unrecognizable from the dilapidated and stark vista that had greeted students in 1980. Construction was underway or planned on several additional capital projects, including the Helix performing-arts centre, offering further proof of the institution's growth and of the momentum generated under O'Hare's leadership.

1999; John R. Healy to Harvey Dale, 28 Sept. 1999 (APA, Grant #8276). Dr Judith Rodin, president of the University of Pennsylvania, was invited to oversee the assessment of the shortlisted candidates in December 1999. Governing authority approved the appointment of Ferdinand von Prondzynski on 27 January 2000 (DCUPO, GA2000/1, 2; APA, Grant #8276).   80 Statute no. 2 of 1999, DCU, came into operation on 11 May 2000 (www.dcu.ie/policies/statutes.shtml). The duties of the director general were defined as follows: 'In the event that the office of President is or becomes vacant, the Governing Authority may appoint an employee of the University to the position of Director General of the University (hereinafter called the "Director General") whose function shall be to manage and direct the affairs of the University in its academic, administrative, personnel, financial and other activities and to act as the accounting officer of the University pending the appointment of a person to the office of President and Chief Officer. A Director General so appointed shall be accountable to the Governing Authority and his/her appointment be subject to confirmation by the Governing Authority unless Governing Authority otherwise directs from time to time. A Director General appointed pursuant to this Section 3 shall hold office on such terms and conditions and for such period as the Governing Authority shall determine by resolution or regulations made by it from time to time provided always that his/her term of office shall not in any event exceed a period of one year.'   81 *Irish Times*, 3 Oct. 1980; *College View*, Feb. 2000; Albert Pratt interview, 19 Oct. 2018. Quotation taken from *College View*.   82 For the purchase of 10 acres of the Eustace estate, completed in 2000, see chapter 6.   83 DCUPO, GA2000/1–3.

4.6 Thomas P. Hardiman (left) and Ferdinand von Prondzynski, pictured at the latter's inauguration as university president (DCU Collection).

Equally important had been the development of the university's national and international reputation for the strength of its teaching and learning, and as a centre of excellence in research.[84] Clashes with senior staff over such a lengthy period as chief officer were inevitable, particularly as he struggled to adapt his management style to suit the university's rapid growth during the 1990s.[85] While there are no buildings on campus named in his honour, O'Hare received an honorary doctorate from the university in 2008 at which time Farrel Corcoran delivered a citation that paid suitable tribute to his legacy:

> Danny is a very modest man, with a tendency to deflect praise towards others. But as he walks around the campus today, he must have much to reflect upon with quiet pride and satisfaction. Very few other people in

84 Exchange and collaboration arrangements were in place with almost 200 universities, spread across six continents. For a list of these universities, see DCU, *Annual report, 1997/8*, pp 433–9. 85 Commenting in 1992, John R. Healy of Atlantic Philanthropies noted that O'Hare had 'enormous strengths and his achievement in building up Dublin City University is substantial. He does, however, show an unwillingness to delegate work and has been reluctant to build a strong management team around him. He is also uncomfortable about projecting himself on the public stage (in sharp contrast to Ed Walsh)' (John R. Healy to Ray Handlan, 23 July 1992 (APA, Folder 'Strategic planning, 1992–2001, 2/2')).

Irish public life can match this contribution. In Christopher Wren's magnificent St Paul's Cathedral in London, there is an inscription in Latin that suits Danny very well: *Si monumentum quaeris, circumspice*. Which roughly translated means: if you are looking for a monument to him, just look around you.[86]

Prior to his arrival at DCU, Ferdinand von Prondzynski had spent a decade at the University of Hull as professor of law and dean of the Faculty of Social Sciences. He was, however, no stranger to Ireland and its higher-education system. Having spent part of his childhood in Ireland, in 1980 von Prondzynski was appointed as a lecturer in the School of Business Studies at Trinity College Dublin.[87] During his eleven years at TCD, the future president was aware of the progress of NIHED/DCU, particularly through his work as national secretary of the Irish Federation of University Teachers, and supported its ambitions for university status.[88] His arrival as president was a pivotal moment, marking the first time that NIHED/DCU would be led by a person whose career had not evolved in tandem with the institution:

> The institution had got big, comparatively … and there were a lot of people working in it who had been there for quite a while. When they had started it was small … [I]f you look at the comparisons with industry start-ups there are quite a lot of similarities … the way in which people worked, the way they saw each other as part of a community, the slight sense of an outside world that wasn't helpful to them. A fairly close-knit kind of operation where people knew each other terribly well, were very much part of the same family. And then suddenly this thing had grown. A lot of other people came in who hadn't shared that particular start-up, who might have come from institutions that had a different outlook, and might have had a different outlook in fact on DCU. And so, you had a quite close-knit group of people on the one hand, who had around them a group of people who didn't particularly have the same experience. And that also led to a moment, I think, in the history of the institution where it wasn't quite sure where it was going.[89]

One of the new president's first priorities was to improve staff morale. Fallout from the initial failed search for O'Hare's successor and its divisive resolution lingered: 'Managing that particular element of it, and in particular persuading people not to take a hostile view of each other … was quite a significant element

86 *DCU News*, 11 Nov. 2008.   87 Ferdinand von Prondzynski interview, 18 Oct. 2018.   88 Ibid. IFUT is a trade union representing university staff, and von Prondzynski served as the union's national secretary in 1983 and 1984 (Marie Coleman, *IFUT: a history, 1963–99* (2nd ed., Dublin, 2010), p. 65).   89 Ferdinand von Prondzynski interview, 18 Oct. 2018.

of my initial period. It wasn't an overwhelmingly dominant element, but it was there and it needed to be addressed.'[90] One method of doing so was to improve staff facilities. As a consequence of the rapid increase in student numbers during the 1990s, the only common room available to all staff was a converted tearoom in the Henry Grattan, offering a limited hot-beverage service. During discussions with Atlantic Philanthropies concerning possible funding opportunities, von Prondzynski identified renovations to Albert College to convert some old chemistry labs into staff facilities as one of his top priorities. Atlantic duly provided €2.25m to cover 90 per cent of the costs. Completed in October 2003, the renovations provided dining facilities, a common room and separate spaces for private, small-scale events – collectively known as the 1838 Club.[91] Despite the obvious boon to staff morale and benefit for hosting guests of the university, the decision to prioritize this project was somewhat curious, given that Atlantic had signalled its intention to fund one final 'bricks and mortar' project at DCU. The alternative, for which Atlantic indicated it would be willing to consider a grant of *c*.€20m, was the construction of a student residential complex with 400 bedrooms.[92]

An additional area in which von Prondzynski showed a willingness to listen to the concerns of staff was that of gender balance and broader issues of inequality in the workplace. Gender balance and equality in the higher-education sector did not then feature as a prominent policy concern, either at national level or within individual institutions. Gemma Hussey's tenure as minister for education during the 1980s had marked the beginnings of change, with the HEA reporting in 1987 on the notable gender imbalance at the upper levels of academic teaching and leadership.[93] However, little was done to address that imbalance over the following decade. In a 1995 white paper, the Department of Education and Science promised a new beginning for gender equality. All third-level institutions would be required to develop and publish policies to promote gender equality. Suggested steps included ensuring an appropriate gender balance on staff-selection boards, encouraging female students to enrol in traditionally male-dominated disciplines, encouraging and facilitating women in applying for senior academic positions and putting in place adequate arrangements for assisting staff and students with young children.[94] The 1997 Universities Act imposed statutory obligations to 'promote gender balance and equality of opportunity among students and employees of the university'.[95]

90 Ibid. **91** APA, Grant #10490. The name was chosen in honour of the opening of the Glasnevin Model Farm/Albert Agricultural College in 1838 – see chapter 1. **92** Colin McCrea to David Walsh and John R. Healy, 4 Oct. 2000 (APA, Folder 'DCU student residences – background only'); 'Grant recommendation summary', June 2002 (APA, Grant #10490, 1/2). **93** HEA, *Women academics in Ireland: report of the committee on the position of women academics in third level education in Ireland* (Dublin, 1987). **94** Department of Education and Science, *Charting our education future: white paper on education* (Dublin, 1995), p. 109. **95** Universities Act, 1997 (no. 24 of 1997), ss 12, 18 and 36; Walsh, *Higher education in Ireland*, pp 357–62.

The need for action on the issue was clear. Statistics compiled by the HEA in 1998 painted a grim picture for the promotion prospects of female academics, prompting demands for change across the sector.[96] In the seven Irish universities and two teacher-education colleges, 95 per cent of professors were male, as were 94 per cent of associate professors and 82 per cent of senior lecturers. The situation in DCU was worse. Despite the fact that 36 per cent of the academic staff were female, there were no women at either professor or associate professor level. Just 17 per cent of senior lecturers were female, yet women accounted for 55 per cent of assistant lecturers, the lowest grade available. More than half of all female academics were employed on temporary contracts, compared to just 17 per cent of their male counterparts.[97]

Anxious to accelerate efforts to redress the situation, female employees at DCU created the Sunrise Group, consisting of academics, administrators, librarians and secretaries 'with an interest in reversing the ongoing effects of gender imbalance' at all levels. Its recommendations (largely accepted by the university's executive) included the establishment of an Equal Opportunities Unit and employment of a unit director.[98] Implementation of these recommendations was, however, delayed until early 2002. In the meantime the university appointed Patricia Barker as its first female registrar in April 2000, while the following year saw the appointment of Jenny Williams (School of Applied Languages and Intercultural Studies), Kathy Monks (DCU Business School), Heather Ruskin (School of Computer Applications) and Anne Scott (School of Nursing) as the first female professors at the university.[99] According to Barker, in the early years of NIHE Dublin 'everything was growing so rapidly, gender equality was not part of our agenda ... It was later, on reflection, we realised how gender-imbalanced it was on the academic side.' Barker illustrated the point by observing that she was the only female member of academic council's standing committee. Noting that the position at DCU merely reflected trends in other universities, industry and wider society, Barker concluded that 'we had to take positive steps to persuade management, which was male dominated, and didn't perceive that there was a problem'.[100] Progress in the area of gender equality in the ensuing years has been uneven, at national and individual institutional level. By 2017, 30 per cent of professors at DCU were female, and the balance at the levels of associate professor (44 per cent) and senior lecturer (43 per cent) were clear improvements on 1998.[101]

96 See, for example, *Irish Times*, 23 and 27 June 1998.   **97** DCU equality director funding proposal, 7 Feb. 2000 (APA, Grant #8048).   **98** Sunrise Group Report, Mar. 1999 (APA, Grant #8048); *DCU News*, Mar. 2002. Mary Ainscough was appointed as the university's first equality director in January 2002.   **99** *Irish Times*, 13 Mar. and 11 Sept. 2001.   **100** *Irish Times*, 11 Sept. 2001. **101** HEA, *Higher education institutional staff profiles by gender* (Dublin, 2018), p. 9. At the end of 2017 DCU had the second highest proportion of female professors, a position held jointly with Maynooth University, behind UL (31%). DCU received an Institutional Athena SWAN Bronze

4.7 John Horgan (right) in conversation with John Hume on the day Hume and Jean Kennedy Smith (left) received honorary doctorates from DCU, 26 March 1994 (DCU Collection).

In addition to enhancing staff facilities, von Prondzynski prioritized building upon the university's existing strengths and emphasizing its impact on Irish higher education:

> The point I was trying to get everyone to remember back in 2000 is, actually quite a lot of Irish higher education is changing, and it's changing because of what DCU did. So, whether it's the INTRA work placement programme, or whether it is creating academic units that were genuinely interdisciplinary ... Virtually every academic unit in DCU is inter-disciplinary, which was not the case in UCD or Trinity.[102]

The first strategic plan of his tenure outlined an innovative vision to reorient the university's research objectives. Adopted by governing authority in February 2001, *Leading change* proposed a research strategy centred on six academic themes.[103] Each theme was intended to provide a framework for interdisciplinary collaboration between the university's schools and faculties, characterized as 'a radical departure from the emphasis of most universities on traditional disciplinary frameworks'.[104] The six themes selected for strategic development

award in 2017 (*DCU News*, 15 Mar. 2017).   **102** Ferdinand von Prondzynski interview, 18 Oct. 2018.   **103** DCUPO, GA2001/1–3.   **104** DCU, *Leading change: DCU strategic plan, 2001–5*.

were: 1) communication, arts and culture; 2) education and learning; 3) business and innovation; 4) science, discovery and technological innovation; 5) life sciences and health in society; and 6) social development and world order. In order to maximize the development and effectiveness of these themes, von Prondzynski proposed the appointment of five academic theme leaders, with a remit to promote and manage the interdisciplinary activities of the university's staff.

Attempts to fully integrate academic themes into the university's research strategy formed one of the pillars of von Prondzynski's presidency. Conceived in part to provide a new direction for the university, the themes were presented as instruments 'for renewing DCU's mission to challenge the traditions of higher education in Ireland'.[105] For von Prondzynski, the concept was underpinned by a desire to allow the university to address society's needs directly.[106] The proposal met with some initial scepticism, both within the university and from potential funders. Much of the doubt concerned the proposed leadership structure, particularly the relationship between theme leaders and deans of faculty, and the extent to which theme leaders would be able to influence the university's overall research direction.[107] Despite these reservations, in what would prove to be its last major donation to the university, Atlantic Philanthropies provided €2.65m to fund the scheme.[108] Progress was, however, slow. By June 2004 just two theme leaders had been appointed, and a full complement was never reached.[109] An external review in 2007 noted a 'clear lack of understanding ... of the roles of the theme leaders' within the university. Moreover, the university's leadership had not adequately communicated the philanthropic source of theme-leader funding, and so some hostility arose from a perception that the programme was a drain on scarce resources.[110] Perhaps most importantly, the scheme was ahead of its time and thus struggled to gain the traction necessary for successful implementation.[111]

Von Prondzynski's presidency provided an apposite moment to remould organizational structures. At the end of the 1990s DCU had thirteen academic schools, divided among seven faculties, with the head of each school reporting

---

105 M.L. Shattock to John A. Healy, 12 Aug. 2003 (APA, Grant #12263).   **106** Ferdinand von Prondzynski interview, 18 Oct. 2018.   **107** See, for example, John A. Healy memo, 21 May 2003 (APA, Grant #12263).   **108** In February 2003, Colin McCrea and John A. Healy met with von Prondzynski and informed him that, given Atlantic's long association with DCU, they were anxious to make one final grant of €3m to the university, which von Prondzynski decided to utilize to implement the academic themes concept (John A. Healy memo, 4 Feb. 2003 (APA, 'DCU policy: background, strategic planning, 1/3')).   **109** The second institutional review of DCU, published in 2010, made no mention of the academic theme leaders programme (DCUPO, AC2004/3; EUA, *Institutional Quality Review of Dublin City University*, pp 6, 11, 19).   **110** 'Report of the external review: Office of the Strategic Themes', 7 June 2007 (APA, Grant #12263).   **111** Most Irish universities later adopted the concept of interdisciplinary themes to provide strategic direction for research policy. See, for example, TCD, *Strategic plan, 2014–19* (Dublin, 2014), pp 60–1.

directly to the president. While each faculty was led by a dean, heads of school maintained responsibility for school budgets and major decisions at school level. That structure was fundamentally revised during the first strategic review process. Schools were consolidated into four executive faculties, each headed by an executive dean with overall responsibility for individual schools/academic groups, accounts, administration and academic leadership. Decisions regarding individual school budgets were now made at faculty level, and heads of school no longer had direct, regular access to the president and senior leadership.[112] Other changes in the university's administrative structure included the decision to reorganize Registry with the creation of a director of registry and vice president for learning innovation.[113] Discussed and implemented during the first half of von Prondzynski's tenure, these changes reflected the ongoing evolution of the university from a tight-knit, small institution to one that reflected – for better or for worse – similar trends across the higher-education sector towards the consolidation of decision-making within small leadership groups.[114] Though the transition enhanced opportunities for interdisciplinary collaboration, other consequences were less benign and were the cause of dissatisfaction among academic staff:

> As a result of the restructuring of the university, the position and role of the Head of School changed … Previously Heads had reported directly to the President/Senior Management in what had been a rather flat structure. When the four Executive Faculties were established, [the School of Applied Languages and Intercultural Studies] found itself in a faculty with four other schools … [A]s the Faculty gradually grew together, there were increasing opportunities for collaboration, beginning with a 'Faculty Degree', the BA in Communication and Cultural Studies. The overall result of the university restructuring, however, was to sideline Heads in the decision-making process.[115]

Nonetheless, when evaluating the new structure in 2005, the European University Association noted that the change had assisted the development of more coherent strategic research priorities, creating opportunities for the university to build upon the successes of its university-designated research centres and national research centres.[116]

---

112 DCU, *Quality assurance/quality improvement programme for academic units, 2006–7: School of Education Studies* (2007), pp 8–9.   113 DCUPO, GA2002/2–7; GA2004/1, 2; AC2002/2–4, 6; AC2003/1–2.   114 For an overview of this trend – often referred to as 'managerialism' – and the extent of leadership restructuring across the Irish university sector in the late 1990s/early 2000s, see Walsh, *Higher education in Ireland*, pp 408–14.   115 Jenny Williams, 'Head of SALIS – Aug. 2004 to July 2007' in Péchenart and Williams (eds), *School of Applied Languages and Intercultural Studies*, p. 53.   116 EUA, *Institutional quality review of Dublin City University*, pp 10–11.

A consummate communicator, von Prondzynski brought a radically different sensibility to the role of the president in public life. While O'Hare was reticent on the public stage, von Prondzynski consciously cultivated a national profile. Working firmly against the grain, von Prondzynski embraced the use of social media to present the university's message and began a blog detailing his experiences as president.[117] That in turn led to a regular column in the *Irish Times* in which von Prondzynski would frequently propose policy for the higher-education sector and air grievances.[118] DCU's profile was enhanced in a manner that wasn't possible through traditional public relations channels, though the tactic was not universally popular. Criticism largely came from other university heads, with some resistance also emanating from within DCU. For von Prondzynski, the benefits of increased exposure outweighed any potential drawbacks: 'We needed to be able to present ourselves in the public. We needed to make a noise. We needed to be visible and audible. We needed to be quite brash about that.'[119]

Von Prondzynski's tenure as president featured considerable advances in addressing equality, as well as consistent levels of success in attracting major research funding. There were also some high-profile missteps in relations with staff and governors. A careless email from the president, critical of the chancellor, Justice Mella Carroll, caught the attention of the national press.[120] Tensions with staff unions concerning the university's commitment to the principle of academic tenure resulted in costly court cases, with the university suffering defeats in both the high court and the supreme court.[121] DCU's reputation and international standing were nonetheless greatly increased under von Prondzynski. Chancellor David Byrne paid tribute to his impact on the university, noting that von Prondzynski had increased the profile of the university and brought its reputation for teaching and research to a new level. Byrne also praised the president's fierce advocacy for the wider higher-education sector, and lauded his leadership on linkage initiatives with other third-level institutions as a positive and agile response to the evolution of national higher-education policy.[122]

117 The blog's first post was published on 5 June 2008, and its final post was published on 30 April 2019 (https://universitydiary.wordpress.com/about/). 118 See, for example, *Irish Times*, 14 Dec. 2010. 119 Ferdinand von Prondzynski interview, 18 Oct. 2018. 120 *Irish Times*, 28 May 2003. 121 Trouble began with the enactment of university statute no. 3, dealing with the suspension and dismissal of employees, in 2001. That statute has since been superseded (DCUPO, GA2002, 5–7; *Dáil Debates*, 14 Nov. and 18 Dec. 2002; *Cahill v. Dublin City University* [2007] IEHC 20; *Cahill v DCU* [2009] IESC 80; *Sunday Independent*, 15 Apr. 2007, 11 Dec. 2009). 122 DCUPO, GA2010/3.

III

The detailed process put in place to find von Prondzynski's successor reflected the harsh lessons learned in 1999. While drawing up the candidate profile, governing authority's search committee consulted the wider university community through focus groups and targeted meetings.[123] The result was the appointment, on 17 December 2009, of Brian MacCraith as the university's president-designate, to succeed von Prondzynski on 14 July of the following year.[124] Having joined NIHE Dublin's School of Physical Sciences in September 1986, MacCraith had risen to the position of professor of physics and gained international recognition for his central role in the establishment and leadership of several major research centres. Founding director of the National Centre for Sensor Research (1999), he later led proposals to establish the Biomedical Diagnostics Institute (2005) and the Nanobioanlaytical Research Facility (2014).[125] The incoming president was, coincidentally, also the second former student of both Dundalk CBS and of NUI Galway to hold the office, following in the footsteps of Danny O'Hare.

In the course of his inaugural address MacCraith noted the uncertain future of the economy. With student numbers set to continue to rise, he warned of the potential damage to Irish higher education if university budgets were slashed further:

> Shrinking budgets, coupled with increasing student numbers, are placing unsustainable pressures on universities. After all the rationalisation and staff cuts that we have applied in recent years, the quality of the education that we can provide is under severe threat. Moreover, the scale of future demand will necessitate a doubling in capacity of the system over the next two decades.[126]

Government support was already on the wane, with the proportion of fee income provided to DCU by the state dropping from 56 per cent to 44 per cent between 2000 and 2010.[127] Beginning in 2008, DCU (along with the entire higher-education sector) was required to cut staff levels by 6 per cent, while maintaining

---

123 The search committee consisted of David Byrne (chancellor), Prof. Jenny Williams, Dr Dermot Egan, Margaret Sweeney, Martin Conry, Larry Quinn (chairman, DCUET), and Dr Louise Richardson (principal, St Andrews University). Recruitment consultancy Saxton Bampfylde was retained to assist with the search. Five candidates were shortlisted for interview, which were held on 7 December 2009 (DCUPO, GA2008/5, GA2009/4, 5).   124 DCUPO, GA2009/6; *DCU News*, 17 Dec. 2009; *Irish Independent*, 23 Dec. 2009.   125 APA, Grant #7900; HEA, *PRTLI impact assessment*, ii, p. 48; DCU, *President's report, 2005*, pp 29–30; DCU, *President's report, 2010–11*, p. 22; Brian MacCraith interview, 1 Oct. 2018.   126 Brian MacCraith's inaugural address, 13 July 2010 (https://www.dcu.ie/president/speeches.shtml, accessed 12 June 2018). 127 DCUPO, GA2010/3.

the same or increased numbers of students.[128] The decade-long investment in research funding, fuelled by PRTLI and SFI, was tapering off dramatically. It soon became apparent that the funding environment would be even more challenging than anticipated. In November 2010, just four months after MacCraith's speech, the government availed of an €85bn bailout provided by the European Union and International Monetary Fund. As such, MacCraith faced challenges with strong echoes of the those that had faced NIHE Dublin during the 1980s. While DCU's facilities were incomparably better than those available to the staff and students of NIHE Dublin, enforced reductions in staff numbers under the HEA's employment control framework threatened the quality of the university's educational experience.[129] As had previously been the case, the university's staff were pivotal to averting that outcome:

> We lost good numbers of staff, student numbers kept increasing and funding kept going down ... It meant that people right across the university were doing more with less ... It has been a very committed and resilient staff that has allowed the university to grow in a significantly under-resourced environment.[130]

Despite the unforgiving financial climate, DCU has experienced profound change during MacCraith's tenure, perhaps best embodied in the further development of socially innovative education strategies (see chapter 7) and the completion of the Incorporation programme. Conceived in 2011 and completed in 2016, Incorporation saw the full integration into DCU of the Mater Dei Institute of Education, St Patrick's College, Drumcondra and the Church of Ireland College of Education – in the process forming Ireland's first university-based Faculty of Education.

Strategic links

The roots of Incorporation lay in the formal linkage agreements negotiated with St Patrick's College, Mater Dei and All Hallows College between 1991 and 2009. All three institutions were well-known for their teacher-education and religious-education programmes and were situated in Drumcondra, adjacent to DCU's Glasnevin campus. Prior to the development of its relationship with DCU, St Pat's had been a recognized college of the National University of Ireland, as were the teacher-education colleges of Mary Immaculate, Limerick and Carysfort, Blackrock. Yet the relationship between the NUI and the teacher-education

---

128 *College View*, 28 Sept. 2011.   129 HEA, 'Employment control framework for the higher education sector, 2011–14' (2011); Walsh, *Higher education in Ireland*, p. 253.   130 Brian MacCraith interview, 16 May 2019.

colleges was never fully satisfactory, with UCD (accrediting university for St Pat's) later blocking the introduction of a master's in education at the Drumcondra college.[131] Proposals for the introduction of a new BA programme at St Pat's, to be accredited by UCD, were blocked in the late 1980s by Mary O'Rourke, minister for education, following a government review of the state's teacher-education facilities. O'Rourke favoured a link with the newly established university in Glasnevin, a proposal supported by members of DCU's governing body.[132]

Resistance to the idea was prevalent within St Pat's, with staff fearful of redundancies and a worsening of working conditions. These concerns were not helped by reports that DCU's interest in a linkage agreement stemmed from its intention to use the Drumcondra campus to expand its own courses and facilities.[133] St Patrick's was administered by the Vincentian Order on behalf of the Catholic archdiocese of Dublin, and the college's leadership was resistant to any change to the status quo. Of particular concern was the preservation of the college's Catholic ethos, as expressed by Jim Cantwell, director of the Catholic Press and Information Office:

> It is obvious that the fundamental consideration of Archbishop [Desmond Connell] must be to protect the identity and the ethos of St Patrick's College. He made it very clear to [Minister O'Rourke] that he is perfectly prepared to co-operate with the government in any future arrangement that would secure those objectives.

Early indications were that the archdiocese preferred to preserve its existing relationship with the NUI. As Cantwell pointedly observed: 'There has been, since the 1970s, a very satisfactory arrangement between St Patrick's and UCD.'[134]

The minister's wishes ultimately held sway, however, and pressure from the Department of Education and the HEA led to the opening of discussions between DCU and St Pat's in early 1991. DCU was represented by Chris Curran (Distance Education), Farrel Corcoran (Faculty of Communications and Human Studies), Peter McKenna (Curriculum Development) and Tony Moynihan (School of Computer Applications).[135] The group met on nine occasions to consider the various options for institutional linkage, with a remit

---

131 Ciaran Sugrue, 'Three decades of college life, 1973–99: the old order changeth?' in James Kelly (ed.), *St Patrick's College Drumcondra: a history* (Dublin, 2006), pp 237–8, 252–7; Bradley, *'Twigs for an eagle's nest'*, pp 137–9.　**132** *Irish Times*, 16 Nov. 1990. A similar proposal for teacher education in Limerick had led to a linkage agreement between UL and Mary Immaculate College (Fleming, *University of Limerick*, pp 103–7).　**133** Sugrue, 'Three decades of college life', p. 252; *Irish Times*, 14 and 15 Nov. 1991.　**134** *Irish Times*, 20 Nov. 1991.　**135** DCUPO, 'St Patrick's College, linkage negotiations, 1991–4'; *Nuacht*, Apr. 1991.

to make recommendations for future development. Its report, delivered on 13 September 1991, proposed that St Pat's should become a college of DCU, which would allow for maximum co-operation while simultaneously allowing St Pat's to retain its individual identity and Catholic ethos. The college's function within DCU would see it continue and enhance its involvement in teacher education, including initial and continuing education, as well as the development of new programmes in the humanities. The arrangements were to be formalized with the creation of a Joint Faculty of Education and Joint Faculty of Humanities.[136]

These recommendations formed the core of the eventual linkage agreement, yet negotiations were not concluded until September 1993.[137] Under the terms of the agreement, the college would now receive its funding from the HEA, via DCU, and the university would accredit its degrees. The archbishop of Dublin retained the power of appointing the president of St Patrick's, as well as the final say in academic promotions within the college. Continuity of the college's Catholic ethos was thus ensured, though this proved to be an area of some concern to staff unions at DCU, who feared a dilution of the non-denominational ethos of the university.[138]

Other issues remained to be ironed out. Neither of the joint faculties integrated as well as had been hoped. Education was described as a 'rather lopsided faculty since the membership from the university was provided by the small number of personnel within its School of Education'.[139] As for humanities, DCU's well-established programmes in communications and languages offered greater scope for innovative programme development: 'However, despite initial efforts to create joint programmes of an interdisciplinary nature … autonomy rather than integration, and collegiality rather than collaboration' characterized the faculty's efforts.[140] Both institutions also tested the limits of their agreement during the mid-1990s. Resistance to certain restrictions on the freedom of St Pat's was evident in actions such as the establishment of an academic council that skirted the boundaries of what was permitted under the terms of the linkage. Diplomatic correspondence between O'Hare and Simon Clyne, president of St Pat's, occasionally reinforced by legal opinions, ensured that such squalls did not blow the agreement off course.[141]

136 'St Patrick's College – DCU working group report', 13 Sept. 1991 (DCUPO, 'St Patrick's College, linkage negotiations, 1991–4'). Despite concern within St Pat's that there was insufficient time to plan and introduce a BA programme, the Department of Education's insistence on the point ensured that the first BA students were admitted to the college in October 1993 (Sugrue, 'Three decades of college life', pp 252–3). **137** DCUPO, 'St Patrick's College, linkage negotiations, 1991–4'; Bradley, *'Twigs for an eagle's nest'*, pp 137–8. **138** DCUPO, 'St Patrick's College, linkage negotiations, 1991–4'; *Irish Times*, 14 Sept. 1993. **139** Sugrue, 'Three decades of college life', p. 257. **140** Ibid. **141** Danny O'Hare to Revd. Simon Clyne, 31 Mar. 1994; John O'Dwyer to Martin Conry, 14 Apr. 1994 (DCUPO, 'St Patrick's College, linkage negotiations, 1991–4'); Sugrue, 'Three decades of college life', pp 254–7.

Linkage between DCU and St Pat's paved the way for similar agreements with All Hallows College and Mater Dei Institute of Education. Discussions with Mater Dei took place over two years, beginning in August 1997. The university was initially represented by Curran and McKenna (veterans of the negotiations with St Pat's), Tony Moynihan and Anthony Walsh. From a strategic point of view, the linkage with Mater Dei was seen as key for the university to increase its footprint in the field of educational studies.[142]

The initial draft agreement ran into difficulty at governing authority and academic council when circulated in March 1999. Both bodies expressed reservations and requested a number of revisions and clarifications. Anxious to ensure that this would not be interpreted as an outright rejection, academic council agreed to convey 'a generally positive and open disposition' towards the proposed linkage.[143] A revised agreement was approved two months later, following the resolution of concerns relating to the governance of Mater Dei, its academic programmes and academic freedom, as well as assurances that the Catholic ethos of the institute would be preserved.[144] Welcoming the linkage, formally signed in August 1999, Archbishop Desmond Connell noted that it allowed for 'the insertion of religious education as a subject and a profession into the Irish university system', and would serve 'as a catalyst in bringing about a much needed dialogue between faith and culture at third-level education'.[145]

DCU's investment in teacher education was further enhanced nine years later, following the completion of the linkage agreement with All Hallows College, a seminary/teacher-education institution located across the road from St Pat's. Negotiated during 2006 and early 2007, the agreement saw All Hallows join Mater Dei Institute and St Pat's as a constituent college of the university.[146] Discussions with All Hallows also prompted a review and strengthening of ties with Mater Dei and St Patrick's, which saw their academic structures more tightly integrated into the university. Welcoming these developments, von Prondzynski noted the university's intention to develop innovative educational policies as part of its strategic vision: 'With its three constituent colleges [the university] is the most significant provider of teaching and research in teacher training, educational policy and related aspects of the humanities.'[147]

Attempts to develop strategic partnerships with other third-level institutions over the past decade, based on geographic proximity, have also informed the

---

142 DCUPO, AC99/2, 3. By the time the agreement was concluded in August 1999, both Peter McKenna and Anthony Walsh had left the university.   143 DCUPO, AC99/M3/2, AC99/M2/15; DCUPO, 'Mater Dei Institute of Education'.   144 DCUPO, AC99/M3/12.   145 DCUPO, 'Mater Dei Institute of Education'; *Irish Times*, 24 Aug. 1999; *College View*, Oct. 1999. 146 Governing authority approved the linkage agreement with All Hallows, and the revised agreements with Mater Dei and St Pat's, at its meeting on 25 June 2007 (DCUPO, GA2007/3). 147 DCUPO, AC2006, AC2007/A1; DCUPO, 'All Hallows'; DCU, *President's report, 2008*, pp 2–3; *Irish Times*, 5 Feb. 2008. The linkage agreement between DCU and All Hallows was signed on

Incorporation process. A memorandum of understanding signed in July 2012 with Dundalk Institute of Technology envisioned joint academic programme development, research and enterprise support and the sharing of services. The agreement – which revived a relationship first established in 1986 – was modelled on the successful partnership between NUI Galway and Galway-Mayo Institute of Technology.[148] Maintaining the theme of establishing regions of knowledge, and concurrent to its discussions with DkIT, DCU also entered into a formal partnership with NUI Maynooth (NUIM) and the Royal College of Surgeons in Ireland (RCSI). Discussions between the three institutions were initiated in 2009 during von Prondzynski's tenure and were facilitated by Don Thornhill.[149]

The formation of regional partnerships within the higher-education sector anticipated and complemented policies advanced by the HEA and Department of Education and Skills, later articulated in the Hunt Report's call for the creation of regional clusters characterized by 'close coordination and cooperation between various types of independent higher education institutions'.[150] The policy aimed to build upon the principles established via joint research initiatives, with inter-institutional collaboration extending to joint course planning, outreach and co-ordinated strategies for regional economic and social development. The old suggestion of mergers between universities, in the name of delivering greater institutional quality, once more raised its head.[151]

In this context, DCU's discussions with NUIM and RCSI were viewed as a tentative step towards protecting the university from expected further rationalizations within the higher-education sector, particularly in the light of the deteriorating global financial position. The challenge was to balance any move towards a federalization of the university sector with the need to maintain DCU's 'radical and innovative image'.[152] Branded the 3U partnership, the collaboration was hailed at its launch as having the potential to become a national and international model for collaboration within the higher-education sector.[153] The 3U Pathways programme, launched in June 2014, aimed to provide a

4 February 2008.   148 In 1986 NIHED and Dundalk RTC had introduced a master's in business administration programme that ran for just one cycle, with 24 students graduating in October 1989 (Danny O'Hare to Gemma Hussey, 7 Jan. 1986, Danny O'Hare to J. Harris, 3 Feb. 1986 (DCUPO, 'Department of Education, 1981–6'); NIHED, *Annual report, 1986/7*, p. 18; *Newslink*, Nov. 1989; DCUPO, AC2011/1, 4, AC2012/2, 4; *Irish Times*, 18 July 2012).   149 DCUPO, GA2010/1. Thornhill was a former secretary general of the Department of Education and executive chairman of the HEA.   150 Department of Education and Skills, *National strategy for higher education to 2030* (Dublin, 2011). Authored by the Higher Education Strategy Group and known informally as the Hunt Report (after its chairman, Colin Hunt). See Walsh, *Higher education in Ireland*, pp 440–9; Siobhán Harkin and Ellen Hazelkorn, 'Institutional mergers in Ireland' in Adrian Curaj et al. (eds), *Mergers and alliances in higher education: international practice and emerging opportunities* (London, 2015), pp 105–23.   151 Department of Education and Skills, *National strategy for higher education to 2030*, pp 98–101.   152 DCUPO, GA2009/5, 6.   153 DCUPO, AC2012/4, 5; DCU, *President's report, 2011–12*; *Irish Times*, 26 June 2012.

bridging programme for foreign students to allow them to meet the requirements for studying at one of the partner institutions.[154] From a research perspective, the partnership produced some innovative, cross-institutional outputs, particularly in the field of biomedical research. Teaching collaborations resulted in the creation of an MSc in humanitarian logistics and emergency management in November 2013, and the partnership also opened a China office the following year, intended to offer Chinese students a guaranteed pathway to undergraduate programmes at DCU and Maynooth University.[155]

Despite this progress, the difficulty of creating tightly interwoven systems and collaborations between independent institutions quickly emerged. Three years after its formation the partnership's senior management team reported that 'the innate competition amongst partners and a desire to protect the distinctiveness of individual institutions … are difficult to overcome. Furthermore, institutions are traditionally focused on their individual success metrics rather than looking at collective metrics for a partnership as a whole.'[156] Such warnings proved to be prescient, with the 3U Partnership succumbing to increasing inertia as the higher-education landscape continued to evolve, with a consequent altering of priorities among the three partner institutions.[157] Perhaps more importantly, while the 3U Pathways initiative broke even financially, it did not generate the expected levels of income.[158] In the absence of appropriate incentives, the partnership was quietly shelved.

Incorporation

The publication of the Hunt Report in January 2011 was soon followed by a general election that swept a Fine Gael/Labour coalition government to power. As the newly appointed minister for education, Ruairi Quinn implemented a reformist agenda largely informed by the Hunt Report's recommendations.[159] Incorporation – perhaps the logical conclusion of the strategic linkage strategy begun in 1993 – was, however, the result of initiatives taken by DCU, St Pat's and Mater Dei. In July 2011 MacCraith addressed the MacGill Summer School, sharing a panel with Quinn, where he first raised the potential of an education research and policy institute to 'address the central challenges of our education

---

154 DCUPO, AC2014/1, 4. The 3U Pathways programme was based at the Emerald Cultural Institute, Milltown.   155 DCUPO, GA2013/7; DCU, *President's reports, 2013–14 and 2014–15*. NUI Maynooth rebranded as Maynooth University in 2014.   156 Ruth Davis and Mary Fenton, 'Partnership and collaboration in the new higher education landscape: the 3U Partnership experience', *All Ireland Journal of Teaching and Learning in Higher Education (AISHE-J)*, 7:1 (2015).   157 The Royal College of Surgeons has, for example, lobbied consistently for the granting of university status (*Irish Times*, 21 Nov. 2017, 7 Feb. 2019).   158 DCUPO, GA2016/3. 159 Walsh, *Higher education in Ireland*, p. 449. Quinn was appointed minister for education on 9 Mar. 2011.

system at all points on the continuum from early childhood to fourth level and play a transformational role in ensuring a world-class education system for Ireland'.[160]

MacCraith's speech reflected the direction of informal discussions between DCU and its linked colleges (St Pat's and Mater Dei) that took place throughout 2011, which had touched upon their shared potential to create a transformative critical mass of research expertise and pedagogical innovation in teacher education.[161] Central figures in these discussions included MacCraith, John Coolahan, Pauric Travers, Andrew McGrady and Daire Keogh, in addition to the secretary general of the Department of Education, Brigid McManus.[162] Within the Department of Education there was widespread recognition of the need to restructure teacher education at all levels. International best practice was at odds with the fragmented Irish system, in which twenty-two different providers offered more than forty programmes.[163]

---

160 Brian MacCraith, 'Transforming our education system to deliver a new Ireland' in Joe Mulholland (ed.), *Transforming Ireland, 2011–16: essays from the 2011 MacGill Summer School* (Dublin, 2011), p. 277. MacCraith specifically drew parallels with the Institute of Education at the University of London, which is now a constituent faculty of University College London. 161 It is important to note that NIHE Dublin opened its doors with a Faculty of Education Studies in place, incorporating a School of Curriculum Development, a School of Staff Development and a School of Instructional Design and Development. The faculty fulfilled a number of roles within the Institute, primarily focused on staff and curriculum development, as well as course design. As non-teaching units, the three schools supported postgraduates but offered no undergraduate degree programmes. The School of Curriculum Development produced position papers on educational issues and conducted research intended to advise on new course developments. The School of Staff Development and the School of Instructional Design and Development ran frequent workshops and staff training courses on the use of innovative media and teaching techniques, principally through the establishment of a Learning Resource Centre. Following a major restructuring of its schools and services, the faculty was abolished in 1989, though the School of Education Studies remained. The school's input into the joint Faculty of Education, created in 1993, was minimal. When the Institute of Education was formed following the completion of Incorporation, it became the first university-based faculty of education in Ireland dedicated to the training of teachers at all levels, from early childhood education through to fourth level (HEA, *The structure of teacher education in Ireland: review of progress in implementing reform* (Dublin, 2019), p. 14; Brian MacCraith, 'DCU Institute of Education: the first Faculty of Education in an Irish university' in Brian Mooney (ed.), *Education matters yearbook, 2016–2017* (Castleisland, 2017), pp 25–30; Sugrue, 'Three decades of college life', p. 257. For NIHE Dublin's Faculty of Education, see NIHED/DCU, *Annual reports, 1978–90*). 162 Brigid McManus was secretary general of the Department of Education from 2005 until 2012. Pauric Travers was president of St Pat's from 1999 until 2012. Daire Keogh would soon be appointed president of St Pat's, while John Coolahan was chairman of the College's governing body and a member of governing body of Mater Dei Institute. As early as 2009 Keogh had raised the possibility of that college's amalgamation with DCU: 'I am convinced that St Pat's days as a stand alone institution must be limited, but there seems to be no stomach to face these implications. Should we be integrated fully within [DCU]? Merged with the four colleges of education in Dublin? Merged with Mater Dei? These are issues which have implications for the future of the College and the University and should be reflected upon, before the [Department of Education and Skills] or Hunt report present them to us' (Daire Keogh to Ferdinand von Prondzynski, 10 June 2009 (email provided to author)). 163 Department of

In February 2012 the HEA initiated consultations with all higher-education institutions regarding the future of the sector.[164] Teacher education formed an important component of this consultation, with Tom Boland, chairperson of the HEA, writing in April to all institutions involved in teacher education to request formal proposals regarding their future roles.[165] DCU, St Pat's and Mater Dei submitted a joint response the following month, outlining their vision for an Institute of Education. That document also formed the basis of a submission to an international review panel appointed by the Department of Education to assess initial teacher education in Ireland. Led by Finnish academic Pasi Sahlberg, the panel's key recommendation was for rationalization of the sector through amalgamation and strategic linkages.[166] Highlighting the close links between the institutions in Drumcondra, the report wholly endorsed the proposal – presented to it by the institutions themselves – to create an Institute of Education at DCU.[167]

Quite unexpectedly, the Church of Ireland College of Education (CICE) joined discussions in late 2012. Following the breakdown of its existing relationship with TCD, CICE first sought to enter into an alternative arrangement with Maynooth University. Given Maynooth's historic identity as the first Catholic seminary established in Ireland, that proposal was soon dropped in light of political and religious objections. A discreet intervention by the minister for education led to a meeting, on 14 July, between MacCraith, Michael Jackson, Church of Ireland archbishop of Dublin, and Prof. Anne Lodge, principal of CICE, to discuss the College's inclusion in the Incorporation process. By the end of the month, CICE had formally committed to Incorporation.[168] The addition of CICE to the process complicated matters, with the proposal now required to devise and embrace a progressively pluralist, multi-denominational teacher-education model. Echoes of negotiations with St Patrick's College were also found in resistance displayed within the Church of Ireland hierarchy, and among the college's staff. Crucially, however, the proposal had the strong backing both of Lodge and Jackson.[169]

Formal negotiations were initiated on 15 October 2012 following a meeting between the heads of the four institutions.[170] Relations between leadership and staff of all four institutions were strained over the next four years as the details of the integration were finalized. Differences in pay and conditions required

Education, *Report of the international review panel on the structure of initial teacher education provision in Ireland* (Dublin, 2012), p. 18. **164** HEA, *Towards a future higher education landscape* (Dublin, 2012). **165** DCUPO, GA 2012/3, 4; MacCraith, 'DCU Institute of Education', p. 26 (quotation). **166** Department of Education, *Report … on the structure of initial teacher education*, p. 13. **167** Ibid., pp 25–30; *Irish Times*, 4 Feb. 2013; Brian MacCraith interview, 1 Oct. 2018. **168** DCU, *Towards a future higher education landscape: DCU response* (Dublin, 2012), pp 18, 21. **169** Walsh, *Higher education in Ireland*, p. 455; John Walshe, *An education: how an outsider became an insider and learned what really goes on in Irish government* (Dublin, 2014), pp 143–4; *Irish Times*, 7 Dec. 2012; Brian MacCraith interview, 1 Oct. 2018. **170** DCUPO, GA2012/4, 5.

harmonization, as did educational ethoses and academic structures.[171] Elements of compromise necessary for the creation of the Institute of Education also required delicate handling:

> We understood very well that if we didn't get the two relevant archbishops onside early in the process, it just wasn't going to end in the conclusion that we wanted. So we knew we had to find the model of addressing the delivery of denominational education for teachers for the two main denominations in a secular environment.[172]

The solution was to provide, particularly for primary-school teaching, a non-denominational core curriculum alongside special modules for teaching in denominational schools, run by discrete centres within the Institute of Education. This strategy was publicly endorsed at an event hosted by the Department of Education and Skills in June 2014, attended by archbishops Martin and Jackson.[173] Maintaining the socially inclusive ethos that had been developed at the university also proved a key component in the formation of the Institute:

> The new Institute of Education will provide a place of mutual respect for the formation of teachers for denominational (Roman Catholic; Church of Ireland/Reformed Christian traditions), non-denominational and multi-denominational schools. In this way, the establishment of the Institute will enable the education of excellent teachers for all dimensions of a 21st century pluralist society.[174]

Incorporation thus required a 'complex balancing act' as DCU absorbed separate institutions with distinct cultural outlooks, academic structures and denominational teacher-education functions.[175] The imprimatur of both churches was vital to the success of the venture. The final legal formalities of Incorporation were completed on 30 September 2016, with the creation of the Institute of Education universally hailed as an important milestone in the evolution of initial teacher education.[176] Harold Hislop, chief inspector with the

171 SIPTU, *A survey of academic staff on working conditions at DCU* (Dublin, 2015), pp 18, 30, 37; IFUT, *Annual report 2017/18*, pp 4–7; *Irish Times*, 27 Jan. 2017; HEA, *The structure of teacher education in Ireland: review of progress in implementing reform* (Dublin, 2019), p. 14.   172 Brian MacCraith interview, 1 Oct. 2018.   173 DCUPO, GA2014/4, 5; DCU, *President's report, 2013/14*, pp 3, 18; *Irish Independent*, 21 June 2014.   174 Brian MacCraith, 'DCU Institute of Education: the first faculty of education in an Irish university' in Mooney (ed.), *Education matters yearbook, 2016–17*, p. 28.   175 Walsh, *Higher education in Ireland*, p. 455. Conscious of the sensitivities associated with Incorporation, DCU sought assistance through external facilitation, funded by the government and led by Price Waterhouse Coopers (DCUPO, GA2013/6 and 7).   176 DCUPO, GA2016/4–6; *DCU News*, 30 Sept. and 23 Nov. 2016; *Irish Times*, 30 Sept. 2016.

Department of Education and Skills, welcomed it as a hugely significant landmark, harking back to the Kildare Place Society and the origins of teacher education:

> This new DCU Institute has the potential to be equally radical and trend setting, not only for the Irish education system, but also in a wider international context. I am glad to pay tribute tonight to Prof. Brian MacCraith's leadership of this development at Dublin City University, to Dr Andrew McGrady and Dr Anne Lodge, and especially to Prof. Daire Keogh whose relentless energy and commitment were critical in bringing about the foundation of the Institute. I would also like to pay tribute to the outstanding leadership that Prof. John Coolahan gave as chair of the governing board of St Patrick's College. John's contribution in this forum, as in every other context in which he works in Irish education, is immense.[177]

The multi-stream approach to teacher education was later noted by the HEA as an innovative solution to the integration of denominational education into a secular university.[178] Somewhat ironically, Incorporation effectively overturned the original vision of NIHE Dublin's first governing body, which had strenuously argued against the development of a multi-campus institution. Nonetheless, the spirit of that argument is embodied in the Institute of Education, which has rejected the clustered, yet physically separated model of teacher education pursued by other universities.[179] All strands of teacher education within DCU are now co-located on the St Patrick's campus.

Incorporation brought an enhanced capacity and consolidation of the humanities and social-science programmes at DCU – an at times uneasy situation for a university accustomed to offering degree programmes tailored to meet specific demands of the job market. The university's geographic footprint was also enhanced. All Hallows College did not feature in plans for Incorporation or the Institute for Education, and during 2014 it was announced that the continuation of All Hallows as an educational institution was not feasible.[180] The decision by the trustees of All Hallows to place its campus up for sale presented an opportunity for DCU to acquire a strategically significant

177 Harold Hislop speech, DCU St Patrick's Campus, 17 May 2017 (https://www.education.ie/ en/Publications/Inspection-Reports-Publications/Evaluation-Reports-Guidelines/A-Co-professional-Approach-to-Inspection-for-Accountability-Improvement.pdf, accessed 4 Jan. 2019). 178 HEA, *Higher education system performance, 2014–16* (Dublin, 2016), p. 62.   179 HEA, *The structure of teacher education in Ireland: review of progress* (Dublin, 2019), pp 3, 14.   180 DCUPO, GA2014/3. For a partial history of All Hallows College, see Kevin Rafferty, 'All Hallows: from a seminary to an institute for mission and ministry', *Colloque: Journal of the Irish Province of the Congregation of the Mission*, 32 (1995), pp 125–37.

location. Briefing governing authority on the importance of the site, MacCraith spoke of the alignment between DCU's mission and All Hallows' legacy as an educational site.[181] The unexpected nature of the opportunity required a nimble response: 'There's always serendipity ... [W]e didn't plan for All Hallows becoming available, and you have to have enough bandwidth to respond to opportunities.'[182] Despite an inability to match the highest bid, DCU had emerged as the preferred bidder by the beginning of 2015. The pre-existing relationship between the two institutions, as well as DCU's declared intent to preserve the site for educational purposes, allowed All Hallows' trustees to prioritize preservation of its heritage ahead of achieving maximum value during the sale process:

> We couldn't match the private bidders ... [W]hat was important to [the trustees] was the legacy, and maintaining that legacy of commitment to education and issues like social justice. There was a very strong alignment in terms of the values articulated in our strategic plan and what we had been doing and continue to do ... It was great that they recognised that there was a value in what we would do and there was a trust that we would do it.[183]

Financial support from the Department of Education and Skills – predicated on a commitment from the university to provide space on the campus for the construction of a school – proved vital.[184] Speaking after the sale had been concluded, the president of All Hallows, Dr Patrick McDevitt, CM, expressed satisfaction at the outcome: 'As a linked college of Dublin City University, we have worked closely together ... and have every confidence that the university has an understanding and respect for our heritage and legacy.'[185]

IV

If the 1980s and 1990s can be characterized as periods of intense growth, the 2000s can be seen as one of renewal and refinement of the university's strategic planning process, with extensive changes to its governance structures. Further growth during MacCraith's tenure saw an upsurge in student numbers, from 11,377 student registrations for the 2009/10 academic year to 17,550 for 2019/20.[186] The addition of All Hallows and St Patrick's College brought the number of DCU campuses to five, including the St Clare's sports facility and the

181 DCUPO, GA2015/1, 2.   182 Brian MacCraith interview, 16 May 2019.   183 Ibid.
184 DCUPO, GA2015/6.   185 *Irish Times*, 8 Apr. 2016.   186 Statistics provided by DCU Quality Promotion Office.

DCU Alpha innovation campus. Three of these were added in the period after the return of economic recession in 2010 and owed much to the vision of the university's leadership and governors, as well as the quality of its academic and administrative staff.[187] The scale of the transformation at DCU over the past three decades can be measured in a variety of ways. International recognition of the university's achievements is evident from its inclusion on a list of the top one hundred universities under fifty years of age since such rankings were introduced in 2011. The university consistently attracted a disproportionate amount of research funding, relative to its size, during the 1980s and early 1990s, a trend that was continued under the PRTLI and SFI funding models.[188] In terms of physical footprint, DCU has evolved from a single-campus institution, largely housed in nineteenth-century buildings, into a multi-campus university. The student profile has also changed dramatically. All 191 undergraduates who enrolled in 1980 were Irish; in 2017 just under one-third of the undergraduate population (some 3,020 students) held non-Irish passports, representing 110 different nations.[189] Under the development plan drawn up in 1977, the student population was to be capped at 5,000. Current planning models anticipate a student population of 20,000 by 2023.

187 As discussed above, All Hallows' board of trustees sold the campus to DCU for less than the highest bid received. With regard to the Alpha campus, the university signed a 99-year lease for the site in January 2013, with an annual rent of just €100 (DCUPO, GA2013/2–6).   **188** For annual amounts of research funding attracted, see fig. A6.2. DCU was included on the QS 'Top 50 under 50' in 2012, and the *Times Higher Education* 'Top 100 under 50' the same year. As of 2019 the university was 94th on the *Times Higher Education* list (*DCU News*, 12 Sept. 2012, 5 Apr. 2017; *Irish Times*, 30 Jan. 2014, 30 Sept. 2016; *Times Higher Education*, World University Rankings, 26 June 2019).   **189** HEA, *Accounts 1980 and student statistics 1980/1* (Dublin, 1981), pp 48–9; DCU, *Talent, discovery and transformation: DCU strategic plan, 2017–22* (Dublin, 2017), p. 7.

5

Notes on the curriculum

Prior to the 1970s the degree programmes at Ireland's third-level institutions primarily evolved on an ad hoc basis, with little government intervention. The autonomy and academic freedoms enjoyed by the universities were largely considered sacrosanct, and the curriculum of the higher-education sector as a whole rarely featured as a policy concern for the Department of Education.[1] That situation changed with the introduction of the regional technical colleges and the NIHEs. The plethora of reports produced during the 1960s and early 1970s, recommending a greater focus on technological education, heralded a turning point of sorts and led directly to sweeping reforms. Yet there was little consensus on what actually constituted a 'technological education'. When the creation of NIHE Dublin was announced in December 1974, few details were revealed regarding the expected nature of its courses. The task of shaping the academic schools and faculties of the Institute, and their degree programmes, fell to the governing body appointed in March 1975. While there was an expectation that the Institute would subsume some of the CDVEC's courses and staff and offer core courses of a technological nature, governing body was otherwise handed a blank canvas. Its deliberations over the following five years were informed by a guiding principle articulated in 1977: 'The needs of industry and the type of course which will meet such needs will be the sole criterion on which the Institute will base its decision on course type.'[2] The Institute arrived at an opportune time for those within higher education who wished to forge links with industry, with a clear appetite for greater alignment evident within both sectors. In its 1981 report on the role of third-level institutions in industrialization, the Confederation of Irish Industry identified several areas in which co-operation could be nurtured. Their recommendations were echoed in reports released during the early 1980s by the National Board for Science and

1 The Department of Education's white paper on education, published in 1995, included a section on curriculum in its chapters on primary and post-primary education yet makes no mention of third-level curriculum at all outside of that for teacher education. Similarly, *The national strategy for higher education to 2030* (Hunt Report) makes little mention of curriculum, beyond vague calls for greater integration of research and teaching, enhanced input from students and 'external stakeholders' in curriculum design, and the development of 'generic skills' at undergraduate level (Department of Education and Science, *Charting our education future: white paper on education* (Dublin, 1995); Department of Education and Skills, *National strategy for higher education to 2030* (Dublin, 2011)). 2 NIHED, *Plan for the future of the Institute*, p. 37. See also DCUPO, GB77/4–6. When used in the Institute's planning documentation, 'industry' served as an umbrella term for

Technology, and the Manpower Consultative Committee.[3] These reports were particularly influential on government policy and the development of degree programmes at NIHE Dublin. The government's *Programme for action in education, 1984–7*, prioritized funding for 'technological studies' at third level, while also promising to 'intensify' links between higher education and industry.[4] In addition to validating NIHE Dublin's initial development, such policy ambitions also bolstered the Institute's resolve to foster links with industry and to prioritize the integration of its commercial research with its teaching programme. These priorities, and their evolution over four decades, have shaped NIHED/DCU's curriculum. The educational values and ethos nurtured during the 1980s and 1990s have proved enduring, notwithstanding the rapidly changing nature of the educational landscape. Early examples of course creation and teaching innovation help to illustrate the wider themes that have threaded through DCU's curriculum development. Trends such as a continued willingness to explore technology as a pedagogical tool, alongside wide-ranging consultation with contacts in industry and private enterprise when developing degree programmes, were apparent from a very early stage.[5]

I

Between 1975 and the summer of 1980 the Institute's education and planning committee devised an academic framework, drawing upon input from various working parties and international bodies to design the Institute's curriculum. Initial recommendations were that the Institute would provide courses at degree, diploma and certificate level, with the latter qualification gradually phased out of the curriculum. Postgraduate and post-experience courses were also envisaged.[6] The curriculum would be tightly focused, embodied by a commit-

industry, commerce and the public service.   **3** CII, *Strategy for Industrialisation: the role of third-level institutions* (Dublin, 1981); NBST, *Education, innovation and entrepreneurship* (Dublin, 1983); Manpower Consultative Committee, *Review of links between industry and third-level education* (Dublin, 1985); White, *Investing in people*, pp 184–6.   **4** Department of Education, *Programme for action in education, 1984–7* (Dublin, 1984); John Coolahan, 'Higher education, 1908–84' in J.R. Hill (ed.), *A new history of Ireland*, vii: *Ireland, 1921–84* (Oxford, 2003), p. 788.   **5** Some elements of the curriculum are explored elsewhere in this book, notably when they have accompanied various inflection points in the university's broader evolution. It would, however, be impractical to provide a detailed account here of every aspect of curriculum development, or of the numerous debates that have shaped DCU's educational philosophy. Such a task would require a detailed analysis of topics such as the university's adaptation to changing workplace demands, experimentation with pedagogical techniques, and the influence of new technologies on the consumption and delivery of course content.   **6** DCUPO, GB76/4, 5; DCUPO, 'Governing body – reports and working papers, 1975–9'; NIHED, *Annual report, 1975–8*, pp 5–6; NIHED, *Plan for the future of the Institute*, pp 63–98, 102. The following working parties were formed: business, professional studies and hotel management; communications and human studies; engineering, environmental studies, art and

ment to clarity in academic planning: 'The tendency towards academic drift which has been a feature of certain institutions in Ireland and abroad will be resisted.' Such clarity would allow for the design and introduction of educational programmes to fulfil the Institute's guiding principle – the preparation of students for work.[7] Planning documentation produced in 1976 had urged 'the devising of syllabi and the implementation of courses ... such as to emphasise their relevance to industry and to the business world in general'.[8] The Institute thus followed the model for curriculum development that was (and arguably remains) dominant within Irish higher education – the creation of degree programmes to meet either economic or social demands, or to develop a reputation for excellence in particular fields of study/research.[9] The student would remain at the centre of curriculum planning. In a submission to government outlining its views on draft legislation to place NIHE Dublin on a statutory basis, governing body confirmed that the Institute would develop courses 'based primarily, though not solely, on "technological" content'. That submission also reiterated, but did not elaborate upon, an aspiration to create a holistic approach to the education of its students: 'The objectives of the Institute generally shall be to advance learning, knowledge and their application through teaching and research, and to enable students to obtain the advantages of a liberal education.'[10]

Proposals for the structure and organization of the Institute were refined by the education and planning committee over the course of 1977, leading to the adoption of the outline presented to the minister for education in the *Plan for the future of the Institute*.[11] The flexibility granted to the Institute's planners was reflected in early proposals – later dropped – for the creation of faculties of humanities, of art and design, and of hotel and catering studies.[12] Degree and postgraduate programmes would be developed primarily – but not solely – with technological content. Certificate, diploma and postgraduate courses would focus on enhancing and augmenting the practical knowledge of those already in employment. Degree programmes would have the objective of preparing school-leavers for a career in industry, with a design that allowed for pedagogical and structural flexibility and facilitated adaptation to changing employment needs.

---

design; science and paramedical studies.   7 *Plan for the future of the Institute*, pp 36–7.   8 Danny O'Hare, 'Future organisation of the Institute: a personal view', Mar. 1976 (Brian Trench Papers). See also 'A discussion paper on an educational philosophy for the National Institute for Higher Education Dublin', Aug. 1977 (DCUPO, 'Governing body – reports and working papers, 1975–9'). 9 Jean Hughes and Morag Munro, 'Curriculum change: achieving institutional cohesion while maintaining individual autonomy' in Jean Hughes and Eloise Tan (eds), *The dynamic curriculum: shared experiences of ongoing curricular change in higher education* (Dublin, 2012), p. 26. 10 'Legislation for the Institute: the views of governing body', Jan. 1979 (DCUPO, 'Governing body – reports and working papers, 1975–9'); NAI, 2009/135/491; Horgan, *Dublin City University*, p. 19. 11 DCUPO, GB77/1–7. 12 'Future organisation of the Institute: a personal view'; DCUPO, GB76/2–4; DCUPO, 'Governing body – reports and working papers, 1975–9'.

A 'distant-study' unit would make the Institute's courses available on a national basis, where feasible, via co-operative arrangements with regional technical colleges, NIHE Limerick and other institutions. The Institute's planners also placed a high level of importance on providing high-quality supports for academic and administrative activities, including computer and educational-technology services.[13]

A preference for five faculties soon emerged: Administration, Business and Professional Studies; Science and Paramedical Studies; Communications and Human Studies; Technology and Design; and Educational Studies. The sheer scale of the Institute's ambition was epitomized in its intention to have these faculties combine, within a decade, to offer more than eighty courses of varying level and duration.[14] Science and Paramedical Studies would, for example, eventually offer diplomas in chemical sciences, biological sciences and physics. Each of these subjects would also be available at certificate level, along with pharmaceutical science and textile sciences. Degrees would be offered in analytical chemistry, applied biology, combined sciences, biological and chemical sciences, medical laboratory sciences, environmental sciences, nursing studies and occupational therapy.[15]

In May 1978 the government provided its imprimatur to governing body's plans to provide courses with a 'mainly technological bias'. Its remit would be national, with students primarily drawn from the greater Dublin area, but also from the 'country generally'.[16] Despite all indications to the contrary, the Department of Education still expected the CDVEC would transfer its degree programmes in commerce, architecture and engineering to the Institute. Those hopes were formally dashed in January 1979 (see chapter 2), thus freeing the Institute's planners from a curricular straitjacket with which it had struggled for almost three years, allowing it to reshape its educational planning. It also permitted a subtle yet important shift towards a focus on degree-level programmes, allowing the Institute to position itself as a pioneering addition to the higher-education sector, sensitive to the needs of industry.[17] This practical focus on applied research and teaching would later be communicated to the wider public through various institutional and staff profiles, as well as targeted advertising features. Interviewed in November 1980, shortly after the Institute opened its doors, Danny O'Hare declared that the curriculum was 'unashamedly applied or technological ... [NIHED] sees its role being more directly and

13 NIHED, *Plan for the future of the Institute*, *passim*; NIHED, *Annual report, 1975–8*, pp 17–18. 14 NIHED, *Plan for the future of the Institute*, pp 63–98. 15 NIHED, *Plan for the future of the Institute*, pp 72–5. See also DCUPO, GB77/1–6; DCUPO, 'Governing body – reports and working papers, 1975–9'. 16 Cabinet minutes, 19 May 1978 (NAI, 2008/148/523). 17 Horgan, *Dublin City University*, pp 20–1. The decision to drop certificate-level courses from the curriculum was partially informed by governing body's preference to repair its relationship with the CDVEC by avoiding any suggestion that it was competing with the Committee's well-established programmes.

immediately responsive to the needs of Ireland's developing industrial and business enterprises.' His comments were echoed the following year by governing body's chairman, Michael MacCormac, who declared that the Institute's outlook was 'practical, hard-headed … and job oriented'.[18] An expensive, three-page advertising feature in the *Irish Independent* highlighted the Institute's links with industry, its focus on applied research and its innovative INTRA programme.[19]

Early faculty structure and degree programmes

When the Institute's first term commenced in November 1980, its faculty structure was almost identical to that envisioned in 1977: Business and Professional Studies; Science and Paramedical Studies; Communications and Human Studies; Engineering and Design; Education Studies; and Computing and Mathematical Studies.[20] With the first two years of its degree programmes having received the imprimatur of the National Council for Educational Awards (NCEA) by the spring of 1980, the Institute's public-relations manager, Reg Hannon, issued its first prospectus to every secondary school in Ireland, as well as to various education correspondents.[21] That November, 191 students registered for six degrees: communications studies (42 students); accounting and finance (16); business studies (30); computer applications (37); analytical science (20); and electronic engineering (46).[22] The following year saw the commencement of degree courses in applied physics, and international marketing and languages. During the 1980s, however, the government was unable to provide the levels of capital investment required to increase the capacity of the higher-education sector.[23] Ambitions to rapidly add additional degrees to the Institute's curriculum were thwarted by the government's repeated postponement of Phase 2 of campus development (see chapter 6). Noting the intake of the first students on the BSc in applied mathematics in October 1984, the Institute's annual report dryly observed that 'to start up a new degree in the present stringent financial environment has not been an easy task'.[24] In an effort to further increase its

18 *Sunday Independent*, 23 Nov. 1980; *Irish Times*, 1 Aug. 1981. See also *Irish Times*, 7 Apr. 1986, 5 Nov. 1987. 19 *Irish Independent*, 5 Nov. 1981. The cost of the feature was offset by selling advertising spaces to a variety of businesses. All had connections to the Institute, as suppliers, contractors and service providers, including Chem-Labs Ltd, Hewett's Travel Agency, A.R. Cameron Ltd, Associated Marketing Ltd, Video Services Ireland Ltd, Wilson Video Ltd and Remidex. 20 The initial faculty structure was decided upon and reaffirmed by governing body on 21 April 1978, 27 November 1981 and 15 January 1982 (NIHED, *Academic procedures* (1987), p. 23). 21 DCUPO, GB80/2–5; DCUPO, 'NIHE Dublin: general, 1/2'. The prospectus was circulated in April 1980. 22 HEA, *Accounts 1980 and student statistics 1980/1981* (Dublin, 1982), p. 33. The degrees initially to be offered had largely been decided by the summer of 1978 and were reported, with a high degree of accuracy, in the *Irish Independent* (DCUPO, GB78/3–5; *Irish Independent*, 14 June 1978; White, *Investing in people*, pp 149–53). 23 Walsh, *Higher education in Ireland*, pp 331–44. 24 NIHED, *Annual report, 1984/5*, p. 21.

5.1 Communications studies students filming Martin O'Donoghue, minister for education, during the formal opening of the Henry Grattan building on 1 June 1982 (DCU Collection).

5.2 Computer applications graduating class of 1984 (DCU Collection).

reach, and to provide pathways to further education for mature students and those already in the workforce, the Institute introduced evening and weekend options for select undergraduate and postgraduate courses, beginning in the 1983/4 academic year with the BBs in business studies.[25]

A decade after opening its doors, and having attained university status, just eleven degree programmes were available to undergraduates, along with taught postgraduates at master's level (journalism, instrumental analysis, and electronic systems) and a professional diploma in accounting.[26] This is not to imply stagnation, however, with degree programmes undergoing regular internal and external review and enhancement. The School of Communications, for example, undertook a major revision of its BA programmes in 1987, while the School of Chemical Sciences altered the core composition of the third and fourth years of its BSc in analytical science.[27] Major revisions to undergraduate programmes were not lightly undertaken, requiring scrutiny by the NCEA, which also subjected the Institute's courses to stringent reviews within four years of initial approval.[28] Moreover, the number of undergraduate programmes, at all levels, had more than trebled by the end of the decade.

Equally important was the Institute's focus on developing courses that were innovative in content. Each of its six original degree programmes incorporated modules and pedagogical approaches that were new to the Irish system. Patricia Barker recalled the ambition guiding course development within the Faculty of Business and Professional Studies:

> We wanted to be different. We wanted to have our own identity, and we really wanted to create a name for ourselves. We set up, for instance, the degree in accounting and finance, which was the first in the country ... That was a risky thing to do, it would have been much less risky to do a degree in commerce, or a degree in Business and Economics, or something that was established and that we could compete [in].[29]

The Faculty of Science and Paramedical Studies adopted an equally ground-breaking approach:

---

25 The BSc in computer applications was added to the list of part-time degrees for the 1985/6 academic year, with taught postgraduate options in computer applications, financial control and instrumental analysis added by the end of the decade (NIHED, *Annual report, 1982/3*, pp 16, 117; NIHED, *Annual report, 1985/6*, pp 22, 153; DCU, *Annual report, 1988/9*, p. 159).   26 DCU, *Annual report, 1990/1*, p. 158. In addition to the eight degrees listed above, the university had added degrees in applied mathematical sciences; applied languages (translating and interpreting); and biotechnology.   27 DCUPO, AC87/1–5; NIHED, *Annual report, 1986/7*, pp 21, 36.   28 'NCEA awards: course approval and review processes', Feb. 1987 (Eugene Kennedy Papers; DCUPO, AC87/2, 3).   29 Patricia Barker interview, 20 Sept. 2018.

Quality control was central to operations in the broad range of Irish industries of the day, and of course still are – pharmaceuticals, food, electronics. The technologies involved relied on chemical, biological and physical principles, but there were no undergraduate programmes where these sciences came together in an integrated manner, with the focus on analysis. The Analytical Science [degree] provided the logical rationale for the development of a Science Faculty here, and Analytical Science became one of the world's first BSc degree programmes in this new and rapidly developing discipline, to be followed soon afterwards by the innovative primary degree course in Biotechnology.[30]

This forward-thinking approach to course creation was not always appreciated outside of the Institute. Its vision for humanities programmes differed from the classical approach found in the established universities. Informally regarded as applied humanities, programmes created by the Faculty of Communications and Human Studies embraced the Institute-wide practice of blending theory, technology and the demands of the job market.[31] When presented with a proposal for a degree in languages and international marketing, the HEA hesitated to grant approval until persuaded by a combined intervention from the Institute's staff – led by Dr Leslie Davis – and from governing body's chairman, Prof. Michael MacCormac, who had been trying to get the staff in the Languages Department and Commerce Department at UCD to work together in a similar fashion for some time.[32]

Significant milestones in postgraduate teaching soon followed. The Institute's first higher degree was awarded on 2 November 1984, when James Brilly received his MSc in applied physics. One year later, on 1 November 1985, the Institute conferred Gerard Byrne and Dermott Pearson with PhDs in biotechnology. These were the first doctorates awarded outside of the university system in Ireland, an achievement viewed as a positive reflection of the Institute's decision to develop as a research-intensive higher-education institution and to integrate its research and teaching programmes.[33] Almost a decade later Seamus Cowman achieved another major milestone when he became the first nurse to be awarded a doctorate by an Irish university, following postgraduate work with the School of Education Studies.[34] Table 5.1 shows the number of graduates per annum between November 1983 (when the first students graduated) and the end of the 2015/16 year.

30 Albert Pratt to author, 2 May 2019.   **31** *Irish Times*, 1 Oct. 1987.   **32** Péchenart and Williams (eds), *School of Applied Languages and Intercultural Studies*, pp 25–7; Danny O'Hare interview, 28 May 2018.   **33** NIHED, *Annual report, 1984/5*, p. 25; *Irish Times*, 2 Nov. 1985; Horgan, *Dublin City University*, p 22.   **34** DCU, *Annual report, 1993/4, appendix*, p. 30.

Table 5.1. NIHED/DCU graduates per annum, 1983–2016

Year	Undergrad	Postgrad (taught)	Master's (research)	PhD
1983	50	31	0	0
1984	150	45	1	0
1985	272	27	2	2
1986	305	21	10	1
1987±	425	27	–	–
1988	448	19	21	2
1989	530	34	–	38*
1990	507	43	–	44*
1991	585	85	–	54*
1992	748	159	–	47*
1993	709	224	–	78*
1994	822	213	–	77*
1995	928	255	–	86*
1996	952	233	8	7
1997	955	453	24	24
1998	1,152	534	35	33
1999	1,265	559	40	42
2000	1,428	560	25	44
2001	1,457	579	18	28
2002	1,527	592	20	40
2003	1,551	657	21	54
2004	1,621	773	30	51
2005	1,371	890	19	59
2006	1,265	877	24	73
2007	1,311	908	21	57
2008	1,354	1,014	10	51
2009	1,439	918	11	81
2010	1,484	1,282	13	63
2011	1,473	1,144	16	89
2012	1,594	949	11	113
2013	1,754	1,151	15	123
2014	1,822	1,055	17	97
2015	1,813	1,039	8	84
2016	1,968	910	13	70

Source: DCU Quality Promotion Office; NIHED/DCU, *Annual reports, 1983–98*.
± Data for 1987 research postgraduates (master's and PhD) unavailable.
* Data for 1989–95 does not distinguish between a master's by research and a PhD. The figure given in the PhD column for these years represents the total number of research postgraduates.

Academic council

Formed on an ad hoc basis during the summer of 1980 (and placed on a statutory footing in January 1982), academic council replaced governing body's education and planning committee, assuming responsibility for directing the institution's curricular and academic development. It has played an integral role in the evolution of DCU's curriculum over the past four decades.[35] The council has taken full advantage of its statutory power to convene subcommittees and working parties to formulate and implement major policy decisions, such as the modularization of degree programmes and introduction of semesterization (see below). Membership of the council initially consisted of the director and registrar, all permanent members of academic staff, the student admissions officer, the librarian and assistant librarian, as well as the heads of student services, industrial liaison, educational technology and curriculum development.[36] As perhaps befitted an emerging higher-education institution with ambitions to expand its course offerings at a rapid pace, the council met at least once a month in in its early years, with proceedings typically lasting three hours.[37]

The importance of academic council to the functioning of NIHED/DCU can be inferred from its prominence within the Institute's establishing legislation, and the vigorous debate on its composition within the Oireachtas.[38] According to the legislation, the council's main function was to assist governing body in the planning, co-ordination, development and oversight of the Institute's educational work. Core responsibilities included the design, development and implementation of 'appropriate programmes of study'; the establishment of the structures necessary to implement those programmes and the development and oversight of the Institute's research programmes. Crucially, academic council was given authority to establish subcommittees as necessary, and to regulate its own procedure – within the constraints of the 1980 legislation (and subsequent acts) and the directions of governing body/authority.[39]

35 DCUPO, GB80/4–6, AC80/1; NIHED, *Academic procedures* (1987); 'General description of staff and facilities', Feb. 1981 (DCUPO, 'NIHE Dublin, institutional reviews, 1980–6'); Horgan, *Dublin City University*, p. 22.   36 As NIHED/DCU grew, it naturally became impractical to include all members of academic staff on the council, and provision was also made for student membership. As of October 2017 membership of the council consisted of the following *ex officio* members: president; deputy president; registrar/vice president for academic affairs; deputy registrar/director of teaching and learning; academic affairs secretariat nominee; academic secretary; executive deans of faculty; directors of each support unit; vice president for research and innovation support; dean of graduate studies; chair of examination appeals board; director, National Institute for Digital Learning; faculty administration representative; and DCUSU vice president for academic affairs. Additionally, each faculty selects 15 members, along with three from DCU's Open Education unit. The student body is also entitled to elect seven representatives (DCU academic council terms of reference, 4 Oct. 2017).   37 'General description of staff and facilities', Feb. 1981, p. 34 (DCUPO, 'NIHE Dublin, institutional reviews, 1980–6').   38 *Dáil Debates*, 21 and 27 May, 18 and 24 June, 29 Oct. 1980; *Seanad Debates*, 2 and 3 July, 19 and 26 Nov 1980; National Institute for Higher Education, Dublin, Act, 1980 (no. 30 of 1980).   39 National Institute

Early in 1983 academic council drafted an overarching mission statement, clearly articulating the Institute's practical objectives and values. Noting its national character, the council declared that the Institute's operations should be concentrated on 'selected sectors' of higher education: 'The main criteria which the Institute will use in choosing these sectors will be Ireland's current and future needs for graduate manpower in the technological, commercial and public service fields.' These sentiments were echoed in the mission statement's articulation of the Institute's purpose, which prioritized research into 'physical and social technology that will accelerate Ireland's economic and social development', as well as the cultivation of 'resources in knowledge and research to solve specific problems for industry, commerce and the public service'.[40] By the middle of the decade the frequency of meetings had been reduced to a bi-monthly schedule yet the administrative demands placed on members continued to grow, particularly in the area of intended course provision. Consideration of specific issues was thus devolved to ad hoc working groups, eventually leading to the formation of a standing committee in 1986.[41] Additional subcommittees included teaching, research and postgraduate studies, discipline, the library and Coiste na Gaeilge.[42] Further efforts to remove some of the administrative burden from academic council saw the formation of the Office for Academic Affairs in 1987, also notable as a significant development in the senior leadership of the Institute. Initially headed by Tony Bradley following his appointment to the new position of assistant registrar, the office was created to manage and develop the Institute's academic operations.[43]

for Higher Education, Dublin, Act, 1980 (no. 30 of 1980), s. 8. Academic council was also vested with various other vital functions, including the formulation of student admissions criteria, the administration of examinations, and the creation and maintenance of the Institute's academic regulations. See also Dublin City University Act, 1989 (no. 15 of 1989), ss 3, 5, and Universities Act, 1997 (no. 24 of 1997), ss 27–30.   **40** DCUPO, AC83/1, 2; NIHED, *Academic procedures* (1987), pp 7–8; *Institutional review, 1980–6*, section 2.3 (DCUPO, 'NIHE Dublin – institutional reviews, 1980–6').   **41** Academic council's standing committee met monthly to deal with routine matters of academic business, and any items that required urgent attention. Its first meeting was delayed until November 1986, due to the pressures associated with preparation for the visit of the international study group appointed to assess the potential for the establishment of a technological university in Ireland (DCUPO, AC84/4, AC85/1–6, ACSC86/1; *Nuacht*, Sept. 1985 and Nov. 1986).   **42** DCUPO, AC82/1–4, AC83/6, AC84/6, AC85/6, AC87/2; NIHED, *Academic procedures*, pp 9–19.   **43** NIHED, *Annual report, 1987/8*, pp 36–8, 186; *Nuacht*, Nov. 1987 and Jan. 1988; Bradley, *'Twigs for an eagle's nest'*, p. 80. Reorganization of these various committees occurred at occasional intervals, representing both the evolution of pedagogical best practice, and the need to accommodate the university's expanding suite of undergraduate and postgraduate programmes. Following the implementation of a strategic planning process in 2005 (the second such process initiated under the presidency of Ferdinand von Prondzynski), academic council simplified its structures, resulting in widespread changes to the composition of subcommittees, including the replacement of the standing committee with the university standards committee in April 2006 (DCUPO, AC2005/2, 3; ACUSC2006/1).

II

Academic council's primary role lay in the development of the curriculum. Prior to the attainment of university status, the creation of new degree programmes required approval at three main stages, one internal and two external. Mindful of the Institute's remit to provide degrees that addressed the social and economic requirements of the country, faculty identified the need for a programme and submitted outline proposals to academic council. Once an outline was approved for further development, the council appointed a programme board to prepare more detailed documentation for consideration.[44] Assistance was also received from the Institute's School of Curriculum Development, whose major responsibility was to ensure a professional approach to the identification of learning needs, the formulation of course objectives and the development of appropriate forms of assessment.[45] Proposals were required to state the rationale behind the programme's creation, the likely demand from students and for graduates, an outline of course content and the human and physical resources required to deliver that content. Second-stage development incorporated a two-step approval process by the NCEA. The third and final stage involved clearance from the HEA, which took into account the national and regional need for the degree, as well as the projected costs of providing the required staff and facilities. In what can be construed as an endorsement of the initial quality-control procedures in place at the Institute, and its ability to identify gaps in the provision of third-level educational programmes, none of its proposed degrees were rejected by the NCEA.

Each of the Institute's courses resulted from a multifaceted approach to content creation. As part of its overall educational remit, the Institute sought to identify the state's social and economic requirements by consulting with industrial and commercial entities. Preparations for the introduction of a BSc in applied physics, by the staff of the School of Physical Sciences, illustrate the point.[46] Beginning in April 1980, the course team sought input on the development of the degree from the Industrial Development Authority (IDA),

---

44 In their initial incarnation, programme boards were subcommittees of academic council, with responsibility for the administration of individual degree programmes. Each board was composed of those who taught on the programme and several *ex officio* members. External experts could also be co-opted to the board. For membership of programmes boards, see NIHED, *Institutional review, 1980–6*, s. 3; NIHED, *Academic procedures*, pp 29–31. 45 The School of Curriculum Development formed part of the Faculty of Education Studies and was headed by Dr Peter McKenna. The faculty was abolished in 1990, with the School of Education Studies established at DCU in 1993 following a period of reorganization coinciding with the linkage agreement with St Patrick's College, which saw the creation of a joint Faculty of Education (DCUPO, 'St Patrick's College – linkage negotiations'; NIHED, *Annual reports, 1978–89*). 46 The lead developers of the BSc in applied physics were Dr Alexander Spowart (head of school), Dr Martin Henry and Dr Eugene Kennedy.

the National Board for Science and Technology (NBST) and the Institute for Industrial Research and Standards.[47] Encouraged by their reaction, the course team wrote to 350 industrial firms using technology in the work place, outlining the broad areas to be covered by the degree. By the end of the year, more than 60 per cent of the firms had responded. Some outlined how the course might meet their particular needs and indicated their willingness to participate in the INTRA scheme (see below), while others provided more general information regarding the difficulties they had experienced in employing staff with sufficient technological and technical training. The course team's detailed CR2 syllabus submission to the NCEA outlined a four-year degree and ran to more than 130 pages. The interdisciplinary nature of the degree was stressed, with courses to be shared or co-taught with the programmes for business studies and analytical science. Submitted for consideration in February 1981, NCEA approval was received in May with the first students enrolled that October.[48]

The standards established by such comprehensive preparatory work formed the bedrock of course development over the following three decades. The principle of engagement with professional bodies and private enterprise was also firmly established; core elements of DCU's curriculum have thus developed following direct consultations with relevant stakeholders, particularly in the private sector, along with other third-level institutions. The School of Biological Sciences designed its biotechnology degree – introduced for the 1982/3 academic year – following input from the IDA, the NBST and various multinational companies. A new concept in Irish higher education, the degree combined relevant aspects of microbiology, biochemistry and process engineering at undergraduate level for the first time, mirroring similar developments at American and European institutions. Alongside its ambition to produce graduates suitable for employment in biologically based industries, it was hoped that the degree would also bring the Institute closer to the pharmaceutical, food and agricultural sectors of the economy.[49] Initial demand for places was high, reflected in the minimum requirement of twenty-four points in the Leaving Certificate examination. The creation of this particular degree neatly illustrated NIHE Dublin's ability to anticipate emerging national economic trends; in late 1981 the IDA released a report emphasising the need for biotechnologists with process engineering training, 'which is precisely in line with the proposed NIHE course'.[50]

47 The IIRS was located in Glasnevin and merged with the NBST in 1987 to form EOLAS.
48 'CR2 submission to NCEA on degree in applied physics', Feb. 1981 (Eugene Kennedy Papers); DCUPO, 'NCEA – National Council for Educational Awards, 1978–89'; NIHED, *Annual report, 1978–82*, p. 18. Similarly intensive preparations were undertaken by all schools and faculties. See, for example, Péchenart and Williams (eds), *School of Applied Languages and Intercultural Studies*, pp 6–7.   49 The analytical-biology component of the analytical science degree was also taught for the first time during the 1982/3 academic year (NIHED, *Annual report, 1982/3*, pp 27–8; *By Degrees*, Oct. 1982).   50 NIHED, *Annual report, 1978–82*, p. 17; O. Ward to Danny O'Hare, 22 Feb. 1982

Other schools undertook similar initiatives. The School of Communications completed a large-scale market-research exercise in the spring of 1980, which played a significant role in shaping its degree in communication studies. National and provincial newspaper editors assessed the school's plans for a postgraduate diploma in journalism and their approbation gave further impetus to the programme, which enrolled its first students in 1982.[51] Dr Tony Coulson, lecturer in the School of Applied Languages (which later added Intercultural Studies to its designation), recalls close consultation with schools of translation in Geneva, Saarbrücken and Mainz as the school prepared its proposal for a degree in applied languages.[52]

Anxious to formalize the Institute's relations with relevant industrial and professional interests, governing body approved the creation of an Industrial Advisory Council under the chairmanship of Richard Burrows, CEO of the Irish Distillers Group, which assembled for the first time on 18 October 1985. Meeting two to three times annually, the council's terms of reference included offering advice on the improvement of NIHED/DCU's curriculum and INTRA programme, facilitating communication with the Irish government and the industrial and commercial sectors, and providing advice and guidance on research and development priorities.[53] Speaking of his decision to join the council, Burrows praised the Institute's willingness to collaborate:

> They were prepared to come to industry and to ask for real input. The Institute was thinking of its customers, the customers who will eventually be employers of NIHE Dublin's graduates ... [O]ne just needs to look through the spread of courses that are run at the Institute to see how effectively they dovetail into so many areas in industry. It really is Industry's university.[54]

There were, nonetheless, those among the institution's faculty who were uncomfortable with industry's influence on the development of NIHED/DCU, which they felt raised difficult questions about the blurring of lines between the university's public-service ethos and its willingness to adapt its curriculum and research programme to the specific needs of the private sector.[55]

(DCUPO, 'NIHE Dublin: general, 2/3'). Quotation taken from Ward letter. **51** T.J. Wheeler to Danny O'Hare, 2 Feb. 1982 (DCUPO, 'NIHE Dublin: general, 2/2'); NIHED, *Annual report, 1982/3*, p. 20. **52** Péchenart and Williams (eds), *School of Applied Languages and Intercultural Studies*, p. 6. **53** 'University Business Advisory Council information note', *c.*1996 (DCUPO, 'B – miscellaneous'); *Nuacht*, Sept. 1985; Horgan, *Dublin City University*, pp 23–4; Bradley, *'Twigs for an eagle's nest'*, pp 37–9. **54** Quoted in Bradley, *'Twigs for an eagle's nest'*, p. 38. Burrows served as chairman of the council for three years. Alongside Burrows, the members of the inaugural council were Bill Ambrose (Business and Finance), Alex Burns (Stokes Kennedy Crowley), Paddy Cummins (Waterford Co-op), Matt McDonagh (Organon), Vincent Daly (Ericsson Information Systems), Harry Lynam (Lake Electronics), Danny O'Hare (director, NIHED) and Terence Larkin (chairman, NIHED governing body). **55** Helena Sheehan, *Living eons in decades: a story of history*

5.3 Students protesting during the visit of Taoiseach Albert Reynolds to open the new DCU Business School building, 27 October 1994 (DCU Collection).

Long-term curriculum planning was also undertaken in response to prompts from the HEA. Curriculum enhancement was envisaged at undergraduate and postgraduate level in the fields of biotechnology, applied languages, accounting and mechanical engineering.[56] The development of engineering courses proved particularly problematic during the 1980s, with the Institute's efforts constrained by the government's inability to deliver the laboratory space and staff promised under the proposed Phase 2 development of the Institute.[57] By the mid-1980s the Faculty of Engineering consisted of only the School of Electronic Engineering, despite the existence of a faculty-development plan outlining courses in information technology, manufacturing and automation.[58] The School of Mechanical Engineering was not formally established until January 1987, following the appointment of Prof. Saleem Hashmi.[59] Even so, while the School

after the end of history (forthcoming); Brian Trench interview, 9 May 2019. I am grateful to Prof. Sheehan for providing me with an early draft of her forthcoming book.   **56** NIHED, *Annual report, 1978–82*, p. 12. See also individual annual reports for the 1980s and 1990s, which provide detailed school reports that occasionally mention ongoing programme development.   **57** The ability of the Faculty of Engineering and Design to deliver programmes was, somewhat ironically, also impacted by a dearth of graduates of the type it proposed to train. In 1986 it reported that 'the joint problems of minimal recruitment, through lack of suitable applicants, and turnover in academic staff has taken the School of Electronic Engineering to crisis point at the end of the 1985/6 academic year – in excess of 50% of established faculty positions in the School are currently vacant' (NIHED, *Annual report, 1985/6*, p. 26).   **58** NIHED, *Annual report, 1984/5*, pp 6, 23–4.   **59** NIHED,

was able to accept postgraduate research students, by the mid-1990s its planned undergraduate course in mechatronics engineering had yet to be approved by the HEA.[60]

If industrial and economic demands were influential in NIHE Dublin's initial curriculum development, its staff and leadership were also cognizant of the need to anticipate and indeed shape the future needs of Ireland's commercial, industrial and public sectors. As part of a review initiated during the 1981/2 academic year, heads of school submitted reports on the demand from all employment sectors for their graduates, as well as courses scheduled for commencement. The Institute's goals, and the attitude of its staff, were encapsulated by the report of Anthony Foley, head of the School of Business Administration: 'We feel that an applied Institute, such as NIHE Dublin, should be concerned to create economic development through its activities and academic programmes and not simply to respond to the manpower needs of economic development ... It is not sufficient that our contribution should end there. We must also, through our activities, assist in accelerating that process of development.'[61]

Perhaps the most important legacy of such an approach was to inculcate a spirit of innovation and risk-taking in the institution's educational planning, particularly during its first two decades. The limited scale of NIHE Dublin's size, along with its youth and concomitant lack of established bureaucratic procedures, permitted greater flexibility. With fewer formal structures in place, staff were bound primarily by budgetary considerations when considering new degree programmes. These flexibilities and freedoms persisted for most of the 1990s, before the growing scale of DCU's operations brought a more controlled approach. During an interview in 1992 for the position of lecturer with the School of Communications, Brian Trench recalls being asked a simple, yet open-ended question: 'What would you like to do when you come here?' The question resonated with Trench (who later served as head of school) as indicative of the kind of institution he was joining: 'That stayed with me because I remember the feeling of inclusiveness, the feeling of accommodation of new ideas as a distinguishing characteristic of NIHED/early DCU.'[62]

Curriculum development in the late 1980s and early 1990s at undergraduate level proceeded with careful iterations of the Institute's existing strengths; new offerings were usually confined to postgraduate study and continuing education.

Annual report, 1986/7, pp 32–3.   **60** The BEng in mechatronics engineering was finally launched in time for the beginning of the 1996/7 academic year (NIHED, *Annual report, 1987/8*, pp 19–20; DCU, *Annual report, 1988/9*, p. 13; DCU, *Annual report, 1996/7*, p. 27).   **61** Anthony Foley, 'Employment aspects of four-year plan programmes of the School of Business Administration', Feb. 1982 (DCUPO, 'NIHE Dublin: general, 2/2').   **62** Brian Trench interview, 9 May 2019. Trench later established an innovative master's programme in Science Communication, jointly delivered with Queen's University Belfast (Brian Trench, 'The rocky road of science communication in Ireland' in Brian Trench, Padraig Murphy and Declan Fahy (eds), *Little country, big talk: science*

Financial difficulties, stalled campus development and staff shortages stifled the introduction of new degree programmes. The attainment of university status in 1989 proved to be a watershed moment, coinciding with an influx of philanthropic and government investment during the 1990s and 2000s that allowed DCU's curriculum to evolve in tandem with the physical growth of the Glasnevin campus. The relationship between the university's physical and curricular development during the 1990s and 2000s was largely symbiotic, with additional teaching and research space allowing each faculty to expand its programmes and to explore new opportunities. A major extension to the School of Computer Applications, completed in 1999 at a cost of *c.*£4.5m, permitted a doubling in the school's undergraduate intake, the further development of the degree programme in applied computational linguistics, and the pursuit of new research priorities. That year also saw the completion of the Chemical Sciences and Biotechnology (Lonsdale) building, enabling the Faculty of Science and Paramedical Studies to introduce new degrees in sports science and health, as well as science education.[63] Earlier in the decade, the completion of the linkage agreement with St Patrick's College, Drumcondra had led to the creation of two new joint faculties, in education and in humanities – though both institutions continued to offer separate degree programmes under the CAO system.[64] Further linkage agreements completed with Mater Dei Institute (1999) and All Hallows College (2007) enhanced the university's offerings in education and humanities. While the 1990s and 2000s thus witnessed rapid growth in DCU's core strengths of STEM subjects, applied humanities and business education, it also heralded the first steps towards the integration of 'traditional' humanities, teacher education and educational studies into the curriculum.[65]

University status also brought significant changes to the work of academic council, allowing for the evolution of the new university's curriculum in unexpected directions. At its first meeting following the announcement of the impending change in status, the council's members were reminded of the additional demands they would face. The need to maintain a reputation for academic quality was paramount for the new university. Moreover, as the only statutory body with members elected by staff, academic council was uniquely representative. Its importance to the new university's operations would be vital, particularly its enhanced role in programme validation and accreditation.[66] Inevitably, some difficulties attended the implementation of the new system of

communication in Ireland (Dublin, 2017), pp 1–25).   **63** DCUPO, AC99/M1/7, AC99/2 and 4; DCUPO, ACSC99/4, 5; APA, Grants #7380, #7237 and #7526; *Irish Times*, 27 Mar. and 4 May 1999; *Newslink*, Apr. 1999.   **64** DCUPO, 'St Patrick's College: linkage negotiations'; DCU, *Annual report, 1993/4*, p. 8 and *appendix*, pp 13–14, 30.   **65** See chapter 4 for the Incorporation within DCU of St Patrick's College, Mater Dei Institute and the Church of Ireland College of Education, which saw the addition of a number of schools to the Faculty of Humanities and Social Sciences, as well as the creation of the DCU Institute of Education.   **66** DCUPO, ACSC89/1; *Nuacht*, Mar. 1989.

self-accreditation. Painstakingly developed connections with various professions and private enterprises had led to widespread recognition of the quality of NIHE Dublin's graduates, and time was needed to convert the exemptions from examinations for professional bodies for DCU graduates.[67] The changeover was otherwise relatively smooth, a testament to the quality of the systems established by NIHE Dublin in partnership with the NCEA and HEA.[68]

The Dublin City University Act made several amendments to the council's existing statutory functions. Alongside the power to advise on the criteria for awarding honorary degrees (which would be drawn up in consultation with governing body/authority), the only other substantive change empowered the council to confer degrees not only on graduates of the university, but also on graduates of 'such other colleges or institutions as the governing body may approve'. As a corollary, the university was permitted to enter into arrangements with other 'relevant' institutions, both nationally and internationally, to offer joint courses. Governing body welcomed this progressive step as one that would have fundamental implications for the university's development.[69]

Those implications were quickly apparent. In October 1990 a proposal was received from Lindsay Armstrong, director of the Royal Irish Academy of Music, for the creation of a joint degree in music performance to be taught by the RIAM and validated by DCU, or taught by both. Welcomed as a new and significant stage in the university's development, the proposed degree's emphasis on performance was seen as complementary to the university's 'applied education' ethos. O'Hare also supported the initiative as part of a wider preference for increased representation of the arts and music on campus in the future – as embodied in the ongoing efforts to locate an arts centre at DCU (see chapter 6). The proposal was subject to a lengthy discussion at academic council's standing committee, particularly on the potential for problems with accrediting an externally taught degree programme.[70] Following close co-operation with the RIAM to refine the programme's parameters and infra-structural supports, the BA in music performance was introduced for the 1992/3 academic year. By 1995, the collaboration had progressed to the creation of an MA and graduate diploma.[71]

67 DCUPO, ACSC90/2. **68** See, for example, 'Proposed system for the validation and accreditation of … programmes leading to qualifications awarded by NIHE Dublin', Dec. 1985 (Eugene Kennedy Papers). See also DCUPO, AC86/1. **69** Dublin City University Act, 1989 (no. 15 of 1989), s. 3; DCUPO, GB89/8, 9; *Nuacht*, Oct. 1989. See appendix 3 for more on the awarding of honorary degrees by NIHED/DCU. **70** DCUPO, GB90/7, ACSC90/11, ACSC91/2. **71** DCUPO, ACSC91/5–7, ACSC93/1–4, ACSC95/7; DCU, *Annual report, 1993/4, appendix*, p. 231. It is worth noting that a degree in music performance and teaching was considered in early curriculum planning. See Danny O'Hare, 'Future organisation of the Institute: a personal view', Mar. 1976 (DCUPO, 'Governing body – reports and working papers, 1975–9'); *Plan for the future of the Institute*, pp 76–7. The *Plan* argued that developing a 'music section' on campus could be justified by the desirability of exposing staff and students to the development of musical skills and

The precedent established with the RIAM allowed academic council to give serious consideration to an approach from the Eastern Health Board, which sought to develop a suite of collaborative courses in psychotherapy, from diploma through to doctoral level.[72] While this initial attempt to add medical studies to the curriculum was not successful, it was not long before DCU ventured into the field. The majority of Irish universities incorporate a medical school, with the exceptions of Maynooth University and DCU. Though the establishment of a full medical school at NIHED/DCU was never seriously considered, the education and planning committee did contemplate the development of a degree-level nursing course. Aware of the nursing profession's ambitions to modernize its training in response to medical and diagnostic innovations, the committee briefly explored the possibility of providing such training in collaboration with regional health boards.[73] Contact with nursing bodies continued throughout the 1980s, including a 1985 proposal to collaborate with the South Eastern Health Board to create a degree in nursing.[74]

The nursing profession had identified a clear need for more formalized training in areas such as physiology and biochemistry and was seeking partners to meet that demand. In 1995 DCU broke new ground with the launch of its diploma in nursing.[75] Originally run in collaboration with Beaumont Hospital and the Royal College of Surgeons in Ireland, the establishment and delivery of its content was primarily overseen by DCU graduate Dr Seamus Cowman, Josephine Bartley and Annette Donnellan.[76] The following year saw the formal creation of DCU's School of Nursing, with Betty Brady appointed as the university's first director of nursing studies.[77] A one-year, part-time bachelor of nursing studies was introduced in 1997, and the programme was quickly expanded to offer six diplomas in general, psychiatric and mental handicap nursing in partnership with six health-care service providers.[78] These developments were among the first steps in the national recognition of nursing as a degree-level profession, formally recommended to the government in a 1998 report delivered by the Commission on Nursing.[79] Following the appointment of Prof. Anne Scott as head of the School of Nursing, DCU's BSc in nursing was

appreciation, and of allowing the Institute to offer courses in music to the local community and to local schools.   **72** DCUPO, ACSC93/1, 3, 4.   **73** NIHED, *Plan for the future of the Institute*, pp 72–5.   **74** Colette Fenelon to unspecified, 7 Aug. 1985 (DCUPO, 'Correspondence: general, 1980–5').   **75** DCUPO, AC95/4–6; ACSC96/3, 4. The University of Limerick enrolled its first nursing students the following year (Fleming, *University of Limerick*, pp 149–50).   **76** DCU, *Annual report, 1994/5*, pp 33–4; DCU, *Annual report, 1995/6*, p. 281.   **77** DCU, *Annual report, 1995/6*, p. 29; DCU, *Annual report, 1996/7*, pp 8, 34–6.   **78** In addition to Beaumont Hospital, partnerships were established with James Connolly Memorial Hospital; St Vincent's Hospital, Fairview; St Joseph's Intellectual Disability Services, Portrane; St Ita's Hospital, Portrane; and St Joseph's, Clonsilla.   **79** Department of Health and Children, *Report of the commission on nursing: a blueprint for the future* (Dublin, 1998). Justice Mella Carroll, future chancellor of DCU, chaired

launched in 2002, followed by the opening in 2003 of the first purpose-built, university-based nursing school in the state.[80]

The current process of course creation, from initial concept through to validation and accreditation, retains many of the core features of the system developed during the 1980s.[81] In what can be viewed as an endorsement of one of the core structures implemented in the early phase of NIHE Dublin's evolution, the university retains a requirement that its accreditation boards include professional experts from outside the academic community, where appropriate, thus continuing the legacy of the Industrial Advisory Council.[82] The most recent review of DCU's programme-approval process noted that its 'internal and external stakeholders were satisfied with the validation and accreditation procedures', with the process commended as appropriate, rigorous and standardized across the university.[83] As can be seen from fig. 5.1, the number of undergraduate programmes on offer at NIHED/DCU has expanded rapidly since the incremental growth of the 1980s. In that first decade of operations just five degree programmes were added to the six originally offered in November 1980. University status coincided with the rapid development of campus facilities, and the curriculum expanded at a similar pace. By the end of the 1990s the university offered forty-four full-time primary-degree programmes, twenty-three full-time postgraduate courses at diploma and master's level, and forty-seven part-time courses.[84] As of the 2015/16 academic year, there were 123 undergraduate programmes alone on offer.[85] Remarkably, despite the steady increase in undergraduate and postgraduate courses available, the number of faculties at the university has actually been reduced, though there have also been numerous changes to faculty designations and internal realignment of schools.[86]

the commission. **80** DCUPO, AC2001/2; M.G. Leavy, 'Managing the nurse tutor transition: a case study of organisational socialisation' (MSc, DCU, 2003), pp 4–17; DCU, *Quality assurance report, School of Nursing, 2004–5* (Dublin, 2005), p. 8; Danny O'Hare interview, 28 May 2018; *Irish Times*, 18 Sept. 2001, 19 Mar. 2002. Prof. Scott later served as deputy President and registrar of DCU between 2006 and 2012. **81** Compare, for example, the procedures laid out in NIHED, *Academic procedures* (Dublin, 1987), pp 27–38, with the latest regulations for validation and accreditation, approved by academic council's education committee in September 2016 (DCUPO, AC2016/6). **82** The name of the Industrial Advisory Council was changed to the Business Advisory Council in November 1989. By the late 1990s the council had fallen into abeyance, but was re-established during the presidency of Ferdinand von Prondzynski, who was keen to involve members of the business community in the university's strategic-planning process, and to provide an 'appropriate forum for regular discussions with business leaders and others in influential positions' (DCUPO, GB89/9; Ferdinand von Prondzynski memo, 28 Aug. 2000 (DCUPO, 'B – miscellaneous')). **83** QQI, *Institutional review report 2019: DCU* (2019), pp 18–19. See also Irish Universities Quality Board, *IRIU report*, pp 14–15, 49. **84** DCU, *Annual report, 1997/8*, pp 440–3. **85** Data provided by DCU Quality Promotion Office. **86** For example, DCU Business School (which has faculty status) was formerly known as the Faculty of Business and Professional Studies (1980–7), and the Dublin Business School (1988–92). It was renamed the Dublin City University Business School in October 1992 (NIHED/DCU, *Annual reports, 1978–93*).

Of the original faculties created at NIHE Dublin, two were abolished during the 1990s: Education Studies, as well as Computing and Quantitative Methods.[87] A number of new faculties have been added to (and later removed from) the university since 1989: Distance Education was accorded faculty status in November of that year (though it no longer has that status), and a joint Faculty of Humanities and a joint Faculty of Education were formed in 1993 with the completion of a linkage agreement with St Patrick's College, Drumcondra. Further evolution of education studies at the university saw the creation in 2016 of the first Faculty of Education (with a focus on teacher education at all levels) in an Irish university, following the Incorporation into DCU of St Patrick's College, Drumcondra; Mater Dei Institute; and the Church of Ireland College of Education.[88]

Fig. 5.1. Total number of undergraduate programmes, 1980–2016[89]

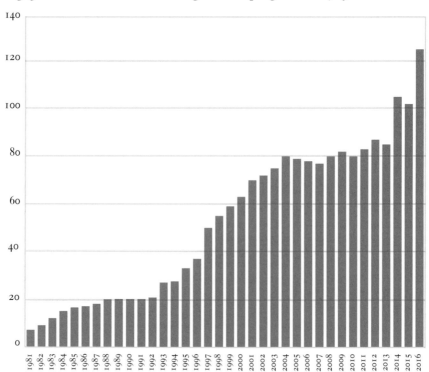

Source: DCU Quality Promotion Office.

87 DCU, *Annual report, 1989/90*, p. 17.   **88** DCUPO, GB89/9, 10; *Nuacht*, Nov. 1989. The university currently consists of five faculties: Humanities and Social Sciences; Science and Health; Engineering and Computing; DCU Business School; and the Institute of Education. See chapter 4 for further details on the Incorporation process and the creation of the Institute of Education. **89** This table includes programmes offered via distance education, part-time and evening study.

5.4 Members of the Fr Ted Appreciation Society during Rag Week (DCU Collection).

Modularization

Embedded during planning in the late 1970s and early 1980s, an interdisciplinary approach to course creation has remained as one of the core pillars of curriculum design. Degree programmes shared course content, with students on the BSc in computer applications studying accountancy alongside those enrolled in applied mathematical sciences or business studies. Inter-school and inter-faculty service teaching facilitated this approach; the School of Accounting and Finance, for example, provided service teaching to as many as ten separate courses.[90] Other instances of inter-school and interfaculty collaboration abounded in the following years. The BSc in applied computational linguistics was introduced in 1991 through a 'novel collaboration' between the School of Applied Languages and the School of Computer Applications, which produced its first graduates in 1995. As was the case with many curriculum innovations, the applied computational linguistics programme developed in response to the changing needs of the workplace and of society – in this case the rapid advancement of information and communications technology.[91]

While the institution encouraged interdisciplinary innovation, the delivery of programme content was otherwise organized along relatively traditional lines.

90 NIHED, *Institutional review, 1980–6*, s. 3.4 and appendix 3 (DCUPO, 'NIHE Dublin – institutional reviews, 1980–6'). Every school in the Institute contributed service teaching to at least one other school.   91 Péchenart and Williams (eds), *School of Applied Languages and Intercultural*

Though cognizant of research arguing against conventional course structures, the Institute's planners were nonetheless wary of the alternative, modular approach. A version of modularization had been introduced to Ireland in the early 1970s by NIHE Limerick, and the system was closely examined by NIHE Dublin's education and planning committee. A discussion paper prepared in August 1977 proved particularly influential in the decision not to emulate Limerick's approach. Highlighting the difficulties experienced by several London polytechnics that had embraced modularization, the document also cited recent research that highlighted student difficulties in moving from one module to another across vastly different disciplines.[92] Rejecting the modular system, the Institute noted that its reservations were based on what it believed to be 'the questionable ability of the average student on any course to progress with any measure of ease from one module to another … A more fundamental reservation is based on the belief that conveying concepts and their appreciation is more important than imparting facts, and that whereas it is possible to modularise facts it is not possible to modularise concepts.'[93]

The issue was, however, not permanently settled. Following pressure from staff members in favour of the modular approach, in 1983 academic council requested a new report from the Faculty of Education on modularization.[94] During the ensuing year, the faculty convened a series of seminars and discussion groups on the topic, featuring guest lectures by academics from NIHE Limerick and Oxford Polytechnic.[95] Consideration of the issue progressed significantly, with individual programme boards asked to review the feasibility of modular reorganization of their courses, and to ensure that no obstacles were placed in the way of any courses that wished to move to a modular structure.[96] While these activities had little immediate impact, the prospect of modularization was raised once again in the early 1990s. Academic council's standing committee established a special working group on modularization, with broad terms of reference to consider both the benefits and the drawbacks of the system and to recommend a formal university policy. Kay MacKeogh was appointed chairperson of the working group, with a first meeting held on 28 May 1992.[97]

Seven months later, two core principles for the implementation of the modular system were agreed: 1) the division of the academic year into two semesters, with three weeks for revision and examination at the end of each semester; and 2) all DCU programmes were to be modularized, with the overall structure to correspond with the European Credit Transfer System (ECTS),

Studies, p. 28.   **92** 'A discussion paper on an educational philosophy for NIHED', Aug. 1977 (DCUPO, 'Governing body – reports and working papers, 1975–9'), p. 14.   **93** NIHED, *Plan for the future of the Institute*, p. 38. For the modular structure of NIHE Limerick's courses, see Fleming, *University of Limerick*, pp 130–2; White, *Investing in people*, p. 74; Walsh, *Higher education in Ireland*, p. 262.   **94** DCUPO, AC83/3, 4; *Nuacht*, Aug. 1983.   **95** DCUPO, AC84/1; NIHED, *Annual report, 1983/4*, p. 26; *Nuacht*, Apr. 1984.   **96** DCUPO, AC84/4, 5.   **97** DCUPO, ACSC92/3, 4.

1 Daniel O'Hare, director and president of NIHE Dublin/DCU, 1977–99. Portrait by
Carey Clarke, RHA (2002) (DCU Collection).

2 Ferdinand von Prondzynski, president, DCU, 2000–10. Portrait by Mick O'Dea, RHA (2010) (DCU Collection).

3 Brian MacCraith, president, DCU, 2010–20 (DCU Collection).

4 Patrick Donegan, chairman, governing body, 1975–9 (DCU Collection).

5 Michael MacCormac, chairman, governing body, 1979–82 (DCU Collection).

6 Terence Larkin, chairman, governing body, 1982–92 (DCU Collection).

7 Eoin O'Brien, chairman, governing body, 1992–7 (DCU Collection).

8 Paddy Wright (DCU Educational Trust), Danny O'Hare and Thomas P. Hardiman
at Hardiman's inauguration as chancellor of governing authority, 10 September 1998.
Hardiman served as chancellor from 1998 until 2001 (DCU Collection).

9 David Byrne, chancellor, governing authority, 2006–11. Portrait by Mick O'Dea, RHA (2012) (DCU Collection).

10 Martin McAleese, chancellor, governing authority, 2011–present (DCU Collection).

11 Aerial photo of the Glasnevin campus, 1981 (DCU Collection).

12 Aerial photo of the Glasnevin campus, 1997 (DCU Collection).

13 The quad of DCU St Patrick's Campus, Drumcondra (DCU Collection).

14 DCU All Hallows Campus, Drumcondra, which was acquired by the university in 2016 (DCU Collection).

15 The Helix Centre for the Performing Arts, opened in 2002 (DCU Collection).

16 Students walking in front of the Albert College building in the 1980s (DCU Collection).

under which each academic year was worth sixty credits.[98] Arguably the most significant and controversial reform to the curriculum and course structure ever undertaken at DCU, the decision to move to modularization was not taken lightly. Internal opposition was fierce. Those in favour of the status quo argued that abandoning the carefully crafted, specialized degree structures had the potential to damage the academic quality and professional reputation of DCU's degrees, and to negatively impact the INTRA programme. There was also resistance to the need to quantify teaching aims (as learning outcomes), to submit programmes to more detailed scrutiny and validation and to the inevitable increase in administrative work.[99]

When modularization was introduced in September 1996, it represented the culmination of a process that had proved both fractious and drawn-out.[100] The academic year was now divided into two semesters of twelve weeks' duration, with exams held at the end of each semester. The system was designed to facilitate inter-institutional student transfers, and to simplify the creation of new courses and degree programmes, as explained by Registrar John Carroll: 'If we want to respond to the needs of industry, say at master's level, it will be much simpler for us to combine existing modules with new modules to create a new title.'[101] It was also a change that reflected government policy, as outlined in the Department of Education's 1992 green paper and 1995 white paper. The shift to a modular structure was later validated, from a policy perspective, by the government's adoption of the Bologna Declaration, a European initiative to facilitate greater ease of transfer between higher-education institutions in different jurisdictions. Despite the significance of the Bologna process, and the far-reaching consequences for Irish higher education, most institutions within the Irish system adapted to the new policy 'with remarkably little internal or public debate'.[102]

Nonetheless, the changes wrought by the Bologna process have been described as a 'paradigm shift' in Irish higher education.[103] Within DCU, further consideration of the modular system during the early and mid-2000s led to a refinement of academic structures, programme content and descriptions, bringing them into greater alignment with Bologna, including conformity with the government's new National Framework of Qualifications (NFQ).[104] As part

98 DCU, *Annual report, 1992/3*, p. 7.   **99** DCUPO, AC92/1–6, AC93/1; *Nuacht*, Jan. 1993; Brian Trench interview, 9 May 2019. The extent of the disagreements and division among staff on the introduction of modularization is not properly conveyed by the documentary record. The strength of feeling might be inferred from one staff member's reference to 'the Modular Wars' (Martin Clynes, 'DCU: the movie', *DCU Times*, c.2005).   **100** DCU, *Strategy for the year 2000* (Dublin, 1995), p. 11; DCU, *Annual report, 1996/7*, p. vi; *Irish Times*, 27 Sept. 1994 and 27 Feb. 1996.   **101** *Irish Times*, 27 Feb. 1996.   **102** Walsh, *Higher education in Ireland*, pp 393–9 (quotation on p. 393); Jim Gleeson, 'The European Credit Transfer System and curriculum design: product before process?', *Studies in Higher Education*, 38:6 (2013), pp 921–38.   **103** Gleeson, 'The European Credit Transfer System', p. 923.   **104** DCUPO, AC2005/1, 2; AC2006/2, 3. The National

of several strategic reviews undertaken in the late 2000s, the university conducted a detailed analysis of all academic structures and its implementation of the modular system – including an in-depth examination of more than 2,500 modules.[105] That process led to the creation of the Academic Framework for Innovation (AFI), developed between 2006 and 2009 specifically to achieve NFQ and Bologna compliance, and to implement the recommendations of academic council's modularization working group.[106] As a result, each module and programme available at DCU shares a common descriptive format, and the systems of assessment and application of grading standards have been redesigned to ensure greater cohesion and consistency across the university. According to a study of the AFI, completed by DCU's Learning Innovation Unit, the 'intangible' outcomes of the AFI process were particularly valuable:

> It is clear that the language of curriculum is used by academics across the campus to a far greater extent than before. Where previously the main focus was on programmes and, more specifically, on content, the curriculum focus is now broader, with discussions about learning outcomes, valid assessment, learning approaches and learning activities becoming more frequent. In the context of DCU's strategic intentions, flexibility is also becoming an increasing focus.[107]

Despite the scale of the exercise, the willingness of the university's staff to shoulder significant additions to their regular workloads over a number of years ensured a successful implementation. The AFI was subsequently lauded by an international review group, which commended DCU for its

> wisdom and foresight in conceiving the AFI project, for the manner in which the project's implementation has been managed, and for … the dedication and energy with which its staff have supported the AFI through developing programme descriptors, revising DCU's stock of taught modules, and developing learning outcomes linked to assessment criteria for modules.[108]

Building upon that framework, the Generation 21 initiative was launched in September 2011 following extensive consultations within the university and with employers. Its intent was to 'change the way the university prepares and shapes graduates for life and work in the 21st century'.[109] Designed to integrate with the

Framework of Qualifications was introduced in 2003, providing a system whereby learning achievements and higher-education qualifications from Irish institutions can be measured against each other and quantified.   **105** DCUPO, AC2008/1–6; AC2009/1–6; Hughes and Munro, 'Curriculum change', p. 31.   **106** Academic council approved the implementation of the AFI on 25 June 2007 (DCUPO, AC2007/4, 5; Hughes and Munro, 'Curriculum change', p. 28). **107** Hughes and Munro, 'Curriculum change', p. 32.   **108** Irish Universities Quality Board, *IRIU report*, p. 32.   **109** *Irish Times*, 8 Sept. 2011.

5.5 One man and his dog watch a football match between graduates and current students in April 1988 (DCU Collection).

Uaneen module and INTRA programme (see below) and in expectation that graduates would require attributes that would enable continuous adaptation to an ever-changing jobs market, the initiative aimed to provide students with core skills in addition to the disciplinary knowledge gained in discrete degree programmes.[110] The university's determination to foreground student employ-ability has been a constant in its curriculum-design principles, encapsulating a long-standing commitment to adapt its degree programmes to reflect the changing nature of the undergraduate experience, as outlined in its 1995 strategic plan:

> DCU has decided to introduce a system of modularisation and semesterisation, which should provide more flexible access to academic programmes for a wider population, a wider range of student choice, credit for related work experience, and easier interchange with other institutions. We will ensure that the design and implementation of this system will enable the development of core transferable skills across all platforms.[111]

110 When launched, the initiative identified six attributes that would prepare students for 'lifetime employability', rather than 'lifetime employment': they should be creative and enterprising, solution-oriented, effective communicators, globally engaged, active leaders and committed to continuous learning (DCU, *President's report, 2010–11*, pp 42, 49; DCU, *Transforming lives and societies: DCU strategic plan, 2012–17* (Dublin, 2012), pp 8, 12; Hughes and Munro, 'Curriculum change', p. 33). 111 DCU, *Strategy for the year 2000*, p. 11.

Modularization, the development of the AFI and the implementation of the Generation 21 initiative are key components in ongoing efforts to meet this commitment, first articulated in 1977 in the *Plan for the future of the Institute*, which has featured as a core objective in every subsequent strategic-planning exercise.

III

While NIHED/DCU has consistently pioneered new directions for third-level study since opening its doors in 1980, it has also introduced groundbreaking pedagogical techniques to enhance the educational experience. Such innovations have focused on the incorporation of practical work experience for under-graduates as a formal part of their education, and a determination to recognize and reward students' extracurricular activities and achievements, and to provide distance-education services as part of a broader strategy to facilitate greater access to higher education. This section examines the INTRA programme and the Uaneen module, as well as the establishment of the National Distance Education Centre.

INTRA – INtegrated TRAining

In a profile of NIHE Dublin published at the beginning of its 1983/4 academic year, the Institute was described as 'unashamedly sold on technology'.[112] While perhaps apt to give a misleading picture of much of the work within the faculties of Business and Professional Studies, and of Communications and Human Studies, both faculties were nonetheless intent on incorporating cutting-edge technology within their teaching and learning environments. Blending these ambitions with a determination to provide workplace-ready graduates necessitated the creation and maintenance of strong ties to the industrial and commercial sectors. One method of doing so was to ensure substantial representation from these sectors on governing body.[113] As noted above, curriculum design has traditionally incorporated close consultation with industrial and professional interests. However, the ability to train and educate undergraduates capable of meeting the changing demands of these sectors required more concerted and widespread levels of contact. Staff would be expected to play a role in these relationships, both through their research work and with the establishment of consultative committees combining staff and

112 Quote from newspaper article 'College for the Future' by Eleanor Petley, *c*.Sept. 1983. I have not been able to identify the newspaper, or the date of publication, from the clipping present in DCU's archive (DCUPO, 'NIHE Dublin: general, 2/2').   113 As outlined in formal government proposals for the establishment of NIHE Dublin. See chapter 2.

members of the private sector. The creation of an Industrial Liaison Unit (ILU) with a remit to co-ordinate these activities featured in early discussions on the structure of the Institute, and duly began operations in January 1981 when Dr Anthony Glynn took up the post of head of unit.[114]

In this area NIHE Dublin was following a well-established international trend, whereby universities had recognized the need to establish meaningful interactions with industry. Such units were generally tasked with – among other things – identifying the training and skills needs of industry, promoting co-operative research and education, attracting research funding, and providing public-relations services to advertise the expertise available to industry within the third-level sector.[115] The first industrial-liaison officer in Ireland was appointed at Trinity College Dublin in 1971 in partnership with the National Science Council. Two years later the Council established a scheme to fund similar initiatives at other higher-education institutions. By 1988 industrial-liaison officers, or equivalent positions, existed at TCD, UCD, NUI Galway, NUI Cork, NIHE Dublin, NIHE Limerick, the CDVEC and the regional technical colleges at Cork and Galway. The HEA also reported that it was considering additional methods to foster relations between industry and third-level education.[116]

In addition to performing the above functions and contributing to the development of content for degree programmes, the Industrial Liaison Unit was central to the creation and implementation of the Institute's inventive take on co-operative education. Pioneered in the first decade of the twentieth century, co-operative education provided academic credit for formal work experience completed during a degree. While work placements were quite common in professional and industrial environments and the concept of integrating work placements in higher education was long established internationally, co-operative education was first introduced to Ireland by NIHE Limerick in the early 1970s.[117] The system embraced a holistic approach to knowledge transfer by recognizing that learning took place outside of the university. For students, there was the obvious benefit of providing first-hand experience of the careers for

---

114 DCUPO, 'Industrial liaison, 1980–92'; NIHED, *An educational philosophy for the National Institute for Higher Education, Dublin* (Dublin, 1977), p. 11; NIHED, *Annual report, 1978–82*, pp 24, 35, 39. 115 HEDEL, 'Policy on higher education–industry interface', 1984 (DCUPO, 'Industrial liaison, 1980–92'). The Higher Education Directors of External Liaison (HEDEL) was a short-lived body, established by the various industrial liaison officers working within the Irish third-level sector. See also Dylan Jones-Evans, Magnus Klofsten, Ewa Andersson and Dipti Pandya, 'Creating a bridge between university and industry in small European countries: the role of the Industrial Liaison Office', *R&D Management*, 29:1 (1999), pp 47–56. 116 European Commission, *COMETT: the training needs of staff in the Community's higher education sector engaged in cooperation with industry* (Luxembourg, 1988), pp 32–48. 117 Fleming, *University of Limerick*, pp 132, 135–6; White, *Investing in people*, pp 74, 158; Yasushi Tanaka, *The economics of co-operative education* (New York, 2015), pp 7–19; *Inside Higher Ed*, 23 Mar. 2007.

which they were training. Theory and practice were closely integrated, providing clear links between work and study. For the university, the attractive qualities of individual responsibility and independence were cultivated among students. Employers stood to gain graduates who were well educated, highly skilled and comfortable in the workplace. Other anticipated benefits included the introduction of new ideas and methods to employers, as well as an opportunity to observe potential future employees and thus refine future recruitment strategies.[118]

The ILU looked to North America for guidance when creating a learning experience that would 'prepare college students for the hard realities of the business world'.[119] The name selected by the Institute for its iteration of co-operative education, INTRA (INtegrated TRAining), was chosen to emphasise the unique nature of NIHE Dublin's implementation, and to distinguish its programme from that of NIHE Limerick.[120] Traditionally, co-op programmes were run by dedicated educational units. By incorporating INTRA into its Industrial Liaison Unit, the Institute created a streamlined mode of contact with industry, commercial and professional entities, and government: 'This allowed us easy access into companies to cover a range of activities, not just INTRA. The ILU was the one-stop shop for [the Institute's contacts with] industry and business.'[121]

Working closely with academic council, the ILU fashioned an innovative element of the curriculum at an unpropitious time. INTRA was established at a time of serious economic hardship. Businesses were not necessarily open to the idea of providing work experience to students. Alongside its own efforts, the ILU was also able to rely on the Institute's staff to establish the necessary connections. Patricia Barker, lecturer in the School of Accounting and Finance, recalls the difficulties of doing so in the midst of a recession:

> We had to go out to employers and say, will you take these unknown quantities into your office, or into your workplace … It was extremely difficult. I can remember literally driving around the country, with my kids in the back of my car … ringing up people that I knew, or half knew, or knew somebody who knew … and saying can I meet with you? They were in a position where they had just laid off half their workforce, and the unions were up in arms. The idea of taking in somebody, and giving them even their expenses, was completely impossible for them.[122]

118 'A discussion paper on an educational philosophy …', pp 8–10 and appendix 3. Early planning for the Institute's educational philosophy noted that the use of the co-operative model by British polytechnic institutions had more than doubled between 1966 and 1972.   119 Anthony Glynn, 'Co-operative education (INTRA): an assessment', Jan. 1982 (DCUPO, 'Industrial liaison, 1980–92').   120 Danny O'Hare to Anthony Glynn, 23 May 1981 (DCUPO, 'Industrial liaison, 1980–92'); Anthony Glynn to author, 4 Mar. 2019.   121 Anthony Glynn to author, 4 Mar. 2019. 122 Patricia Barker interview, 20 Sept. 2018.

The INTRA programme placed its first students in 1981, when less than twenty participated. Within three years that figure had increased to 400, spurred not just by the rise in enrolments at the Institute, but also by a marked increase in connections between the Institute and the private sector. By the mid-1980s the overall placement rate of students on eligible degree programmes was 90 per cent, regarded as 'better than expected in such recessionary times'.[123] Placement numbers remained consistently high, with statistics for 1998 showing that 604 students had been placed with 260 companies, representing 99 per cent of eligible students. Average student earnings were £180 per week, with 7 per cent of students working overseas.[124] Some teething problems surfaced, including the reluctance of students to temporarily re-locate for their placement, the relative immaturity of students, as well as a lack of knowledge of basic workplace etiquette.[125] The workload of the ILU's staff was highlighted as excessive – during the 1982/3 academic year the unit dealt with almost 300 company contacts per week, to which could be added student and staff contacts, as well as standard administrative duties. In common with the Institute's other units and faculties, a lack of finance meant that the ILU suffered from spartan facilities. Just one word was used to describe the situation regarding the unit's telephone system in 1984: 'Crazy'.[126]

Despite these obstacles, the INTRA programme was quickly established as an integral part of the NIHE Dublin curriculum. Students were assessed via reports from their employers and the observations of staff tutors who conducted workplace visits. Placements were typically three to six months in duration, though from 1997 some programmes introduced year-long options.[127] As might be expected from a unit that initially included public relations in its portfolio, annual reports on the INTRA programme highlighted various successes.[128] Such positive reports were supported by annual reviews of the programme, which routinely noted employer-satisfaction rates of 90 per cent or higher. By the end of the 1990s, 95 per cent of participating companies were of the opinion that INTRA was beneficial to their operations.[129] Early reports also included details of participating businesses, which included Apple Computers in Cork, dairies in Rathfarnham, Dundalk and Drogheda, Coras Iompair Éireann, Bank of Ireland, Bord na Móna and numerous accountancy firms.

Feedback gathered via informal channels in the early years also painted a positive overall picture. Writing in 1987, Tom Mooney highlighted the

---

123 Industrial Liaison Unit report, 15 Nov. 1983 (DCUPO, 'Industrial liaison, 1980–92'). The report noted that the figure of 400 compared very favourably with NIHE Limerick, which had been running a similar programme for more than a decade. 124 DCU, *Annual report, 1997/8*, pp 61–2. 125 Industrial Liaison Unit report, 15 Nov. 1983 (DCUPO, 'Industrial liaison, 1980–92'). 126 Anthony Glynn, 'Industrial Liaison Unit: summary of position', Apr. 1984 (DCUPO, 'Industrial liaison, 1980–92'). 127 DCU, *Annual report, 1996/7*, p. 53. 128 NIHED/DCU, *Annual reports, 1980–98*. 129 DCU, *Annual report, 1997/8*, p. 61.

importance of INTRA to his children's education. Two had gone on to jobs as electronic engineers, and a third was then in the midst of his studies at the Institute:

> One of the course elements at NIHE, Dublin, which impressed me most was the opportunity your students get at their third-year stage to engage in a practical application of their education through the INTRA placement … Both of my working sons owe their positions in no small part to the impression they made during their INTRA placement.[130]

Employers also voiced their support for the programme, with Brian Reynolds, managing director of Microsoft Ireland, noting that the applied nature of DCU's courses ensured that it attracted the 'cream of young Irish students'. His views were shared by John Beatty, managing director of Raleigh Ireland, while the Institute for Industrial Research and Standards declared INTRA to be an 'essential ingredient' of DCU's undergraduate courses.[131] A report on the participation of communications studies undergraduates in January and February 1989 noted the diversity of their placements, including RTÉ, Bord Fáilte, Channel 4, the Irish Farmers' Association and the Arts Council: 'We have received several unsolicited calls from employers praising the high quality of our students and their commitment while on placement. A number of students have been offered jobs in the advertising and public relations areas as a result of the programme.'[132]

Perceptions of the INTRA programme among the student body were occasionally more nuanced. Their experiences often depended on the relevance of the placement to their field of study. In the early 1990s Emmet Ryan, a fourth-year business studies student, observed that '[O]verall the placement was good and worthwhile, as I got experience of working with people on a daily basis … but as for learning stuff related to the course, it was of no value.' Ryan's sentiments were echoed by Mark Sheridan, another fourth-year student: 'I think INTRA is very worthwhile if you have a relevant job but I wasn't all that impressed with my placement … [M]y employer was unhelpful and therefore I learned little.'[133] DCUSU opinion polls nonetheless revealed a largely positive take on the initiative. A study conducted in 2000 suggested that almost two-thirds of students who chose a degree in DCU as their first preference did so because of the INTRA programme.[134]

In addition to its educational functions, INTRA served as a valuable calling card for NIHED/DCU within the Irish commercial and industrial sectors. Graduate employment rates benefitted from the connections established during

---

130 Tom Mooney to Danny O'Hare, 5 Apr. 1987 (DCUPO, 'Correspondence: general, 1986–8'). 131 *DCU Bull Sheet*, Jan. 1992.   132 Paul McNamara to Farrel Corcoran, 14 Feb. 1989 (DCUPO, GB89/3).   133 *DCU Bull Sheet*, Jan. 1992.   134 *College View*, Mar. 2000.

placements, and INTRA also increased the level and regularity of interaction between the university and industry, which in turn generated research contracts. During the early 1990s the changing needs of the economy, the steady increase in student numbers at DCU and greater levels of competition from work-placement programmes at other third-level institutions increased pressure on DCU to alter its own approach. With an undergraduate population of close to 10,000 predicted by the year 2000, the INTRA programme was facing serious capacity issues.

One potential solution offered was to remove INTRA from some degrees. That option was, however, met with strenuous opposition from the university's leadership. The most promising avenue of catering to increased student numbers was to expand INTRA's international placements. While DCU sent between 8 per cent and 10 per cent of its placements abroad, UL had a significantly higher proportion of their placements overseas, and had recently appointed a full-time international placement manager:

> From our experience, particularly over the last two years, there will be problems with obtaining full INTRA placements over the coming years. This will be as a result of the present economic climate and the increase in student numbers ... Given that we are already locked into the present system for the next three years, the expansion of our international placement appears to be the path to be followed.[135]

Placement of students constituted a near perennial administrative challenge. On average, the creation of a single INTRA placement required contact with twelve companies, and dozens of communications from the private sector were processed daily.[136] Economic circumstances have also traditionally dictated the ease (or difficulty) of securing INTRA placements. At the turn of the millennium, biotechnology and journalism were the only two degree programmes experiencing difficulty in securing employment for all students. At the height of the Celtic Tiger economy, employers competed to attract the best candidates.[137] Yet following the relative economic prosperity of the 1990s and 2000s, the difficult economic climate that prevailed after 2008 saw placement difficulties resurface.[138]

In spite of these challenges, successive quality reviews of the university have repeatedly highlighted the INTRA programme as one of DCU's distinctive strengths.[139] As the university matured and expanded, the ILU was restructured

135 DCUPO, 'Industrial Liaison, 1980–92'. 136 DCUPO, AC89/9. 137 *College View*, Mar. 2000; DCU, *Quality assurance report, programme for administrative units, 2006–7* (Dublin, 2007), p. 22. 138 DCUPO, AC2012/2–5. 139 QQI, *Institutional Review Report 2019: DCU* (Dublin, 2019); Irish Universities Quality Board, *IRIU report*; EUA, *Institutional quality review of Dublin City University*.

and rebranded on numerous occasions.[140] Core duties such as responsibility for public relations, international affairs and fundraising were devolved to dedicated units. Rising student numbers during the 1990s eventually led to the transfer of INTRA administration to Student Services and Development, where it is currently handled by a dedicated team.[141] The legacy inherited and enhanced by the INTRA Office is considerable. During the late 1970s the Institute's planners showed considerable foresight in embracing the concept of co-operative education, then in its infancy in Ireland. Bestowing responsibility for its implementation on the ILU proved an inspired decision and provided the nascent institution with a superb means of establishing links with employers and potential research funders. INTRA remains an integral part of the under-graduate experience for the vast majority of DCU's students.[142]

Uaneen module

Some twenty years after the introduction of the INTRA programme, academic council once more sought ways to provide academic credit for student activities completed outside of lecture theatres and laboratories. On this occasion, however, the activities to be rewarded were of a very different nature to those undertaken on INTRA placement. Introduced to the curriculum in 2004, the Uaneen module enables students 'to demonstrate learning achieved through involvement in sporting, social and citizenship activities' and provides academic credit for their efforts.[143]

Methods of encouraging and promoting extracurricular activities among the student body had previously focused on supporting the Students' Union (DCUSU), student societies and sports clubs. In April 1999 the *College View*, produced by DCUSU, published an editorial calling for academic credit for society activities. Perhaps unaware of nascent discussions at academic council for the introduction of a similar scheme, the editorial dismissed its own proposal as fantasy due to the 'infinite number of assessment headaches it would cause'.[144] Planning for a mechanism to reward extracurricular activity actually began in earnest in 2000, initially driven by Prof. Patricia Barker, university registrar.[145]

140 DCUPO, 'Industrial Liaison/Intra/IIA/IBR/Invent'.   **141** DCU, *Quality assurance report, student support and development, 2012*, p. 12.   **142** Three-quarters of the degree programmes at DCU currently offer a work-placement option. Certain programmes (such as those incorporating nursing and education) operate schemes that are tailored specifically to the needs of those disciplines and are not part of the INTRA programme. The most recent strategic plan published by the university has committed to reviewing INTRA, with the intention of incorporating it into all degree programmes (*Talent, discovery and transformation: DCU strategic plan, 2017–22*, p. 20). **143** Unless otherwise noted, the following draws upon Jean Hughes and Una Redmond, 'Learning from life: the Uaneen experience at Dublin City University' in McIlrath et al. (eds), *Mapping civic engagement within higher education in Ireland* (2009), pp 116–23.   **144** *College View*, Oct. 1999. **145** *DCU News*, 6 Feb. 2004.

Introduced in its initial incarnation in spring 2001, Ferdinand von Prondzynski presented the university's first extracurricular awards before the 2001 graduation ball. Though yet to offer academic credit for participation and open only to those in the final year of their studies, more than 70 students received awards in that first year. The potential of the scheme was obvious, though participation dropped significantly the following year. In response, academic council convened a subcommittee on extracurricular awards in November 2002 to examine ways of promoting participation, which recommended a re-launch of the scheme and a formalization of its administrative duties. A partnership was subsequently formed with the Irish Business and Employers Confederation (Ibec). Following consultation with her family, the scheme was named in honour of Uaneen Fitzsimons, a television and radio presenter with RTÉ and graduate of DCU's communications studies degree, who had died in a car crash in November 2000.[146]

Further tweaks to the awards system were designed to widen its appeal to students. In what proved a significant step, in 2004 academic council approved the module awards (though on an additional credit basis), and inclusion of the module results on a student's academic transcript. Two years later council formally approved the module as an elective option for students entering the final year of their studies, thus opening up participation to any student enrolled on a degree programme with elective modules in its final year – provided that programme had the necessary academic structures in place.[147]

The creation of the Uaneen module saw DCU become the first university in Ireland to award academic credit for its students' extracurricular activities. Speaking in 2004, Prof. Barker outlined the rationale behind the module's creation:

> Employers are increasingly looking for graduates with experience and skills that set them apart from those with academic qualifications alone. Students who participate in sport, work with charitable organisations, play an active role in clubs and societies or in other Student Union activities, develop a range of valuable skills that are of benefit not just to employers but to society in its broader sense.[148]

Assessment of student participation in sporting, social and citizenship activities is enabled through the submission of a reflective-learning portfolio, a pedagogical tool far from widely incorporated at third level in the early 2000s, but now considered a core element of active-learning techniques. Students are also not restricted to completion of the module with activities or organizations

---

146 *Irish Times*, 25 Nov. 2000; *College View*, Nov. 2000; *Irish Independent*, 20 Apr. 2003. 147 DCUPO, AC2003/5, 6, AC2005/2–4, AC2006/3, 4, AC2007/3, 4; Patricia Barker to author, 4 Oct. 2017. 148 *DCU News*, 6 Feb. 2004.

directly linked with DCU: 'Care has been taken to avoid limiting the scope of activities which can be incorporated into the Uaneen Module, because it is believed that all extracurricular activity enables the development of a variety of skills which complement those developed through formal learning.'[149] Since the redesign and relaunch of the module for the 2003/4 academic year, more than 1,000 students have participated.[150] Significantly, since the launch of the module there is a high correlation between completion of the Uaneen module and receipt of the university's Chancellor's Medal – awarded to students who have achieved excellence in both their academic and extracurricular activities.[151]

Distance education

The provision of adult and continuing education has long been a core feature of the curriculum at NIHE Dublin/DCU. Its roots lay in the publication of the 1973 Murphy Report on adult education.[152] The establishment of the Open University in 1969 had brought with it a new era of respectability and sophistication in distance education, and provided a base model for NIHE Dublin's initiative.[153] As a means of providing continuing education for professionals, improving the social and geographic accessibility of the Institute's courses and promoting the concept of lifelong learning, distance education featured in governing body's plans from an early stage. Though the definition of distance learning, and the methodology of its delivery, has dramatically altered over the past four decades, the Institute's original vision called for an educational system where the learner and teacher were separated by time and space for the majority of the study period, with teaching mediated through correspondence and audio-visual media.[154] The 1977 *Plan for the future of the Institute* touched briefly on the topic, noting that a distance-education unit had the potential to be of 'major service to the nation', particularly by providing learning packages tailored to the needs of different sectors of society. Co-operation with other third-level institutions was also anticipated, to facilitate the establishment of a tutorial system on other campuses, and by providing localized access to libraries, computer facilities and laboratories.[155]

---

149 Hughes and Redmond, 'Learning from life', p. 119. 150 Statistics provided by DCU Quality Promotion Office, with additional information obtained from published reports on Uaneen module graduations (https://www.dcu.ie/uaneen/receptions.shtml, accessed 12 Apr. 2019). 151 For the Chancellor's Medal, see appendix 5. 152 Kay MacKeogh, 'Encouraging distance education? An analysis of EU policy on distance education, 1957–2004' (PhD, NUI Maynooth, 2005), pp 44–5. Unless otherwise noted, the following information on distance education relies on MacKeogh's thesis, and Chris Curran, 'Co-operative networks in higher distance teaching' in Urban Dahllof and Staffan Selander (eds), *New universities and regional context* (Uppsala, 1994), pp 161–76. 153 Jennifer Sumner, 'Serving the system: a critical history of distance education', *Open Learning*, 15:3 (2000), p. 276. 154 NIHED, *Distance education: an international review and directions for development* (Dublin, [1982]), p 2. 155 NIHED, *Plan for the future of the Institute*, pp 95–6.

A more detailed report was completed in 1979, which firmly recommended the addition of distance education to the Institute's activities on the basis that it would mark an innovative step in terms of Irish higher education, while also allowing the Institute to disseminate skills, knowledge and academic qualifications in a convenient and cost effective manner.[156] John Wilson, minister for education, announced the creation of NIHE Dublin's distance-education unit in May 1981. Its brief was to 'deliver qualifications through distance education to adult students throughout Ireland, in co-operation with the universities and other third-level institutions' – thus distinguishing Ireland from several other European countries that had adopted a single-institution model.[157] Collaboration with RTÉ and the Open University's Belfast team was anticipated, with two pilot programmes scheduled to begin the following year.[158] Implementation of these pilots was, however, slightly slower than anticipated. Chris Curran was appointed as head of the Distance Education Centre in February 1982, with a lecturer and secretary making up the remaining staff.[159] A single pilot programme on computer programming enrolled 600 students later that year, largely with the intention of testing key elements of a national system, including student administration, course materials, tutorial support, the study-centre network and, most importantly, potential demand.[160] A variety of media were also employed during the pilot, including the broadcast of six television programmes by RTÉ.[161] Discussions with the newly established ACOT, a national advisory and training body for the agriculture sector, took place concurrently, with the intention of introducing a distance-education programme in agriculture in 1983.[162]

Despite the appointment of Curran and his staff, and the strong support of government for the distance-education initiative, there was no budget to cover administrative costs or to purchase some of the most fundamental equipment required – computers. Drawing inspiration from the Institute's founding principles of engagement with industry, O'Hare delegated to Tony Glynn and Peter McKenna the task of sourcing commercial sponsorship for equipment.[163] Using his contacts in Apple, Glynn arranged a meeting with Steve Jobs in Jury's Hotel, Cork, during which Jobs agreed to donate 120 Apple IIe computers to the Institute. Working closely with Curran, Glynn and O'Hare later met senior executives at Guinness Ireland and secured a gift of £100,000 to cover the centre's administrative costs.[164] When seeking further donations from Guinness

156 Ibid.; NIHED, *Annual report, 1978–82*, p. 29.   **157** MacKeogh, 'Encouraging distance education?', pp 45, 195 (quotation on p. 195).   **158** *Irish Times*, 14 May 1981.   **159** NIHED, *Annual report, 1978–82*, p. 29.   **160** *Irish Times*, 8 Oct. 1982.   **161** Chris Curran to author, 7 Sept. 2018. RTÉ broadcast the first programme, titled 'Distance education: an introduction', on 6 and 9 October (*Irish Times*, 6 and 9 Oct. 1982).   **162** NIHED, *Annual report, 1978–82*, p. 29.   **163** Peter McKenna was the Institute's Head of the School of Curriculum Development. Following that School's dissolution, he was appointed as director of special projects at DCU, and later joined Eolas as Director of its Collaborative Research Centre.   **164** Anthony Glynn to author, 6 Nov. 2018; *Irish*

a decade later, Dorothy Barry recalled the importance of the company's previous support: 'What is clear to us all is that the Guinness donation made over ten years ago which facilitated the development of the National Distance Education Centre was truly a transforming gift.'[165]

Initial progress was promising, even if the rollout of the pilot projects was slightly slower than anticipated.[166] Yet their potential was clear. More than 7,000 applications had been received by the end of 1983, and 1,520 students enrolled.[167] This was swiftly followed by the government's mention of the Distance Education Centre in its *Programme for action in education, 1984–7*. Alert to the success of the unit's pilot programme, the government publicized its plans to extend the programme on a modular basis.[168] In June 1985 the Department of Education formally requested that the Institute establish the National Distance Education Council, with the intention of introducing a national, co-operative distance-education programme.[169] Membership of the council was drawn from a variety of stakeholders across higher-education, the private sector and the public sector. The minister for education, Gemma Hussey, addressed the first meeting of the Council, held at the Institute on 24 September 1985.[170] Noting that the Distance Education Centre had just completed the first phase of its pilot programme, involving thirty-three separate study centres, more than 2,400 students and the close co-operation of RTÉ, Hussey committed her Department to a further £226,000 in financial support for the second phase.[171] Within just a few short years the renamed National Distance Education Centre had become

Times, 14 June 1982; NIHED, *Annual report, 1982/3*, p. 6; speech by Gemma Hussey at NIHED, 24 Sept. 1985 (DCUPO, 'Department of Education, 1981–6'). Verbatim and Amdahl were also among the companies that provided logistical and financial support.   **165** Dorothy Barry to Patrick Barry, 14 June 1993 (DCUPO, 'DCUET Proposals/Approaches, 1989–94'). Dorothy Barry was chief executive officer of DCU Educational Trust.   **166** *Irish Times*, 19 Dec. 1984.   **167** DCUPO, GB83/10, GB84/1; *Nuacht*, Jan. 1984; NIHED, *Annual report, 1982/3*, pp 35–6.   **168** Department of Education, *Programme for Action in Education, 1984–7* (Dublin, 1984), section 2.17.   **169** Department of Education to Danny O'Hare, 28 June 1985 (DCUPO, 'Department of Education, 1981–6'); DCUPO, GB85/6; *Nuacht*, July and Oct. 1985; NIHED, *Annual report, 1984/5*, p. 36; Bradley, '*Twigs for an eagle's nest*', p. 48.   **170** Membership of the first National Distance Education Council, as listed in NIHED, *Annual report, 1985/6*, pp 177–8: A. Munnelly (Arts Council); R. Griffin (RTC Waterford); W. Fitzsimons (RTC Letterkenny); M. Ó Murchú (Bord na Gaeilge); L. Connellan (Confederation of Irish Industry); D. O'Connor (Council for Development in Agriculture (ACOT)); B. Meehan (Department of Education); K. Warner (Department of Justice); P. Cullinane (Department of Labour); M. O'Donnell (DIT); Prof. R. O'Connor (ESRI); John Hayden (HEA); L. Heffernan (Holy Child Community School, Sallynoggin); W. Brosnan (IDA); Dr A. O'Reilly (Industrial Training Authority (AnCO)); M. O'Halloran (ICTU); L. Kavanagh (Irish Vocational Education Association); T. Collins (Aontas); Dr V. O'Gorman (National Board for Science and Technology); P. MacDiarmada (NCEA); Chris Curran (NIHED); Dr Danny O'Hare (NIHED); P. Colgan (NIHEL); Dr Michael Gilheany (NUI); V. Finn (RTÉ); C. Duignan (RTÉ); P. Lynam (Regional Management Centre, Limerick); Dr P. Carr (St Patrick's College, Maynooth); C. Sugrue (St Patrick's College, Drumcondra); Prof. J. Scattergood (TCD); Dr M. Mortell (UCC); Dr John Kelly (UCD); and S. Ó Cathail (UCG).   **171** Speech by Gemma Hussey at NIHED, 24 Sept. 1985 (DCUPO, 'Department of Education, 1981–6').

5.6 Minister for Education Gemma Hussey with (l–r): John Hayden (HEA),
Chris Curran and Danny O'Hare at the inauguration of the National Distance
Education Council on 24 September 1985 (DCU Collection).

'the central hub of a national network of co-operating universities and regional
colleges, with a dedicated budget from the HEA'.[172]

Building upon the experience gained over the course of its pilot studies, the
NDEC launched its first degree and diploma programmes in information
technology in October 1986.[173] The multitude of partner organizations involved
in the delivery of the programmes illustrates the extent to which the Centre used
its base at NIHED/DCU to build a national co-operative model for distance
education. Membership of the programme team was drawn from TCD, UCD,
UCC, the University of Ulster, DIT, RTC Dundalk, RTC Sligo, RTÉ and the
Irish Sugar Company, as well as staff from DCU and the NDEC. Study centres,
which allowed students to attend tutorials and practical study sessions, were
hosted by DCU, UCC, UL and the RTCs at Letterkenny, Dundalk, Sligo and
Waterford.[174]

172 Chris Curran to author, 7 Sept. 2018. See also NIHED/DCU, *Annual reports, 1986–98.*
Funding for the centre came from the HEA (*c*.30% of its annual budget), student fees and project
income (MacKeogh, 'Encouraging distance education?', p. 195).   **173** NIHED, *Annual report,
1986/7*, p. 48; MacKeogh, 'Encouraging distance education?', p. 195.   **174** The programme's

The Centre's method of programme development mirrored the principles of close co-operation with industry and professional bodies that had been fostered at NIHED/DCU. Working with the Institute of Chartered Accountants in Ireland during the late 1980s, the NDEC created a course in microcomputers and accounting, completion of which was necessary for qualification as a chartered accountant. The twenty-week course included an introduction to information technology, database and accounting software, microcomputers, financial modelling and spreadsheet creation.[175] Formally launched by Minister for Education Mary O'Rourke in February 1989, by the end of the following year 2,063 students had registered for the course.[176] That year also saw the Centre enter into an innovative collaboration with RTÉ to deliver the EuroPACE programme of continuing education in the fields of software engineering, telecommunications, microelectronics, technology management and advanced manufacturing technologies. EuroPACE created content designed by leading figures from across the European industrial and university sectors, disseminated via satellite transmission and broadcast on RTÉ's television network (on Monday, Wednesday and Friday mornings). The NDEC provided the necessary supporting infrastructure.[177] Further course innovation during the early 1990s saw the launch of Ireland's first humanities degree by distance education, with more than 500 students registered in October of that year. Co-ordinated from the NDCE, the programme was developed and administered in conjunction with St Patrick's College, Maynooth, TCD, UCC, UCD, NUI Galway and UL. Modules in literature, philosophy, psychology and sociology were initially offered, with plans to introduce further modules in history, economics and politics. The launch of the degree marked a major milestone in the Centre's development and was exceptional in that it was accredited by six universities, 'from any one of which students could receive their degree'.[178]

In addition to its contributions to the curriculum and educational ethos of the Institute, the NDEC also made its mark in establishing the Institute's reputation. Following a luncheon meeting with the Institute's senior staff, John Wilson, former minister for education and then minister for tourism and transport, praised the Centre's development: 'As you know, it is an aspect of the

academic subject leaders were Prof. H. Harrison (UCD), Dr S. Laverty (University of Ulster), A. Mulally (Irish Sugar Company) and Prof. M. Taylor (UCC) (DCU, *Annual report, 1989/90*, p. 19). **175** The software to be used was Pegasus Integrated Accounting; dBASE III; and Open Access Spreadsheet (DCUPO, GB89/2). **176** NIHED, *Annual report, 1986/7*, p. 50; DCU, *Annual report, 1988/9*, p. 18; DCU, *Annual report, 1989/90*, p. 19; *Irish Times*, 17 Feb. 1989. **177** DCUPO, GB89/6, 7. The EuroPACE programme was modelled on similar initiatives in the United States of America, but proved largely unworkable in Europe due to the high cost of international telecommunications. The programme was abandoned in 1993. See MacKeogh, 'Encouraging distance education?', p. 157. **178** Chris Curran to author, 29 Aug. 2018; DCU, *Annual report, 1993/4*, p. 9 and *appendix*, p. 34; *Irish Times*, 1 June 1993; Curran, 'Co-operative networks in higher distance teaching', pp 172–3.

Institute's work in which I am very interested. I was delighted to hear of the success of the Unit's work. It is heartening to hear of the large numbers availing of the degree programme. I must say that I was both surprised and pleased to learn that we in Ireland are at the leading edge of distance education in the new information technology ... Chris and his team deserve our congratulations for their excellent work.'[179]

The importance of the NDEC to the university was reflected in the granting of faculty status in November 1989, a move designed to clarify the centre's position within the university.[180] In the decade that followed the NDEC entered into a number of formal collaborations with similar institutions, including the Open University, and developed innovative degree programmes in nursing and the humanities in addition to its suite of diploma, certificate and degree courses in various aspects of information technology.[181] Participation in European Community programmes such as COMETT and DELTA allowed the centre to develop closer links with other European distance-teaching institutions.[182] Taking note of distance education in its white paper on adult education, published in 2000, the Department of Education observed that its contribution to the third-level sector, and its potential for greater impact, were not fully appreciated. At the turn of the millennium some 7,000 students were enrolled in distance-education programmes, primarily through the Open University and the National Distance Education Centre (then known as Oscail).[183] Numbers enrolled with NDEC/Oscail had increased from 940 in 1988 to 2,806 in 1997, a growth of 198 per cent in less than a decade.[184]

In an effort better to reflect DCU's embrace of new platforms for the dissemination of online learning material, in 2004 Oscail dropped National Distance Education Centre from its title in favour of DCU Online Education. Nine years later a further restructuring saw Oscail integrated into the new National Institute for Digital Learning (NIDL). Incorporating new online teaching platforms (Loop and DCU Connected) and the university's pedagogical research centre (the Teaching Enhancement Unit), the NIDL represented the next step in the university's attempts to create and provide new approaches to online, distance education and blended learning.[185] The Institute's director, Prof. Mark Brown, was appointed as the first chair of digital learning in Ireland.[186] The completion of a strategic partnership with FutureLearn, an

179 John Wilson to Danny O'Hare, 31 Mar. 1988 (DCUPO, Correspondence: general, 1986–8). 180 DCUPO, GB89/9, 10; *Nuacht*, Nov. 1989. 181 DCU, *Annual reports, 1989–98*. 182 DCU, *Annual report, 1989/90*, p. 19. 183 Department of Education and Skills, *Learning for Life: White Paper on Adult Education* (Dublin, 2000), p. 75. 184 Ibid., p. 144. MacKeogh provides alternative figures for enrolments at NDEC/Oscail over a seventeen-year period: 1987 (290), 1990 (3,500), 1994 (2,911), 1997/8 (3,651), 2004 (3,000) (MacKeogh, 'Encouraging distance education?', p. 78). 185 DCUPO, GA2013/6, 7; *DCU News*, 28 Nov. 2013; DCU, *President's report, 2013/14*, pp 3, 19 and 30. 186 DCU, *President's report, 2013–14*, p. 19; *Irish Times*, 9 Dec. 2013, 7 Aug. 2014.

online education platform, later allowed for the introduction in January 2018 of 'Irish 101', the first massive open online course (MOOC) offered by DCU.[187]

Given the dramatic evolution of DCU's distance-education unit over four decades, it is easy to overlook its significant achievement in establishing distance education as a viable alternative to traditional models of higher-education delivery. With limited resources, Chris Curran and the staff of the NDEC pioneered an innovative, cost-effective model for the delivery of educational programmes of comparable quality to on-campus courses. Moreover, the work of the NDEC/Oscail over the course of the 1980s, 1990s and beyond proved internationally influential, helping to shape European policy on distance learning.[188]

IV

The case studies presented above offer insight into the overall direction of curriculum development and focus at NIHED/DCU over four decades, yet do not fully capture the many innovations that have refined and broadened the university's educational focus. While many of these innovations focused on the university's core strengths in STEM education and collaborations with industry, languages and the humanities were also prominent. The completion of the Incorporation process in 2016 added a suite of traditional arts subjects to its curriculum, an eventuality cautiously welcomed in the 1977 *Plan for the future of the Institute*: 'Technological institutes frequently have faculties of the Humanities, Fine Art and Social Studies … and university institutes contain technologically-based faculties. Neither combination can be criticized, in principle.'[189] The status of the Irish language within the university was also transformed with the establishment in 1993 of Fiontar, which aimed to promote the Irish language through an innovative, interdisciplinary programme of teaching and research, with a focus on the intersection of the Irish language with entrepreneurship and technological advancement.[190]

187 FutureLearn is a subsidiary of the Open University. In September 2018 the university became a global strategic partner of FutureLearn, leading to a grant of €1.4m from the HEA's Innovation and Transformation Fund for the implementation of teaching and learning initiatives and projects through the partnership. By the end of 2019 more than 40,000 learners had registered for a DCU course through the FutureLearn platform (DCU, *Annual institutional quality assurance report, 2019*, p. 16; QQI, *Institutional review report 2019: DCU* (2019), p. 34; *Irish Times*, 1 Feb. 2018). 188 MacKeogh, 'Encouraging distance education?', pp 81–109.   189 NIHED, *Plan for the future of the Institute*, p. 37.   190 Within a year of Fiontar's establishment, DCU had introduced its BSc in airgeadas, ríomhaireacht agus fiontraíocht (finance, computing and enterprise), thus becoming the only university in Ireland to teach a primary degree through the Irish language (excluding courses on the language itself). The MSc i ngnó & i dteicneolaíocht an eolais (business and information technology) was introduced in 2000. Among Fiontar and Scoil na Gaeilge's key achievements has been the development of a computing terminology for Irish, ensuring that the

5.7 Minister for Education Niamh Bhreathnach at the launch in 1993 of Fiontar, DCU's centre for teaching and research through the medium of Irish. Also pictured are (l–r): Danny O'Hare, D.J. McCullough, Finbarr Bradley and Micheál Ó Muircheartaigh (DCU Collection).

As a new entrant to the higher-education sector in the late 1970s, NIHE Dublin enjoyed the advantage of adaptability and flexibility in the creation and evolution of its curriculum. Initial course developments in STEM education were dictated by the identification of industry needs. Gaps in the human sciences and applied humanities were also identified, allowing for the development of courses in new and innovative fields, including applied languages and communication studies. When coupled with a relentless and continuing drive to establish meaningful connections with the industries and professions within which its graduates would work, such perceptive readings of current and future educational needs allowed NIHED/DCU to develop its reputation as an innovator in practical education. Over the past four decades the university's curriculum has evolved in a manner that is, in some ways, in marked distinction to the vision laid down by NIHE Dublin's governors and planners in the late 1970s and early 1980s. Economies of scale have meant that as the

language keeps pace with modern technology. It has also been at the forefront of recent efforts to preserve the Irish language and its heritage, particularly in the area of digital humanities. See logainm.ie, ainm.ie and dúchas.ie (Caoilfhionn Nic Pháidín, 'University education through Irish: place or space?' in Caoilfhionn Nic Pháidín and Donla uí Bhraonáin (eag.), *University education in Irish: challenges and perspectives* (Dublin, 2004), pp 77, 85; DCU, *Annual report, 1993/4*; DCU, *Annual report, 2000/1; Irish Times*, 17 Apr. 2001).

university has grown and the broader educational landscape has changed, the freedom of individual staff members to experiment with degree-programme creation has waned.[191] Nonetheless, the core ambitions of providing courses of relevance to industry and the business world, and of preparing students for the workplace, remain intact. Linkage agreements with other third-level colleges and the eventual completion of the Incorporation process have seen significant additions in the fields of teacher-training and humanities, building upon the original 'applied humanities' model that existed in the 1980s, as well as the tradition of educational innovation embodied in the INTRA programme and the Uaneen module. While outlining the government's vision for the type of education that NIHE Dublin would provide, minister for education John Wilson spoke of the need to guard against 'academic drift'. Such a restrictive approach to the development of NIHED/DCU's educational platform was, rightfully, rejected from an early stage. Variety and flexibility in curriculum development were, in fact, embedded in the university's very first strategic plan, which called for a curriculum that could develop in whatever manner was necessary to produce suitably qualified graduates.[192] Published in 1977, that planning document articulated the simple philosophy that any attempt to adhere to a rigid curriculum would be foolhardy: 'We must also accept from the outset that it is very likely that our philosophy and projections arising therefrom will be wrong, particularly if we speak of 20/25 years in the future. Consequently, the notion of a structured flexibility must be inherent in the planning approach.'[193] Over the past four decades, the university's adherence to the principle of structured flexibility has allowed it to grow in ways both unforeseen and necessary.

191 Brian Trench interview, 9 May 2019.   192 NIHED, *Plan for the future of the Institute*, pp 36–7. 193 'An educational philosophy for the National Institute for Higher Education, Dublin', Aug. 1977 (DCUPO, 'Governing body – reports and working papers, 1975–9').

6

Building a university, 1980–2019

When asked to report on proposals for a new higher-education institution at Ballymun, on the old Albert Agricultural College site, the Higher Education Authority concluded that there were compelling grounds for government support. Steady population growth was predicted for the north-west of the county, and there was also a need to redress the concentration of third-level institutions south of the River Liffey. Sites in the city centre were also considered, in terms of their ability to satisfy immediate needs and future projections of demand for student places. From a long-term perspective, however, the city centre was largely unsuitable. Any new institution would need to be located on a site that allowed for future growth and expansion:

> In view of the extent to which in other institutions of higher education demand for student places has far exceeded the accommodation available therein, it would be prudent to ensure that a central site should be large enough to allow for expansion of buildings and facilities well in excess of those recommended for the current decade.[1]

These were prescient words for, despite the decision to locate NIHE Dublin on what appeared to be an ample, 50-acre greenfield site, within two decades the campus was straining to accommodate a rapidly expanding university.[2] The construction boom that occurred on campus during the 1990s marked a considerable improvement in the fortunes of NIHED/DCU, which had seen its building plans repeatedly delayed by the constrained public finances of the 1980s. Those financial considerations played a major role in shaping the campus-development plans drafted in the 1980s by renowned architect Arthur Gibney – plans that continued to inform the university's master planning during the following decade and, indeed, to the present day.

The physical development of NIHED/DCU's Glasnevin campus has been driven by a flexible, modular approach to the expansion of teaching, research and student facilities as the institution has adapted to fluctuating levels of capital investment. Early planning for a rapid expansion of NIHE Dublin's student capacity and research facilities was guided by a development framework published in 1978. Implementation of the framework's goals proved next to

---

1 HEA, *Report on the Ballymun project* (Dublin, 1972), p. 55.   2 See chapter 2 for the selection of the Albert College site as a home for NIHE Dublin.

impossible during the straitened economic circumstances of the 1980s, leading to increasing pressures of space on staff and students. The Institute's fortunes dramatically improved during the 1990s, with the piecemeal, meagre expansion that characterized the preceding decade replaced by a programme of rapid construction that saw the campus building footprint quintupled by the end of the millennium. Several signature projects envisaged in 1978 were completed during this time, following almost two decades of tortuous fundraising, including the sports centre and the Helix. Such was the pace of construction that the Glasnevin campus rapidly approached saturation point in terms of its ability to accommodate new buildings, necessitating several strategic land purchases that were vital to allow the university's continued growth.

I

Among the many tasks facing governing body following its appointment in March 1975 was to predict the infrastructural needs of the Institute during its first decade. Building a campus to accommodate a student population expected to reach 5,000 by 1991, as well as the research needs of staff, required careful statistical modelling – a resource in short supply during the mid-1970s. Perhaps unwisely, the Institute's planners framed their intended building programme within parameters set by the British Department of Education and Science, which decreed that a gradual rise in student population should be 'exactly matched by expansion of the physical facilities needed to house them':

> In practice, an institution's stock of accommodation can only increase in a series of steps, as new building projects are completed. These completions cannot always coincide with the rise in student numbers … Some imbalance is inevitable, but the desirable aim is clearly that the opening of new courses and the taking into use of new accommodation should be kept in step.[3]

The planning committee also operated under the impression that, while the demand for third-level places in Dublin would increase by at least 10,000 over the course of the 1980s, there would be several other higher-education institutions established to cater for the demand. That much was implicit in a presentation made by the Institute's staff to members of the Oireachtas in June 1980. Following that presentation, Senator Noel Mulcahy welcomed the establishment of NIHE Dublin but warned that greater capacity was needed in the region:

---

3 DCUPO, 'Governing body – reports and working papers, 1975–9'; NIHED, *Plan for the physical development of the Institute*, p. 9. The British Department of Education and Science's development parameters had been defined in 1972.

The new institute in Dublin is not sufficient. We all know that some four regional technical colleges spread around the developing areas of the city will be required. I am looking forward to a healthy network of education in the applied area of technology, of business and communications operating throughout Dublin, with NIHE Dublin as its peak and the regional technical colleges there side by side working in a collaborative stance.[4]

Governing body thus proposed to cap the Institute's undergraduate enrolment at 5,000 in total.[5] In what turned out to be a wildly optimistic assumption, plans for the Institute's expansion during its first decade were predicated on the basis that it was 'reasonable and acceptable to propose that new buildings can be provided each two years to 1988'.[6] By the end of the 1980s it was anticipated that the Institute's buildings would encompass an area totalling 76,120 sq.m. At almost half of the anticipated requirement, teaching space easily counted as the largest allocation. Other key space requirements included the library (7,500 sq.m.), computer facilities (2,800 sq.m.), central administration (3,525 sq.m.) and communal/social areas (3,500 sq.m.). Research space accounted for 3,440 sq.m., assuming the presence of 200 research-active staff and 132 postgraduate students in the sciences and engineering. The Institute's planners discounted any requirement for dedicated research space for staff working in other disciplines, anticipating that their needs would be adequately served by the library, computer services and their individual offices.[7] The cost of providing the Institute with its required space in a five-stage, biennial process was estimated at £33.5m.[8]

As outlined in chapter 2, while the Institute's governors were investigating potential sites for its campus, the Department of Education had quietly progressed its own plans for the Ballymun site. The Department's buildings unit presented a draft development plan to Minister Richard Burke in June 1976, prepared by Philip Doyle, its senior architect.[9] Doyle's design envisaged the construction of six four-storey structures, on either side of a covered pedestrian

4 *Seanad Debates*, 26 June 1980. See also NIHED, *Plan for the physical development of the Institute*, p. 11.   5 While that figure now appears to be conservative, governing body's information in terms of population growth and projected demand for third-level places came from cutting-edge, commissioned research, as well as statistical analyses supplied by the HEA and Dublin Corporation (DCUPO, 'Governing body – reports and working papers, 1975–9'; NIHED, *Plan for the physical development of the Institute*, p. 11; NIHED, *Plan for the future of the Institute*, pp 12–35; Danny O'Hare interview, 28 May 2018; John Hayden interview, 1 Jan. 2010). The HEA's first commissioned study of educational trends and predicted demand in the capital city was published in 1979 (Patrick Clancy and Ciaran Benson, *Higher education in Dublin: a study of some emerging needs* (Dublin, 1979)).   6 NIHED, *Plan for the physical development of the Institute*, p. 12.   7 DCUPO, 'Governing body – reports and working papers, 1975–9'; NIHED, *Plan for the physical development of the Institute*, pp 23–40.   8 NIHED, *Plan for the physical development of the Institute*, pp 12–19.   9 This plan was sent to governing body in June 1976 (DCUPO, 'Governing body – reports and working papers, 1975–9'; NIHED, *Annual report, 1975–8*, p. 14).

6.1 Construction of the Restaurant and Henry Grattan buildings was completed in
1981 (DCU Collection).

arcade and located to the east of the original Albert College building. The
engineering faculty and library would be located on the south side of the arcade,
with separate buildings for commerce and architecture/surveying located to the
north.[10] Two further buildings were also envisaged on the north side, to
accommodate the Institute's growth. The Albert College building would be
connected to the new campus by means of the arcade, and would accommodate
catering facilities and administrative offices. A sports hall and associated hard-
surface playing areas were to be located to the south of Albert College (in space
currently occupied by Tennis Ireland). Roughly half of the site would be retained
for playing fields, with parking spaces provided for almost 1,300 cars.[11] While
Doyle's plan bore little resemblance to the development framework later
approved by the Institute's governing body, it is striking in a number of respects,
not least the proposal to build to a height of four storeys. Had that original
concept been maintained, later constraints on DCU's expansion would have

10 Doyle's plan situated the library in roughly the same location as the present Hamilton building
and Interfaith centre, while the student centre and sports complex occupy the space originally
earmarked for engineering. To the north of the arcade, a large commerce building was envisaged in
the space now taken by the Henry Grattan building and the Helix, with the space reserved for
architecture/surveying currently occupied by the Dublin Business School, McNulty building and
Terence Larkin theatre. Pedestrian and vehicular entrances were to be located on Collins Avenue
Extension, in almost their precise current locations.   11 Department of Education, NIHE Dublin

been somewhat ameliorated. Doyle's visualization of a covered pedestrian arcade connecting the campus may also have influenced the development master plan later created by the Institute's architect, Arthur Gibney, in 1985.

In May 1978 the government approved a plan for the physical development of the Institute in three separate phases, with Phase 1 consisting of the refurbishment of Albert College and the construction of a restaurant and new building with capacity for 800 students. The projected cost of the three phases was put at £11.5m and represented a significant downgrading of governing body's development ambitions. A sum of £1.1m was considered necessary to complete the first phase, with approximately one-quarter of this initial outlay to be provided via a World Bank loan.[12] Though work did not begin until the end of 1979/beginning of 1980, refurbishment of Albert College was completed in time for the commencement of the Institute's first academic year in November 1980, at a cost of *c.*£250,000.[13] With completion of Phase 1 due in time for the beginning of the 1981/2 academic year, the Institute appeared set to achieve its target of providing places for 5,000 students within a decade.

II

Construction of the restaurant and a new teaching/research building was completed by the summer of 1981, at a cost of *c.*£2.5m.[14] Total floor space stood at approximately 14,000 sq.m. (see table 6.1), allowing for a new cohort of 401 undergraduates to enrol in September 1981.[15] The expansionary momentum provided by the new buildings was, however, fleeting. Plans to increase student capacity to approximately 3,000 places within three years were submitted to the HEA in January 1981. The HEA's response was conservative, warning that the Institute's goals were not feasible due to their projected capital cost, as well as the cost of providing the necessary extra staff: 'The Authority considers that the target should be 2,000 extra places by 1990/1 and believes this figure to be in accordance with the intention expressed in the White Paper on Education.' The Institute was also advised that this expansion should be accomplished in two discrete phases that would each increase capacity by 1,000 places.[16]

Coming so early in its existence, this news represented a considerable setback and a sharp alteration of government policy. Speaking in the Dáil just three months previously, the minister for education, John Wilson, had mapped out the Institute's immediate future: 'The next phase of buildings will concentrate

draft development plan, June 1976 (Brian Trench Papers). **12** Department of Education memo, 10 May 1978 (NAI, 2007/50/72, 2008/148/523); NIHED, *Annual report, 1975–8*, p. 14. **13** *Dáil Debates*, 20 Feb. 1980. **14** HEA, *General report, 1974–84* (Dublin, 1985), p. 50. **15** For statistics related to student enrolment, see appendix 6. **16** J.F. Dukes to Danny O'Hare, 10 Feb. 1981 (DCUPO, 'NIHE Dublin: physical matters, 1978–86, 1/2'). The government presented its white paper on educational development to both houses of the Oireachtas in December 1980.

heavily on the provision of places for technology – science and engineering – and will provide 2,700 places.'[17] Yet the potential for the public finances to undermine Wilson's promises was soon apparent. Just six weeks after this statement was made, the HEA began preparing the ground for bad news by intimating that Wilson's figure of 2,700 might not be attainable.[18] Undeterred, governing body had appointed a design team for Phase 2 by April 1982, consisting of Ove Arup & Partners, J.A. Kenny & Partners, and Healy Kelly & Partners. The reality of the financial constraints under which the Institute operated, as well as the refusal of the HEA to sanction any financial outlay for development works, ensured that it was not until early 1985 that the next additions were made to the campus. Moreover, ambitions had been scaled back considerably, with Phase 2 now due to be completed in two stages.[19]

In the meantime, frustrations at the slow pace of development and the Institute's inability to progress its building programme had led to the loss of the Institute's original architects, Robinson, Keefe & Devane, who had been engaged to oversee the completion of Phase 1. The core issue was that the Institute was wholly reliant on government funding and approval. There were, at the outset, four different stakeholders involved in the Institute's planning process: the HEA, the Department of Education, the Institute and the Institute's architects. Under the terms of its establishing legislation, the formal approval of the minister for education and HEA were required for the development of the Institute's land and buildings.[20] This was an arrangement destined to lead to conflict, with the Department's building unit retaining ultimate authority over the Institute's developmental and architectural plans. Delays in the beginning of Phase 1, coupled with the building unit's modifications to the design and fitting-out of the new teaching/research building, prompted an exasperated response from Andrew Devane.[21] Referring to his 'dreadful' experience with the Department, Devane advised Danny O'Hare to adopt two approaches to future development: 1) to find a way to ensure NIHE Dublin fully controlled its own building programme; and 2) to employ an architectural firm to draw up a comprehensive master plan for the Institute's physical development. Devane was unsparing in his criticism of the Department of Education:

17 *Dáil Debates*, 29 Oct. 1980.　18 DCUPO, GB82/1.　19 DCUPO, GB82/2, 3 and GB85/3, 4; Danny O'Hare to John Hayden, 15 Apr. 1985 (DCUPO, 'NIHE Dublin: physical matters, 1978–86, 2/2'); *By Degrees*, 28 Apr. 1982.　20 National Institute for Higher Education, Dublin, Act, 1980 (no. 30 of 1980), s. 4.　21 Andrew Devane (1917–2000) was one of Ireland's foremost architects, having worked with Frank Lloyd Wright during the late 1940s. Among his many iconic works, he was responsible for the design of St Patrick's College campus in Drumcondra (Ellen Rowley (ed.), *More than concrete blocks: volume II, 1940–72 – Dublin city's twentieth-century buildings and their stories* (Dublin, 2019), pp 346–57; Patrick Long, 'Devane, Andrew ('Andy') (1917–2000)' in *DIB*; *Irish Times*, 29 Jan. 2000).

> As you are aware, we have done our best to initiate – in isolation, in a virtual vacuum, and with extreme difficulty – the start of your new campus, but one has only to glance at our original proposals, limited and spare though they were, to see how sadly they have been depleted and emasculated, through no fault of ours or yours. It is absolutely heartbreaking when one reviews the time which has been taken to start building and to measure actual results against what might have been, in terms of content and inflation costs.[22]

Notwithstanding Devane's frustrations at the depletion of their plans, the completion of Phase 1 was cautiously welcomed by the architectural community. A critique of the new campus, published at the end of 1982, commended the architects and noted the promise that existed on what was a relatively large, green-field site:

> The new buildings by Robinson, Keefe & Devane had to face up to the challenges of a relatively flat and featureless site and surroundings, the need for large areas of varied accommodation to be provided quickly, and the establishment of a visual and physical link between the existing building and a new campus … Considerable attention has been paid to external layout and landscaping, including the courtyards, and when matured this should prove to be a major feature of the campus.[23]

When construction was completed on the Henry Grattan building in October 1981, it became the first major new addition to the Institute's facilities. Despite the excitement generated by its opening, the Institute's staff were disappointed with the spartan nature of the building's internal fixtures and fittings. Multiple requests for an increased allocation from the Department of Education were ignored, even in the light of concerns raised over the inadequacy of access arrangements for disabled staff and students.[24] Nonetheless, the new building contained much-needed classrooms and lecture theatres, a computer centre, a purpose-built library, language laboratories, studios for TV, radio and graphics, as well as a games room and other student leisure areas.[25] Perhaps more importantly, the Institute was able to accommodate almost 600 students on campus.

Operations were swiftly moved into the new building, which now required a name. Internal memoranda still referred to it as the College of Commerce

---

22 Andrew Devane to Danny O'Hare, 17 July 1981 (DCUPO, 'Correspondence: general, 1980–1'). RKD Architects, as they are now known, later designed DCU's Nanobioanalytical Research Facility, completed in 2014. 23 *Plan: The Architectural Magazine*, Nov. 1982. 24 DCUPO, 'Department of Education, 1981–6'. 25 Aide-memoire on new building, 27 May 1982 (DCUPO, 'Department of Education, 1981–6'); National Institute for Higher Education, floor plans [*c.* 1987] (DCU Estates

building, a reference to previous plans to transfer courses to NIHE Dublin from the CDVEC.[26] In the lead-up to its formal unveiling on 1 June 1982 by Martin O'Donoghue, minister for education, several options were considered. Intriguingly, suggestions were dominated by two figures from the early modern era. Jonathan Swift proved popular, due to his well-known association with Delville House in Glasnevin.[27] The myriad of topics covered in Swift's corpus of published work were considered most appropriate, given that the new building would host teaching on business studies, accounting and finance, and communications.

Swift was, however, rejected in favour of another eighteenth-century luminary. The choice of Henry Grattan (1746–1820) seems at first glance somewhat incongruous given the Institute's avowed focus on scientific and technological education and research. On closer inspection, however, Grattan's record as a parliamentarian and leading member of the Patriot movement, during the late eighteenth century, spoke to certain elements of the Institute's ethos. The Patriots agitated for and attained, in the late 1770s, the removal of trade restrictions imposed on Ireland by the British government. Following that success, Grattan spearheaded efforts to achieve legislative independence for the Irish parliament, removing the right of the British parliament to pass laws for Ireland, and of the British government to veto Irish legislation.[28] Most importantly, those aims were achieved in 1782. NIHE Dublin's governing body thought it appropriate to mark the 200th anniversary of Grattan's achievement: 'In naming its major business-based building in honour of Henry Grattan, the Institute commemorates the 200th anniversary of the Grattan Parliament together with Grattan's significant contributions to the development of Irish trade.'[29]

Three other buildings were named at this time: the former library and plant pathology buildings of UCD's agriculture faculty, and a prefab building constructed in 1980 and provisionally known as the Weldon. Intended as a temporary fixture, the main consideration for naming the Weldon was that it was not given a name that might be wanted for any future building, as it would disappear in time. Two possibilities were proposed: Westfield, after Westfield

Office, unsorted collection).   **26** Robinson, Keefe & Devane had completed the design of the building by April 1979, with formal plans submitted to the Department of Education that month (NAI, 2007/50/72). For a discussion of the government's unsuccessful attempt to transfer courses from the CDVEC to NIHED, see chapter 2.   **27** DCUPO, 'Governing body – reports and working papers, 1975–9'; NIHED, *Annual report, 1975–8*, p. 12. Delville House was demolished in the early twentieth century. The site, on Glasnevin Hill, is now occupied by the Bon Secours Hospital. Dublin Corporation had taken note of Swift's association with Glasnevin when naming several streets in the area. Drapier Road, Dean Swift Road and Delville Road are all located directly opposite DCU's Ballymun Road entrance.   **28** For more on Grattan, see James Kelly, 'Grattan, Henry (1746–1820)' in *DIB*. The Irish parliament was abolished in 1800 by the Act of Union. **29** DCUPO, GB82/4/7; DCUPO, 'NIHE Dublin: general, 2/2'.

House, located between Albert College and the Ballymun Road, or Hamstead, after a local farm associated with the Institute's grounds. Hamstead was duly chosen.[30] The library was named after John Barry, a former principal of the CDVEC's College of Technology on Bolton Street, and a member of NIHE Dublin's governing body at the time of his death in 1979.[31] Another deceased member of governing body was commemorated when naming the plant-pathology building. A noted artist, Bea Orpen was a niece of Sir William Orpen and received her artistic education at the Dublin Metropolitan School of Art, the Royal Hibernian Academy and the Slade School of Fine Art (London). Bea Orpen was also an educator and founding member of the Irish Countrywomen's Association's adult-education centre in Termonfeckin, Co. Louth.[32] One of the original appointees to governing body in March 1975, Orpen remained in office until her death in 1980, despite her inability to attend meetings after 1978 due to illness. Along with Albert College and An Grianán, the Bea Orpen is one of just three buildings that have survived from the old Albert Agricultural College.[33]

III

The architectural firm Arthur Gibney & Partners had replaced Robinson, Keefe & Devane by the end of 1982, when planning began for the construction of the 'skirt' building, a large extension to Albert College intended to provide an additional 1,000 sq.m. of laboratory space.[34] In the interim, a former residence for the agricultural college, dating from the end of the nineteenth century and known as An Grianán, formally became part of the Institute's campus. When approving the sale of the Albert College site to the Department of Education in February 1980, Dublin Corporation had at the last minute removed An Grianán from the deal. Given the already limited accommodation available to the Institute, this had been a considerable blow to plans for housing senior faculty and administrative offices within An Grianán. Writing to the Corporation, Danny O'Hare recorded the Institute's disappointment with the decision: 'If the house is not made available to us … this will involve considerable additional

---

30 DCUPO, 'NIHE Dublin: general, 2/2'. The public park located beside DCU's campus is variously known as both Albert College Park and Hampstead Park. **31** The John Barry and Hamstead buildings were demolished at the turn of the century to make way for the postgraduate residences, while the Bea Orpen building is still extant and houses the National Institute of Digital Learning. **32** Lawrence W. White and Aideen Foley, 'Orpen, Beatrice Esther ('Bea') (1913–80)' in *DIB*; *DCU News*, 24 Mar. 2010. Orpen's son, Brian Trench, later became a member of DCU's faculty and a senior lecturer in the School of Communications. **33** In 2017 the university renamed six buildings, honouring renowned public figures and simplifying a naming convention of applying letters to buildings that had long confused new students and visitors. See table 6.1. **34** The Albert College extension was completed in 1985 (NIHED, *Annual report, 1982/3*, pp 48–9; NIHED,

expenditure and will certainly render an already difficult start-up phase increasingly difficult and jeopardise that beginning.'[35] The dispute was finally resolved three years later following the purchase of An Grianán by the Department of Education, on behalf of NIHE Dublin, though the Institute had been permitted use of the house in the meantime.[36] Drawing upon a grant of €950,000 from Atlantic Philanthropies, the house was later converted into the university president's residence.[37]

Following the acquisition of An Grianán and the beginning of construction on the 'skirt' building, the Institute's architects undertook a thorough site analysis in preparation for drafting a master development plan.[38] Arthur Gibney presented his vision to governing body on 6 December 1984. Rejecting the Department of Education's 1976 plans as utilitarian, Gibney proposed a much larger built environment on campus. Drawing inspiration from the University of Trondheim, Gibney sought to create a signature feature by linking individual buildings with a series of glazed streets. While representing a visually striking, unifying spine for the Institute, the glazed streets were also intended to economize expenditure on perimeter wall construction and reduce energy consumption, thus reducing operating costs.[39] Specially commissioned research confirmed that constructing the Institute around a series of glazed streets would not only serve as an architectural enhancement, but would also 'reduce the energy requirements of the [campus] significantly'.[40]

The first opportunity to implement this concept arose with the construction of a large extension to the Henry Grattan building, completed in 1987. Consisting of a block of academic offices, teaching facilities and library accommodation, the extension was unified by a glass-fronted and glass-roofed street.[41] EEC funding was secured in 1987 to study whether the Henry Grattan extension provided proof of concept. Later design schematics outlined the ambition of this concept, with a glazed central mall equivalent in width to O'Connell Street.[42] Reviewing the completed building, Desmond Doyle

Annual report, 1984/5, pp 48–9). **35** Danny O'Hare to Frank Feely, 1 Feb. 1980 (*Minutes of the Dublin City Council, 1980* ([Dublin, 1981]), pp 78–80). **36** The Corporation also retained an interest in the Ballymun Road entrance to NIHED, which was not relinquished until August 1986 (DCUPO, 'NIHE Dublin: general, 2/2' and 'Dublin Corporation, 1982–2000'; *Nuacht*, July 1983; *Minutes of the Dublin City Council, 1983* ([Dublin, 1984]), p. 68; *Minutes of the Dublin City Council, 1986* ([Dublin, 1987]), p. 313. For staff recollections of the accommodation in An Grianán during the early 1980s, see chapter 3. **37** The renovation and extension of An Grianán was overseen by Shay Cleary Architects and the McKeon Group. The building is currently listed by Dublin City Council as a protected structure (APA, Grant #8276; *Dublin City development plan: record of protected structures* (Dublin, 2010), p. 18). **38** *Dáil Debates*, 24 May 1984; DCUPO, GB84/8; *Nuacht*, Oct. 1984. **39** 'Development control plan 10', [1985] (DCUPO, 'NIHE Dublin: physical matters, 1978–86, 1/2'). **40** 'A consideration of the possible reduction in energy consumption in … NIHE, Dublin', Aug. 1985, p. 43 (DCUPO, 'NIHE Dublin: physical matters, 1978–86, 1/2'). **41** Gibney's design for the Henry Grattan extension was heavily influenced by Henning Larsen's work on the University of Trondheim's Dragvoll campus. **42** R. Meijer to Danny O'Hare, 10 Mar.

6.2 An Grianán, which originally housed offices, was renovated in 2000 to serve as the president's residence (DCU Collection).

6.3 View of the mall from the Henry Grattan building, 1991. The Interfaith Centre and Student Centre are visible on the right, with construction underway on the Larkfield student residences (DCU Collection).

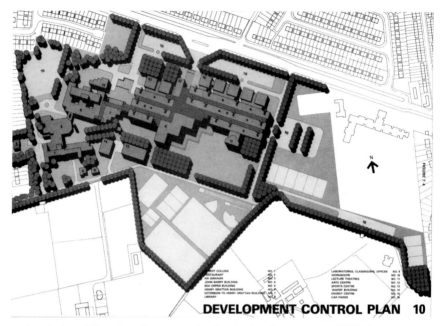

DEVELOPMENT CONTROL PLAN 10

6.4 Arthur Gibney's 1985 master plan for the development of NIHED's campus,
incorporating a glazed street connecting all buildings (DCU Collection).

commended the extension as designed and executed 'with deftness and skill'.
Strained finances, however, meant that the extension's surroundings were not
finished to a similarly high degree: 'It is a pity that the landscaping has been
curtailed. A building is incomplete without its planting and the space both in and
around this building in particular is suffering from this lack.'[43]

Despite gradual improvements in accommodation brought by the Albert
College and Henry Grattan extensions, as well as the completion of the
restaurant extension (the Pavilion) in 1986, a lack of space continued to be a
problem. In the six years following the completion of Phase 1 in 1981, just 4,000
sq.m. of teaching, research, administrative and social space were added to the
campus, making a total of *c.*20,000 sq m. (table 6.1). During the same period, the
total number of students on campus had risen from 191 to 2,432.[44] No further
educational or research buildings were added by the end of the decade. Pressures
of space were a recurring theme in discussions at governing body and the
Institute's reports to the minister for education, with particular reference to the
fact that the accepted norms per student fell far short of the minimum standards
specified by the HEA. Throughout the 1980s (and indeed well into the 1990s),
space at Glasnevin hovered at around 60 per cent of the recommended level.[45]

1987 (DCUPO, 'NIHE Dublin: physical matters, 1978–86, 1/2'). **43** Desmond Doyle, 'NIHE
Dublin', *Irish Architect: The Bulletin of the Royal Institute of the Architects of Ireland*, 64 (Nov.–Jan.
1987/8), pp 13–15. **44** See appendix 6, fig. A6.5. **45** DCUPO, GB90/1; DCUPO, 'NIHE

Due to increased undergraduate admissions, by the end of the 1980s the Institute's space norm per student had actually fallen from 7.5 sq.m. to 6 sq.m.. This compared unfavourably with 12.5 sq.m. per student at NIHE Limerick, and more than 15 sq.m. per student at the universities. Research space was similarly constrained, with estimates placing the Institute's absolute minimum need at close to 3,000 sq.m.[46]

Six years after the HEA had advised splitting plans for Phase 2 into two stages, neither Phase 2A nor 2B had commenced. Hopes for 1988 were dashed when, in October 1987, the government announced its decision to postpone any further capital investment across the third-level sector, particularly for projects designed to increase student capacity. As explained by Mary O'Rourke, minister for education, this was a result of straitened economic circumstances. Defending the decision, O'Rourke highlighted recent significant investment in the third-level sector. Little of that investment had been allocated to NIHE Dublin, however, with Phase 2 identified as one of the deferred projects.[47]

The news did not come as a surprise. For much of the 1980s, successive governments had struggled to reconcile the growth in demand for higher education with a fiscal reality that demanded retrenchment in public spending.[48] Reports in the press during the summer of 1987 had hinted at the government's need to cut £300m from the public-expenditure bill. Education was high on the list of departments in the firing line, with plans for the establishment of regional technical colleges at Blanchardstown, Thurles, Castlebar and Tallaght also due to be shelved.[49] Danny O'Hare sought reassurances from the chairman of the HEA, Liam Ó Laidhin, that NIHE Dublin would not be disappointed yet again.[50] Highlighting the constraints under which staff and students operated, O'Hare observed that NIHE Dublin had just 60 per cent of the space of the next most tightly planned third-level institution. Put another way, the Institute had an enrolment of more than 2,300 students on a campus designed for 1,300. Among the litany of drawbacks that failure to implement Phase 2 entailed, O'Hare instanced the conditions at the Institute's Biotechnology Process Laboratory – which only weeks earlier had been designated a national centre for excellence.[51] Yet the lab was housed in utterly unsuitable premises, consisting of

Dublin: physical matters, 1978–86, 2/2'; *Nuacht*, Jan. 1990; NIHED, *Annual reports, 1982–9*. **46** Tony Glynn, 'Research policy and developmental constraints', Apr. 1989 (DCUPO, 'DCUET Proposals/Approaches, 1989–94'); NIHED, *Annual report, 1983/4*, p. 44; NIHED, *Annual report, 1987/8*, p. 51. While the Institute had embraced computerized timetabling and room-booking systems at an early stage to help alleviate problems allocating space to teaching, research and social activities, it did not represent a solution to the increasing strain on facilities (see NIHED, *Annual report, 1982/3*, pp 47–9; NIHED, *Annual report, 1987/8*, p. 50). **47** DCUPO, GB87/6, 7; *Nuacht*, Nov. 1987; *Dáil Debates*, 22 Oct. 1987; *Irish Times*, 23 Oct. 1987. **48** John Walsh, *Higher education in Ireland, 1922–2016*, p. 198. **49** See, for example, *Irish Times*, 13 July 1987. **50** Danny O'Hare memo, 10 July 1987 (DCUPO, 'NIHE Dublin: physical matters, 1978–86, 2/2'). **51** On 11 June 1987, Seán McCarthy, minister of state for science and technology at the Department of Industry

'a roofed-in courtyard with the chimney stack from our boiler house running vertically through it'. Some of the lab's essential facilities were located one hundred yards away in huts erected against the external wall of another building. O'Hare appended a memorandum outlining NIHE Dublin's need in greater detail, and concluded with a pointed query:

> NIHE Dublin is entitled to ask how serious anyone is about its welfare! Or is it merely that we are near Ballymun and that the North Dublin profile of an inadequate and poor environment – being traditional in this area – must be maintained?[52]

O'Hare's frustrations can be placed in the context of the imminent publication of a government report recommending university status for both NIHEs – a conclusion widely anticipated (see chapter 3). In light of these findings, awareness of the under-resourced state of the Institute's campus and facilities became ever more acute among staff and governors – particularly when compared with Limerick. Though Ed Walsh's institution was also underfunded, it was eight years further along in its development and could boast facilities far more advanced than those in Dublin.

The effects of the lack of investment in NIHE Dublin were beginning to take their toll. Prof. Eugene Kennedy, dean of the Faculty of Science, drafted a memorandum in April 1989 to convey the problems created by his faculty's inadequate facilities. Temperatures in the laboratories had been known to fluctuate from a few degrees Celsius to more than thirty in a single day, which had implications for the accuracy of instruments and data. Perhaps more worrying was that the Institute's radiation store was in actual fact a cubby hole located under a stairwell.[53] The majority of his faculty's complaints could be ascribed to the dilapidated nature of the Hamstead building, an intermittently extended prefab erected in 1980, originally intended to be used for just a couple of years. Housing teaching and research labs for physics and chemistry on the ground floor, with offices above, Hamstead's design shortcomings were the source both of amusement and frustration for staff and students. A tale told about its construction, quite possibly apocryphal, illustrates the point. As a member of staff walked past the site he overheard a conversation between two construction workers: 'Any idea who has the plans for this building?' 'Ask the

---

and Commerce, announced funding for the creation of a national centre of excellence for cell culture at NIHED (DCUPO, 'Correspondence: general, 1986–8'; *Irish Times*, 12 June 1987). 52 Danny O'Hare to Liam Ó Laidhin, 28 July 1987 (DCUPO, 'NIHE Dublin: physical matters, 1978–86, 2/2'). Liam Ó Laidhin (1919–2002) joined the Department of Education in 1939, and was appointed secretary of the Department in 1979. 53 Eugene Kennedy to Danny O'Hare, 27 Apr. 1989 (DCUPO, 'NIHE Dublin: physical matters, 1978–86, 2/2'). Intended to be used for just five years, until the completion of Phase 2 of the Institute's development, Hamstead remained in use until 2000 when it was demolished to make way for postgraduate student residences.

foreman.' 'I am the foreman', came the reply.[54] Some could at least see the funny side of things. When a sizeable hole developed in the floor of one of the prefabs, quick-witted students lost no time in erecting a sign welcoming people to the 'Open University'.[55]

Michael Ryan, head of the School of Computer Applications, lodged a similar complaint just days later. Having received a donation of an IBM System 36 minicomputer, a lack of floor space prevented the school from installing the new equipment.[56] Martin Clynes, director of the National Centre for Cell and Tissue Culture, warned of the damaging consequences for the Institute's competitiveness, without immediate funding for expansion and improvement of its facilities. He noted that several international companies had recently visited the campus to discuss the establishment of research and development links. Having inspected the laboratory facilities, the companies expressed serious reservations about the Institute's capacity to conduct cutting-edge research:

> The frustrating aspect of this is that they were impressed with our proposals and expertise, and impressed with the calibre and enthusiasm of the research staff, at all levels. The level of equipment was considered just about adequate and in need of improvement, but wasn't on balance a major negative factor. The *quantity* and *quality* of the laboratory space, however, were seen as a very significant limitation on our ability to deliver R&D services to an internationally acceptable level … It is really a great pity when we have the ideas, the expertise and the excellent people on board that we are losing out for want of a building of adequate standard.[57]

A similar report came from Prof. Alistair Wood, who informed O'Hare of the Institute's recent success in securing a prestigious and valuable two-year contract from the European Community's Fusion Committee. However, Wood noted that the contract allowed for the employment of two research assistants, for whom there was no office space available on the entire campus. Wood's frustration was clear: 'What do I do? Do I turn down this contract, which is only the second ever awarded to Ireland by the EC Fusion Committee?'[58]

Despite the sense of grandeur surrounding the Institute's inauguration as Dublin City University in September 1989, there was little sign of any major government investment in the new university's short-term future. The difficulties of trying to meet competing demands from faculties, each desperate

54 Martin Clynes, 'DCU: the movie', *DCU Times, c.*2005.   **55** DCUPO, GB89/4.   **56** Michael Ryan to Danny O'Hare, 1 May 1989 (DCUPO, 'NIHE Dublin: physical matters, 1978–86, 2/2'). **57** Martin Clynes to Danny O'Hare, 9 Mar. 1989 (DCUPO, 'NIHE Dublin: physical matters, 1978–86, 2/2'). The companies that expressed reservations included Beckman, Intergen-Armour Biochemicals, Cambridge Med-Tech and Medical and Veterinary Services.   **58** Alistair Wood to Danny O'Hare, 5 Sept. 1989 (DCUPO, 'NIHE Dublin: physical matters, 1978–86, 2/2').

for a greater allocation of limited and meagre resources, undoubtedly took their toll on the university's leadership. In October 1989, the *Irish Times* reported on remarks made by O'Hare at DCU's conferring ceremony, in which the president noted that the university suffered from a 'crippling lack of space'.[59] The report prompted O'Hare to write to Taoiseach Charles Haughey, expanding upon his observations and drawing attention to the impact of the government's continued lack of capital investment in DCU. A short, enclosed document detailing the problems facing NIHE Dublin showed that, if anything, the situation had worsened since O'Hare's letter to Liam Ó Laidhin in July 1987.[60]

Just a few weeks later the *Irish Press* published its annual guide to third-level courses. Commenting on DCU's degrees in computer applications and applied physics, the *Press* noted that while job prospects for graduates of both were excellent, the university's facilities for these courses were considered substandard. Frustrated with the potential damage to its reputation, governing body used these negative comments to increase the pressure on the government for greater investment in DCU.[61]

Intent on keeping the plight of Ireland's newest university fresh in the minds of the HEA and the Department of Education, and with Phase 2A yet to commence by the end of the 1989/90 academic year, O'Hare gathered submissions from deans and heads of school, outlining the various ways in which this lack of infrastructural investment was inhibiting the university. Most worryingly, Donal Keating identified a problem with staff morale: '[There is a] general sapping of initiative in the university. People are slow to put forward new ideas for courses and research because they know that the space and facilities are not available to carry them out.'[62] Eugene Kennedy echoed Keating's assessment when commenting that most of the university's activities in supporting staff (such as the allocation of lab space and teaching facilities) was driven by crisis management: 'Staff are continuously occupied by a survival approach rather than imaginative plans for the future. It is difficult when one is unsure of how to live with and cater for existing student numbers to conceive too readily of new courses/directions.'[63]

There were a host of practical problems. The dispersal of schools across multiple buildings (biotechnology was housed in no less than four) led to a lack of coherence, and major inconvenience to staff and students. There was no accommodation for visiting academics, and research space continued to be inadequate. What little did exist was shared between staff, undergraduates and

59 *Irish Times*, 21 Oct. 1989; *Nuacht*, Nov. 1989.   **60** Danny O'Hare to Charles Haughey, 3 Nov. 1989 (DCUPO, 'NIHE Dublin: physical matters, 1978–86, 2/2').   **61** Con Power to Danny O'Hare, 29 Jan. 1990 (DCUPO, 'NIHE Dublin: physical matters, 1978–86, 2/2'; GB90/1). **62** Donal Keating to Danny O'Hare, 2 May 1990 (DCUPO, 'NIHE Dublin: physical matters, 1978– 86, 2/2').   **63** Eugene Kennedy to Danny O'Hare, 14 May 1990 (DCUPO, 'NIHE Dublin: physical matters, 1978–86, 2/2).

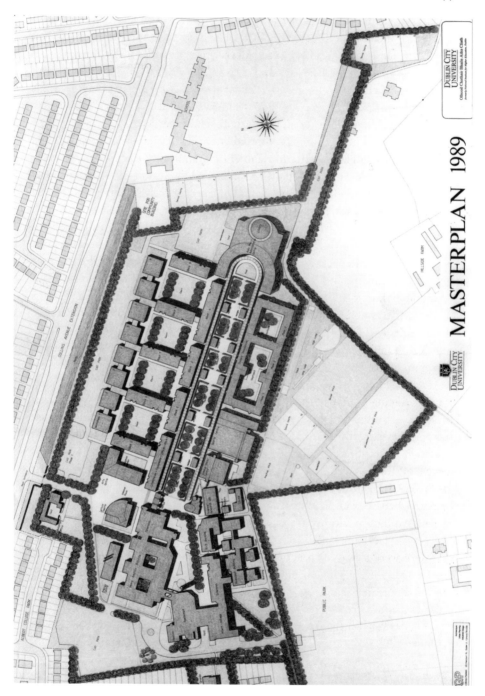

6.5 Revised campus development master plan, 1989 (DCU Collection).

research students, leading to the rapid deterioration of equipment due to overuse. The university's campus still had no indoor sports facilities and lacked sufficient communal space for the size of the student body. Health services were cramped – a portion of a classroom had to be converted to create enough space for a person to lie down. No central, fireproofed archive for storing important university documents or backup disks and tapes existed.[64]

Some relief was, however, at hand. At the end of February 1990, Minister O'Rourke announced a capital programme for third-level institutions, designed to enhance the state's facilities in science, technology and business studies. Over the following three years, the government planned to invest £72.5m in a number of major projects, including new science and technology facilities for DCU.[65] The level of financial support DCU was set to receive had yet to be confirmed, but initial indications suggested a total of £6m.[66] Consultation with heads of schools led to the prioritization of these funds to improve undergraduate activity in the School of Mechanical Engineering, and for permanent accommodation for the School of Physical Sciences, the only school then wholly housed in temporary accommodation.[67] This much-needed injection of capital would soon be augmented by the first of many large philanthropic donations received over the next decade. DCU was now entering a sustained era of expansion, largely fuelled by philanthropic funding, that would see its campus develop beyond recognition.

Given the somewhat ad hoc nature of the extensions and additions to the campus during the 1980s, and in light of ongoing and potential construction projects, Arthur Gibney reviewed his campus master plan at the end of 1989. Informed both by the financial reality of restricted government funding, and the university's intention to build student residences, Gibney delivered his updated master plan in January 1990. The update was especially necessary given that a successful implementation of the 1985 master plan – particularly the central organizing concept of glazed streets – was heavily reliant on steady construction progress, which could not be guaranteed in the absence of concrete funding assurances. Drawing upon design cues both from United States and Europe, Gibney's revised plan called for the alignment of the university's spine along an open, longitudinal arrangement, with a quad-based design for student residences and research and teaching buildings.[68] However, the core of the 1985 master plan – the stunning, glazed-street linking each building on campus – would have to

---

64 'NIHE Dublin: the experience on campus of shortage of space', 28 July 1987 (DCUPO, 'NIHE Dublin: physical matters, 1978–86, 2/2').   65 Mary O'Rourke to Danny O'Hare, 28 Feb. 1990 (DCUPO, 'NIHE Dublin: physical matters, 1978–86, 2/2'). See also DCUPO, GB90/2; *Nuacht*, Mar. 1990; *Irish Times*, 28 Feb. 1990.   66 Michael Gleeson to Danny O'Hare, 28 Feb. 1990 (DCUPO, 'NIHE Dublin: physical matters, 1978–86, 2/2'); *Nuacht*, Mar. 1990.   67 DCUPO, GB90/2; *Nuacht*, Mar. 1990.   68 For the development of the central mall concept in university-campus design, see Paul Turner, *Campus: an American planning tradition* (Boston, 1984), pp 50–70.

be abandoned, with a significant scaling back of ambitions in terms of external detailing of buildings. The central mall would now be open-air, but landscaped in such a fashion as to promote a 'groves of academe' atmosphere.[69] As he had done in 1985, Gibney continued to rely upon the Institute's 1978 *Plan for the physical development of the Institute* when drafting his new master plan. One of the defining features of the design, which has endured to the present day, was Gibney's decision to group all student-related buildings on the south side of the mall, with teaching and research buildings opposite. The crowning feature of the campus was to be a U-shaped building incorporating a new library and aula maxima, linking the north and south aspects of the mall at its eastern apex.

Reviewing Gibney's new designs, following the addition of the student social centre and Research and Development building to the campus, architect Richard Hurley noted that the key to successful campus planning was flexibility to adapt to future needs while maintaining central coherence. In that respect, Hurley applauded the change of axis for the campus from the Albert College building into the main mall:

> The promise of a great tree-lined mall evokes dreams of Thomas Jefferson's University of Virginia plan as a model ... Recognising the need for future buildings which may not conform to the space as established in the master plan, the architects have approached the planning problem at DCU on a modular basis so that the green spine can be preserved as an element unifying both sides of the mall.

Hurley was less enamoured with the bland detailing of the student centre's interior and exterior, though he had some sympathy for the difficulty of working with restricted budgets. Overall, however, Hurley approved of Gibney's determination to embody the ideals of a university through his vision for DCU's physical development:

> The main role of a university is to develop the intellect, to foster creative thought, scholarship and research as well as training professionals. University architecture should embrace these ideals and there is every indication that DCU has embarked along that road, having already declared its intentions in the extension to the Henry Grattan building ... some years ago.[70]

---

69 DCUPO, GB89/5 and 90/1; *Nuacht*, Sept. 1989 and Jan. 1990. It was still intended to provide a covered walkway around the mall.   70 Richard Hurley, 'Dublin City University master plan, 1991: critique', *Irish Architect*, 85 (1991), pp 20–3.

IV

During the 1980s and 1990s the architects and planners with responsibility for campus development strove to attain a number of goals based around the provision of specific facilities for staff and students, as well as the greater integration of the university with its surrounding locality. The strategic acquisition of an additional 47 acres of land during the 1990s, as well as two key individual building projects – the sports centre and the Helix – reflected the core strategic objectives and values pursued by the university from its earliest planning stages.

The sports centre

In relation to its sports facilities, the Institute's framework development plan called for 1,670 sq.m. of indoor sports facilities, along with 11.3 hectares for outdoor activities. Comprehensive and well-equipped leisure facilities, would, if provided, prove to be a considerable asset both to the Institute and the wider community. Initial costings for these facilities, which included a swimming pool and athletics track, were put at £350,000.[71] In the absence of a major building programme, which ensured that much of the Institute's campus remained greenfield, playing fields were not an issue until the mid-1990s. Indoor facilities were, however, a permanent fixture on the Institute's wish list between 1980 and 1991. NIHE Limerick's needs in that area were met shortly after its first students arrived on campus, with the opening of the National College of Physical Education – though that building was not without its problems.[72] Just two months after NIHE Dublin opened its doors, UCD's new sports centre opened in Belfield. Built at a cost of £2m, the state-of-the-art facility had taken fifteen years to complete from the time plans were originally drawn up, a wait that did not bode well for NIHE Dublin's ambitions.[73]

Improvements to the Institute's outdoor sports facilities were sporadically completed during the 1980s, including the addition of an all-weather playing surface, new soccer and GAA pitches, and multi-gym equipment (housed in prefabricated buildings).[74] As the student body grew, bringing with it greater variety in sports clubs and growing numbers participating in sporting activity, the Student Services Unit highlighted the difficulties caused by the lack of indoor sports facilities with increasing urgency: 'The major disappointment [this year] was the continued failure to make any significant impression on the disadvantages suffered by Institute students compared to their counterparts in other Irish universities.'[75]

---

71 NIHED, *Plan for the physical development of the Institute*, pp 33–4, 38.   72 See Fleming, *University of Limerick*, pp 265–7.   73 *UCD News*, Jan. 1981.   74 NIHED, *Annual report, 1986/7*, pp 57–8; NIHED, *Annual report, 1987/8*, p. 45.   75 NIHED/DCU, *Annual reports, 1982–9*.

6.6 DCU's long-awaited sports centre opened in 1993, providing vital facilities for staff and students (DCU Collection).

Student facilities were, without doubt, relatively low on the list of priorities for the Institute's governors during the 1980s. John Kerrane, sport and recreation officer, rejected O'Hare's suggestion that the lack of a strong student lobby for indoor facilities was proof that students were not interested in the issue. Kerrane's arguments for improved sporting facilities drew upon the same reasoning advanced by the Institute's planners in 1978, emphasizing the benefits provided by sports for academic and personal development.[76]

However, while it is broadly true to say that O'Hare and the Institute's governors favoured development of teaching and research facilities over those for student life, such decisions were generally taken in difficult economic circumstances. Governing body rejected a 1984 proposal, advanced by Student Services, to build indoor facilities on a phased basis, preferring instead to lobby

Quotation from annual report for 1987/8, p. 45. **76** John Kerrane to Danny O'Hare, 19 June 1985 (DCUPO, 'Student Services, 1980–7'); NIHED, *Plan for the physical development of the Institute*, pp 33–4; NIHED, *Plan for the future of the Institute*, p. 48.

the HEA and Department of Education for support, and to investigate alternative methods of financing a large-scale project.[77] A window of opportunity briefly opened in 1985 when the minister for sport, Donal Creed, proposed the development of a national sports centre and invited expressions of interest for its location and management. Following tentative discussions with Dublin Corporation, the Institute submitted its proposal for a national indoor athletics centre for Albert College Park, adjacent to the campus on the Ballymun Road, to Cospóir and the Department of Education. Convincing the government to locate a national sports centre in Glasnevin, with preferential access for the Institute's students, would have been a significant coup, but such hopes disappeared when the government's plans foundered.[78]

DCU's difficulties in securing funding for a sports centre ended with the arrival of support from Atlantic Philanthropies.[79] Armed with the knowledge that Atlantic were prepared to supply £600,000 in funding, O'Hare was able to leverage a National Lottery grant of £500,000 from the government, on the basis that DCU would supply the remaining £1.5m required. Though negotiations with the government came down to the wire, with O'Hare required to sign contracts before the end of 1991 or face delays and escalating costs, the government contribution was confirmed at Christmas, with construction beginning in January 1992.[80] Atlantic's eventual contribution came to £900,000, with DCU providing the balance of the final cost of £2.4m.[81] Designed by Arthur Gibney, the centre was opened in January 1993 and comprised 3,775 sq.m. of facilities, including a multi-purpose main hall, squash and handball courts, changing facilities, a gym and a spectators' gallery.[82]

Kerrane highlighted the new centre's positive impact on the university, noting a 'huge increase' in sports participation among staff and students, the formation of new sports clubs and the ability to host indoor inter-varsity competitions. Equally important was the accessibility of the centre to the local community: 'It

---

77 DCUPO, GB84/7, 8.   78 DCUPO, GB85/7, 8; *Nuacht*, Oct. 1985; DCUPO, 'Dublin Corporation, 1982–2000' and 'Sports complex'; *Dáil Debates*, 5 Feb. and 25 June 1986; *Irish Independent*, 19 Feb. 1986; *Sunday Independent*, 4 May 1986, 25 Jan. 1987. Established in 1978, Cospóir was the forerunner of the current Irish Sports Council.   79 For an overview of Atlantic Philanthropies' support of DCU, see chapter 4.   80 Danny O'Hare to Frank Fahey, 19 Dec. 1990 (APA, Grant #7115; DCUPO, 'Sports complex'). The outstanding amount would be raised via student capitation fees, student-centre bar profits and other revenue streams. The government's grant was confirmed at Christmas 1991 (John R. Healy memo, 19 Dec. 1991 (APA, Grant #7115); Danny O'Hare interview, 13 Oct. 2005; DCUPO, 'Sports complex').   81 'DCU Sports complex grant request', Feb. 1992 (APA, Grant #7115; DCUPO, 'Sports Complex'). Atlantic had originally hoped to obtain a commitment from Joe Lyons to provide £300,000, but was unsuccessful on this occasion. Lyons had previously visited DCU's campus and had donated £175,000 to the Research and Development (Hamilton) building, completed in 1990.   82 Brief to architects for DCU sports complex [1991]; DCU Sport and Recreation Service, *Annual report, 1992/93*; John R. Healy to Chuck Feeney, 7 Apr. 1993 (APA, Grant #7115; DCUPO, 'Sports complex'). The formal opening ceremony was performed by Bertie Ahern, minister for finance, on 5 April 1993.

is very much geared towards all parts of the outside community as well as our own student body. That is central to our philosophy regarding the centre.' Just six months after opening, public membership numbered 500, bringing both revenue and an important point of contact with community groups and sports clubs.[83] Improved facilities also brought improved performances for the university's sports teams. DCU won both the men's and women's volleyball inter-varsity championships in 1994 (the competition was hosted in the new centre), while the badminton and men's basketball teams finished as runners-up.[84] Kerrane's focus for the development of DCU's sporting facilities now switched to the acquisition of a swimming pool and reversing the diminution of the university's space for outdoor sports. In the face of a rapidly expanding built environment, Kerrane warned of an 'urgent need' for additional grass pitches, though he acknowledged that these would almost certainly have to be provided on land purchased by the university, and located off-campus.[85]

Land purchases

As the pace of construction work on campus accelerated during the 1990s, these welcome developments brought pressures of space of a different kind to those experienced during the 1980s. If that decade was characterized by undeveloped green space on campus, the 1990s saw DCU's landscape develop its distinctive, red-bricked facade. Between 1990 and 1993 nine buildings were added to the campus, including a student centre and student residences, along with the Business School and the Computer Applications building (see table 6.1). As feared when Albert College was first selected as the site for NIHE Dublin, its relatively small size was now constraining the university's development. More land was urgently required, but, with the university located in a highly developed urban landscape, opportunities for acquiring suitable greenfield sites adjacent to the campus were few and far between.[86]

Such land did, however, exist. While not directly linked to the campus, the Eastern Health Board's nursing home at St Clare's was situated across the Ballymun Road within easy walking distance, surrounded by *c.*35 acres of

---

83 DCU Sport and Recreation Service, *Annual report, 1992/3* (APA, Grant #7115). 84 DCU Sport and Recreation Service, *Annual report 1993/4* (APA, Grant #7115). 85 *Irish Times*, 27 Apr. 1993; DCU Sport and Recreation Service, *Annual report 1992/3*; (APA, Grant #7115). The university incorporated a swimming pool in its updated campus-development plan, drawn up in 1999, at a time when DCU was lobbying aggressively for the National Aquatic Centre to be located on campus. While those efforts were unsuccessful, the sports centre now incorporates a 25m indoor swimming pool (DCUPO, 'Swimming pool'). 86 It is worth juxtaposing this situation with that facing NIHE Limerick in the 1970s. During attempts to co-locate the National College of Physical Education with NIHE Limerick, an additional 122-acre site was acquired in 1973 with a minimum of fuss, thus increasing the campus to 195 acres from an initial 73-acre site (Fleming, *University of Limerick*, pp 264–5).

undeveloped land. Initial approaches to the Board were rebuffed until the university 'pulled some political strings', opening up the possibility of a sale in 1994.[87] Eager to secure financial support from Atlantic Philanthropies, the university's secretary, Martin Conry, showed John Healy around the grounds of St Clare's in August 1994. Suitably impressed, Healy requested that a full proposal be prepared for submission to Atlantic's board.[88] Valued at between €5m and €6m and zoned for residential development, purchase of the land was identified as a strategic priority for the university, a rare opportunity to acquire a substantial greenfield site within touching distance of the main campus. The need for the facilities was particularly pressing. The university had just three sports pitches remaining on its campus, which would be swallowed up by the end of the decade as the university's building footprint increased. From a long-term perspective, the potential benefits to the university were enormous. If rezoned for building development, acquisition of the land would represent an increase of approximately 70 per cent to existing campus lands – though medium-term plans were to utilize the grounds for playing pitches.[89]

Negotiations with the Eastern Health Board progressed well, allowing Conry to report to governing body that agreement on the sale had been reached by the summer of 1995.[90] The purchase was fully funded by Atlantic Philanthropies, which donated £5m for the purpose.[91] Support from the government to develop St Clare's as playing pitches was expected, with O'Hare arguing that as the land had been obtained at no cost to the public finances, there was a 'moral obligation' on the Department of Education to do so.[92] Nonetheless, no government funding was provided. Submitting a final report on the development of St Clare's to Atlantic almost a decade later, Martin Conry noted that the price of €100,000 per acre represented exceptional value, with conservative estimates placing the land as worth €2.5m per acre in 2003. More pertinently, the intervening decade had witnessed the completion of a number of building projects on the Glasnevin campus, including the O'Reilly Library, the Lonsdale building and the expansion of student residences. As a result, just one sports pitch remained on the original campus, highlighting just how important the purchase of St Clare's had been for

87 Danny O'Hare initially broached the possibility of support from Atlantic Philanthropies for purchase of the land in November 1992 (John R. Healy memos, 20 Nov. 1992 and 12 Aug. 1994 (APA, Grant #7710). Quotation from Aug. 1994 memo.)   88 Martin Conry memo, 11 Aug. 1994 (DCUPO, 'DCUET: general, 1994–5').   89 APA, Grant #7710; DCUPO, 'Student affairs – sport and recreation'.   90 Governing body approved the purchase of the land at its 6 July 1995 meeting (DCUPO, GB95/5, 6, 7; *Nuacht*, Dec. 1995).   91 Atlantic Philanthropies grant-request summary, 7 Feb. 1995 (APA, Grant #7710). The purchase price was £4.3m, with £700,000 set aside for development of the land. While the expectation was that the government would provide additional funding, a second grant of £3.4m was eventually provided by Atlantic in 1998 to enable the university to complete the St Clare's facilities.   92 John R. Healy to Chuck Feeney, 22 Dec. 1994; John R. Healy memo, 17 Jan. 1996; St Clare's House proposal [to HEA/Department of Education, *c.*1995] (APA, Grant #7710).

the university's sporting and extracurricular activities. Development of the site had provided two GAA pitches, two rugby pitches, a floodlit all-weather pitch and a cricket crease, along with 1,000 sq.m. of indoor facilities.[93]

In the meantime, DCU had further added to its stock of land with the purchase of 10 acres of the Eustace estate.[94] At the time the land was put up for sale, DCU's building programme was on course to leave just 20 per cent of the original 50-acre campus free of buildings. During its consideration of the planning application for the Helix (see below), Dublin City Council noted the density of development on campus and warned that this might mitigate against future planning applications.[95] Seeking the HEA's support for purchase of the Eustace lands, Martin Conry drew attention to the university's existing policy of strategic land acquisitions, and that the estimated price of €25m was roughly equivalent to the cost of a single building with capacity for 1,500 students. Drawing parallels with UCD's Belfield campus, Conry pressed home the need for DCU to acquire more land if it was to continue to grow:

> The decision to acquire Belfield in the 1950s was truly visionary and has facilitated a huge expansion of UCD which would never have been possible in its previous diffused sites … [S]uch is our determination to acquire this land that we are committed to raising a significant portion of the cost from the private sector.[96]

While the diminution of DCU's green space was clearly evident to the naked eye, the need for land acquisition had also been highlighted by the university's architects. Having grown somewhat disillusioned with Arthur Gibney's vision, the university retained Anthony Reddy Associates in 1999 to update its master plan to guide development until 2010.[97] Though the recommendation was not included in the published master plan, for reasons of confidentiality, the architects strongly urged governing body to prioritize acquisition of any land that became available in the vicinity of the campus. Aside from an obvious need for greater space, there were also strategic research and collaboration considerations behind DCU's intent to obtain the land. The completion of the M50 motorway had created ideal conditions for the development of industrial and business parks between Ballymun and the new motorway. Demand for greenfield

93 Final report on St Clare's, Apr. 2003 (APA, Grant #7710).   94 A satellite overview of DCU's campus reveals a significant greenfield area directly adjacent to the south-east of the campus, *c.*80 acres in total. This land has been owned and farmed by the Eustace family since the early nineteenth century, and they also operate a number of private health care facilities there. Hampstead Hospital was opened by the Eustace family in 1825 for the care of mentally ill patients (http://www.highfieldhealthcare.ie/about/family-history, accessed 12 Dec. 2018).   95 Martin Conry to Colin McCrea, 14 Apr. 2000 (APA, Grant #8024).   96 Martin Conry to John Hayden, 2 Mar. 2000 (APA, Grant #8024).   97 O'Hare had grown disillusioned with Gibney's master plan by the end of 1992 (John R. Healy to Chuck Feeney, 25 Sept. 1992 (APA, Folder 'DCU policy: background,

sites in the area was only likely to intensify.[98] The Eustace lands had extensive road frontage on Griffith Avenue, and their acquisition would mean that the remaining Eustace estate (*c*.75 acres in total) would share a substantial border with DCU, putting the university in a strong position to acquire any future parcels of land put up for sale.[99]

Given their prime location the Eustace lands were not expected to be cheap, prompting the university to broker an agreement that would see the cost of acquisition shared equally between the government and Atlantic Philanthropies.[100] There was a further complication, however, in that relations between the Eustace family and the university were poor.[101] When, as expected, the Eustace family refused to sell to DCU, the university implemented a prepared and creative solution. Acting through a company owned by property developer Charles Kenny, who also served as a trustee with DCU Educational Trust, the university submitted a blind tender of £31.1m (€39.5m) plus fees, which was accepted.[102] Atlantic's contribution to the purchase price totalled €20.5m, its largest grant to the university by a significant margin and a compelling declaration of faith in an institution that was, at the time, in the middle of a disruptive search for a successor to Danny O'Hare. Within just five years DCU's campus had almost doubled in size, from 50 acres to 95 acres, at a cost of £36m. In an interview with DCU's student newspaper, Conry justified the price paid for the Eustace land by pointing to the dearth of space available for DCU's development and expansion: 'We have a total of 85 acres here. Contrast that with UCD or Limerick who have over 300 acres and you see that we just don't have enough land … In terms of our long term strategy you can't say that it was expensive.'[103] Though the university intended to create an industry-linked research park on the site, immediately after the sale the land was leased back to the Eustace family.[104] Development of the site in the ensuing years

strategic planning, 3/3')). 98 'DCU master-plan presentation', 14 Nov. 2002 (DCU Estates Office, unsorted collection); APA, Grant #8024. See chapter 7 for DCU's collaborations with Ballymun Regeneration Ltd in this area. 99 Ronan Smith to John Hayden, 2 Mar. 2000 (APA, Grant #8024). Smith, one of the directors of Anthony Reddy Associates, concluded his letter with the observation: 'As the university master planners, we consider that the acquisition of this site is of such strategic importance to the long-term development of the campus that every effort should be made to ensure that it is purchased for DCU and not allowed to fall into private hands.' 100 Martin Conry to Colin McCrea, 14 Apr. 2000; grant-request summary, 20 Apr. 2000 (APA, Grant #8024). 101 Michael Gleeson to governing body, 26 Mar. 1990 (DCUPO, GB90/3). The Eustace family objected to the development of a large third-level institution next to their lands. Relations in the early days of NIHED, when it occupied just the Albert College and Henry Grattan buildings, were more cordial, with members of the family visiting the Institute in March 1981 (*By Degrees (NIHE Diary)*, 31 Mar. 1981). 102 'Griffith Avenue lands – strategy', 29 Mar. 2000 (APA, Grant #8024); The *Irish Times* incorrectly reported, on 21 Sept. 2000, that DCU had initially been outbid by Kenny's company. Though the price was several million pounds higher than Conry intimated to the HEA, the Valuation Office placed an open-market value of £28m on the site in March 2000 (Patrick Conroy to Martin Conry, 27 Mar. 2000 (APA, Grant #8024)). 103 *College View*, Oct. 2000. 104 Ongoing difficulties in developing the site eventually led to a decision to put

proved difficult, in part due to the fact that it was separated from the main Glasnevin campus. Early plans for Metro North included a stop underneath the site, further complicating matters.[105] The site was eventually put back up for sale in November 2019.[106] This was not, however, a major setback for the university. Relations with the Eustace family improved significantly during Brian MacCraith's presidency, allowing for the simultaneous purchase of an alternative 10 acres of the estate directly behind the O'Reilly Library, this time contiguous to the campus boundary and thus more suitable for development.[107]

The Helix

Utterly unique in terms of its function on campus, and in its design principles, the Helix performing-arts centre began life as a proposal to construct an aula maxima for convocations and other large gatherings. When calculating future space needs for NIHE Dublin, the Institute's planners envisaged construction of a 750 sq.m. 'large hall cum theatre' suitable for a range of activities, such as examinations, graduation ceremonies, dances, concerts, theatrical performances and use by the local community.[108] Mere months after the Institute opened its doors, however, the possibility of locating an arts centre on campus to serve the greater north Dublin area was also raised. It was not until the mid-1990s that the combination of both projects into one was advanced, out of which DCU's most architecturally ambitious building emerged.[109]

A campus arts centre first appeared on the Institute's wish list in January 1981. The initial design, drawn by Andrew Devane from a brief prepared by Barry Kehoe, blended performance spaces for theatre, cinema, music and the visual arts across a floor area of 882 sq.m., with an estimated cost of £500,000.[110] Somewhat incongruously, the centre would also incorporate a bank branch. The combination of the two was quite deliberate, however, with sponsorship for construction and running costs for the arts centre to be provided by the bank in return for an exclusive campus banking licence.[111]

the land back up for sale in late 2019 (*Irish Times*, 6 Nov. 2019). See also Arup, *Campus connectivity study* (Dublin, 2016).   **105** *Metro North: updated detailed business case* (July 2010).   **106** *Irish Times*, 6 Nov. 2019; *College View*, 13 Nov. 2019.   **107** Brian MacCraith to all staff, 23 Dec. 2019 (email provided to author).   **108** NIHED, *Plan for the physical development of the Institute*, p. 35.   **109** It is worth noting that Arthur Gibney's original campus master plan, developed in late 1984, featured just an arts centre, which would double as an aula maxima when needed. Under direction from Danny O'Hare, who was a strong advocate of having both, the 1989 master plan – which formed the basis for 1990s development on campus – incorporated a separate arts centre and aula maxima. **110** Andrew Devane to Barry Kehoe, 22 Jan. 1981; 'Proposal for the provision of an Arts Centre on the campus of NIHE Dublin', 23 Jan. 1981 (DCUPO, 'Arts centre – DCU'). The proposal document suggested that the best site for the centre would be on Collins Avenue, opposite Shanowen Avenue. This is precisely where the Helix is now situated.   **111** Due to the relatively unattractive size – from a commercial perspective – of NIHED's staff and student population, the plan for bank branch on campus, and thus bank sponsorship, fell through. Following a competitive

By May 1982 sufficient planning progress had been made to allow for mention of the intended arts centre in the Institute's annual report to the minister for education. Acknowledging that a lack of facilities for social and cultural activities presented a recurring difficulty for students, the report noted that an arts centre would 'expose students to the liberal arts in an integrated way and … provide theatre and arts facilities for the Northside of Dublin City and County', thus assisting the Institute's integration into the local community.[112] A meeting in October 1982 between Danny O'Hare and Frank Feely, city manager for Dublin Corporation, focused on the planning and financial support that the Institute required. While their discussions were positive, O'Hare left without any commitment of financial support for an arts centre – a frequent result of fundraising meetings over the ensuing thirteen years.[113]

Prospects were improved by the inclusion of Section 32 in the 1984 Finance Act, which provided for tax relief on contributions of between £100 and £10,000 made by any person to an artistic institution.[114] This was a significant improvement on the limited circumstances available for philanthropy in 1980, when the Institute had inquired as to the possibility of obtaining tax relief on donations 'for purposes relating to the arts'.[115] Adrian Munnelly, education officer with the Arts Council, met with O'Hare to discuss the implications of the 1984 Finance Act, and to advise on how financial support might be raised from the EEC, the government, Dublin Corporation and the Arts Council itself – provided that the arts centre be made readily available to the wider north Dublin community.[116]

Arthur Gibney's appointment as the Institute's architect saw designs for the arts centre evolve into a distinctive L-shape, with an outdoor amphitheatre and sculpture garden.[117] In a small but telling illustration of the Institute's

tendering process in the mid-1980s, Allied Irish Banks (AIB) was awarded an exclusive campus banking licence, which they operated until 2013. A dedicated banking building was located on DCU's campus for several years, at the east end of the mall close to the present site of the O'Reilly Library. It was demolished at the end of 2005. Bank of Ireland replaced AIB as the campus bank in December 2013 (DCUPO, 'AIB'; *Irish Independent*, 23 Jan. 2013; *DCU News*, 13 Dec. 2013). 112 NIHED, *Annual report, 1978–82*, pp 26, 31 (quotation on p. 31). 113 Danny O'Hare to Frank Feely, 22 Oct. 1982 (DCUPO, 'Correspondence: general, 1980–5'). O'Hare and Feely were on good terms, with O'Hare later advising Feely's daughter on her choice of postgraduate school in America (DCUPO, 'Dublin Corporation, 1982–2000'). 114 The section's provisions referred specifically to donations for the advancement of the practice of architecture, art and design, music and musical composition, theatre arts, film arts, or any other subject approved of by the minister for finance (Finance Act, 1984 (no. 9 of 1984), s. 32). 115 Barry Kehoe was advised that any such donation had to be made to the minister for finance in the first instance, and had to be for a purpose or towards defraying a cost usually covered by public finances (Adrian Munnelly to Barry Kehoe, 15 July 1980 (DCUPO, 'Arts centre – DCU')). 116 Laurence Cassidy to Danny O'Hare, 23 May 1984; J.P. Wright to Danny O'Hare, 10 July 1984 (DCUPO, 'Arts centre – DCU'). Dublin Corporation quickly made it clear that it was in no position to make a financial contribution. 117 Barry Kehoe visited several arts centres in Northern Ireland and England in 1982, including those at the University of Bradford, the University of Ulster and The Albany, Deptford.

commitment to the project, a scale model of Gibney's design was commissioned to enhance funding applications.[118] It was a shrewd move, with the model helping to convince the Arts Council to allocate a grant of £60,000 towards the centre's construction costs in November 1984.[119]

As with so many of the Institute's building projects during the 1980s, progress was slow. Fresh impetus was provided in 1987 as the Institute sought ways to participate in Dublin's millennium celebrations. By that stage £300,000 had been raised, though inflation had driven the expected overall cost to *c.*£1m.[120] O'Hare embarked on a sustained campaign to raise the outstanding amount, soliciting support from various stakeholders and private enterprises, including Dublin Corporation, Taoiseach Charles Haughey, the Guinness Group and Bank of Ireland. His efforts were in vain. NIHE Dublin's arts centre proposal received no funding under the National Lottery's 1988 allocation, despite a total of £8m being made available for arts and culture projects.[121]

The Institute now faced a choice: to hold its £300,000 in reserve while continuing to lobby for a major capital injection from the government or private sources, or to use the funds for equally pressing building projects, such as R&D facilities or the planned indoor sports centre. As O'Hare wrote in a pointed letter to the Arts Council:

> Our dilemma is this – whether to hold this money for the Arts Centre or to succumb, so to speak, to the extreme pressure on us to use the funds to support … much needed facilities on campus … I have still a personal commitment to establishing an Arts Centre in North Dublin, but I feel I must be somewhat more realistic in relation to the prospects of realising this ambition for our local community … I am loath nonetheless to let go of a progressive idea but after some six years I am firmly of the opinion that I must establish whether this project is 'on' or not.[122]

Information relating to these centres, including plans, was then forwarded to Gibney, whose 1985 development plan located the arts centre to the north of the campus, roughly where the McNulty building is now. Gibney's design called for a building with combined floor space of 1,650 sq.m. (DCUPO, 'Arts centre – DCU'). 118 Arthur Gibney charged £13,699.12 for drafting the design. The scale model, crafted by Gerard Crowley Modelmakers, cost £1,120.50 (Mary Boucher to Danny O'Hare, 11 Sept. 1984 (DCUPO, 'Arts centre – DCU')). 119 DCUPO, GB85/2 and 'Arts centre – DCU'; *Nuacht*, Mar. 1985. 120 Danny O'Hare to Ted Nealon, TD, 9 Feb 1987; 'The Millennium Arts Centre: A proposal to Dublin Corporation', May 1987 (DCUPO, 'Arts centre – DCU'). Dublin Corporation celebrated the city's millennium in 1988, and included the NIHED arts centre in a 'shopping list' of projects requiring support that was circulated to 400 potential sponsors in the Dublin area during planning for the millennium celebrations. 121 Statement by Ray MacSharry, TD, minister for finance, 19 Nov. 1987 (DCUPO, 'Arts centre – DCU'). 122 Danny O'Hare to Adrian Munnelly, 15 Dec. 1987 (DCUPO, 'Arts centre – DCU'). NIHED was, at that time, the only higher-education institution in Ireland without an indoor sports complex.

Just two months later Haughey refused to meet with a delegation from the Institute to discuss the project. O'Hare was informed that little would be gained by meeting, as no amount of special pleading would change the fact that government funding for the centre was unlikely to materialize in the foreseeable future.[123]

The enormous potential for an arts centre at DCU to enhance the greater north Dublin area was confirmed by the *Dublin arts report*, published in February 1992 by a working group drawn from the Arts Council, Dublin Corporation and Dublin County Council.[124] Local sentiment largely echoed the report's findings. Glasnevin North Community Council and Glasnevin Musical Society both expressed strong support.[125] There was, however, some opposition. Responding to the *Dublin arts report*, Labour Party councillor Tommy Broughan declared DCU an unsuitable location because it was an 'elitist and socially isolated university'.[126] Yet with local and national government unable to commit the resources necessary, the prospect of an arts centre on campus seemed remote.

Early in 1996 O'Hare sought feedback from staff and students on proposals to build an aula maxima on campus, which was regarded as a separate project to the arts centre. Barry Kehoe's response epitomized those of many others when he wryly observed that he was not sure what an aula maxima actually was. Kehoe proposed that the relationship between an aula maxima and arts centre should be examined, and that it might perhaps be more practical to design a facility that could accommodate the functions intended for both.[127] That suggestion was enthusiastically backed by Martin Conry and Marie Louise O'Donnell, DCU's director of arts and performance, prompting a reorientation of building plans.

Though Atlantic Philanthropies had been providing significant financial support to DCU's infrastructural and research development plans since 1990, it was not until DCU had incorporated the aula maxima into its arts centre design that the university made a formal application for funding. As was by now his custom, Danny O'Hare sought John Healy's opinion.[128] Initial reaction within Atlantic was cautious, particularly with regard to the financial viability of the building. Atlantic were conscious of the Arts Council's decision not to provide annual funding for UL's concert hall (another Atlantic-supported project), and the fact that there were six theatres of varying size all due for completion in Dublin before the end of the decade.[129] If funding were forthcoming, it would

---

123 Pádraig Ó hUigínn to Danny O'Hare, 22 Feb. 1988; Michael Barrett, TD, to Danny O'Hare, 2 Mar. 1988 (DCUPO, 'Arts centre – DCU').   124 *Dublin arts report* (Dublin, 1992); DCUPO, 'Arts centre – DCU'; *Dáil Debates*, 19 Feb. 1992; *Irish Times*, 7 Feb. 1992.   125 See, for example, *Dublin Tribune*, 15 Nov. 1990.   126 *Northside People*, 25 Mar. 1992. Formerly a teacher at St Aidan's CBS, located adjacent to DCU's campus, Broughan was elected to Dublin Corporation in 1991, and to Dáil Éireann in 1992, as a member of the Labour Party.   127 Danny O'Hare to all staff, 12 Jan. 1996; Barry Kehoe to Danny O'Hare, 31 Jan. 1996 (APA, Grant #7616). Kehoe's advice was repeated by John Healy (John R. Healy to Danny O'Hare, 28 May 1996 (APA, Grant #8037, 1/3)).   128 John R. Healy to Danny O'Hare, 22 Feb. 1996 (APA, Grant #7616).   129 Colin McCrea to

have to wait until the library and computer building extension – two major projects to which Atlantic was already committed – had been fully financed and construction was underway.[130]

In the meantime, alternative sources of major donations were actively sought by DCU Educational Trust. Impressed by the university's commitment to improving the facilities of north Dublin City, Tim Mahony of Killeen Investments Ireland expressed an interest in supporting DCU's plans.[131] Mahony's intervention was timely in light of the Arts Council's decision to withdraw its own commitment to contribute £310,000 to fund the arts centre.[132] That decision itself was unsurprising, given the Arts Council's original financial commitment to the project had been made eleven years previously, and the growing role of the Department of Arts, Culture and the Gaeltacht in the distribution of funds for arts-related capital projects.

By December 1997 Atlantic had agreed to contribute £10m towards the construction of the aula maxima/arts centre, with the condition that DCU secure a further £5m from another donor. Initial indications were that Tim Mahony would provide the remaining £5m.[133] The tax implications of Mahony's donation were, however, crucial, with their determination to use Section 16 of the 1997 Finance Act necessitating government approval for the extension of the section to universities. Delays on this issue ran for several months, threatening Mahony's involvement and thus the project as a whole.[134]

Andrzej Wejchert, of A&D Wejchert Architects, presented his plans for the combined aula maxima/arts centre in June 1998. Incorporating 11,700 sq.m. of space across a 1,200-seat concert hall, 400-seat theatre with fly tower and orchestra pit, a small theatre for experimental work, studio space and facilities for conferences and workshops, Wejchert's design promised a stunning addition to the university.[135] Its location, directly inside what was then the university's main campus entrance, was deliberately chosen to offer a buffer zone between the community and the university's academic functions:

> This pivotal location between main entrance and central mall allows the building to form the link between town and gown. The building has been

John R. Healy, 28 Aug. 1997, John R. Healy to Colin McCrea, 1 Sept. 1997 (APA, Grant #8031, 1/3). **130** John R. Healy to Danny O'Hare, 22 Feb. 1996 (APA, Grant #7616). **131** Danny O'Hare to Tim Mahony, 20 Apr. 1995; Tim Mahony to Danny O'Hare, 26 Apr. and 15 May 1995 (DCUPO, 'Arts centre – DCU'). **132** Danny O'Hare to Colm Ó hEocha, 19 Nov. 1991; Adrian Munnelly to Danny O'Hare, 6 Mar. 1995 (DCUPO, 'Arts centre – DCU'). The Arts Council's financial commitment had been raised from £60,000 to £310,000 in late 1989 (DCUPO, GB90/1, 2; *Nuacht*, Jan. 1990). **133** Colin McCrea memo, 1 Dec. 1997 (APA, Grant #8037, 1/3; Grant #7616). **134** Bertie Ahern to Paddy Wright, 18 Feb. 1998; Paddy Barrett to Martin Conry, 23 June 1998 (APA, Grant #8037, 1/3). Tax clearance was received from the Revenue Commissioners to use Section 16 (which became Section 485 of the 1997 Taxes Consolidation Act) in September 1998. **135** Danny O'Hare to Colin McCrea, 7 Jan. 1999 (APA, Grant #7616); DCUPO, 'Arts centre –

designed in response to this role with an open transparent appearance
facing the main entrance and with a curving wall and linear feature
columns directing people along the axis between the Main Campus
Entrance, the Arts Centre and the Central Mall. This is precisely the role
for which the Arts Centre was originally intended in the original university
master plan.[136]

One of the most eye-catching features was Wejchert's determination to work
against the 'logical, rational and sciences-oriented campus' by using the
building's form to mirror the contradictions and conflicts inherent in the arts.[137]
Approval for construction was granted by Micheál Martin, minister for
education and science, on the basis 'that no direct Exchequer expenditure will
arise ... in any circumstances', and planning permission was received in March
1999.[138]

Eighteen months later the project encountered a potentially devastating
setback when Tim Mahony wrote to Conry to formally withdraw his support.[139]
The loss of almost a quarter of the project budget would make the arts centre
impossible to complete and entail the loss of previous investments in the design
process. Mahony had been unhappy for some time at the lack of communication
from DCU concerning important developments, including budget overruns, the
government's intention to locate an Irish Academy of Performing Arts at DCU
and the lack of assurances that Danny O'Hare's departure from the university
would not affect the project.[140] Following the intercession of John Healy, and a
meeting with Martin Conry, Mahony's fears were assuaged and his support
reaffirmed.[141]

Mahony's concerns regarding the project budget were understandable, given
an escalation from £15m in December 1997 to £22.9m by January 1999.[142] By

DCU' and 'The Helix'; *A&D Wejchert & Partners* (Kinsale, 2008).   **136** Andrzej Wejchert to
Martin Conry, 23 Oct. 1998 (APA, Grant #8037, 1/3). Wejchert was responding to suggestions that
the arts centre (Helix) would be moved from its present location to the one currently occupied by
the multi-storey car park. While the Helix was in its design stage, the main campus entrance on
Collins Avenue was located where the pedestrian entrance currently stands. The present main
entrance was, at that time, used for construction-vehicle access. When opened, the Helix was thus
the first building visible when entering the campus.   **137** Marie-Louise O'Donnell, 'The Helix',
Irish Arts Review, 19:3 (2002), pp 90–7.   **138** John Hayden to Danny O'Hare, 25 Sept. 1998 (APA,
Grant #8037, 1/3); Colin McCrea memo, 8 Apr. 1999 (APA, Grant #8037, 2/3). Quotation from
Hayden letter.   **139** Tim Mahony to Martin Conry, 4 Feb. 2000; Tim Mahony to John R. Healy,
4 Feb. 2000 (APA, Grant #8037, 2/3).   **140** John R. Healy to Martin Conry et al., 22 Dec. 1999;
John R. Healy memo, 14 Feb. 2000 (APA, Grant #8037, 2/3); DCU Estates Office, unsorted files.
The proposal to establish a National Academy of Performing Arts at DCU, which dated back to the
end of 1999, aroused trenchant opposition within the arts community and was later abandoned. See,
for example, *Irish Times*, 6 and 11 Dec. 1999, 29 Apr. and 15 June 2002.   **141** John R. Healy memo,
14 Feb. 2000 (APA, Grant #8037, 2/3); DCUPO, 'Arts centre – DCU'.   **142** Construction of the
Helix began in March 2000 (*Irish Times*, 11 Apr. 2000; *College View*, Apr. 2000).

the time the Helix was completed, costs had spiralled to £28.75m. With £15m of philanthropic funding secured, DCU also entered into an arrangement with RTÉ to host its concert orchestra, for a contribution of £2m, and later secured £5m from the government.[143] The university's accountants also designed a special-purpose tax arrangement to recoup more than £2m in VAT payments. An additional grant of almost €1m was also sanctioned by Atlantic to cover the escalating costs, bringing Atlantic's total investment to just under €15m.[144]

On 21 October 2002 the president of Ireland, Mary McAleese, performed the formal opening ceremony for the Helix Centre for the Performing Arts – known simply as the Helix (see plate 15).[145] Following the example set with the university's first graduation ceremony, composer Colin Mawby was commissioned to write a unique piece of music for the occasion.[146] The ceremony marked the launch of a varied programme of musical and theatrical performances, including RTÉ's Living Music Festival, and represented a remarkable achievement for a university better known for its excellence in STEM-related teaching and research.[147]

Some operational teething issues were inevitable, given the scale of the undertaking and lack of experience in running such a facility within the university. Despite the appointment of an artistic director, attendances at shows were poor in the first six months of operations, during which the Helix operated at a substantial loss. DCU staff and students were initially slow to embrace the new facility.[148] The completion of the Helix nonetheless marked the culmination of a planning process that had lasted more than twenty years, and its value to the university has been proven with time.[149] Over the past eighteen years the venue has established itself as an integral feature of the north Dublin arts scene – exactly as intended when planning began in January 1981.

---

143 Relations with RTÉ subsequently broke down when the broadcaster attempted to attach a host of ancillary conditions to their financial contribution, leading to the cancellation of their arrangement with DCU and the payment of no money (APA, Grant #8037, 2/3 and 3/3). 144 APA, Grant #8037, 2/3 and Grant #7684. Atlantic's supplementary grant covered the cost of designing and constructing a basement to increase the overall size of the Helix, in view of the overall pressures of space on campus. Figures are given in a mix of Euro and £IR in this paragraph due to the nature of the surviving records. 145 The original name for the Helix was The University Arts Centre at DCU – favoured by Atlantic but rejected by Ferdinand von Prondzynski, who preferred a name that suggested the facility was open to all, not just to those involved with the university (Ferdinand von Prondzynski to John R. Healy and Colin McCrea, 8 Nov. 2001 (APA, Grant #8037, 3/3)). 146 DCUPO, 'Conferring, 1983' and 'Helix'. Colin Mawby was appointed choral director at RTÉ in 1981, and was one of the founders of RTÉ's philharmonic, chamber and children's choirs. 147 *Irish Times*, 22 Oct. 2002. 148 'Final report on The Helix', Apr. 2003 (APA, Grant #8037, 3/3); Ferdinand von Prondzynski interview, 18 Oct. 2018. By 2017 turnover at the venue had risen to €3.2m, with pretax profits recorded at just over €0.5m (*Irish Times*, 24 Aug. 2017). 149 In a signal that the Helix had evolved into a landmark project both for DCU and Atlantic Philanthropies, the majority of Atlantic's Irish staff attended the opening ceremony – something they rarely did. Von Prondzynski also arranged personal tours of the facility for Chuck Feeney and Atlantic's board members (APA, Grant #8037, 3/3).

Table 6.1. **Building completions and accommodation capacity (Glasnevin),
1980–2018**

Name	Year	Floor Space (sq.m.)[150]
Albert College (refurbishment)	1980	c.3,500
John Barry (refurbishment)[151]	1980	Unknown
Bea Orpen (refurbishment)	1980	1,350[152]
An Grianán[153]	1980/1983/2000	400
Hamstead building[154]	1980/1986	Unknown
Henry Grattan building	1981	6,090
Restaurant	1981	2,125
Albert College extension	1985	1,000
Pavilion (restaurant extension)[155]	1986	260
Creche[156]	1986/1999	305
Henry Grattan extension	1987	c.2,500
Estates office and workshops	1989	390
Research and Development (Hamilton)[157]	1990	2,975
Interfaith centre	1990	240
Student centre/The Hub/The U	1990/2000/2018	1,200/3,450/5,500
Terence Larkin lecture theatre	1991	570
Larkfield residences	1991	5,095
Computer Applications (McNulty)[158]	1992	c.2,000
DCU Business School	1992	6,570
Sports centre	1992/2004	3,775/4,530
Physics[159]	1993	5,210
Library extension[160]	1996	c.500
Administration (MacCormac) building[161]	1998	1,125
Hamstead residences	1998	7,440
Computer Applications extension	1999	c.3,000
Chemical Sciences and Biotechnology (Lonsdale)[162]	1999	13,470
Sports pavilion (St Clare's Grounds)	2000	1,210
Multi-storey car park	2000	21,000
Postgraduate residences	2000	4,600
John and Aileen O'Reilly Library	2000	10,065
DCU Invent	2000	2,670
Engineering and Research (Stokes) building[163]	2002	11,000
The Helix	2002	11,900
Nursing and Human Sciences	2003	7,100
College Park residences	2004	15,475
National Institute for Cellular Biotechnology	2006	3,630
Biomedical Diagnostics Institute	2008	2,500
Nanobioanalytical Research Facility	2014	3,000

Sources: DCU Estates Office; Atlantic Philanthropies Archive, Cornell University; NIHED/DCU, *Annual
reports, 1980–98, 2005–14*.

As can be seen in table 6.1, by the end of the 1990s the Glasnevin campus had largely taken shape. Fourteen new buildings were completed that decade, as well as a second extension to the Henry Grattan building in 1996, to provide further library space. Plans for a dedicated library building, incorporating the latest in information technology, were at that point well advanced.[164] The opening of the John and Aileen O'Reilly Library in 2000 marked a significant improvement in the facilities available to staff and students at DCU, trebling the university's previous library seating capacity. Funded by a mix of state investment and philanthropy, including major donations from Atlantic Philanthropies and Anthony O'Reilly, the new library (named for O'Reilly's parents) was situated at the opposite end of the mall to the Helix and provided over 10,000 sq.m. of space, with 1,500 reader places – all capable of full internet connectivity – alongside 400 public computer terminals.[165] In addition to the Helix and the

150 Floor-space calculations for certain buildings include minor extensions completed after initial construction.   **151** Built *c.*1900, briefly home to NIHED library and later utilized for laboratory work. Demolished along with Hamstead in 2000 to make way for the construction of postgraduate residences.   **152** Incorporates minor extensions in 1993 and 2000.   **153** Use permitted by Dublin Corporation from 1980 until 1983, when it was bought by the Department of Education, on behalf of NIHED. Converted into the president's residence in 2000.   **154** Two-storey prefab located to the rear of the Bea Orpen building. Extended in 1986. Demolished along with the John Barry building in 2000 to make way for the construction of postgraduate residences.   **155** Formerly home to Student Services, Students' Union offices and social space. Currently home to the Centre for Talented Youth, Ireland.   **156** Permanent creche building completed in 1999. Housed in a temporary building between 1986 and 1999.   **157** Renamed Hamilton in 2016 in honour of mathematician Sir William Rowan Hamilton (David Spearman, 'Hamilton, William Rowan (1805–65)' in *DIB*; *DCU News*, 5 July 2016, 5 July 2017).   **158** Renamed the McNulty building in 2016 in honour of pioneering computer programmer Kathleen McNulty (Linde Lunney, 'McNulty, Kathleen (Kay) (1921–2006)' in *DIB*; *DCU News*, 5 July 2016, 5 July 2017).   **159** Renamed the Marconi building in 2017, in honour of Guglielmo Marconi, inventor of the radio telegraph system (*DCU News*, 5 July 2017).   **160** A further extension of the Henry Grattan building, currently home to Information Systems Services.   **161** Formally renamed the MacCormac building in 2016 after Prof. Michael MacCormac, chairman of NIHED's governing body 1979–82 (*DCU News*, 5 July 2016).   **162** Formerly known simply as the X Block. Renamed in 2016 in honour of Dame Kathleen Lonsdale, a crystallographer born in Newbridge, Co. Kildare and the first female professor appointed at University College London (Enda Leaney and Linde Lunney, 'Lonsdale, Kathleen (1903–71)' in *DIB*; *DCU News*, 5 July 2017).   **163** Renamed the Stokes building in 2017 in honour of Sir George Gabriel Stokes (1819–1903), mathematician and physicist. A major extension of the Stokes building was completed in 2018, with capacity for an additional 1,400 students (Linde Lunney and Enda Leaney, 'Stokes, George Gabriel (1819–1903)' in *DIB*; *DCU News*, 5 July 2017, 9 July 2018).   **164** DCU became the first university in Ireland to receive the QMark from Excellence Ireland, which was awarded for its plans for a new library. Designed by Scott Tallon Walker architects, construction on the library began in January 1999. It was completed the following year and opened in time for the 2000/1 academic year, but the ceremonial opening was not held until April 2002 (*Newslink*, Apr. 1999; *Irish Independent*, 16 Jan. 1999, 23 Apr. 2002; *Irish Times*, 23 May 1998, 16 Jan. 1999).   **165** Paul Sheehan, 'Dublin City University new library – a library for the information age', *Liber Quarterly*, 10:2 (2000), pp 84–93; HEA, *Reports, accounts and student statistics, 1996–8*, p. 146. O'Reilly's donation amounted to *c.*€3m, with Atlantic

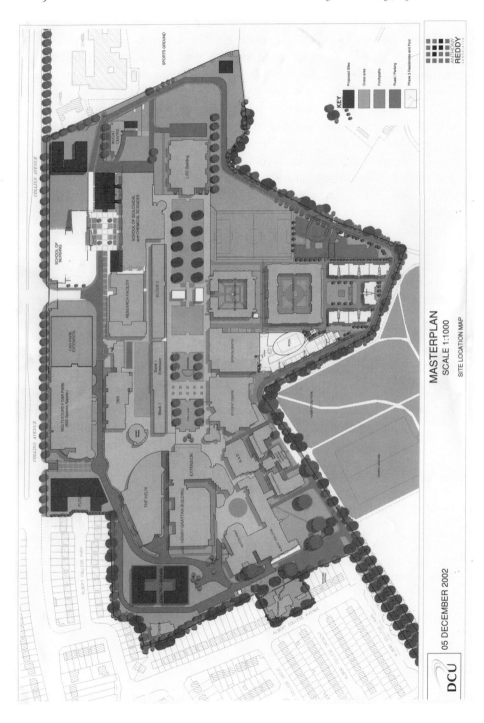

6.7 Revised campus development master plan, December 2002 (DCU Collection).

O'Reilly Library, as the new millennium approached construction was also underway or nearing completion on the Hub, DCU Invent and the Engineering and Research (Stokes) building. Together, these twenty additions increased the university's built footprint by 540 per cent, from *c*.18,000 sq.m. to *c*.97,000 sq.m.[166] Priorities for the first decade of the new millennium centred on the construction of a nursing school (completed in 2003) and the National Institute for Cellular Biotechnology (completed in 2006).

Engaged to update the university's campus plan in 1999, it is notable that Anthony Reddy Associates returned a design that adhered to the principles outlined by Arthur Gibney, but with specific refinements geared towards public-area enhancements and the development of the Collins Avenue frontage. The gradual development of the campus along its south-east axis had led to the creation of a new main entrance in front of the Engineering and Research (Stokes) building. The old main entrance, situated further west on Collins Avenue opposite the Helix, became accessible only to pedestrians. Improvement of the new main entrance, which lacked the grandeur of the Helix as the first sight to greet visitors to the campus, became a priority for MacCraith during the early years of his presidency. Working on a collaborative design project, Collins Maher Martin Architects and ZAP Architecture combined in 2014 to produce an award-winning entrance feature with an array of glue-laminated timber posts (rising up to sixteen metres tall), accompanied by two-metre precast concrete letters spelling DCU, in the same style as the logo designed by Barry Bödeker.[167]

Development of the Collins Avenue area of the campus had previously been a delicate subject, given the impact of DCU's construction programme on surrounding housing estates.[168] In addition to the Eustace Estate and a public park, the campus shared a boundary with a local school and housing estates, with high-density development located directly opposite its Collins Avenue frontage. One of the key themes that emerged during planning for the Helix was the university's desire to use the building to strengthen its links with the surrounding community. Continuous construction on campus for much of the 1990s had, however, strained relations with local residents. Matters were worsened in 2000 when the decision to locate a new five-storey car park on Collins Avenue added to the disruptions already caused by work on the Helix.[169]

Philanthropies contributing €6.5m to the library project between 1994 and 1997. Other significant donors to the library, which had a total cost of *c*.€28m, included Aon Corporation, Citigroup, Nestle, Fyffes, while there were also significant donations from the Dolan, Kenny, Levin, MacDougall, Marron, Mitchell and O'Halleran families (APA, Grant #7411; DCUPO, 'Library'; *Irish Times*, 11 May 2000, 15 June 2002; *Irish Independent*, 23 and 24 Apr. 2002).   **166** The multi-storey car park, completed in 2000 with a floor space of *c*.21,000 sq.m., is not included in this calculation.   **167** For Bödeker's design, see appendix 1. The concrete lettering at the main entrance on Collins Avenue won an Elemental Award at the Irish Concrete Society's 32nd Annual Awards (DCUPO, GA2014/2).   **168** 'DCU master plan presentation', 14 Nov. 2002 (DCU Estates Office, unsorted files).   **169** Ferdinand von Prondzynski to John R. Healy and Colin McCrea, 8 Nov. 2001

Writing in the *Irish Times*, Frank McDonald observed that the car park was redolent of the Berlin Wall and gave the university the appearance of a fortress.[170] Residents on the avenue complained about the impact of construction on their daily lives, labelling the car park a 'monstrosity', with the new Chemical Sciences and Biotechnology (Lonsdale) building dismissed as resembling a stack of shipping containers in Dublin Port.[171] Regarding potential pollution from the latter, Paddy Horgan of the Westfield Residents' Association questioned DCU's decision not to put student residences on Collins Avenue instead: 'DCU is like the Angel of Justice in Dublin Castle, she's got her arse facing the people of Collins Avenue.'[172] Residents also complained about a lack of communication from the university and that they were only made aware of new building projects once construction had started.[173] Ciarán O'Kelly, director of buildings for the university, acknowledged some of these complaints but insisted that the building work would benefit the community by increasing house values and rental incomes and providing local employment.[174] Residents' fears that the new multi-storey car park would not solve the problem of students parking in their estates were realized when a charge of £60 was introduced for use of the facility, prompting an increase in student parking on Collins Avenue.[175]

V

Under the presidency of Brian MacCraith, development planning for the Glasnevin campus has reflected the fact that little of the site remains as green-field development space. The focus has accordingly switched to the consolidation of already developed land, incorporating extensions to and refurbishment of existing buildings. Teaching and learning infrastructure have also been targeted for improvement as part of ongoing efforts to create a digital campus.[176] As a corollary to this objective, the university has also invested in the development of

(APA, Grant #8037, 3/3).   **170** *Irish Times*, 15 June 2002.   **171** The facade referred to is now largely obscured from Collins Avenue by the Nursing and Human Sciences and Stokes buildings. **172** The Westfield Residents' Association wrote to Dublin Corporation requesting information regarding the chemicals that would be stored in the new buildings (Francis Healy to David Dunne, 9 Mar. 1996 (DCUPO, 'Dublin Corporation, 1982–2000'); *College View*, Mar. 2000). Quotation from *College View*.   **173** A residents' liaison group had been proposed in the mid-1990s but was not established until the beginning of 1999, when DCU appointed a contact person for each housing estate adjoining its Glasnevin campus and St Clare's sports ground. Additional measures to alleviate the problem included the hosting of public meetings to inform residents of its development plans (*DCU News*, Apr. 1999; Brendan Brady to Danny O'Hare, 10 Dec. 1998 (DCUPO, 'Dublin Corporation, 1982–2000'); Eilis O'Brien to Eileen Brady, 22 May 2002 (DCUPO, 'Dublin City Council, 2002–15')).   **174** *College View*, Mar. 2000. Ciarán O'Kelly was director of buildings at NIHED/DCU from 1985 until 2003.   **175** *College View*, Oct. 2000 and Oct. 2001. The charge was introduced before the multi-storey car park had been finished. See chapter 7 for an overview of the university's community-based initiatives.   **176** DCUPO, GA2017/4; DCU, *Transforming lives and societies*, p. 21; *DCU News*, 29 Apr. 2016, 20 Sept. 2017,

DCU Alpha, a commercial-innovation campus established in 2013 and located in the former headquarters of Enterprise Ireland on the Old Finglas Road, close to the Glasnevin campus.[177] Plans for the establishment of a university-linked, enterprise-oriented campus had been in existence since the late 1980s but had failed to come to fruition.[178] During his inauguration speech, MacCraith signalled his intention to revive these efforts:

> The Eastern Corridor between Dublin and Belfast is and will continue to be the largest and fastest growing centre of population and economic activity on the island of Ireland. This corridor, stretching north from DCU, through Fingal, Dublin Airport, Drogheda, Dundalk and across the border to Belfast, offers massive untapped potential to DCU ... DCU will be a key force in this region and play a pivotal role in the next wave of its economic, social and cultural development ... I am committed to working with partners in the establishment of a significant Science & Technology Park in this region with a focus on knowledge-based industries.[179]

Following Enterprise Ireland's decision to relocate, the university entered lengthy negotiations to acquire the site from the Department of Jobs, Enterprise and Innovation. A 99-year lease was signed in January 2013, with an annual rent of just €100.[180] By 2019 the campus was considered to be operating at capacity and was host to more than 100 companies, with over 800 people employed on site.[181]

Since the mid-2010s, state investment in the third-level sector has gradually returned to its pre-recession levels, though it has not kept pace with the national increase in student numbers. One of the main priorities pursued by DCU in recent years is the enhancement of student life, including the redevelopment of the student centre and provision of additional residences, alongside improved transportation links between the university's campuses.[182] Another key feature of the most recent campus development plan is the intention to refine its visual appeal, particularly the mall, which received extensive improvements in 2019.[183] In this there are echoes of an ambition expressed in the university's 1995

18 Sept. 2018. **177** The campus is located beside the National Botanic Gardens. The university has had an association with the site since the first days of NIHE Dublin, when the site was home to the Institute of Industrial Research and Standards (IIRS). NIHE Dublin's staff formed research links with the IIRS, which was established by the government in 1946 (Industrial Research and Standards Act, 1946 (No. 25 of 1946)). **178** DCUPO, 'Science Park – Proposed (1987–1998)', 'Software Park – Proposed (1991–97). **179** Brian MacCraith inauguration speech, 13 July 2010 (https://www.dcu.ie/president/speeches.shtml). **180** Continuation of the lease was predicated on certain performance indicators, which have consistently been met. Originally known as the DCU Innovation Campus, it was rebranded as DCU Alpha in 2015 (DCUPO, GA 2013/2–6, GA2015/6, GA2016/6, GA2017/5). **181** DCUPO, GA2018/6; Makerspace People, *The creation of an Institute of Making* (2019). **182** DCUPO, GA2013/6. The newly renovated student centre, known as the U, opened in November 2018. **183** *College View*, 2 Oct. 2019.

strategic plan, which was not blind to the Orwellian aesthetic then prevalent on campus: 'Buildings have been very utilitarian in nature ... We are now entering a more mature phase of development during which we aim to place more emphasis on amenities and landscaping and can facilitate a more "joyful" approach to our existing buildings.'[184] Planning for the future, DCU's governing authority instigated a risk-management committee with responsibility for maintaining an institutional-risk register, which highlighted the threat to the university's future presented by a lack of space for future growth.[185] This risk was reduced, in the short term, by the completion of the Incorporation process, which has also prompted major renovations and additions to the St Pat's campus, and refurbishment of elements of All Hallows.[186] Further campus development was ensured when funding was secured from the Ireland Strategic Investment Fund and the European Investment Bank – which had provided €800m to support education investment across Ireland – in late 2015. Combined with earlier agreements, these facilities provided DCU with the ability to borrow €130m for the progression of Phase 1 of its new campus development plan, which promised overall investment of €300m.[187] Echoing his predecessors and, indeed, the *raison d'être* of NIHED/DCU as articulated by its first governing body, MacCraith welcomed the ISIF/EIB funding as crucial investment in DCU's graduates and its research programme, fundamental factors in the creation of a sustainable Irish economy.[188]

Located in an eclectic and unique urban environment and squeezed between a public park, farmland, housing estates and a secondary school, DCU's campus enjoys none of the verdant space or classical architectural notes evident at the 'traditional' Dublin universities. Its stately nineteenth-century buildings are tucked away in the south-west corner of the campus; narrower planning foresight might have seen ill-informed attempts to orient the campus around the Albert College building. Resisting that temptation, DCU's planners and architects have ensured the evolution of a campus that reflects the university's core value of practicality in education. Conceived in an era of constrained public finances, Arthur Gibney's 1989 development master plan gave greater prominence to function rather than form, allowing for modular development. More crucially, his decision to structure the campus around a central mall has allowed this densely developed, tightly planned campus to maintain a coherence and sense of community often lacking in universities with more abundant space for growth. Retention of this central feature in more recent master plans echoes the university's founding commitment to fostering dialogue and interdisciplinarity in teaching and research.

---

184 DCU, *Strategy for the year 2000*, p. 16.   185 See, for example, DCUPO, GA2015/1.
186 DCUPO, GA2015/4, 6, GA2016/2; *DCU News*, 29 Apr. 2016.   187 DCUPO, GA2015/3 and GA2016/1; *DCU News*, 29 Apr. 2016.   188 *Irish Times*, 30 Apr. 2016.

7

The university in the community

The transformation of Irish educational policy during the 1960s was spurred by a variety of factors, particularly the need to widen the range of subjects and training opportunities available to students in response to the changing demands of the labour market. There was also a broader recognition that the potential progression of students to third-level study was influenced by various considerations, particularly socio-economic status. Tacit acknowledgment of this fact came in a speech by Donogh O'Malley, minister for education, on 10 September 1966. Though the speech is better known for the surprise announcement of the government's intention to provide free second-level education for all, O'Malley also made a bold commitment to ensuring equality of access to university education by eliminating financial barriers: 'I am glad to be able to announce that I am drawing up a scheme under which, in future, no boy or girl in this State will be deprived of full educational opportunity – from primary to university level – by reason of the fact that the parents cannot afford to pay for it.'[1] O'Malley's commitment was, to some extent, embodied in the 1971 legislation that established the HEA. Among the functions bestowed on the authority was a duty to promote the 'attainment of equality of opportunity in higher education'.[2] Yet responsibility for implementing this commitment was soon devolved onto third-level institutions themselves. Though the state introduced student grant schemes in the 1970s, these were largely ineffective in promoting participation in higher education across all sectors of society, even at a time when the number of student places steadily increased.[3] It was not until the mid-1990s that the government began to draft and implement formal policies on widening access to third level, with a particular focus on disadvantaged students.[4] Those policies were significantly influenced by the success of two programmes initiated at DCU in 1990 – the direct-access scholarships and BITE: Ballymun Initiative for Third-Level Education. It was not entirely accidental that both of

1 Quoted in Brian Fleming and Judith Hartford, 'Irish educational policy in the 1960s: a decade of transformation', *History of Education*, 43:5 (2014), p. 648. O'Malley's announcement of free second-level education had not been approved by the cabinet, and provoked a furious reaction from the Department of Education.   2 Higher Education Authority Act, 1971 (No. 22 of 1971), s. 3. 3 HEA, *Progressing the action plan: funding to achieve equity of access to higher education* (Dublin, 2005), pp 4–16.   4 The term 'disadvantaged' is used here to refer to students from lower socio-economic groups, mature students, students with disabilities, and those from ethnic-minority backgrounds. For a detailed discussion of how to define disadvantage and access in the university context, see Andrew Loxley, Fergal Finnegan and Ted Fleming, *Access and participation in higher*

these schemes were conceived as NIHE Dublin transitioned to DCU, taking its place as the only university in north Dublin. As the institution enjoyed a subsequent period of significant and rapid expansion, it increasingly came into contact with economically disadvantaged communities in close proximity to its campus. BITE and the direct-access scheme played a pivotal role in increasing DCU's awareness of the challenges that faced these communities, leading to the formulation of ad hoc community-outreach programmes, their later incorporation into the university's strategic goals and the creation of the Access Service. DCU's civic-engagement strategy and interaction with the community that exists beyond its campus, both locally and nationally, has thus been focused on two ambitions – widening access to higher education for disadvantaged students, and assisting north Dublin's general economic and social development.

I

Increased investment in the third-level sector from the 1960s allowed for a major expansion of the number of places available to students. During the 1960s and 1970s enrolment at third-level institutions more than doubled. Despite this increased level of participation, the student population in the 1980s was still overwhelmingly drawn from among the upper socio-economic groups.[5] Research conducted in the late 1970s and early 1980s by the Economic and Social Research Institute, as well as the Organisation for Economic Co-operation and Development, suggested that many potential third-level students were unable or unwilling to further their education due to the associated costs.[6] Means-tested subsidy schemes, provided by local authorities such as the vocational-education committees, as well as the Higher Education Authority, went some way towards addressing the needs of those from socio-economically disadvantaged backgrounds. There was, however, growing recognition that merely increasing the third-level sector's ability to enrol students did not create greater equality of access: 'The financial stringency of the present system is such that it does not adequately compensate those from less well-off homes.'[7]

When formulating the educational philosophy of NIHE Dublin, the Institute's governing body acknowledged the need to develop 'an awareness ... of [the Institute's] place, both socially and physically, as an element within the community at large', and to 'make a real and meaningful contribution to the

education (London, 2017), pp 45–87.   **5** Fleming, Loxley and Finnegan, *Access and participation in Irish higher education*, p. 47.   **6** See, for example, A.C. Barlow, *The financing of third-level education* (Dublin, 1981); Maureen Woodhall, *Review of student support schemes in selected OECD countries* (Paris, 1978). For a summary of the work of Patrick Clancy, one of the leading Irish scholars on participation trends and policy development in higher education, see his *Irish higher education: a comparative perspective* (Dublin, 2015).   **7** Barlow, *The financing of third-level education*, p. 4.

equalisation of educational opportunity for students from all social and cultural backgrounds'.[8] Those ambitions were further developed in the 1977 *Plan for the future of the Institute*, which also contained a commitment to lifelong education through the 'abolition of artificial distinctions between formal and informal qualifications and between young and old students'.[9] The Institute's mission statement, ratified by academic council on 8 June 1983, stated its intent to 'assist in the equalisation of educational opportunity across all socio-economic groups; to be a responsible member of its local community; [and] to make its facilities and resources available, wherever possible, for community development'.[10]

Lifelong learning, and the opening up of non-traditional educational opportunities, were pursued through the establishment of distance education as a core feature of the Institute's curriculum.[11] With regard to providing equal opportunities to attend the Institute, particularly for students from disadvantaged socio-economic backgrounds, there were few models upon which governing body could draw in formulating strategies. Irish universities had traditionally offered a limited number of undergraduate scholarships and fee waivers, based on academic merit and financial hardship. It was in this context that governing body established a working group on disadvantaged students in 1982.[12] While the Institute already remitted course fees for individual students on a case-by-case basis, governing body was concerned that a noticeable number of students were abandoning their studies due to financial pressure. The working group began its deliberations by collating information on financial-aid schemes from within the Irish higher-education sector, as well as universities in France and the United States of America. Subsequent deliberations considered a wide range of potential measures to ease the burden on students deemed to be in financial hardship. As a corollary to discussing measures to assist its own students, the group also briefly considered how the Institute might take a lead role in framing a coherent national policy on financial assistance for disadvantaged students.

This second objective was quickly discarded as an unrealistic ambition, a recognition that as a new institution still struggling to provide adequate facilities for its own staff and students, it was beyond their resources to address the wider inadequacies of government policy on student support and higher-education funding. A number of options for supporting the Institute's students were presented to governing body, including working with the banking sector to arrange student loans at favourable rates; sourcing industry-sponsored

8 NIHED, *An educational philosophy for the National Institute for Higher Education, Dublin*, pp 5–6. 9 NIHED, *Plan for the future of the Institute* (1977), p. 8. 10 Academic council also adopted a general resolution, in early 1984, that the Institute should 'aim at increasing the participation rate of those from lower socio-economic groups' (DCUPO, AC83/5–7, AC84/3, 4; *Nuacht*, Apr. 1984; NIHED, *Academic procedures*, p. 3). 11 For a discussion of distance learning at NIHED/DCU, see chapter 5. 12 Susan Folan to Carmel Ryan, 22 Nov. 1982 (DCUPO, 'Governing authority

scholarships; and establishing an educational trust fund.[13] George Hegarty, Students' Union president, continued to press for the development of policies on student financial assistance that could be presented to the government for implementation on a national scale. While sympathetic to Hegarty's arguments, governing body nonetheless endorsed the working party's recommendation to focus on the Institute's current and future students.[14]

Precedent for industry-sponsored scholarships already existed. Under the guidance of Anthony Glynn, the Institute's Industrial Liaison Unit had already secured funding for several scholarships and prizes. Over the course of the 1982/3 academic year, the Unit maintained contact with more than 200 commercial and industrial firms. While these contacts were primarily driven by attempts to place students on the INTRA scheme, they also allowed Glynn and his staff to solicit research contracts and consultancy fees, gifts of equipment, scholarships and other financial donations. By the time the working party reported, the unit had sourced six scholarships from the private sector, while a further six scholarships had been made available through formal linkage agreements with California State University and the University of Kentucky.[15] With the Irish economy in the grip of a deep recession, staff were conscious of the pressure on students to make ends meet, and of the value of these prizes and scholarships. Writing to a student to inform him he had placed first in his class, Tim Wheeler, head of the School of Communications, noted that the achievement brought with it a prize of £30 from RTÉ: 'I hope that the rigours of life on a building site have not taken their full toll and I look forward to seeing a financially healthy student returning to us.'[16]

In recommending the formation of an educational trust fund, the working party was influenced by American and British models of student funding. Barry Kehoe, head of Student Services, drafted a detailed outline for the proposed fund. A passionate advocate for the Institute's students – which frequently led him to clash with the Institute's executive – Kehoe framed the fund as an 'expression of the Institute's concern for student welfare and the equalisation of educational opportunity'. Conscious of the fact that the Institute had very limited cash reserves and was almost wholly dependent on state funding, Kehoe proposed a pilot project lasting eighteen months. The fund would complement

working groups'). 13 'Report of Working group on disadvantaged students', 22 June 1983 (DCUPO, 'Governing authority working groups'). 14 DCUPO, GB83/5; DCUPO, 'Governing Authority Working Groups'; *Nuacht*, July 1983. 15 DCUPO, 'Industrial Liaison, 1980–92'; NIHED, *Annual report, 1982/3*, pp 40, 98. Coopers and Lybrand Associates provided three scholarships to the value of full course fees to first-year students on the BA in accounting and finance; Digital Equipment Ireland, Ltd, provided two postgraduate scholarships to the value of £2,000 each and Irish Shell agreed to finance a year's study abroad for a languages and international marketing student. A number of cash prizes, awarded for examination performance, had also been secured both from the private and public sectors. 16 T.J. Wheeler to Pat O'Mahony, 30 July 1984 (Pat O'Mahony Papers); NIHED, *Annual report, 1983/4*, p. 97.

existing grants and scholarships but would subsume the Institute's fees-remission scheme into its own operations. Kehoe identified several potential sources of income for the fund, including grants from industry and commercial interests (which could qualify for a tax deduction with some creative accounting), INTRA earnings of sponsored students, donations from Institute alumni and annual contributions from the Institute and student-finance committee. Approximately £4,000 had already been raised from the first two sources, through the efforts of the Industrial Liaison Unit, including a donation of £2,500 from Fruit Importers of Ireland, Ltd.[17] Kehoe's advocacy for the trust fund typified his keen awareness of student-welfare issues. In addition to his ardent support for the fund, he repeatedly lobbied for improved student facilities. He also proposed the creation of a strong alumni association during the Institute's early years, not just as a means of fundraising, but also for its potential to foster industrial links and support the Institute's public-relations work.[18]

Governing body's attention was further focused on the issue of student finances by the government's decision in 1983 to change qualification criteria for student medical cards, leading to demonstrations by students' unions across the country.[19] While cognizant of the added financial burden the decision would place on the Institute's students, governing body nonetheless refused to endorse a motion brought by the Students' Union urging that no disciplinary action would be brought against students peacefully protesting against the decision.[20] Following intense debate, members agreed to seek further recommendations from the working group on disadvantaged students.[21] Yet the group was not reconvened, and consideration of student finances at governing body over the next five years largely focused on the setting of fee levels.

Nonetheless, the establishment of the student-assistance fund (briefly known as NIHE Educational Trust Fund) in 1983 created a vital resource for students, particularly those who experienced difficulties meeting the shortfall between grants and the actual cost of education.[22] Some statistics for the early 1990s amply demonstrate the point. During the academic year 1991/2, more than

17 Barry Kehoe, 'Educational trust fund proposal', June 1983 (DCUPO, 'Governing authority working groups'); *Nuacht*, July 1983; NIHED, *Annual report, 1982/3*, p. 100. Fruit Importers made their donation to formally mark the bicentenary of the Dublin Chamber of Commerce.   18 See, for example, Barry Kehoe to Danny O'Hare, 17 Jan. 1984 (DCUPO, 'Student Services, 1980–7').   19 *Irish Times*, 24 Feb., 2 and 14 Mar. 1984.   20 The motion was proposed by governing body's two Students' Union members, George Hegarty and Ciaran Ó Maoileoin (DCUPO, GB84/1; *Nuacht*, Feb. 1984).   21 DCUPO, GB84/2; *Nuacht*, Mar. 1984. Marie Honan, Students' Union welfare officer at NIHED, published a letter in the national press reminding students of both NIHEs that they were eligible for grants both from Dublin Corporation (or their home county council), and vocational-education committee grants (*Irish Times*, 30 Aug. 1984).   22 During the 1980s and 1990s the Institute's annual reports recorded donations received, and their purpose. There was no donation for the specific purpose of alleviating student hardship recorded over those two decades. Finance was provided by the government during the 1990s following the establishment of a Student Hardship Fund, which distributed funds to third-level institutions (DCU, *Annual*

£10,000 was distributed by the fund. Two years later, Student Services reported that it had provided financial support to 179 students through the provision of an interest-free loan (average amount £141) or top-up grant (average amount £155), while an additional forty students had availed of financial advice from the service. The number of students using this service gradually increased for the remainder of the 1990s, with Student Services highlighting in particular the struggles of mature students.[23]

Together with the fees-remission programme, administered by Student Services on an ad hoc basis, the student-assistance fund remained the Institute's primary tool for offering financial support for students until its inauguration as Dublin City University. The boost this provided to north Dublin, coupled with the advent of European Community funding and a growth in community activism in Ballymun, led directly to the creation of both DCU's direct-entry scholarships and the BITE programme.

Since the publication of the Department of Education's 1995 white paper, creating alternative pathways to university and increasing participation rates in third-level education – across all sectors of society – has become a central tenet of educational policy.[24] Alongside a focus on the provision of lifelong learning opportunities (a consideration that was a key factor in the creation of the Distance Education Unit at NIHE Dublin), access initiatives have traditionally emphasized the importance of engaging with areas of social deprivation and socio-economic disadvantage, as well as increasing educational opportunities for mature students and those with disabilities.

Higher-education participation rates had steadily risen during the 1970s and 1980s, following the establishment of multiple regional technical colleges, the NIHEs and broader expansion of the third-level sector. Between 1980 and 1992 admission rates among 18- to 22-year-olds increased from 20 per cent to 36 per cent. The increase was not, however, spread evenly across all sectors of society. Rates of participation continued to be heavily skewed in favour of those from better off socio-economic groups: admission of students from the higher professional demographic increased from 67 per cent to 89 per cent. While the socio-economic demographic of unskilled manual workers also saw a significant increase in admissions of 10 per cent over the same period, this merely brought the total admission rate from that grouping up to 13 per cent.[25]

---

report, 1994/5, p. 50).   **23** DCU, *Annual report, 1991/2*, p. 16; DCU, *Annual report, 1993/4: appendix*, p. 46; DCU, *Annual report, 1994/5*, p. 51; DCU, *Annual report, 1995/6*, p. 51; DCU, *Annual report, 1996/7*, p. 59. Mature students were ineligible for non-adjacent maintenance grants if they lived outside of the Dublin area.   **24** Fleming, Loxley and Finnegan, *Access and participation in Irish higher education*, p. 1. For example, the National Office of Equity of Access was established in 2003 to direct national policy for lifelong learning and access programmes.   **25** Department of Education and Science, *Charting our education future*, p. 104; Fleming, Loxley and Finnegan, *Access and participation in Irish higher education*, pp 46–8.

NIHE Dublin's immediate hinterland incorporated areas with contrasting economic fortunes. Ballymun town, one of the most economically deprived areas in Ireland during the 1980s, was located less than two kilometres to the north of its campus. The fourteen years between the establishment of its governing body and the attainment of university status saw NIHE Dublin maintain a steady inward focus on the development of its campus and curriculum. When its attention turned to external connections, the Institute targeted links with industry and universities in other countries as it sought to establish its reputation. Though understandable given the seriously constrained economic climate within which the Institute operated, that narrow focus also ensured that few links were formed with the local community. However, when that community came looking for assistance in improving the future of its youth, the new university's response was transformational – both for DCU and for disadvantaged students across north Dublin.

Following the announcement of university status in January 1989, DCU's governing body sought ways to increase the university's connections with the surrounding communities. Academic council also approved the formation of a working group to consider mechanisms for encouraging and supporting applications to attend DCU from students from the locality – once more led by Barry Kehoe.[26] Institutional memory emphasizes the role of the university's staff and governors as primary instigators of these initiatives, driven by a longstanding acknowledgment that few students from the local community were to be seen on campus:

> From the beginning [NIHED/DCU] had been very aware of its hinterland – Ballymun was right on its doorstep. It was supposed to be a university for all, so staff were wondering why so many people from the local community would pass by the gates without ever considering the possibility of coming inside to study.[27]

The roots of the Access programme were, however, slightly more complex. The initial impetus for the formation of the working group is found in an approach from within the Ballymun community. That approach, prompted by the awarding of university status, arose in turn from an announcement by the Irish government that it was seeking applications for European Regional Development Funds for projects in the greater Dublin area. Concurrently, the Irish American Partnership, which had well established links with NIHED/DCU, was also seeking to increase its philanthropic efforts in Ireland. All of these factors came together to create a synergistic partnership that led to the beginnings of DCU's Access programme.

26 DCUPO, GB89/4; *Nuacht*, May and Sept. 1989.   27 Ita Tobin, former director of the Access Service at DCU, quoted in *Irish Times*, 21 Feb. 2012.

The Irish American Partnership, a body established to encourage the Irish American community to contribute to the economic development of Ireland, had worked closely with NIHE Dublin during the late 1980s. The Institute hosted visiting delegations from America on behalf of the Partnership in 1987 and 1989 and would do so throughout the 1990s. Given its proximity to Ballymun, and the Partnership's interests in supporting disadvantaged communities, these initial visits were of particular importance to the development of the Access programme. While in Dublin, the Partnership's delegations met with local community organizations and assisted in raising funds for the Ballymun Community Coalition and Ballymun Job Centre Co-op.[28]

Built in the mid-1960s, Ballymun town had marked a new departure in the development of Dublin's urban landscape. Incorporating 5,000 homes, split between housing estates and tower blocks, the population of Ballymun reached 25,000 during the 1970s, before declining to approximately 20,000 by the end of the 1980s. From the very beginning, it had suffered from poor town planning and an almost complete lack of amenities. The unemployment rate stood at 61 per cent in 1985 (three times the national average), with corresponding financial hardship leading to a rise in drug addiction, crime rates and homelessness.[29] Those trends continued throughout the late 1980s and early 1990s, with school-completion rates also much lower than the national average.[30]

The emergence of the Ballymun Job Centre Co-op in the late 1980s was emblematic of the community-led response to the rapid deterioration of Ballymun. Within the community there existed a widespread belief in the indifference of local and national government to the plight of the town and its residents, symbolically represented by Bank of Ireland's decision to close its branch in Ballymun Shopping Centre.[31] The bank justified its decision by noting that an abnormally high level of its business came in the form of cashing social-welfare cheques, an area of business in which the bank had little interest: 'We recognise that we have a social responsibility to the country, but we wouldn't confuse a social responsibility with a commercial one ... The problems [in Ballymun] are more fundamental than cashing a cheque for local people once a week.'[32] The bank's decision was greeted with outrage, prompting locals to stage a mock funeral procession from Ballymun to Bank of Ireland's headquarters on Baggot Street on 5 October 1984, the day that the branch closed for the last time.[33] The loss of banking services acted as a catalyst for local activists,

28 DCUPO, 'Irish American Partnership, 1987–98'.   29 Ballymun Job Centre Co-op submission to the National Programme of Community Interest for the greater Dublin area, Jan. 1989 (DCUPO, 'B – Miscellaneous').   30 'IAP/DCU/Ballymun pilot programme proposal', Mar. 1990 (DCUPO, 'BITE – Ballymun Initiative for Third Level Education').   31 *Irish Times*, 21 Aug. 1984; Robert Somerville-Woodward, *Ballymun, a history: volumes 1 and 2, c.1600–1997, synopsis* (Ballymun, 2002), pp 54–5.   32 Sean McQuaid, Bank of Ireland public-relations officer, quoted in *Irish Times*, 27 Sept. 1984.   33 *Irish Times*, 6 Oct. 1984; Mark Boyle, 'Sartre's circular dialectic

The Chairman and Committee of BITE

invite

Dr. D. O'Hare
....

to attend the launch of

The Ballymun Initiative for Third Level Education

by Mrs. Mary O'Rourke, T.D., Minister for Education

at 3.15 p.m. on Friday, March 22nd 1991

in the Junior Comprehensive School, Ballymun Road

RSVP
by March 15th 1991

JUNIOR
COMPREHENSIVE
SCHOOL,
BALLYMUN ROAD,
DUBLIN 9
TEL: 421195 / 426297

7.1 Invitation to the formal launch of the Ballymun Initiative for Third Level Education (BITE), 22 March 1991 (DCU Collection).

providing the spark for the formation of the Ballymun Community Coalition. Established to increase employment and to promote local development, over the next three years the Coalition was central to the establishment of a community-controlled credit union, the Job Centre Co-op (which was the first community-owned job centre in Ireland) and the Ballymun Housing Task Force.[34]

In February 1989 Fr John Sweeney SJ, secretary of the Job Centre Co-op, wrote to Danny O'Hare requesting NIHE Dublin's assistance in revitalizing the Ballymun community. Sweeney enclosed a copy of the Co-op's submission to an advisory group that had been appointed by the government to draft a National Programme of Community Interest, with specific reference to the greater Dublin area.[35] Ten of the Co-op's proposals related to the community's educational needs. Noting that the Institute possessed expertise and resources that were otherwise non-existent in Ballymun, Sweeney requested its observations on the Co-op's submission, as well as a meeting 'to discuss ways in which a closer relationship could be established between the Ballymun community and the New University'.[36]

O'Hare circulated Sweeney's request to all senior staff, seeking suggestions: 'This is a rare opportunity to be asked to help our local community. I hope you

and the empires of abstract space: a history of space and place in Ballymun, Dublin', *Annals of the Association of American Geographers*, 95:1 (2005), p. 185.   **34** *Ballymun Job Centre Newsletter*, 1 (Spring, 1989); DCUPO, 'Irish American Partnership, 1987–98'; Boyle, 'Sartre's circular dialectic', p. 185; Somerville-Woodward, *Ballymun, a history*, p. 55.   **35** National Programmes of Community Interest were established by European Community member states, using the EC's Regional Development Fund. See Andrew Evans and Stephen Martin, 'EC regional policy and the evolution of the structural funds' in Stephen Martin (ed.), *The construction of Europe* (Florence, 1994), pp 57–9; Combat Poverty Agency, *Submission on the National Programme of Community Interest for the greater Dublin area* (Dublin, 1988).   **36** Fr John Sweeney to Danny O'Hare, 3 Feb. 1989 (DCUPO,

agree that we ought to do our best to help in a real way, despite our own lack of resources.'[37] Drawing upon the Co-op's ideas, the response of NIHE Dublin's staff to this request for assistance was critical to DCU's future engagement with Ballymun's community, and the development of the Access programme.[38]

Working with the Co-op and various local groups, the Institute's staff drafted a policy that led to the creation, in 1990, of the Ballymun Initiative for Third level Education (BITE) programme – the first of its kind in Ireland. In the absence of a national strategy for increasing third-level participation rates from among lower socio-economic groups, the programme was created from scratch. The initial proposal was drawn up by a working party that drove the project's development and were instrumental in its establishment: Revd Patrick Crowe, SJ; Peter Davitt (Ballymun Job Centre Co-op); Barry Kehoe (DCU); Eileen Lucey (Ballymun Senior Comprehensive); Helen McCormack (Ballymun Girls' Comprehensive); Patrick Nolan (Goldstar Meats); and Robert Rooney (Ballymun Boys' Comprehensive).[39] Under their guidance, BITE's remit was focused on the specific goal of improving the completion rate of second-level education among Ballymun's residents, and encouraging progression to third level.

A key element of that ambition would be to change negative attitudes within the community towards education. At the time of BITE's inception, figures for second-level completion rates at Ballymun's comprehensive schools were particularly stark. Of the 358 students who enrolled in first year in September 1984, almost one-third had dropped out of school before sitting the Intermediate or Group Certificate.[40] A further third had dropped out before completing the Leaving Certificate examination in 1989. Of those who made it that far, 15 per cent went on to third-level education at diploma level, and just 0.5 per cent (2 of 358) enrolled in a degree-level programme.[41]

Set up as an independent company with charitable status, BITE established a number of structures to achieve its aims and support second-level students, including the provision of evening-study facilities, summer camps at DCU, information sessions for parents and special teaching assistance from the university's staff and students.[42] Working with prominent community members such as Gerry Hoey and Robert Rooney of Ballymun Junior Boys' Comprehensive school, Barry Kehoe and Anthony Foley were the first to serve as DCU's representatives on BITE's management committee.

'B – miscellaneous').   **37** Danny O'Hare to several, 14 Feb. 1989 (DCUPO, 'B – miscellaneous'). **38** 'Ballymun Job Centre proposals – a tentative response', *c*.Apr. 1989 (DCUPO, 'B – Miscellaneous').   **39** DCUPO, 'BITE – Ballymun Initiative for Third Level Education'.   **40** The Intermediate Certificate and Group Certificate examinations were typically taken by students aged 14 or 15. They were replaced in 1989 by the Junior Certificate examination.   **41** DCUPO, GB92/3/7; 'BITE – Ballymun Initiative for Third Level Education'.   **42** DCUPO, AC90/A6/18; GB90/6; 'BITE – Ballymun Initiative for Third Level Education'.

NEWSLETTER No. 3　　　　　**JANUARY 1993**

BALLYMUN INITIATIVE for THIRD-LEVEL EDUCATION

BITE enters third successful year

In Autumn 1992 nine students from Ballymun Senior Comprehensive School began third-level courses with the assistance of BITE. Of these, three started Business or Science Degrees in Dublin City University, five commenced Business or Technical Certificates or Diplomas in the Dublin Institute of Technology (DIT), and one gained entry to a Business Studies Certificate in the new Regional Technical College in Tallaght.

These nine students joined fourteen other BITE grant recipients who obtained third-level places in the previous two years in Dublin City University, The Dublin Institute of Technology, Trinity College, and Galway Regional Technical College.

The range of degrees includes Electronics, Accounting & Finance,

Biotechnology, Arts (French/Russian), Analytical Science and Applied Mathematical Sciences, while among the diplomas are courses in Hotel and Catering Management, Electronics, Building Services, Business Studies and Aquaculture.

Last Autumn also saw the continuance of the BITE grant schemes for students in the third year of the junior cycle (twenty grants) and in the senior cycle (ten grants in each of the two year-groups).

Bite grants (£320 per year in junior cycle, £640 per year in senior cycle and £954 per year at third-level) are just one feature of the BITE programme. BITE stands for Ballymun Initiative for Third-Level Education, and was set up in 1990 to encourage students from

the Ballymun Comprehensive Schools to complete their second-level education and go on to third-level courses. In addition to providing financial support for students, the programme has a wide range of other activities, which are summarised on page 3 of this newsletter. So, if you're a Ballymun parent or student or if you would be willing to help financially or otherwise, read on. ◆

Over ninety Ballymun Comprehensive School students attended the BITE awareness day at DCU last March. The topics included were personal and career development, study skills, student life at third-level and graduate careers. There were also tours of the academic and social facilities. Among those giving the day were five of the BITE third-level grant holders.

7.2　Front page of the BITE newsletter, January 1993 (DCU Collection).

Many of BITE's initiatives relied on voluntary work. However, implement-ation of the whole BITE programme would not have been possible without adequate funding. It was at this point that the Irish American Partnership came to the fore, with a grant of £200,000, spread over a four-year period – support that was supplemented by several grants from the Department of Education during the 1990s, as well as further private fundraising initiatives.[43] As noted by Niall Power-Smith, the Partnership's deputy chief executive, one of BITE's challenges was to raise awareness within the Ballymun community of the clear link between third-level education and improved economic development.[44]

Boosted by this financial support, in September 1990 BITE announced scholarships of between £300 and £900 to assist the parents of second-level students in meeting the costs of their children's education.[45] The provision of financial support at second-level was considered somewhat controversial, but deemed necessary to combat the extraordinarily high school dropout rate in Ballymun, which remained steady at 64 per cent up to Leaving Cert level during the early 1990s.[46] Top-up grants of up to £900 were also available to third-level students, once certain criteria were met: demonstration of high academic achievement and potential; a clear desire to progress to third level; financial hardship; and successful completion of an interview.[47]

One of the key features of BITE was that, though DCU was an integral partner in the scheme, students receiving support from the programme could enrol at any third-level institution.[48] During BITE's pilot phase (1990–5), the university accepted fifteen students from the programme. Apart from an annual scholarship, these students were also given a range of supports during their studies, including the presence on campus of a full-time administrator and support network.

Early assessments of the BITE programme pointed to the main factors behind its success. Plans for the scheme had been worked out in considerable detail in advance of its implementation and had been pitched at a realistic and achievable level.[49] Support from the staff at Ballymun's comprehensive schools

43 DCUPO, 'BITE – Ballymun Initiative for Third Level Education'.   44 *Nuacht*, Sept. 1990; *Partnership News: Journal of the Irish American Partnership*, 8 (1990/1), p. 1 (DCUPO, 'Irish American Partnership, 1987–98'.). The IAP also funded UL's equivalent scheme, the Limerick Community Based Educational Initiative (LCBEI), which began operations shortly after BITE. 45 *BITE Newsletter*, 2 (10 Sept. 1990) (DCUPO, 'BITE – Ballymun Initiative for Third Level Education'). See also DCUPO, AC90/6.   46 *Irish Times*, 2 Mar. 1993.   47 DCUPO, AC90/ A6/18; 'BITE – Ballymun Initiative for Third Level Education'.   48 For example, of the five students granted a BITE award in September 1990, four attended DCU and one attended Galway Regional Technical College. In 1991, DCU accepted five BITE scholars, with four more attending other institutions (DCUPO, GB92/3/7; DCUPO, 'BITE – Ballymun Initiative for Third Level Education').   49 'IAP/DCU/Ballymun pilot programme proposal', Mar. 1990 (DCUPO, 'BITE – Ballymun. Initiative for Third Level Education'). See also Scott Boldt, *BITE: Ballymun Initiative for Third-Level Education, research evaluation* (Dublin, 2000).

had been acquired from an early point in the process. Concentration on the specific aim of increasing participation rates in third level, rather than on tackling wider issues of socio-economic disadvantage, had also been an important factor. A study undertaken in 1995 by Mark Morgan of the Educational Research Centre at St Patrick's College, Drumcondra, concluded that BITE had been successful in changing attitudes, expectations and beliefs regarding third-level education. Each of the features of the programme had been found to contribute to this change, and to the increased academic achievement of participants. It was important, Morgan noted, for similar schemes to have strong links with third-level institutions, and to receive state funding while still being managed by local stakeholders.[50]

A review commissioned on the tenth anniversary of BITE, specifically concentrating on its impact on the progression of secondary-school students to third level, echoed these findings. Placing the academic achievements of BITE scholars within the context of their family and social background, the report noted the programme's positive impact on family life and the broader community. The report also singled out the programme's innovative combination of financial assistance with academic and other supports: 'The high frequency with which scholarship holders have reported that, without BITE, they would not have attended third level is a clear indication of success and a solid endorsement of BITE.'[51]

Reporting to governing body on the programme's early successes, Barry Kehoe emphasized the importance of DCU's role: 'Besides the contribution of the university at the level of ideas, the tangible help given by staff and students in terms of involvement in tuition and supervised study enhances the project considerably.'[52] Staff support for the project was reflected in their close monitoring of students who were admitted to the university through the BITE programme:

> Some good news in these days of gloom and despondency ... [T]he first of the scholarship students to complete her degree has achieved an honour in the BA Accounting and Finance ... She was a very hardworking student and was a delight to teach. I think she is a wonderful role model for the scholarship students who will come after her.[53]

50 Mark Morgan, *Ballymun Initiative for Third Level Education (BITE) and Limerick Community-Based Educational Initiative (LCBEI): an evaluation of projects supported by the Irish American Partnership* (Dublin, 1995), pp 88–90.   51 DCUPO, 'BITE – Ballymun Initiative for Third Level Education'; Boldt, *BITE*; *Irish Times*, 9 May 2000.   52 DCUPO, 'BITE – Ballymun Initiative for Third Level Education'. See also *Irish Times*, 18 Jan. and 17 June 1994.   53 Pat Barker to Danny O'Hare et al., 8 July 1993 (DCUPO, 'BITE – Ballymun Initiative for Third Level Education'). BITE scholars continued to attend DCU and other institutions during the 1990s. For example, 18 BITE scholars graduated with a diploma or a degree in 1998. Four of these graduated from DCU,

A decade after the establishment of BITE, its programme director wrote to Prof. Albert Pratt, then director general of DCU, to pay tribute to the university: 'The continued support BITE receives from DCU is particularly important. As a DCU graduate myself ... your personal interest and offer of assistance is really appreciated.'[54] Though DCU has continued to work with BITE and to make its facilities available to the programme, the majority of its focus in the area of equality of access has been channelled into its own initiatives, which included the establishment of the North Dublin Access Programme in 1996.

By the 1990s, the university had amassed a considerable amount of data relating to the cost of living and studying at university in Dublin. Tracked annually by the Student Services unit, its estimates rose to over £3,000 per annum by the end of the 1980s. While the unit's estimate was typically lower than that provided by the Union of Students of Ireland, DCU's figures nonetheless demonstrated that, by 1990, students in receipt of a full maintenance grant from the Department of Education received less than half of what was required to attend college.[55] Barry Kehoe was particularly critical of the government's failure to keep the value of student maintenance grants in line with economic trends. Commenting on BITE's decision to top up the maintenance grant by providing an additional £950 to its students, Kehoe used the national press to drive home the message that the government grant was inadequate: 'If you are poor enough to qualify for the maximum government grant, you're too poor to take it up.'[56] By the turn of the millennium matters had yet to improve; while inflation had risen by 121 per cent since 1982, the maintenance grant had risen by just 77 per cent. Distinguishing between those who worked to survive at college, and those who worked to fund their social lives, Kehoe expressed concern about the plight of the former: 'From our work in North Dublin, we see a group of low-paid workers who are receiving no supports ... [T]his group is really hurting financially.'[57]

The need for financial assistance for students from lower socio-economic groups was undoubted. Though the timeline is not fully clear, it seems as though work on the BITE programme prompted a deeper engagement by the university with second-level students in Ballymun. This engagement would complement BITE, but would also apply specifically to students who wished to attend DCU. Following unanimous endorsement both by academic council and governing body, the university implemented a separate entry scholarship programme with three main elements: 1) awarding up to five scholarships of £750 per annum to students matriculating from Ballymun Senior Comprehensive; 2) awarding two

including one with a master's in financial mathematics ('BITE graduates 1998', 11 Dec. 1998 (ibid)).   **54** Emma Kiernan to Albert Pratt, 9 Feb. 2000 (DCUPO, 'BITE – Ballymun Initiative for Third Level Education').   **55** DCUPO, 'Student Services/Student Affairs'; DCU Access Service, historic files; *Irish Times*, 25 Aug. 1992.   **56** *Irish Times*, 2 Mar. 1993.   **57** *Irish Times*, 16 Aug. 2000, 9 Jan. 2001. Quotation from 9 Jan.

scholarships each year to mature applicants; and 3) offering four places on the university's part-time degree programme to Ballymun residents.[58]

In order to be eligible, students from Ballymun Comprehensive had to qualify for a maintenance grant. Prospective entrants also had to complete an aptitude test and attend a formal interview. They also had to matriculate from Ballymun Comprehensive with the minimum academic standard for admission to a DCU course (set at receipt of a minimum of four honours in the Leaving Certificate), but without achieving the points required by the CAO system for their preferred course. This latter consideration was one of the key parameters of the scholarship programme, recommended by academic council's working group as a form of 'active compensation' for students without the required entry points that took account of the difficulty of their circumstances. Several of that group's recommendations were also incorporated into BITE's operations, including the intensification of DCU's liaison with local schools and the provision of a mentoring service for second-level students.[59]

While DCU's adoption of the direct-entry scholarship programme in parallel with BITE occasionally caused some confusion for administrators, it also had unexpected benefits. When the BITE awards for September 1991 were made, it transpired that the five recipients had also been given DCU direct-entry scholarships, which allowed BITE to fund an additional four students.[60] The direct-entry scheme was, in some respects, a continuation of a long-standing policy at NIHED/DCU, which regarded the Leaving Certificate as an important indicator of ability, but not the sole arbiter of potential.[61]

The direct-entry scholarship programme was first introduced for the 1990–1 academic year.[62] Seven scholarships were awarded in that first year, with students securing financial support and places in business studies, analytical science, accounting and finance, applied mathematical sciences and international marketing and languages. Due to its success, the scheme was expanded the following year to eleven scholarships for students successfully completing the Leaving Certificate at Ballymun Senior Comprehensive, and six further scholarships for Ballymun residents who were returning to education.[63]

BITE and the direct-entry scholarship scheme were the forerunners of DCU's current Access programme. As early as 1993 plans were drawn up for the expansion of the scheme beyond Ballymun Comprehensive.[64] Notwithstanding

58 DCUPO, ACSC90/4, 9; *Nuacht*, Oct. 1990. **59** DCUPO, AC90/A4/4, AC90/A6/18; GB90/5; 'BITE – Ballymun Initiative for Third Level Education'; *Nuacht*, Dec. 1990. The working group's members were John Carroll; Anthony Foley; Michael Gleeson; Jane Horgan; Barry Kehoe; Eileen Lucey; Micheál MacConmara; Charles McCorkell; Annette McGee; Fr Pat McManus; Sean Marlow; Edel Maguire; Malachy Murphy; and Michael Ryan. **60** DCUPO, GB92/3/7; 'BITE – Ballymun Initiative for Third Level Education'. **61** Aptitude tests and admission interviews had been utilized by NIHED from its first admissions. See chapter 5. **62** *Nuacht*, June and Oct. 1990. **63** DCUPO, 'BITE – Ballymun Initiative for Third Level Education'; *Nuacht*, Mar. 1991. **64** Danny O'Hare to Richard Bruton, TD, 11 July 1994 (DCUPO, 'BITE – Ballymun Initiative for

the clear benefits brought by both programmes, some remained to be convinced by DCU's commitment to the locality. Dublin City Councillor Eamonn O'Brien criticized the university's engagement with BITE as tokenism, eliciting a sharp response from Danny O'Hare, who pointed to the university's role in securing the funding that allowed BITE to begin operations, as well as its own direct-entry scholarship programme and ongoing work in developing further community-outreach initiatives.[65]

Attempts to broaden the reach of the direct-access entry scheme proceeded slowly at first. In 1993 the university secured sponsorship from AIB Capital Markets, which was initially used to create scholarships worth up to £1,000 per annum for three students from the north inner-city who intended to pursue careers in financial services. The bank also guaranteed INTRA places for the students. Candidates had to live within the Custom House Docks Development Authority catchment area and have already attained a place on a DCU course. By the end of 1997 the bank had increased its commitment to enable the attendance of ten students at DCU.[66]

II

DCU's innovations in the field of access did not go unnoticed in government circles.[67] The Department of Education's 1995 white paper identified equality of access to higher education, 'irrespective of social class, age or disability', as one of its major policy objectives. Prior to that, policy decisions were driven by a desire to simply increase overall student numbers, without regard to the socio-economic backgrounds of students.[68] This new policy direction required all higher-education institutions to put in place structures and programmes to achieve 'equality of access, participation and benefit for students'.[69] Drawing upon the practice already established at DCU (and other institutions that had

Third Level Education'). **65** Danny O'Hare to Eamonn O'Brien, 21 Dec. 1994 (DCUPO, 'BITE – Ballymun Initiative for Third Level Education'). **66** DCU, *Annual report, 1993/4: appendix*, p. 46; DCU, *Annual report, 1994/5*, p. 51; DCU, *Annual report, 1995/6*, p. 52; DCU, *Annual report, 1996/7*, p. 60; *Irish Times*, 12 June 1992. **67** The university (then still NIHED) had previously hosted, in May 1988, the first conference specifically dedicated to access to higher education in Ireland. The conference was attended by Mary O'Rourke, minister for education, Dr Finbarr Ó Ceallacháin, assistant secretary at the Department of Education, and John Hayden, chief executive of the HEA. Proceedings were published in the *Journal of Higher Education Studies*, 3:2 (1988). The *Journal of Higher Education Studies* was established by NIHED's Faculty of Education Studies in 1985 (NIHED, *Annual report, 1985/6*, p. 33). **68** Nicola Maxwell and Claire Dorrity, 'Access to third level education: challenges for equality of opportunity in post Celtic-Tiger Ireland', *Irish Journal of Public Policy*, 2:1 (2009); Emer Smyth and Damian Hannan, 'Education and inequality' in Brian Nolan and Christopher Whelan (eds), *Bust to boom? The Irish experience of growth and inequality* (Dublin, 200), pp 109–11. **69** Department of Education and Science, *Charting our education future*, pp 98–7 (quotation p. 98); O'Reilly, 'The evolution of university access

followed its lead, including UL and TCD), the Department urged third-level institutions to promote the benefits of higher education through the establishment of formal links with designated second-level schools. Among the suggestions contained in the white paper were the hosting of 'awareness seminars' on campus for second-level students, and the creation of 'care programmes' to assist first-year undergraduates to transition from second level – elements already integral to the BITE and direct-entry programmes at DCU.[70]

For the first six years of its outreach work, DCU concentrated on its immediate hinterland in Ballymun and the north inner-city. The presence of just a single school in Ballymun allowed for the targeted implementation of access initiatives. That area of concentration was expanded in November 1996 with the launch of the North Dublin Access Programme, which adopted the core principles that underpinned BITE.[71] Formal links were established with fifteen schools in three partnership areas: Ballymun, Finglas/Cabra and Northside (Coolock/Darndale).[72] Each school had to satisfy a number of criteria, including designation as a disadvantaged school by the Department of Education, little to no tradition of student progression to third level and no restrictions on student enrolment.[73]

Governing body considered and approved the implementation of the North Dublin Access Programme in the summer of 1996, with a formal launch by Niamh Bhreathnach, minister for education, on 28 November. Áine Galvin was appointed as the university's Access officer.[74] Drawing upon the previous five years of experience in working with disadvantaged students, the Programme adopted an integrated approach to achieving its aims of improving perceptions of third-level education, providing alternative routes to university courses and offering enhanced supports for students during their undergraduate studies. Four main elements were put in place to achieve these aims, drawing on proven structures: 1) school-liaison programmes that included mentoring and information sessions for parents; 2) a direct-entry policy with up to fifty places available per year for students who did not achieve their potential in the Leaving Certificate examinations for reasons of disadvantage; 3) a three-week summer school to prepare students academically and socially for undergraduate life; and 4) undergraduate supports in the form of a £1,000 scholarship, extra tuition and

programmes in Ireland', p. 12.   **70** Department of Education and Science, *Charting our education future*, pp 105–6.   **71** DCU, *Annual report, 1996/7*, pp vi, 59–60.   **72** Area-based partnerships were established by the Irish government in 1991 in areas designated the most disadvantaged in the country. Each partnership was set up as a limited company with a remit to promote social and economic inclusion (Department of Education, *Report of the action group on access to third-level education* (Dublin, 2001), p. 103).   **73** DCUPO, 'Access'; DCUPO, 'BITE – Ballymun Initiative for Third Level Education'; APA, Grant #8043; Department of Education, *Report of the action group on access to third level education*, pp 171–6. Restrictions on school enrolment were typically implemented by faith-based schools, though also included other screening mechanisms based around academic performance.   **74** DCUPO, GB96/5/7; DCU news release, 28 Nov. 1996; *Irish*

7.3 Students performing on the mall during Arts Week, February 1996 (DCU Collection).

the assistance of DCU's Access officer.[75] The Programme also implemented a number of schemes in order to create connections with younger second-level students and to provide information on the benefits of further education. Fifth-year students shadowed first-year undergraduates at DCU, and a tuition scheme saw DCU undergraduates voluntarily giving grinds to Junior Certificate students.[76]

Funding for the North Dublin Access Programme was initially provided by the HEA, through its targeted-initiatives scheme, along with support from the university itself and small levels of philanthropic funding.[77] Seeking to expand the programme in 2000, the university sought a major donation from Atlantic Philanthropies, which approved a grant of €445,500 in 2000, with the proviso that DCU Educational Trust raise a matching €152,500.[78] Noting DCU's longstanding commitment to widening access to third-level education, the grant recommendation highlighted the commitment of the Access Programme's staff, particularly its director, Maeve O'Byrne.[79] By the end of 2004 the matching funds had largely been acquired, with donations totalling €137,000 secured from Marks and Spencer, Musgrave Group, Hewlett-Packard, Management Catering Services, the Irish American Heritage Society and the Society of St Vincent de

Times, 29 Nov. 1996.   **75** DCUPO, 'BITE – Ballymun Initiative for Third Level Education'. **76** DCUPO, 'Access'; DCU Access Service, historic files.   **77** Atlantic Philanthropies grant recommendation summary, 17 May 2000 (APA, Grant #8043, 1/2); HEA, *Report, accounts 1997 and 1998 and student statistics, 1996/7 and 1997/8*, pp 32, 62.   **78** John Healy to Peggy Kim Meill, 28 June 2000 (APA, Grant #8043, 2/2).   **79** Grant recommendation summary, 17 May 2000 (APA, Grant #8043, 2/2).

Paul.[80] Financial support for the programme largely continues to derive from private funding. During the academic year 2016/17, DCU Educational Trust secured over €1.1m in donor funding to support Access scholars.[81]

To coincide with the opening of its second block of student accommodation in 1997, which increased the number of student rooms on campus from 250 to 550, the university launched a scheme offering five of its rooms free of charge, and five more at a 50 per cent discount. The scheme was introduced in recognition of the fact that the maximum accommodation grant available from the HEA was 'significantly less' than the amount required to support students at university, thus restricting opportunities for students from socio-economically disadvantaged backgrounds. In order to avail of free or reduced-cost accommodation, students had to have already qualified for admission to DCU, live beyond reasonable commuting distance and live in a household with a parental income below a set level.[82] Michael King, principal of Liberties College in Dublin, wrote to say that though his students would not qualify for free accommodation due to their proximity to DCU, the initiative was very welcome: 'I would like to note the appreciation of a school like ours for the pioneering role of DCU in forging supportive links with local second level schools. We have benefitted from a more outward-looking approach by both DIT and TCD, inspired in both cases I think by the example of DCU.'[83] As King observed, the success of BITE and DCU's direct-access scheme had clearly been noted by other universities. UCC's access programme, established in 1996, was modelled on those at DCU and TCD.[84]

A major Department of Education report on access to third-level education, published in 2001, highlighted BITE and the North Dublin Access Programme as highly successful examples of community outreach.[85] DCU operated the Programme between 1996 and 2000 with an exclusive focus on students from the north of the city. Efforts to expand the scheme to students from any part of the country began towards the end of 2000.[86] Approved by academic council and implemented in 2001, applications were invited from seventy-five schools designated as disadvantaged and not already formally linked with any other third-level institution.[87] In a related development, DCU collaborated with six other higher-education institutions to create and launch the Higher Education Direct Access Scheme (HEDAS).[88] That scheme's development was driven by a

80 Colin McCrea to Patrick McDermott, 15 Oct. 2004 (APA, Grant #8043, 1/2; DCUPO, 'Access'; DCU Access Service, historic files). 81 DCUPO, 'Access'; DCU, *Access impact report, 2016/17* (Dublin, 2017), p. 17. 82 APA, Grant #7405; *Irish Times*, 7, 11 and 27 Mar. 1997. 83 Michael King to Danny O'Hare, 13 Mar. 1997 (APA, Grant #7045). 84 Department of Education, *Report of the action group on access to third level education*, p. 164. 85 Ibid., p. 171. 86 The need for DCU to advance its Access programme through collaboration with other institutions was identified both internally and by the Department of Education (DCUPO, 'Access'; Department of Education, *Report of the action group on access to third level education*, p. 172). 87 DCUPO, AC2000/6; DCU Access Service, historic files. 88 DCUPO, AC2002/1. The other participating institutions were

desire to move beyond the concentration of individual institutions on specific regional areas. By pooling their reserved access places and participating in a centralized application process, run in conjunction with the CAO system, each of the institutions increased their geographic base and greatly enhanced student mobility for disadvantaged students.[89] The effect of the scheme's implementation, allied with the allocation of increased funding from private sources, can be seen in the marked increase in Access admissions from 2004, a year that saw DCU's intake almost double, from 78 students to 141 students (fig. 7.1 and table 7.1).

Fig. 7.1. DCU Access programme, annual student intake 1990–2018

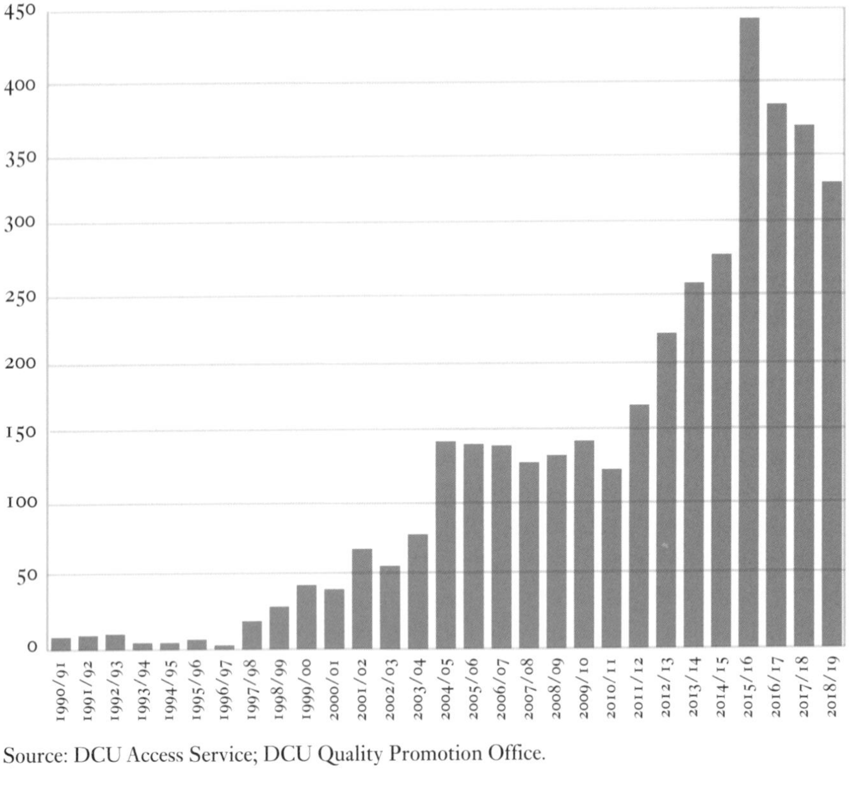

Source: DCU Access Service; DCU Quality Promotion Office.

NUI Maynooth, UCC, UCD, TCD, UL and DIT. Access routes for disadvantaged students are currently administered by the Central Applications Office, in collaboration with participating institutions, under its Higher Education Access Route (HEAR) programme, which replaced HEDAS.   89 DCU Access Service, historic files; HEA, *Report of the high level group on university equality policies* (Dublin, 2004), p. 33; Patricia O'Reilly, 'The evolution of university access programmes in Ireland', UCD Geary Institute Discussion Paper Series (Dublin, 2008), pp 24–5; Cathy McLoughlin, 'The impact of gender, school status and geography on degree outcomes: a study on the academic performance of Access students in Dublin City University, 2009/10' in

Since the introduction of the various access schemes at DCU, 3,717 students have availed of the opportunities provided to enrol at the university. Early numbers were small, in keeping with the pilot programme status both of BITE and the direct access scheme. Table 7.1 and fig. 7.1 provide a breakdown of Access admissions since 1990. The implementation of the North Dublin Access Programme allowed for an increase in admissions from September 1997, with twenty students admitted to DCU via Access programmes that year; a figure that rose seven-fold over the following decade. Access students represented 7.2 per cent of the total undergraduate enrolments in 2006.[90]

Some limited comparisons with other universities are possible for the late 1990s and early 2000s. Over the five-year period covering 1997 to 2001, DCU admitted 165 students from disadvantaged backgrounds, or almost one out of every four such students admitted to Irish universities. During that period, the university's Access programme was the largest in operation in the country.[91] As can be seen from fig. 7.1, there were three large spikes in Access admissions, relative to previous years: 1997, 2004 and 2015. The tenfold increase in admissions in 1997 was a result of the implementation of the North Dublin Access Scheme. The second increase, which saw admissions rise from 78 to 141, was a result of the expansion of DCU's participation in HEDAS. The surge in registrations that occurred in the 2015/16 academic year was linked with Incorporation and was a result of Access students entering programmes within the new Institute of Education, as well as the new suite of bachelor of arts programmes. It is also worth noting that the number of Access students enrolling per annum since the onset of economic depression in 2009 has grown. The ensuing drastic retrenchment of government funding across the third-level sector increased pressure on resource allocation in each university, yet increased fundraising efforts by the DCU Educational Trust has allowed the Access programme to more than double in size since 2010. For Brian MacCraith, this is an illustration of the university's values:

> People have passion for what the university stands for … Right through the recession, our numbers of Access student were growing. We never cut [that programme] back. It would have been a relatively easy though sad decision to take, to actually cut down our Access programme or indeed stop it. We could have said we can't afford this. No one ever contemplated that.[92]

HEA, *How equal? Access to higher education in Ireland* (Dublin, 2013), p. 73. **90** Statistics quoted above provided by DCU Access Service. I am indebted to Cathy McLoughlin and Colette Keogh of the Access Service for their generous assistance and for clarifying various points relating to DCU's Access programme. **91** HEA, *Report of the high level group on university equality policies* (Dublin, 2004), p. 26. DCU's Access programme intake over the period amounted to 194 students, a total that included mature students, refugees, Travellers and students with disabilities. **92** Brian MacCraith interview, 16 May 2019.

Table 7.1. Annual intake of DCU Access students as a per cent of all students

Year	Total first-year admissions	Access admissions	% of admissions
1990/1	588	6	1%
1991/2	678	7	1%
1992/3	766	9	1.2%
1993/4	980	4	0.4%
1994/5	1,030	4	0.4%
1995/6	1,097	5	0.4%
1996/7	1,178	2	0.2%
1997/8	1,442	20	1.4%
1998/9	1,480	25	1.7%
1999/00	1,648	44	2.7%
2000/1	1,584	40	2.5%
2001/2	1,557	65	4.2%
2002/3	1,490	55	3.7%
2003/4	1,645	78	4.7%
2004/5	1,825	141	7.7%
2005/6	1,762	140	7.9%
2006/7	1,917	138	7.2%
2007/8	1,984	122	6.1%
2008/9	2,052	125	6.1%
2009/10	2,139	138	6.5%
2010/11	2,113	122	5.8%
2011/12	2,242	171	7.6%
2012/13	2,493	217	8.7%
2013/14	2,637	255	9.7%
2014/15	2,481	282	11.4%
2015/16	3,452	437	12.7%
2016/17	3,473	385	11.1%
2017/18	3,415	360	10.5%
2018/19	3,364	320	9.5%

Source: DCU Access Service; DCU Quality Promotion Office.

In terms of academic performance, research conducted by the Access Service demonstrates that students who entered DCU under the reduced-CAO-points dispensation performed better than the general undergraduate population. Between 1990 and 2011, 89.5 per cent of Access students graduated with an honours degree, compared to 79.7 per cent of those who enrolled through the traditional route.[93] More than half of Access students progressed to a post-graduate course after completion of their primary degree, while just 7 per cent failed to complete their undergraduate studies, either at DCU or at another higher-education institution.[94] As a percentage of undergraduate enrolments, Access students reached a high point of 12.7 per cent (437 students) in 2015. Such numbers provide firm vindication of the foresight of the community groups, schools and DCU staff who embraced the challenge of providing equality of opportunity for as many students as possible. The funding model for DCU's Access Service, and those of other third-level institutions, stands as an indictment of the failure of successive governments to create equality of educational opportunity for all students. Each Access student at DCU relies upon philanthropic support, not just for direct financial assistance, but also for the ancillary services that the university provides – a situation repeated across the country.[95]

III

In addition to providing direct financial assistance and academic supports to disadvantaged students in north Dublin and beyond, NIHED/DCU has also engaged in various community-outreach activities. Prior to the 1990s, these efforts were generally low-key in nature. General public access to the Institute's library was allowed during the early 1980s, though this was curtailed as student numbers increased and pressure on library facilities grew. Local groups made use of other Institute facilities, including various residents' associations and the Glasnevin Musical Society.[96] Awareness that the Institute was open to such arrangements was not, however, widespread. When the matter was raised by the Students' Union, governing body adopted a rather non-committal resolution reaffirming the Institute's ambition to play a positive role within the community.[97]

Targeted community engagement, paying heed to the concept of lifelong learning, emerged in response to approaches from community groups in the early 1990s. The university's arts committee worked with the Dublin City of Culture celebrations to organize the university's first Arts Day in May 1991,

93 That figure rose to 97% for the period 2011–17 (Access Service Key Facts, https://www.dcu.ie/access/about.shtml, accessed 29 Nov. 2018).   94 Elaine Keane, 'Widening participation in higher education in the Republic of Ireland: report submitted to HEFCE and OFFA' (Bristol, 2013), p. 34; DCU, *Celebrating success: 21 years of DCU Access Service* (Dublin, 2011), pp 12–13; *Irish Times*, 21 Feb. 2012.   95 DCUPO, 'Access'; DCU, *Access impact report, 2017/18*, pp 10–15, 21. 96 Newspaper article 'College for the future' by Eleanor Petley, c.Sept. 1983. I have not been able to identify the newspaper, or the date of publication (DCUPO, 'NIHE Dublin: general, 2/2'). 97 DCUPO, GB85/3; *Nuacht*, Apr. 1985.

featuring performances by students, staff and invited guests. Such was its success that the following year saw the introduction of Arts Week, a three-day event co-ordinated by staff members, including Marie-Louise O'Donnell and Carmel O'Sullivan. Local community groups were also invited to participate.[98] Continuing its interest in employment initiatives, DCU also supported Kilbarrack Local Education for Adult Renewal (KLEAR), a community-based project that provided opportunities for those unable to access traditional education channels, and were interested in developing a model of education based on self-directed learning. DCU's expertise in distance education made it a natural fit. KLEAR had been established in 1982 and operated as an out-centre in the CDVEC system in St Mary's National School, Kilbarrack. Intrigued by the possibilities suggested by KLEAR, DCU supported a successful application to Atlantic Philanthropies for the completion of a feasibility study. Several members of the university's staff lent their weight to the collaboration, including Chris Curran, Barry Kehoe, Kay MacKeogh and Peter McKenna. While a promotional video for the initiative was created with the assistance of the School of Communications, the inability of all parties to draft a satisfactory development plan meant that collaboration did not extend beyond 1994.[99]

Further collaborations were fostered following the creation of the DCU Community Office in 1996, funded by a FÁS community-employment scheme and created as part of the NorDubCo initiative (see below). Intended as a point of contact for community organizations seeking to tap into the expertise available within DCU, the community office concept was based upon community/university interface models that had been pioneered in the Netherlands.[100] The office at DCU taught computer and information technology skills to people from economically disadvantaged backgrounds, as well as children with special needs. English language lessons were provided for refugees, and campus tours were run for local children to enhance their awareness of DCU and its facilities. Postgraduate research students assisted community groups in developing policies and funding applications to address issues such as drug abuse, domestic violence and Travellers' rights. Postgraduates also briefly taught a variety of extra-mural adult-education courses, at off-peak times when the university's facilities were available. All courses experienced high demand, and adults who had little or no prior experience of learning in a university environment were the

98 DCU's arts committee was established in 1983 when John Pratschke voiced his concern about the 'glaring cultural void' in the Institute. The committee (also known as the Visual Arts Group) were responsible for various attempts to bring arts and culture to the campus, including arranging loans of works of art and organising staff/student art exhibitions. The Institute's first commissioned art work was a tapestry, created by Patrick Scott and manufactured by V'Soke Joyce in 1985 (DCUPO, 'Arts: general'; *Nuacht*, Oct. 1985; DCU, *Annual report, 1990/1*, p. 20; *Irish Times*, 27 Feb. 1996, 15 Jan. 2002; *College View*, 24 Sept. and 29 Nov. 2011).   99 APA, Grant #7200; DCUPO, 'K – miscellaneous'.   100 DCUPO, 'NorDubCo – up to 2004'; NorDubCo information note, Mar. 1996 (APA, Folder 'DCU policy: background, strategic planning, 3/3').

7.4 Seamus Heaney and Maighread Ní Dhomhnaill perform on campus during Arts Week (DCU Collection).

7.5 Mary Robinson during a visit to DCU on 31 October 1991, shortly after her inauguration as President of Ireland (DCU Collection).

majority of participants.[101] In spite of the evident success of the Community Office in cultivating links with the university's surrounding area, it was closed in 2003 following cuts in its funding levels, both from government resources and the university.[102]

Nonetheless, the benefits to the university of continued community engagement had now been well established. Civic engagement was formally incorporated in DCU's strategic-planning process in 2005. Linked to the adoption of academic themes as the guiding force of the university's development, civic engagement fell within the remit of the Internationalisation, Interculturalism and Social Development Office, led by Prof. Ronaldo Munck.[103] The loss of the university's Community Office was soon offset by the creation and development of the DCU in the Community initiative, formally launched in 2006. The opening of outreach offices in Ballymun in June 2008, built and funded in collaboration with Ballymun Regeneration Limited, enabled the initiative to create closer ties with local residents and community organizations.[104] Its first project investigated mental-health inequalities among ethnic-minority communities.[105] Commenting on the linked establishment of the DCU Science Shop – which aimed to make the university's knowledge and resources more readily available to the community – Munck reiterated the university's belief that it needed to be 'embedded in society':

> The subtitle of our science shop is 'community knowledge exchange' … Environmental science students can be working on carbon emissions; business studies students can be working with local community groups, helping them develop a business plan; computing students can do websites. There's a whole raft of ways in which the university can engage.[106]

Munck also acknowledged the difficulty of changing the traditional, inward-focused nature of university teaching and research. This challenge was particularly acute in an institution that had branded itself as the university of enterprise: 'A science shop's participatory ethos, fostering dialogue among equals, runs up against success stories from the for-profit sector.'[107] That tension could, however, be turned to an advantage by creating conditions for engagement

101 DCU Community Office: proposal by NorDubCo, 2003 (DCUPO, 'NorDubCo – up to 2004'). 102 DCU, *Annual reports, 1996–2003*; DCU Access Service, historic files.   103 DCU, *Leadership through foresight: DCU strategic plan, 2006–8* (Dublin, 2005); DCU, *Leading through challenge: university strategy, 2009–11* (Dublin, 2009).   104 DCUPO, AC2008/3; DCU, *President's reports, 2006–8; DCU, Leading through challenge: university strategy, 2009–11* (Dublin, 2009).   105 The project received €66,000 in funding from the European Commission and was conducted in association with Cáirde, a non-governmental organization committed to reducing health inequalities among ethnic minorities.   106 *Irish Times*, 1 Sept. 2008.   107 Ibid. See also Ronaldo Munck, 'Community-based research: genealogy and prospects' in Ronaldo Munck, Lorraine McIlrath, Budd Hall and Rajesh Tandon (eds), *Higher education and community based research* (New York,

between the university, private enterprise and the non-profit sector. Such considerations were to the fore in the university's involvement in NorDubCo and Ballymun Regeneration Limited, two community-based initiatives that sought to develop untapped commercial and economic potential within north Dublin.

IV

Building on their successful implementation of the North Dublin Access Programme, DCU and the Ballymun, Northside and Finglas/Cabra partnerships agreed to expand the range of their activities. Joined by Dublin Corporation and Fingal County Council, in 1996 they established a company dedicated to promoting the social, economic and civic development of the north Dublin region. Named North Dublin Development Coalition (NorDubCo), the company was jointly owned and funded by each stakeholder. To accomplish its goals, the initial vision for NorDubCo was to act as the focal point for a programme of research, analysis and debate that would form the basis of a strategic plan for the region.

NorDubCo's mission statement emphasized the Coalition's ambition to ensure sustainable economic and social development in the region, and to act as a catalyst for the transformation of north Dublin into a cohesive community with a sense of common interest. One of its primary aims was to advocate for the level of structural investment necessary to revive an area that, at the turn of the millennium, still had some of the highest levels of unemployment and social deprivation in the country.[108] The design and implementation of DCU's input was initially led by Frank Moran, of the Business School, and Chris O'Malley, the university's director of strategic development. Moran and O'Malley were assisted by a team of graduates seconded to the local-area development partnerships, where they conducted research and analysis. Three graduates were also retained on campus, where they formed the DCU Community Office (see above). The Coalition (which identified as a regional think tank during the early 2000s), modelled its public-dialogue programme on the Boston Seminars series, hosted by Boston College in the 1950s and 1960s, which had provided a platform for a number of initiatives that revitalized Boston.[109]

In tandem with its concentration on the local development areas, NorDubCo's management committee also devoted considerable time to the development of the greater north Dublin area. Working closely with Ferdinand von Prondzynski and senior DCU academics, the Coalition drafted environmental investment strategies for North Dublin, and a submission for the

2014), pp 11–26. **108** NorDubCo, *Towards a vision for North Dublin* (Dublin, *c.*2000), p. 1. **109** DCUPO, 'NorDubCo – up to 2004'.

7.6 The National Chamber Choir during a performance in Albert College
(DCU Collection).

government's *National development plan, 2000–6*.[110] NorDubCo's vision for the
development of the region was thus influenced by various plans and initiatives
that had been gestating at DCU for several years. One such development,
included in early drafts of the Coalition's strategic plan, called for the creation
of a research and development park for computer software, echoing a proposal
first advanced by Prof. Michael Ryan in the early 1990s. Ryan had envisioned a
software R&D park near DCU's campus, both to capitalize on the government's
decision in 1990 to establish a Centre for Software Engineering at DCU, and to
encourage established companies and start-ups to collaborate with the
university's academic staff.[111] Other proposals identified by Chris O'Malley as
of interest to DCU included the creation of an employers' skills and training
forum, as well as the creation of a network of small arts centres across the region,

110 Ibid.; NorDubCo, *Consolidating North Dublin: an Environmental Investment Strategy for North Dublin* (Dublin, 2001); Government of Ireland, *Ireland: national development plan, 2000–6* (Dublin, 1999). 111 In 2014, the university finally realized this proposal with the opening of the Alpha innovation campus. The Centre for Software Engineering operated as a unit within DCU, sharing resources with the School of Computer Applications, and was envisioned as a major component of the government's strategy to support software development. The centre was largely funded through the government's National Software Directorate. When Ryan first proposed a software R&D park, employment in the Irish software industry had grown by 30% per annum between 1986 and 1988, and was estimated to grow by a further 20% per annum until the mid-1990s (DCUPO, 'Software park – proposed (1991–7)'; *Newslink*, June 1990; *Silicon Republic*, 28 Feb. 2003 (https://www.siliconrepublic.com/innovation/dcu-software-facility-to-close-down, accessed 3 Jan. 2019).

for which the DCU Arts Centre (later called the Helix, under construction at the time) would act as a lynchpin.[112]

NorDubCo identified the knowledge economy and the development of sustainable industrial clusters as an integral part of any future regeneration of north Dublin, with DCU and the Institute of Technology, Blanchardstown, well positioned to lead the Coalition in that area. Much of DCU's subsequent input into the Coalition's activities has focused on the university's ability to attract R&D funding to the region, its capacity for the creation of innovative spin-off companies through its research, and the provision of highly trained workers.[113] DCU also contributed heavily to NorDubCo's attempts to establish a venture-capital fund, with a focus on biotechnology, specifically for the north Dublin region. The Coalition acted as facilitator for exploratory talks, which were ultimately fruitless, between Dublin City Council, Fingal County Council and DCU – represented by Martin Conry, Patrick McDermott (CEO, DCU Educational Trust), Chris O'Malley and Dr Leonora Bishop.[114]

DCU's community-engagement initiatives were conceived and implemented in a strategic vacuum until their articulation in the university's strategy document *Leadership through foresight, 2006–8*. This second strategic plan of von Prondzynski's tenure as president emphasized the importance of the university's role in the community, and prompted a series of initiatives with public agencies working in north Dublin in the following years.[115] Much of this initial success was driven by the university's engagement with local stakeholders through NorDubCo, led by its chief executive, Deiric Ó Broin.

During the strategic-planning overhaul of the university initiated by von Prondzynski, responsibility for the university's community engagement fell under the remit of Ronaldo Munck, who joined the Coalition's management committee in 2005 as DCU representative.[116] His ability to engage fully with NorDubCo, and indeed to implement the university's community-engagement strategy, was hampered by delays in hiring support staff. Acknowledging the enthusiasm and professionalism that DCU brought to community-engagement projects, Ó Broin nonetheless expressed his dissatisfaction with the university's failure to fully honour its strategic commitment to community engagement, and the apathy this was generating among the university's staff:

112 Chris O'Malley to Ferdinand von Prondzynski, 9 Nov. 2000 (DCUPO, 'NorDubCo – Up to 2004'). 113 Pauline Logan, 'Knowledge based regeneration in North Dublin', May 2002 (DCUPO, 'NorDubCo – up to 2004'; 'NorDubCo, 2005–16'). 114 One international study of national research and development investment, conducted in 2003, ranked Ireland 104th out of 125 countries surveyed (Deiric Ó Broin to Ferdinand von Prondzynski, 5 May 2004 (DCUPO, 'NorDubCo – up to 2004'); *Sunday Times*, 18 Apr. 2004). 115 See, for example, DCU, *Annual report, 2006*, pp 42–8. 116 Ferdinand von Prondzynski to Deiric Ó Broin, 24 Aug. 2005 (DCUPO, 'NorDubCo, 2005–16').

The Theme Leaders Office has never had a full complement ... and appears unlikely to have in the near future. This has had a very significant impact on the credence and credibility accorded to the university's community engagement strategy by units, schools and faculties ... [F]ollowing an initial period of success and goodwill, the strategy appears to have become bogged down.[117]

The academic theme leaders concept was never fully implemented during von Prondzynski's tenure. Ó Broin successfully refocused NorDubCo as an external advisory panel for the university's community-engagement strategy, while DCU in the Community continues to engage with local area partnerships.[118]

Though not a community-engagement programme in the traditional sense, the ambitious plan to regenerate Ballymun town, initiated in 1998, also incorporated significant involvement by the university. The project was overseen by Dublin City Council through the establishment of Ballymun Regeneration Ltd (BRL), with Danny O'Hare appointed as chairman of the company's board. Launching the redevelopment project, Liz McManus, minister for housing and urban renewal, noted that its aim was to create a town that 'caters for all local needs, attracts public and private investment, provides employment and secures a better mix of housing in a rejuvenated physical environment'.[119] The regeneration of its largest adjacent town offered obvious benefits to DCU, while also presenting it with an opportunity to reinforce its connection to the community. Welcoming the publication of the project's draft master plan for Ballymun, O'Hare highlighted the need for further educational supports in the area to enhance prosperity, and the role that DCU could play in providing those supports.[120]

In addition to educational supports, BRL's plans for the development of a technology/business park on a land bank of c.105 acres was also of interest to DCU, particularly in the light of the research priorities identified in its 2001 strategic plan.[121] From a national perspective, the creation of large centres of technological innovation and research aligned with the priorities for government investment in science and technology, as described in plans for national development during the first five years of the new millennium.[122] The Irish Council for Science, Technology and Innovation had published a report in 1999

117 Deiric Ó Broin to Anne Scott, 21 June 2007 (DCUPO, 'NorDubCo, 2005–16'). 118 Northside Partnership and Dublin North West Area Partnership, *North Dublin Joint Partnership submission to DCU strategic plan, 2018–22* (Dublin, 2018); DCU, *DCU in the Community: strategic plan, 2013–17* (Dublin, 2013). 119 Department of the Environment press release, 11 Mar. 1997 (DCUPO, 'Ballymun regeneration, 1997–2010'). 120 *Ballymun Redevelopment News*, Feb./Mar. 1998. 121 APA, Grant #12263; DCU, *Leading change: DCU strategic plan, 2001–5*. The land bank consisted of undeveloped land located alongside the M50 motorway, between the IKEA store on St Margaret's Road and the Ballymun Road/R108. As of the end of 2018 this land remained undeveloped. 122 Government of Ireland, *National development plan, 2000–6*.

outlining its vision for the future of such investment, highlighting the need for the creation of centres of excellence in a number of industries, as well as improved collaboration in research and development between the industrial and third-level sectors.[123]

Intensive discussions between DCU and BRL took place during the early 2000s about the possibility of locating research facilities on BRL's land bank, where the company hoped to develop a medical technology park and associated centres of excellence in the pharmaceutical and biotechnology sectors. By 2002 a tentative agreement was in place with BRL to synchronize the development of a Ballymun innovation park with DCU's research objectives, in order to 'create an environment which optimally exploits this relationship to the mutual benefit of both parties and creates the fundamentals for innovation and growth'.[124] DCU's commitment to the project was seen as vital to attracting investment in the project from US multinational companies – and indeed to the wider regeneration of Ballymun. BRL had been attempting to develop the land bank for several years, with its original plans for a business park failing due to a slump in the commercial property sector and a disagreement with the development company.[125] Delays to the innovation park were caused by difficulties securing the necessary planning permission, and by 2008 the project had stalled in the face of investor hesitancy as the economic outlook worsened. In an attempt to kickstart development, DCU and BRL opened preliminary discussions for collaboration with Enterprise Ireland. As the organization with responsibility for developing Irish businesses in world markets, Enterprise Ireland had called for the provision of industrial wet-lab space in the Dublin area.[126] Despite a positive preliminary response, discussions between DCU and BRL were ultimately fruitless and the collaboration was quietly shelved. The onset of a global recession shortly afterwards led to subsequent major cuts in funding, ensuring that the development of the Ballymun land bank never ensued prior to Dublin City Council's decision to wind-up BRL. The regeneration of Ballymun ultimately fell far short of expectations, hampered by planning difficulties, fluctuations in the economy and spiralling costs. While there is no doubt that contributing factors included a lack of funding, and the occasional hesitance of local and national government to commit resources to the project, it could also be argued that its ambitions were too great.[127] From DCU's perspective, the

123 ICSTI, *Technology Foresight Ireland: an ICSTI overview* (Dublin, 1999), p. 16.   124 Robert Windborne to Ferdinand von Prondzynski, 2 and 10 Oct. 2002 (DCUPO, 'Ballymun regeneration, 1997–2010'). Quotation from letter of 10 October.   125 DCUPO, 'Ballymun regeneration, 1997–2010'; *Irish Times*, 1 June 2005.   126 Ciaran Murray to Martin Conry, 11 Dec. 2008 (DCUPO, 'Ballymun regeneration, 1997–2010'); *Irish Times*, 14 Nov. 2008. DCU and Enterprise Ireland would later collaborate in the creation of An tSlí Glas (*Irish Times*, 17 Dec. 2010).   127 Ballymun Regeneration Ltd, *Ballymun regeneration completion report* (Dublin, 2008); *Committee of Public Accounts proceedings, Oireachtas*, 1 May 2008; *Irish Examiner*, 3 Aug. 2015; *Irish Times*, 18 Sept. 2016.

failure of several proposals to develop the main land bank as a site for research and innovation projects constituted a disappointment, though the university's commitment to community engagement remained unaffected.

VI

DCU's engagement with BRL was emblematic of the stated ambitions of NIHE Dublin's governing body to contribute to the development of north Dublin. This long-standing commitment to maintaining an active and positive engagement with the local community has been reinforced during the presidency of Brian MacCraith. In addition to supporting various community-based activities and initiatives, MacCraith has also strengthened direct connections with the primary-education sector, continuing a legacy first established with BITE. A memorandum of understanding was signed with Educate Together in 2013, marking an important step in DCU's evolving approach to educational pluralism and the development of innovative approaches to teacher education.[128] MacCraith's tenure has also brought a greater focus on the deployment of socially innovative education strategies, intended to deepen the university's engagement with disadvantaged communities:

> People within the university really resonate with its values, it's part of what keeps people attached to it. The fact that we had this very strong focus on Access was certainly one of the things I was always proud of … That value system of actually reaching out to the disadvantaged, and saying that access to higher education should be about your ability and nothing else, really permeates [the university] and is called out in all our strategic plans.[129]

That focus on social innovation, including its commitment to widening of participation led to DCU's designation as a Changemaker Campus by Ashoka U in 2013, one of just two universities in Europe with that distinction. Subsequent initiatives have seen DCU designated as Ireland's first University of Sanctuary, the world's first Age Friendly University, and the world's first Autism Friendly University.[130] The principles underpinning Age Friendly and Autism Friendly status were developed by staff and students at DCU, in collaboration with relevant charities and advocacy groups, and have been adopted worldwide.

Assessing the success or otherwise of DCU's engagement with the local community over the past four decades is a difficult task. While some initiatives

128 DCUPO, GA2013/2, 3; *DCU News*, 15 Apr. 2013; DCU, *President's report, 2012/13*, pp 3, 9, 41.   129 Brian MacCraith interview, 1 Oct. 2018.   130 DCUPO, GA2017/1; *DCU News*, 21 Dec. 2016 and 23 Mar. 2018; *Irish Times*, 27 Nov. 2012; 22 Mar. 2018; *Irish Independent*, 21 June 2018; Brian MacCraith interview, 1 Oct. 2018. See also ashoka.org.

have fallen victim to funding cutbacks, a loss of momentum or poor planning, others have had the kind of impact that no metrics can properly assess. This is especially true in the area of access to higher education. At national level, participation rates of disadvantaged students in higher education have steadily increased.[131] The importance, and necessity, of DCU's continued efforts to assist students from disadvantaged socio-economic backgrounds is amply demonstrated by the number of students admitted to the university via the Access programme since 1990 (fig. 7.1 and table 7.1). A decade after the establishment of BITE and the direct-access schemes, the number of disadvantaged students attending DCU stood at 583. By the beginning of the 2017/18 academic year that number had risen to 2,566,[132] an increase of 340 per cent. DCU's overall undergraduate population increased by 74 per cent in the same period. Nor was the effect of DCU's initiatives confined to north Dublin. Its participation in the BITE programme and pioneering adoption of direct entry and compensatory access in the early 1990s helped to shape national policy for increasing participation in third-level education across all sectors of society.

For more than two decades, NorDubCo and DCU in the Community have played a central and important role in formulating a strategy for community engagement and civic enterprise, while working as advocates for the university within the north Dublin region. DCU in the Community's efforts continue to focus on social regeneration through education.[133] In more recent years, NorDubCo has played a valuable role in keeping DCU's leadership and senior management informed of ongoing and planned local development and infrastructural investment.[134] Its applied research activities have produced numerous reports for regional stakeholders and national bodies, including an analysis of the economic and social value of higher education, using DCU as a case study, a report that broke new ground by providing metrics to measure the qualitative value of civic engagement.[135] DCU's current commitment to its locality is demonstrated by the continued engagement of its staff with a multitude of community projects, and their contributions to the shaping of national policy on tackling wealth inequality and social disadvantage. NIHE Dublin was slow to engage meaningfully with its surroundings during the 1980s, hampered by its own lack of facilities and funding. The attainment of university status in 1989 provided the confidence necessary to explore and implement

---

131 Fleming, Loxley and Finnegan, *Access and participation in Irish higher education*, p. 28. See also Clancy, *Irish higher education*. **132** Disadvantaged refers here to mature students, students with a disability and those attending via the Access programme. Statistics provided by DCU Human Resources and DCU Quality Promotion Office. I am grateful to Martin Leavy for his assistance with these statistics. **133** DCU, *DCU in the Community: strategic plan, 2013–17*. **134** The coalition produces four or five infrastructure and development reports per annum, which are forwarded to DCU's President's Office (DCUPO, 'NorDubCo – up to 2004'; 'NorDubCo, 2005–16'). **135** DCU, *Capturing the economic and social value of higher education*.

community outreach initiatives. Much of the impetus for these initiatives has come from within the communities themselves, epitomized by the highly successful BITE programme. Supported by philanthropic funding, the commitment of the university's governors, staff and students has ensured that the traditions laid in the early 1990s continue to the present day.

8

Conclusion

NIHED/DCU emerged as part of a broader reimagining of higher education in Ireland in the 1960s and 1970s, one that increasingly looked to the sector as a key driver of national economic development and expansion. Unlike its counterpart in Limerick, which opened its doors in 1972, NIHE Dublin was not the product of a grassroots campaign demanding the establishment of a university to meet regional needs. Nor did it have the benefit of a pre-existing infrastructure and well-established educational mission, as was later the case with Dublin Institute of Technology. Plans to establish the Institute as a recognized college of either UCD or TCD were abandoned almost as soon as they were articulated by the Department of Education. The Institute was created in the absence of any clear direction from the Department or the Higher Education Authority, emerging from the 'technological tangle' engendered by the government's inability to articulate a clear policy for technical education in Dublin during the 1970s. Governing body was instead handed a blank canvas, with few clues as to the kind of institution it was expected to fashion. Despite the uncertainty that pervaded the planning process undertaken between 1975 and 1980, by the end of its first academic year NIHE Dublin was hailed by John Boland, minister for education, as an institution 'designed for modern times and for the future'. He went on to express the hope that governing body would generate an Institute 'whose academic repute, its flexibility in responding to the changing needs of Irish society, its openness to change, its dynamism and foresight in anticipating change – and, indeed, in promoting change – will do honour to Ireland.'[1]

Flexibility and adaptability were embedded from the outset as core institutional characteristics. The university that has evolved at Glasnevin is radically different from that originally envisaged. The *Plan for the future of the Institute*, published in 1977, had called for a maximum student population of 5,000, housed on a single campus. Forty years later the student population at Dublin City University is rapidly approaching 20,000, spread across three academic campuses in Glasnevin and Drumcondra. After four decades of educational innovation, the suite of degree programmes on offer has diverged significantly from that mapped out in the 1970s, reflecting exponential growth in student participation, rapid changes in technological development and the changing demands of the workforce.

1 Boland was speaking at the inauguration of the first statutory governing body of NIHED, 31 July 1981 (DCUPO, 'NIHE Dublin: general').

Though it occurred less than a decade after the admission of the Institute's first students, the attainment of university status in 1989 remains the most important moment in DCU's history. University status had loomed as an unspoken aspiration from NIHE Dublin's early days. That goal had not been achieved since the formation of the state in 1922 yet was accomplished by the Institute in less than a decade. Coinciding with the arrival of the first tranche of financial support from Atlantic Philanthropies, the beginnings of greater government investment in higher education, and the first meaningful engagement with its local community, university status created a powerful momentum that propelled DCU into the new millennium. Given the subsequent development of the Glasnevin campus and evolution of the university, it is easy to forget that in 1989 the campus comprised just a handful of buildings, the majority of which were either prefabricated or built in the nineteenth century, largely unfit for purpose. That a university could emerge from such unpromising facilities was a testament to the staff and leadership of NIHE Dublin. If success is to be measured by growth alone, DCU has comfortably outstripped initial expectations. The parameters by which the institution itself intended to measure success were laid down in 1982, when it set a target of providing 'a new technological and entrepreneurial generation of graduates who will be central to the future dynamism and wellbeing of this nation'.[2] The steady introduction of innovative degree programmes and pedagogical techniques over four decades, several of which have been replicated across the Irish university system, suggest a continued commitment to that ambition and provide an alternative measure of success than metrics as limited and narrow in scope as international university rankings.

One of the common themes underlying the history of NIHED/DCU has been the effect of funding – or lack thereof – on the university's development. Adverse economic conditions that have restricted government investment in higher education have defined much of DCU's existence. While unwelcome, these difficult financial circumstances have proven to be major factors in shaping the university. Its distinctive focus on serving the employment and research needs of private industry and the national economy was both a response to the challenges of Ireland's entry to the EEC in 1973, and to the severe recession of the 1980s. The entrepreneurial spirit that infused staff endeavours in programme creation, and research development, resulted from imaginative responses to the lack of resources as much as from stated educational aims. Increased investment during the 1990s and 2000s, funded by philanthropy and a thriving economy, brought far-reaching changes to the character of the university. Modularization and semesterization presented new challenges to staff. Organizational structures were streamlined to bring the university into

2 NIHED, *Annual report, 1978–82*, p. 32.

greater alignment with national contemporaries, conforming with an international trend towards consolidation of power within university executives and leadership teams.

Renewed economic recession during the 2010s brought retrenchment in government investment. By 2014 funding for third-level education had suffered a 25 per cent cut in just five years.[3] While rising student numbers should have brought an increase in staff and improved facilities, cuts to academic staff were mandated across the higher-education sector. Funding for capital projects receded. Successive reports commissioned to examine the future of the higher-education system characterized the sector as drastically underfunded. In 2015 the Irish Universities Association estimated that an immediate capital investment of €2bn was required for the entire university sector.[4] The Cassells Report, commissioned by the Department of Education and Skills in 2014 and published in 2016, delivered a stark assessment of the future of higher education, warning that an increased annual investment of *c*.€1bn in core higher-education funding would be required by 2030.[5] Yet state expenditure on third-level education continued to fall even as university enrolments continued to grow, placing serious strains on the sector's capabilities.[6] Between 2008 and 2016 the student population at DCU rose by more than 3,000, despite a precipitous drop in state funding from €39.6m in 2008 to €16.7m in 2015 – which rebounded to €27.6m in 2016 but still fell far short of what was required.[7]

From an early stage in its development, DCU has offset shortfalls in state grants by implementing alternative revenue streams to allow for growth and expansion. Investment from the European Investment Bank and the Ireland Strategic Investment Fund in 2015, to help fund a €300m investment in the university's infrastructure, has provided much-needed funds for capital development.[8] Non-exchequer revenue continues to rise in importance, with more than 50 per cent of university income now derived from alternative sources.[9] At DCU, tentative first steps in the early 1990s into providing campus student accommodation proved popular with students and demonstrated an ability to generate revenue. The latest campus development plan provides for an additional 1,240 student beds on campus.[10] Reporting on meetings with DCU's

3 Oireachtas Library and Research Service, *Higher education in Ireland: for economy and society?* (Dublin, 2014), p. 2. 4 DCUPO, GA2015/4. 5 Department of Education and Skills, *Investing in national ambition: a strategy for funding higher education* (Dublin, 2016), p. 7. 6 Department of Education and Skills, *National strategy for higher education to 2030* (Dublin, 2011), pp 15–16, 42–3; idem, *Investing in national ambition*, pp 6–10. 7 See appendix 6, figs. A6.1 and A6.3. Sharp increases in student population and state funding recorded in 2016 reflect the completion of the Incorporation process. 8 Additional government investment in the form of €24m to aid construction of a new STEM facility was announced in September 2018 (DCUPO, GA2015/4, 6; *DCU News*, 14 Sept. 2018; *Irish Examiner*, 14 Sept. 2018; *College View*, 3 Oct. 2018). 9 Oireachtas Parliamentary Budget Office, *An overview of tertiary education funding in Ireland* (Dublin, 2019), p. 14. 10 DCUPO, GA2018/6; *College View*, 7 Feb. 2018; *Irish Independent*, 24 Sept. 2019.

leadership as part of its strategic dialogue process in 2017, the HEA commended the university for its adoption of an 'expansive research agenda', noting that its ambitions in this area would be 'largely shaped by [its] capacity to generate funding through commercialization and increasing international student growth'.[11] The long term effects of this ongoing pivot towards prioritization of commercial revenue and fees from international students remain to be seen.

The financial difficulties of the 2010s reprised those of the 1980s, though the university was far better resourced in terms of facilities and experience. The response of the university's staff was to emulate their predecessors at NIHE Dublin: 'People right across the university were doing more with less. Everyone worked harder, and people innovated.'[12] Challenges nonetheless remain, particularly those arising from the rapid growth in student population and the university's expansion into a multi-campus institution. One is of transport, and the necessity of making travel from one campus to another as easy as possible. Another is the creation and maintenance of a sense of community and common ethos among hitherto discrete entities and staff cohorts. The last decade has also witnessed a rapidly changing higher-education sector, with the emergence of the technological university model and the intent to create a new technological university sector in Ireland.[13] As highlighted in a recent institutional review, this development poses 'a particular challenge given DCU's historic profile and programme portfolio'.[14] The diversification of programmes has already been enhanced with the completion of Incorporation, the greatest evolution of the institution since 1989. The full impact of the integration into DCU of St Patrick's College, Mater Dei Institute and the Church of the Ireland College of Education has yet to emerge. Internal growth has presented numerous challenges, not least the emergence of Humanities and Social Sciences as the university's largest faculty, as well as the creation of an entirely new faculty in the Institute of Education. These developments represent a substantial pivot away from the university's traditionally narrow focus on technological or applied education and the ambition of fulfilling the employment needs of the Irish economy.

As DCU prepares to enter its fifth decade of operations, it does so in an education sector radically different from that which existed in 1980. NIHE Dublin had represented a new departure in third-level education, designed to be different from the traditional universities. As a now well-established university,

11 HEA/DCU strategic dialogue bilateral session, 25 Sept. 2017 (https://hea.ie/assets/uploads/ 2017/04/Dublin-City-University-Strategic-Dialogue-Cylce-4-Minute-and-Assessment- Findings.pdf, accessed 30 Mar. 2019). 12 Brian MacCraith interview, 16 May 2019. 13 Department of Education and Skills, *National strategy for higher education to 2030*, pp 103–9; Technological Universities Act, 2018 (No. 3 of 2018). 14 QQI, *Institutional review report, 2019: Dublin City University* (Dublin, 2019), p. 16.

this is a role it no longer occupies. Indeed, Incorporation has brought the university's character even closer to those of the 'traditional' universities that viewed the arrival of NIHE Dublin with a degree of scepticism. Yet no institution can flourish if it remains static, and the pace of growth and evolution at NIHED/DCU over the past four decades has been remarkable. While the future of Irish higher education remains in flux, it can be said with certainty that the creation of an internationally respected university in just forty years, from the most meagre of resources, is a testament to all who contributed to the development of DCU.

Appendix 1

Logos and crests: creating a visual identity

Under the legislation enacted in 1980 to establish NIHE Dublin on a statutory basis, the Institute's governing body was required to provide and maintain a formal seal for the authentication of official documents.[1] Initial proposals to meet this legal requirement centred on the adoption of a coat of arms, which could be used not only as the basis for a seal but also for the Institute's visual identity.[2]

Authority for the creation of new coats of arms in Ireland has, since the mid-twentieth century, been vested in the Office of the Chief Herald of Ireland. Shortly after the first meeting of NIHE Dublin's statutory governing body, Danny O'Hare wrote to Gerard Slevin, then chief herald, requesting some draft designs. The only guidance O'Hare was able to give Slevin was that the Institute had a national remit and would be regarded in other European countries as a technological university, with a focus on the future needs of industry, business and the community. Slevin's proposals, which never advanced beyond initial drawings, were drafted before his retirement at the end of 1981. Working in a traditional heraldic style, Slevin proposed arms featuring a black and white wavy background, representing Dublin (Dubh Linn, the 'black pool'). Emblazoned throughout is a pile (wedge shaped), representing energy and progress. Two drafts of the pile were prepared, both featuring charges (symbolic devices) representing different aspects of education.[3]

O'Hare was not wholly satisfied with the design, particularly the allusion to Dublin in the background, as his preference was to emphasize the Institute's national remit. Moreover, the Institute's director had doubts as to the suitability of a traditional coat of arms for an institution that was avowedly modern in its educational philosophy. Distracted by more immediate concerns regarding curriculum and campus development, consideration of Slevin's draft and the question of a formal seal for the Institute were shelved for more than a year. However, a seal was still a legislative necessity. In March 1983 O'Hare tasked the Institute's arts group, chaired by John Pratschke, dean of the Faculty of Business and Professional Studies, with revisiting the issue.[4] By that time the Institute had adopted its distinctive 'N' logo (fig. A1.1) for use on stationery and in its marketing and publicity material. Showing regard for the distinctiveness of the visual identity already established, the Institute incorporated the logo into its formal seal, featuring the 'N' encircled by the Institute's name, embossed on red wax. Created by the

1 National Institute for Higher Education, Dublin, Act, 1980 (no. 30 of 1980), s. 5.   2 Danny O'Hare to Gerard Slevin, 10 Sept. 1981; B. McKenna to O'Hare, 23 Nov. 1981 (DCUPO, 'NIHE Dublin: general, 2/2'; NLI, Genealogical Office (GO) Archive, Arms and Genealogy Files). I am indebted to Ciara Kerrigan, assistant keeper at the NLI, for her assistance in locating relevant files in the Genealogical Office.   3 Hand-painted, coloured drafts were sent to the Institute in November 1981. A photocopy of poor quality survives in the DCU President's Office Archive, which is unsuitable for reproduction. The location of the original drafts is currently unknown (DCUPO, 'NIHE Dublin: general, 2/2').   4 Danny O'Hare to John Pratschke, 1 Mar. 1983 (DCUPO, 'NIHE Dublin: general, 2/2').

Institute's designer, Brendan Matthews, the seal was formally adopted by governing body in June 1983.[5]

In deciding against the adoption of a coat of arms, the Institute had deliberately emphasized the modernity of its ethos and curriculum. It was, then, surprising that the announcement of NIHE Dublin's impending inauguration as Dublin City University was accompanied by a loss of nerve with respect to the university's visual identity. Seven corporate-image consultants tendered for the job of reinterpreting the institution's image.[6] Following a presentation to governing body that emphasized a timeless and classical style, Imagebank Group was handed responsibility for crafting a look suitable for the new university.[7]

The new crest featured a blue shield on a white background, emblazoned with the overlapping letters 'DCU' in gold, using the Times Roman serif font (fig. A1.2). Clearly influenced by Dublin city's coat of arms, the crest was topped by the famously enigmatic three castles, with the name of the university situated below in both Irish and English. Hewing closely to a classical heraldic style, the selected design for DCU's new logo ran contrary to the conceptual thinking that underpinned the sleek modernity of the 'N' logo. The new status gave rise to a belief that, as a new university, DCU needed to place itself in the same category as its more well-established counterparts – each of which had a crest in the classical style.[8]

By the turn of the millennium that classical style had itself fallen out of favour. Viewed as staid and unreflective of the university's determination to reposition itself as a radical and innovative institution, a complete redesign took place soon after Ferdinand von Prondzynski's inauguration as president: 'We needed to create a logo that would look totally different … If you look at the Irish Universities' Association website and line up the logos, ours [now] stands out.'[9]

Following a competitive selection process, Barry Bödeker (of Corporate Graphics, a Dublin-based company) was appointed to develop a new identity that would better reflect the university's evolution. Bödeker's brief was to create a logo that was visually attractive, indicative of the university's corporate objectives and core values, and versatile enough to be used in conjunction with the various pre-existing identities established by the colleges, schools and centres that were linked with DCU:

> The design brief I was presented with used words like 'dynamic', 'leading' and 'cutting edge'. The university wanted to be perceived more as a forward-thinking technology/incubation hub rather than as a traditional place of study. The sweeping circular shapes slicing through the typography in the logo were developed precisely with the wording from that brief in mind.[10]

While developing the concept, Bödeker worked closely with several members of the university's staff, particularly Eilis O'Brien, Karl Grimes of the School of

5 DCUPO, 'NIHE Dublin: general, 2/2', GB 83/A4/8; *Nuacht*, July 1983.   6 Within weeks of the announcement of DCU's inauguration, enterprising designers had already submitted speculative proposals to Danny O'Hare (Danny O'Hare to Michael Gleeson, 31 Jan. 1989 (DCUPO, 'NIHE Dublin: general, 2/2')).   7 DCUPO, GB89/M4.   8 *Newslink*, no. 18 (Nov. 1989); DCU press release, 21 May 2001 (https://www. dcu.ie/news/press/2001/p0501d.shtml, accessed 29 Nov. 2018).   9 Ferdinand von Prondzynski interview, 18 Oct. 2018; DCU, *Leading change*.   10 Barry

A1.1 Logo, NIHED (1980–9) (DCU Collection).

A1.2 Logo, DCU (1989–2001)
(DCU Collection).

A1.3 Logo, DCU (2001–present)
(DCU Collection).

Communications and von Prondzynski. Bödeker also toured the campus for inspiration, including the building site of the Helix, with the rounded architecture of the soon-to-be-completed concert hall exerting considerable influence on the final design.

Bödeker's design (fig. A1.3) embraces clean lines through the placement of the DCU acronym, using a custom version of the Optima font, lifted by the three sweeping 'rings'. Von Prondzynski was particularly taken with the three 'rings': 'I really wanted those rings, because that's really what gives it the dynamic sense.'[11] The primary colours used continued the blue and gold theme of the previous logo, with the current iteration of the crest featuring slate blue and burnt gold. Bödeker's design met the requirement of presenting a dynamic visual identity that was markedly different from DCU's contemporaries. The new logo was a radical departure from the crests used by the other six Irish universities, and has become an integral part of DCU's image.[12] During a review of its branding, conducted in 2017 by its communications and marketing department, the university found that, other than a slight adjustment in colouring, the logo was too recognizable to change.

Bödeker to author, 6 Jan. 2019.   11 Ferdinand von Prondzynski interview, 18 Oct. 2018.   12 It is worth noting that UCD followed DCU's lead in launching a redesigned, simplified crest in 2005 (http://www.ucd.ie/news/ aug05/crest.htm, accessed 13 Dec. 2018).

Appendix 2

Members of governing body/governing authority, 1975–2019[1]

Governing body/authority
1st governing body, 1975–81[2]
1st statutory governing body, 1981–2[3]
2nd statutory governing body, 1982–7
3rd statutory governing body, 1987–92
4th statutory governing body, 1992–7
5th statutory governing authority, 1998–2001[4]
6th statutory governing authority, 2001–6
- Three-year term: 2001–4
- Five-year term: 2001–6
7th statutory governing authority, 2006–11
8th statutory governing authority, 2011–16
9th statutory governing authority, 2016–

Members
Dr Thomas Ambrose (1981–92): Kevin Street College of Technology
Fiona Barbagallo (1999–2000): postgraduate student representative, DCU
Dr Patricia Barker (2000–3): registrar, DCU
Vikki Barnett (1998): women's rights officer, DCU Students' Union
John K. Barrett (1982–92): NIHE Dublin
Dr John D. Barry (1975–9): principal, Bolton Street College of Technology
Niall Behan (2017–18): president, DCU Students' Union
Alan Bermingham (1989–90): education officer, DCU Students' Union
Astrid Bilberg (1992–7): guidance counsellor, Holy Faith Secondary School, Killester
Eoin Bolger (2008–9): president, St Patrick's College Students' Union
Dr John Bradley (1992–5): RTC Galway

1 Information supplied by the President's Office and the Office of the Chief Operations Officer. My thanks to Fina Akintola, Gaye Crowley and Yvonne Duff for their assistance.   2 The first governing body of NIHED was appointed on an ad hoc basis on 5 March 1975, for an initial term of three years. That term was twice extended, first to 30 June 1979, and then until such time as the Institute had been established on a statutory basis (NAI, 2011/127/807).   3 The term of office of the first statutory governing body was limited to one year by the provisions of the National Institute for Higher Education, Dublin, Act, 1980 (no. 30 of 1980). Though that act was signed into law by the president of Ireland on 3 December 1980, it was not implemented by statutory instrument until 17 June 1981 (S.I. 213/1981). The first meeting of statutory governing body took place on 31 July 1981.   4 Following the enactment of the Universities Act, 1997 (no. 24 of 1997), governing body was renamed as governing authority.

Hugo Brady (2000–1): president, DCU Students' Union

Joe Brennan (2006–11): postgraduate student representative, DCU

Shane Brodbin (2001–11): graduate representative, Eircom/Vodafone

Kenneth Browne (2014–15): president, DCU Students' Union

Dr Cathal M. Brugha (1981–7): College of Marketing and Design

Michael Burke (2017–present): Faculty of Science and Health, DCU

Gareth Burns (2001–2): president, St Patrick's College Students' Union

Cllr Ciaran Byrne (2010–14): Fingal County Council

Cillian Byrne (2010–12): deputy president, DCU Students' Union

David Byrne (2006–11): chancellor, DCU governing authority

Eoin Byrne (2006–7): education and welfare officer, DCU Students' Union

Monica Byrne (1994–7): School of Biotechnology, DCU

Gerard Callan (1986–7): education officer, NIHED Students' Union

Anton Carroll (1981–92): principal, Greendale Community School

Prof. John Carroll (1997–2000): registrar, DCU

Justice Mella Carroll (2001–6): chancellor, DCU governing authority

Stephen Carty (1982): education officer, NIHED Students' Union

Donal Clarke (1981–2): registrar, NIHE Dublin

Robert G. Clarke (1975–82): personnel director, Brooks Thomas Ltd

Aaron Clogher (2012–14): deputy president (2012–13) and president (2013–14), DCU
    Students' Union

Revd Simon Clyne, CM (1998–9): president, St Patrick's College, Drumcondra

John Paul Coakley (1982–3): education officer, NIHED Students' Union

P.J. Coghill (1987–97): member of board, Athlone Regional Technical College

Ann Coleman (1998–2006): head of Business Studies, Whitehall Senior College

Eileen Colgan (1998–2001): School of Applied Language and Intercultural Studies,
    DCU

Michael Colgan (1998–2001): director, The Gate Theatre

Shaun Conaghan (2006–7): president, St Patrick's College Students' Union

Charlene Connolly (2006–7): president, DCU Students' Union

Dr Peter J. Connolly (1982–7): chief executive officer, Co. Louth Vocational Education
    Committee

Martin Conry (1998–2012): secretary/chief operations officer, DCU and secretary, DCU
    governing authority

Prof. Farrel Corcoran (2001–6): School of Communications, DCU

James Corcoran (2011–present): financial consultant; former president of Junior
    Chamber Ireland

Patricia Jo Corr (1975–82): vice principal, Dominican Convent, Sion Hill

Dr Shirley Coyle (2011–13): CLARITY: Centre for Sensor Web Technologies, DCU

Cllr Anthony Creevey (1998–9): St Kevin's Community College, Clondalkin

Martin Crehan (1988–9): education officer, NIHED Students' Union

Doirín Cremer (1992–7): head of Irish Department, Loreto Abbey, Dalkey

Aleck Crichton (1975–81): director, Irish Distillers Group Ltd

Dr Martin J. Croghan (1982–7): School of Communications, DCU

Ciarán Cunniffe (2004–5): president, St Patrick's College Students' Union

Colin Cunningham (1994–5): president, DCU Students' Union

Clare Daly (1988–90): president, NIHED/DCU Students' Union

Clíodhna Daly (2014–15): president, St Patrick's College Students' Union

Vincent Daly (1987–9): chairman, Ericsson Holdings Ltd

Shane Davis (2005–6): president, St Patrick's College Students' Union

Deirdre Davitt (1998–2003): deputy chief executive, Bord na Gaeilge

Hugh de Lacy (1975–81): principal, Kevin Street College of Technology

Francis Plunkett Dillon (1975–7): solicitor

Paul Doherty (2012–13): president, DCU Students' Union

Patrick Donegan (1975–9): chairman, NIHED governing body; CDVEC

Senator Michael Donnelly (1978–81): chartered accountant

James Donoghue (2015–17): education officer and academic affairs officer, DCU
    Students' Union

Donal Downing (1987–97): chief operations officer, Aer Lingus

Liam Doyle (1984–5): education officer, NIHED Students' Union

Ciaran Duffy (1995–6): president, NIHED Students' Union

Mairead Dunne (2011–16): Enterprise Ireland

Denise Egan (1998–2001): Institute of Technology, Tallaght

Dr Dermot Egan (2011–14): former chair, National Concert Hall

Michael Egan (1992–3): president, DCU Students' Union

Aisling Fagan (2018–present): vice president for welfare and equality, DCU Students'
    Union

Melanie Farrell (2009–10): campaigns and information officer, DCU Students' Union

Sarah Farrell (2005–6): president, DCU Students' Union

Dr Sean Farren (2011–16): School of Education, University of Ulster; MLA

Desmond Fay (1975–81): chartered accountant, member of CDVEC

Lynette Fay (2015–present): producer and media presenter

Thomas Fennell (1987–91): College of Marketing and Design, DIT

Dr David Fenton (1985–7): principal, Athlone Regional Technical College

Ciara Fitzpatrick (1995–7): education officer (1995–6) and president (1996–7), DCU
    Students' Union

Alan Flanagan (2007–8): president, DCU Students' Union

Frank Flanagan (1987): chief executive, Killeshandra Co-operative Agricultural and
    Dairy Society, Ltd

Pauline Flanagan (2010–11): president, St Patrick's College Students' Union

Philip Flood (1977–81): head of Department of Marketing Studies, CDVEC College of
    Marketing and Design

Aileen Flynn (1987): education officer, NIHED Students' Union

David Flynn (1998–9): president, DCU Students' Union

Fintan Foy (1992–3): administrative assistant, Faculty of Science, DCU

Nora French (1992–7): head of Department of Communications, Rathmines College of
    Commerce/DIT

Cllr Karen Furlong (2017–19): councillor, Dún Laoghaire-Rathdown County Council

John Gallagher (1975–81, 1987–92): principal, Carlow Regional Technical College

Peter Gallagher (1975–84): principal, Letterkenny Regional Technical College

Dr Margaret Gibbon (2001–4): School of Applied Language and Intercultural Studies, DCU

Colm Gibbons (2009–10): president, St Patrick's College Students' Union

Ita Gibney (1983–7): director, Murray Consultants, Ltd

Kevin Gildea (1986–7): president, NIHED Students' Union

Pat Gilroy (2016–present): managing director, Designer Group; All Ireland Football winning manager and player

Dr Otto Glaser (1981–7): managing director, Technico (Communications), Ltd

James Glynn (1982): president, NIHED Students' Union

Dr Tony Glynn (1987–92, 1998–2004): director, Industrial Liaison Unit/Industrial and International Affairs, DCU

Brian Gormley (1990–2): president, DCU Students' Union

Bernie Gray (2016–present): management consultant; chairwoman, Coillte

Lorna Greene (2003–4): president, DCU Students' Union

Ray Griffin (1987–92): principal, Waterford Regional Technical College

Gerry Grogan (1998–2001): joint director, The National Centre for Partnership

Veronica Guerin (1982–92): Guerin Public Relations, Ltd; journalist

Prof. Eithne Guilfoyle (2012–present): vice president for academic affairs/registrar, DCU

Don Hall (1992–7): managing director, The Hall Company, Ltd

Mary Hanlon (1998–2001): Community Development Office, Dublin Corporation/Dublin City Council

Dr Thomas P. Hardiman (1998–2001): chancellor, DCU; chairman, IBM International Treasury

Edward Harney (1982): education officer, NIHED Students' Union

Hazel Hayes (2007–8): deputy president, DCU Students' Union

Daniel Heffernan (1992–7): School of Physical Sciences, DCU

George Hegarty (1982–3): president, NIHED Students' Union

Cllr Deirdre Heney (1999–2004): Dublin City Council

Áine Hickey (2000–1): women's rights officer, DCU Students' Union

Anita Hogan (2000–1): president, St Patrick's College Students' Union

Ann Horan (2006–11): trustee, DCU Educational Trust; Financial Advisor

Bríd Horan (2014–present): deputy chief executive, ESB

Dr Jane Horgan (1998–2006): School of Computer Applications, DCU

Prof. John Hurley (2000–1): DCU Business School

Susan Hurley (2008–9): deputy president and education and welfare officer, DCU Students' Union

Rachel Hussey (2017–present): partner and Head of Business Development, Arthur Cox

Deborah Hutchinson (1993–4): education officer, DCU Students' Union

Paul Hyland (2013–14): president, St Patrick's College Students' Union

David Irwin (1992–7): Tallaght Regional Technical College

Celine Jameson (2001–4): administrator, DCU Business School

Gary Joyce (2011–14): Genesis Ireland

Michael Keating TD (1975–81): member, CDVEC

Alan Keegan (2009–10): president, DCU Students' Union

Owen Keegan (2014–16): chief executive, Dublin City Council

Dylan Kehoe (2016–17): president, DCU Students' Union

Dr Patrick Kehoe (1981–2): managing director, MLH Consultants

Dr John Kelly (1981–7): dean of Faculty of Engineering and Architecture, University College Dublin

William Kelly (1998–2011): DCU Business School

Prof. Dorothy Kenny (2016–present): School of Applied Languages and Intercultural Studies, DCU

John Keogan (1998–2006): management consultant

Daire Keogh (2012–present): deputy president, DCU

Aidan Kerins (2006–11): European Commercial Director (Manufacturing and Life Sciences), Fluor Corporation

Eve Kerton (2014–15): vice president for Welfare, DCU Students' Union

Michael Keville (1998–9): president, St Patrick's College Students' Union

Dr Anthony Killard (2007–10): Biomedical Diagnostics Institute, National Centre for Sensor Research, DCU

Sally Anne Kinahan (2003–6): director of Advocacy and General Services, Irish Congress of Trade Unions

Mary King (1987–97): First National Building Society

Dr Dermot Lane (1999–2012): president, Mater Dei Institute of Education

Denis Larkin (1975–81): former secretary, Workers' Union of Ireland

Terence A. Larkin (1981–92): chairman, NIHED/DCU governing body (1982–92); managing director, Irish Glass, PLC

Elaine Lawless (1998): Education Services, DCU

Robert Lawlor (1975–81): principal, Dublin College of Catering

Ed Leamy (2011–12): president, DCU Students' Union

Prof. Anne Lodge (2015–16): principal, Church of Ireland College of Education; Director, Church of Ireland Centre, DCU Institute of Education

Dermot Lohan (Diarmuid Ó Leocháin) (1997–8): president, DCU Students' Union

Karl Lombard (1983): education officer, NIHED Students' Union

Darragh Lucey: (2002): postgraduate student representative, DCU

Berni Lynch (1992–7)

Patrick Lynch (1998–2001): chairman, FÁS

Sean Lyons (1977–81): Kevin Street College of Technology

Prof. Michael J. MacCormac (1975–82): chairman, NIHED governing body, 1979–82; dean of Faculty of Commerce, University College Dublin

Prof. Brian MacCraith (2010–present): president, DCU

Eoin MacCrosáin (1990–1): education officer, DCU Students' Union

Dr Ciaran Mac Murchaidh (2010–13): dean of Research and Humanities, St Patrick's College, Drumcondra

Sean MacPhilibín (1987–92): library, DCU

Seamus MacSuibhne (1987): education officer, NIHED Students' Union

Meabh Maguire (2001–2): vice president and Welfare Officer, DCU Students' Union

Thomas Joseph Maher, MEP (1975–81): president, Irish Agricultural Organisation Society, Ltd; member of the European Parliament, 1979–94

Liavan Mallin (2002–6): chief executive, Shopdirect Group

Vito Maloney Burke (2018–19): president, DCU Students' Union

Patrick Marron (1998–2004): managing director, Nestlé Ireland

Shane Martin (1999–2001): postgraduate student representative, DCU

Paul May (2004–5): president, DCU Students' Union

Dr Martin McAleesse (2011–present): chancellor, DCU governing authority

Orlaith McBride (2007–16): director, NAYD

Thomas McCarthy (1975–87): education and training officer, Irish Transport and General Workers' Union

Tom McCarthy (2013–16): Chartered Accountant

Niall McClave (2008–9): president, DCU Students' Union

Sharon McCooey (2016–present): senior director of International Operations/Head of LinkedIn Ireland

Thomas McCormack (2012–13): president, St Patrick's College Students' Union

Dr Patrick McDevitt (2011–15): president, All Hallows College

Dr Sean McDonagh (1975–87): principal, Dundalk Regional Technical College

Thomas McDonald (1984–5): president, NIHED Students' Union

Farrell McElgunn (1982–97): vice principal, Marymount College, Carrick-on-Shannon

Damian McEvoy (1998–2004): DCU graduate representative; PFPC International Ltd

Dr Kara McGann (2018–present): senior labour market policy executive, Ibec

David McGee (1991–2): education officer, DCU Students' Union

Dr Andrew McGrady (2013–16): director, Mater Dei Institute of Education

John McKay (1981–2): chief executive officer, Co. Cavan Vocational Education Committee

Padraig McKeon (2011–14): managing director, Drury Communications

Barry McKimm (1987–8): education officer, NIHED Students' Union

Damien McLoughlin (2004–5): vice president, DCU Students' Union

Denise McMorrow (2011–12): Student Support and Development, DCU

Phylomena McMorrow (2012–16): director of registry, DCU

Prof. Caroline McMullan (2011–present): DCU Business School

Paula Melvin (2011–12): Oifigeach na Gaeilge, St Patrick's College, Drumcondra

Carol Moffett (1981–6, 2007–9): managing director, Moffett Engineering Ltd

Kevin Mollaghan (2002–3): president, St Patrick's College Students' Union

Cllr Andrew Montague (2004–9): Dublin City Council

Regina Moran (2011–16): managing director, Fujitsu Ireland

Sean Moriarty (1992–7): marketing executive, Roadstone

Dr Jean-Paul Mosnier (2016–present): School of Physical Sciences, DCU

Mary Mosse (1995–7): Waterford Regional Technical College

Donal Motherway (1998–2001): DCU Business School

Declan Moylan (2014–15): DCU Educational Trust

Prof. Anthony Moynihan (2001–4): School of Computer Applications, DCU

Kieran Mulvey (1987–97): general secretary, Association of Secondary Teachers, Ireland; Chief Executive, Labour Relations Commission

Alan Murphy (1987–8): president, NIHED Students' Union

Prof. Gary Murphy (2011–present): vice president for Research, DCU

Dr Noel Murphy (2011–present): School of Electronics Engineering, DCU

Justin Naughton (1996–7): education officer, DCU Students' Union

Holly Ní Chiardha (1999–2000): women's rights officer, DCU Students' Union

Máirín Ní Loideáin (1998–9): women's rights officer, DCU Students' Union

Orla Nic Aodha (2017–present): associate director, library, DCU

Siobhán Nic Thaidhg (2017–18): vice president for Engagement and Development, DCU Students' Union

Dr Robert J Nichol (1981–2): deputy director general, Institute for Industrial Research and Standards

Margaret Nolan (1998–2002): director, Education and Training Services, Irish Congress of Trade Unions

Fr Mark Noonan (2008–11): president, All Hallows College

Michelle Noonan (2002–3): welfare officer, DCU Students' Union

Eoin O'Brien (1992–7): chairman, DCU Governing Body; Director, English Language Institute, Dublin

An tUasal Dáithí Ó Broin (2006–11): deputy principal, Ard Scoil Rís

Cormac Ó Cleirigh (2003–5): postgraduate student representative, DCU

Ciarán O'Connor (2013–14): deputy president, DCU Students' Union

Deirdre O'Connor (2016–present): assistant general secretary, Irish National Teachers' Organisation

John O'Doherty (1987–92): managing director, Squibb (Ireland) Ltd

Richard O'Doherty (2003–4): welfare officer, DCU Students' Union

Daibhí Ó Donnabháin (1999–2000): president, DCU Students' Union

Prof. John P O'Donnell (1975–81): Department of Chemical Engineering, University College Dublin

Michael O'Donnell (1979–97): principal, Bolton Street College of Technology; Deputy President, DIT

Michael O'Donnell (April–May 1983): president, NIHED Students' Union

Eliza O'Driscoll (February–March 1983): president, NIHED Students' Union

Pauline O'Gorman (2001–4): Computer Services, DCU

Dr Eunan O'Halpin (1992–2000): senior lecturer, DCU Business School

Dr Daniel O'Hare (1975–99): director/president, NIHED/DCU

Dr Richard O'Kennedy (1992–7, 2001–4): School of Biological Sciences/Biotechnology, DCU

Norman O'Mahoney (1998–2000): Buildings Office, DCU

Ciaran Ó Maoileoin (1982–4): NIHED Students' Union Education officer (1982/3) and NIHED Students' Union President (1983/4)

Dr Liam Ó Maolchatha (1975–7): acting director, NIHED

Monsignor John M. O'Regan (1975–6): CDVEC

Dr Maurice O'Reilly (2001–6): Department of Mathematics, St Patrick's College, Drumcondra

Megan O'Riordan (2010–11): president, DCU Students' Union

Terence O'Rourke (2013–present): chairman, Enterprise Ireland; President, Institute of Chartered Accountants in Ireland

Riocard Ó Tiarnaigh (1981–2): president, NIHED Students' Union

Dr Jennifer Pearson (1998–2001): School of Applied Language and Intercultural Studies, DCU

Enda Peoples (1993–4): president, DCU Students' Union

Dr Con Power (1987–90): director of economic policy, Confederation of Irish Industry

John Power (2014–present): certified chartered accountant (FCCA, FCIS)

Prof. Albert Pratt (1998–2001): School of Chemical Sciences, DCU and director general, DCU

Paul Quigley (1981–2): general manager, Shannon Free Airport Development Company and Chairman, NIHE Limerick governing body

Kathy Quinn (2017–present): head of finance, Dublin City Council

Larry Quinn (2016–17): chairman, DCU Educational Trust

Dr Declan Raftery (2012–present): chief operations officer, DCU

Prof. Fiona Regan (2011–16): School of Chemical Sciences, DCU

Patrick J. Rock (1975–81): senior specialist, Irish Management Institute

Sandra Rothwell (2005–6): postgraduate student representative, DCU

Dr Vincent Ruddy (1987–92): School of Physical Sciences, DCU

Prof. Heather Ruskin (2006–11): School of Computing, DCU

Carmel Ryan/O'Sullivan (1982–7): library, DCU

John Ryan (1992–3): education officer, DCU Students' Union

Dr Pierce Ryan (1981–7): director, An Foras Taluntais

Vanya Sargent (1994–5): education officer, DCU Students' Union

Dr Ann Saunders (1981–7): chief information officer, Institute for Industrial Research and Standards

Sean Scally (2002–3): president, DCU Students' Union

Derek Scanlon (2001–2): president, DCU Students' Union

Prof. Anne Scott (2001–4, 2009–12): School of Nursing, DCU and deputy president/ registrar, DCU

Lil Sheehy (2006–11): nurse

Dr Mary Shine Thompson (2006–10, 2017–present): dean of Research and Humanities, St Patrick's College, Drumcondra; chair, Reparations Panel for the Restorative Justice Service

Prof. Maria Slowey (2004–9): registrar/vice president for Learning Innovation, DCU

Dr John Smith (2014–16): Online Teaching and Learning, St Patrick's College, Drumcondra

Paul Smith (2001–16): Computer Services, DCU; director of equality, DCU

Prof. Malcolm Smyth (1998–2001): Faculty of Science and Paramedical Studies, DCU

Dr Peter Smyth (1976–81): Department of Medicine and Therapeutics, University College Dublin

Allan Stevenson (2016–18): postgraduate officer, DCU Students' Union

Mark Stewart (1985–6): education officer, NIHED Students' Union

Dr Ciarán Sugrue (1998–2001): St Patrick's College, Drumcondra

Kim Sweeney (2015–16): president, DCU Students' Union

Margaret Sweeney (2001–16): deputy chief executive, Aer Rianta; Chief Executive, Fortis

Deirdre Thornton (1992–6): deputy manager, Irish Intercontinental Bank Ltd

Jonathan Tiernan (2003–4): president, St Patrick's College Students' Union

John Tierney (2011–14): Dublin City Council

Joanne Toal (2007–8): president, St Patrick's College Students' Union

Prof. Michael Townson (1998–2001): School of Applied Language and Intercultural Studies, DCU

Dr Pauric Travers (1999–2012): president, St Patrick's College, Drumcondra

Beatrice Orpen Trench (1975–80): artist; president, Irish Countrywomen's Association

Ruairí Tubrid (2015–16): president, St Patrick's College Students' Union

Ray Tumulty (1987–92): personnel director, Calor Teoranta

James Tunney TD (1975–8): vice chairman, CDVEC

Yvonne Tuohy (2005–6): education officer, DCU Students' Union

Marian Vickers (2001–4): CEO, Northside Partnership

Prof. Ferdinand von Prondzynski (2000–10): president, DCU

Declan Wallace (2016–19): assistant chief executive, Dublin City Council

Dr Edward Walsh (1982–97): director/president, NIHE Limerick/University of Limerick

James Walsh (2003): postgraduate student representative, DCU

Dr Pádraig Walsh (1998–2004): School of Biotechnology; DCU, Director of Quality Promotion

Dr Owen P. Ward (1982–7): School of Biological Sciences, NIHED

Dora Weafer (1992–7): lecturer, College of Catering/DIT

Anne Wheatley (1998–2006): St Wolstan's College, Celbridge

Prof. Paul Whelan (2006–11): School of Electronic Engineering, DCU

Prof. Jenny Williams (2004–6): School of Applied Language and Intercultural Studies, DCU

Prof. Barbara Wright (1975–82): Department of French, Trinity College Dublin

Patrick Wright (2001–2): chairman, RTÉ

Appendix 3

Honorary members and graduates, 1986–2019

Honorary degrees have their historical origins in the granting of dispensations from the requirements normally associated with the attainment of an academic degree. Modern practice has evolved to allow universities to mark the contributions of distinguished guests to their fields of study, or to wider society.

Under the terms of the legislation establishing NIHE Dublin on a statutory basis, the Institute was empowered to grant membership of the Institute to anyone not otherwise so entitled.[1] Speaking in the Dáil, Edward Collins, Fine Gael TD for Waterford and a vocal critic of several aspects of the legislation, argued that without a corollary honorary degree, honorary membership was a meaningless gesture. John Wilson, minister for education, disagreed:

> People who have made distinguished contributions in the field of technology may never have had a formal degree conferred upon them. This is the one area in the history of science and technology where such a person has very often made a mark. It should be open to the National Institute for Higher Education to confer membership of the Institute on such a person.

Wilson also noted that, if it were thought necessary, governing body could recommend the recipient for an honorary degree from the National Council for Educational Awards. The debate also featured a contribution from John Horgan, Labour Party TD for Dublin County South and spokesperson for education, and later professor of journalism at DCU. Noting that the Irish constitution prohibited the state from granting honours and titles to its citizens, Horgan observed that honorary degrees had effectively become a substitute for such distinctions: 'I must record my disappointment with our further removal from the republican ideal that titles and honours do not need to be conferred on citizens of this state.'[2]

The Institute's governing body took advantage of this power just once, on 9 October 1986, when it bestowed honorary membership on Dr Koji Kobayashi and Paul Quigley. Both men were honoured for their contributions to Irish and international industry: Kobayashi was chairman and CEO of NEC Corporation, while Quigley had served as chairman of NIHE Limerick, and general manager of the Shannon Free Airport Development Company (SFADCo).[3] Patrick Hillery, president of Ireland, presided over

---

1 Membership of the Institute was automatically granted to members of governing body, academic council, Institute staff, registered students, and to graduates (National Institute for Higher Education, Dublin, Act, 1980 (no. 30 of 1980), s. 3). 2 *Dáil Debates*, 21 May 1980. While the debate referred to provisions within the bill for NIHE Limerick, the relevant provision was reproduced in the NIHE Dublin legislation. 3 Nippon Electric Company established its Irish operations at Ballivor in Co. Meath in 1975, and SFADCo played an integral role in the

A3.1 Koji Kobayashi, Paul Quigley, Patrick Hillery (President of Ireland) and Danny O'Hare at the awarding of honorary membership of NIHED to Kobayashi and Quigley on 9 October 1986 (DCU Collection).

A3.2 Jean Kennedy Smith and John Hume (pictured with Danny O'Hare) received honorary doctorates from DCU on 26 March 1994 (DCU Collection).

the conferral ceremony. Commenting that it was his first visit to the Institute, Hillery expressed his admiration for an institution that had 'already won for itself a golden reputation'.[4]

Following the attainment of university status, DCU became empowered to 'confer honorary degrees on persons in such manner and subject to such conditions as the governing body, after consultation with academic council, may deem appropriate'.[5] Criteria for the awarding of an honorary doctorate were subsequently drawn up by a subcommittee of academic council, with Taoiseach Charles Haughey the first recipient.[6] Governing body also resolved to convert the two honorary memberships of NIHE Dublin into honorary doctorates. For reasons that are not clear that process was not put in train for several years, with Paul Quigley receiving his distinction in October 1996. Dr Kobayashi was absent from the ceremony due to illness. After his death the following month, the university hosted a private memorial ceremony, on 4 December 1996, at which Dr Kobayashi's honorary degree was accepted by Kaneo Suzuki, chairman of NEC Europe.[7]

Under current guidelines, nominations for honorary doctorates are submitted to a subcommittee of governing authority, consisting of the chancellor, university president and vice president for academic affairs/registrar. Five broad areas govern the deliberations of the committee, which considers outstanding contributions or services to: 1) scholarship, especially in areas of interest to the university; 2) particular professions or fields of endeavour; 3) the arts, literature and culture; 4) the community, particularly the promotion of peace and reconciliation; and 5) the university itself and its associated bodies.[8]

Dr Koji Kobayashi
Honorary Membership, NIHE Dublin
9 Oct. 1986
&
Doctor of Philosophy (DPhil, *honoris causa*)
4 Dec. 1996

Paul Quigley
Honorary Membership, NIHE Dublin
9 Oct. 1986
&
Doctor of Philosophy (DPhil, *honoris causa*)
25 Oct. 1996

Charles J. Haughey
Doctor of Philosophy (DPhil, *honoris causa*)
19 Sept. 1990

Brian Friel
Doctor of Philosophy (DPhil, *honoris causa*)
6 Nov. 1991

Peter Sutherland
Doctor of Philosophy (DPhil, *honoris causa*)
6 Nov. 1991

Prof. Ernest T.W. Walton
Doctor of Philosophy (DPhil, *honoris causa*)
6 Nov. 1991

Mother Teresa
Doctor of Philosophy (DPhil, *honoris causa*)
5 June 1993

John Hume
Doctor of Philosophy (DPhil, *honoris causa*)
26 Mar. 1994   →

---

development of Shannon airport.   4 *Newslink*, Dec. 1986.   5 Dublin City University Act, 1989 (no. 15 of 1989), s. 3.   6 DCUPO, GB90/M4; *Nuacht*, Mar., June and Sept. 1990.   7 Danny O'Hare to several, 6 Nov. 1996 (DCUPO).   8 For guidelines, see: https://www.dcu.ie/governance/honorary-degree-committee.shtml, accessed 1 Mar. 2019. The original criteria are recorded in DCUPO, GB90/M4.

Timothy Mahony
Doctor of Philosophy (DPhil, *honoris causa*)
26 Mar. 1994

Jean Kennedy Smith
Doctor of Philosophy (DPhil, *honoris causa*)
26 Mar. 1994

Prof. James G. March
Doctor of Philosophy (DPhil, *honoris causa*)
26 Mar. 1994

John Pilger
Doctor of Philosophy (DPhil, *honoris causa*)
11 Mar. 1995

Dr Thomas Kenneth Whitaker
Doctor of Philosophy (DPhil, *honoris causa*)
20 Oct. 1995

Nuala Ní Dhomhnaill
Doctor of Philosophy (DPhil, *honoris causa*)
20 Oct. 1995

John F. Mitchell
Doctor of Philosophy (DPhil, *honoris causa*)
25 Oct. 1996

President Mary Robinson
Doctor of Philosophy (DPhil, *honoris causa*)
21 Apr. 1997

Patrick A. Toole
Doctor of Philosophy (DPhil, *honoris causa*)
24 Oct. 1997

Prof. Wesley Cocker
Doctor of Philosophy (DPhil, *honoris causa*)
24 Oct. 1997

Roddy Doyle
Doctor of Philosophy (DPhil, *honoris causa*)
7 Mar. 1998

Louis le Brocquy
Doctor of Philosophy (DPhil, *honoris causa*)
20 Mar. 1999

Neil V. McCann
Doctor of Philosophy (DPhil, *honoris causa*)
20 Mar. 1999

Maurice Whelan
Doctor of Philosophy (DPhil, *honoris causa*)
20 Mar. 1999

Fr Peter McVerry, SJ
Doctor of Philosophy (DPhil, *honoris causa*)
2 Nov. 2001

Mary Davis
Doctor of Philosophy (DPhil, *honoris causa*)
4 Nov. 2003

David Hammond
Doctor of Philosophy (DPhil, *honoris causa*)
5 Nov. 2003

John McGahern
Doctor of Philosophy (DPhil, *honoris causa*)
8 Nov. 2003

Patrick J. Wright
Doctor of Philosophy (DPhil, *honoris causa*)
20 Mar. 2004

Dr Martin McAleese
Doctor of Philosophy (DPhil, *honoris causa*)
29 Mar. 2008

President Mary McAleese
Doctor of Philosophy (DPhil, *honoris causa*)
29 Mar. 2008

Owen Keenan
Doctor of Philosophy (DPhil, *honoris causa*)
10 Mar. 2010

Seamus Heaney
Doctor of Philosophy (DPhil, *honoris causa*)
10 May 2011

Charles F. Feeney
Doctor of Laws (LL.D., *honoris causa*)
(Jointly conferred by all Irish
universities)
6 Sept. 2012

Br Colm William O'Connell
Doctor of Philosophy (DPhil, *honoris causa*)
19 Oct. 2012

→

John E. Kelly, III
Doctor of Philosophy (DPhil, *honoris causa*)
5 Nov. 2012

Páid McGee
Doctor of Philosophy (DPhil, *honoris causa*)
10 Nov. 2012

Brian O'Dwyer
Doctor of Philosophy (DPhil, *honoris causa*)
11 June 2013

John Fitzpatrick
Doctor of Philosophy (DPhil, *honoris causa*)
11 June 2013

David Trimble
Doctor of Philosophy (DPhil, *honoris causa*)
8 Oct. 2013

Seamus Mallon
Doctor of Philosophy (DPhil, *honoris causa*)
8 Oct. 2013

Dr Tony Scott
Doctor of Philosophy (DPhil, *honoris causa*)
9 Nov. 2013

Katie Taylor
Doctor of Philosophy (DPhil, *honoris causa*)
13 Nov. 2013

Brian O'Driscoll
Doctor of Philosophy (DPhil, *honoris causa*)
13 Nov. 2013

Sean Kelly
Doctor of Philosophy (DPhil, *honoris causa*)
13 Nov. 2013

George J. Mitchell
Doctor of Philosophy (DPhil, *honoris causa*)
13 Dec. 2013

Prof. Muhammad Yunus
Doctor of Philosophy (DPhil, *honoris causa*)
18 Oct. 2014

Dr Dermot Lane
Doctor of Philosophy (DPhil, *honoris causa*)
6 Nov. 2014

Justice Susan Denham
Doctor of Philosophy (DPhil, *honoris causa*)
6 Nov. 2014

Dr Margaret MacCurtain
Doctor of Philosophy (DPhil, *honoris causa*)
26 Feb. 2015

Dr Pearse Lyons
Doctor of Philosophy (DPhil, *honoris causa*)
26 Feb. 2015

Brian Cody
Doctor of Philosophy (DPhil, *honoris causa*)
26 Feb. 2015

Dame Jocelyn Bell-Burnell
Doctor of Philosophy (DPhil, *honoris causa*)
5 Nov. 2015

Olwen Fouéré
Doctor of Philosophy (DPhil, *honoris causa*)
2 Apr. 2016

Tomi Reichental
Doctor of Philosophy (DPhil, *honoris causa*)
2 Apr. 2016

Sonia O'Sulllivan
Doctor of Philosophy (DPhil, *honoris causa*)
12 Sept. 2017

Prof. John Coolahan
Doctor of Philosophy (DPhil, *honoris causa*)
12 Sept. 2017

Labhrás Ó Murchú
Doctor of Philosophy (DPhil, *honoris causa*)
12 Sept. 2017

Martin Naughton
Doctor of Philosophy (DPhil, *honoris causa*)
17 Oct. 2017

Sr Stanislaus Kennedy
Doctor of Philosophy (DPhil, *honoris causa*)
17 Oct. 2017

President Bill Clinton
Doctor of Philosophy (DPhil, *honoris causa*)
17 Oct. 2017

→

Steve Myers
Doctor of Philosophy (DPhil, *honoris causa*)
3 Nov. 2017

Willie Walsh
Doctor of Philosophy (DPhil, *honoris causa*)
4 Nov. 2017

Dr Amal Al Qubaisi
Doctor of Philosophy (DPhil, *honoris causa*)
21 June 2018

Paula Meehan
Doctor of Philosophy (DPhil, *honoris causa*)
21 Mar. 2019

Joe Schmidt
Doctor of Philosophy (DPhil, *honoris causa*)
30 Apr. 2019

Micheál Ó Muircheartaigh
Doctor of Philosophy (DPhil, *honoris causa*)
30 Apr. 2019

Appendix 4

Presidents of NIHED and DCU Students' Union, 1981–2020

NIHED SU Presidents

1981/2: Riocard Ó Tiarnaigh
1982/3: James Glynn and Michael O'Donnell
1983/4: George Hegarty
1984/5: Ciaran Ó Maoileoin

1985/6: Thomas McDonald
1986/7: Kevin Gildea
1987/8: Alan Murphy
1988/9: Clare Daly

DCU SU Presidents

1989/90: Clare Daly
1990/1: Brian Gormley
1991/2: Brian Gormley
1992/3: Michael Egan
1993/4: Enda Peoples
1994/5: Colin Cunningham
1995/6: Ciaran Duffy
1996/7: Ciara Fitzpatrick
1997/8: Dermot Lohan
1998/9: David Flynn
1999/2000: Dáibhí Ó Donnabháin
2000/1: Hugo Brady
2001/2: Derek Scanlon
2002/3: Sean Scally
2003/4: Lorna Greene
2004/5: Paul May

2005/6: Sarah Farrell
2006/7: Charlene Connolly
2007/8: Alan Flanagan
2008/9: Niall McClave
2009/10: Alan Keegan
2010/11: Megan O'Riordan
2011/12: Ed Leamy
2012/13: Paul Doherty
2013/14: Aaron Clogher
2014/15: Kenneth Browne
2015/16: Kim Sweeney
2016/17: Dylan Kehoe
2017/18: Niall Behan
2018/19: Vito Moloney Burke
2019/20: Christine Farrell

Appendix 5

Chairman's Medal and Chancellor's Medal
recipients, 1981–2018

Created in 1981, the Chairman's Medal (renamed the Chancellor's Medal in 1998) is presented to students who have excelled both academically and in their contribution to the extracurricular and social life of the university.[1] A second medal was inaugurated in 1995 for presentation to outstanding postgraduates.[2]

1981: Lt David Doogan
1982: Not awarded
1983: Michael Dwyer
1984: Stephen O'Brien
1985: Margaret Ward
1986: Siobhán Bergin
1987: David Gerard Heneghan
1988: Miriam Aoife Gallagher
1989: Susan Russell
1990: Aidan McGettigan
1991: Not awarded
1992: Shane Dowdall
1993: Martin O'Gorman
1994: Not awarded
1995: Robert Damien Mulhall (undergraduate) and Fergal Stack (postgraduate)
1996: Not awarded
1997: Not awarded
1998: Tim Culhane (undergraduate) and Anthony Killard (postgraduate)
1999: Wesley Browne (undergraduate) and Dónal Fitzpatrick (postgraduate)
2000: Edward Taylor Mee
2001: Ciara Peelo
2002: Katrina Keogh and Cara Green
2003: Not awarded
2004: Michael Moriarty (Uaneen module)
2005: Eoin Kavanagh (Uaneen module)

1 Where known, recipients of the Chancellor's Medal who also completed the Uaneen module are noted. For the Uaneen module's introduction to the DCU curriculum in 2004, see chapter 4. 2 DCU, *Annual report, 1994/5*, p. 243. I am indebted to Phylomena McMorrow, Valerie Cooke and Orna Heuston of DCU Registry for their assistance in compiling this list, particularly for the period 2000 to 2018.

A5.1 Lt David Doogan receiving the inaugural Chairman's Medal from Michael MacCormac in 1981 (DCU Collection).

2006: Not awarded
2007: Fionnuala Britton
2008: Cianan Clancy (Uaneen module)
2009: Allan Dixon
2010: Jennifer Tweed (Uaneen module)
2011: David McMullin (undergraduate and Uaneen module) and Paul Conroy (postgraduate)
2012: Rebecca Townsend (undergraduate and Uaneen module) and Colin Moran (postgraduate)
2013: Abdul Ali Hassan (Uaneen module)
2014: Rónán Ó Dálaigh (undergraduate and Uaneen module) and Ann Reilly (postgraduate)
2015: Paula-Avril Jatariu (Uaneen module)
2016: Trina Mawuena Dzidonu (undergraduate and Uaneen module) and Sarah Gilgunn (postgraduate)
2017: Not awarded
2018: Zeynep Naz Tugrul (undergraduate) and Claire O'Connell (postgraduate)

Appendix 6

Select statistics

Fig. A6.1 State grant income (€'000s), 1980–2017[1]

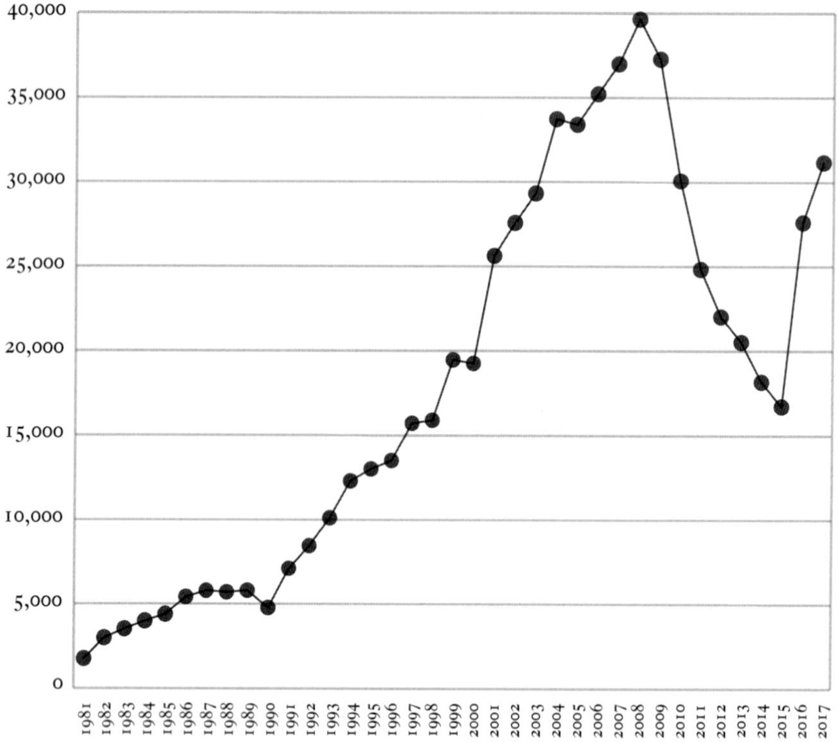

Source: DCU Finance Office.

---

1 The figure for 1981 incorporates state grants received in 1980.

262

Fig. A6.2 Research grants and project income (€'000s), 1990–2017[2]

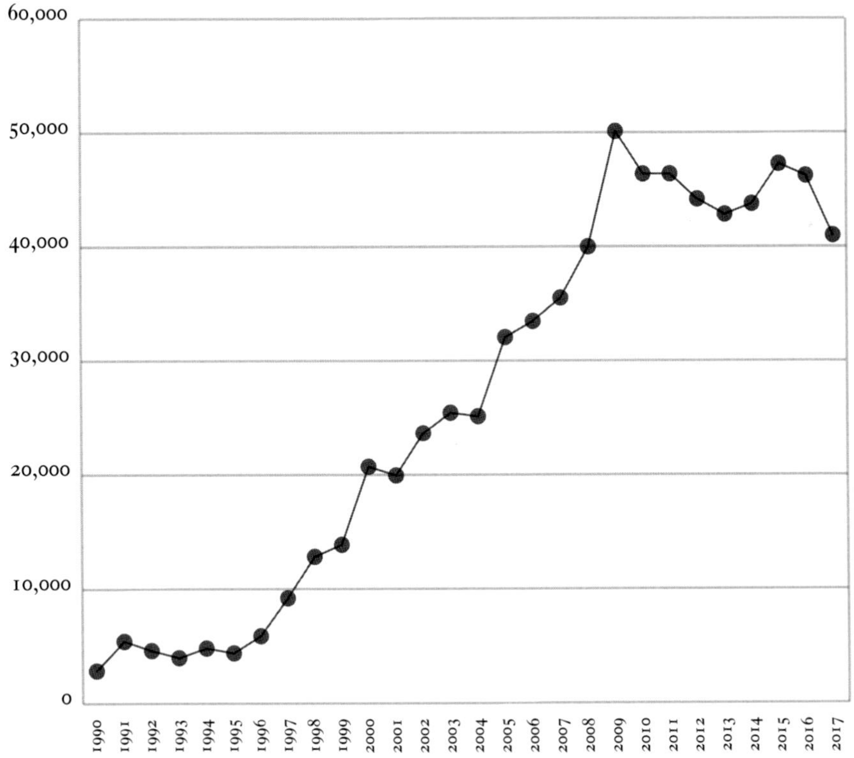

Source: DCU Finance Office.

2 Data provided by DCU Finance Office excludes figures for 1980 to 1989. Alternative sources indicate that *c.*£12m in research income was accrued during that period (e.g. *Newslink*, Feb. 1989).

Fig. A6.3 Academic fees income (€'000s), 1980–2017[3]

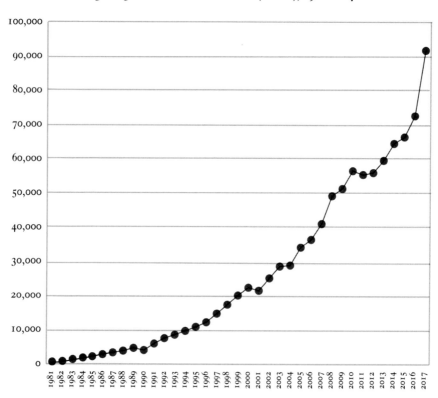

Source: DCU Finance Office.

3 The figure for 1981 incorporates academic fees received in 1980. Free fees were introduced in 1995 under the ministerial tenure of Niamh Bhreathnach. A large proportion of the university's academic fee income is thus technically a state grant, but is treated as a separate entry for accounting purposes. For more details on the HEA's funding model, see https://hea.ie/funding-governance-performance/funding/how-we-fund/. For the introduction of the 'free fees' scheme, see Walsh, *Higher education in Ireland*, pp 207–8.

Fig. A6.4 Other operating income (€'000s), 1980–2017[4]

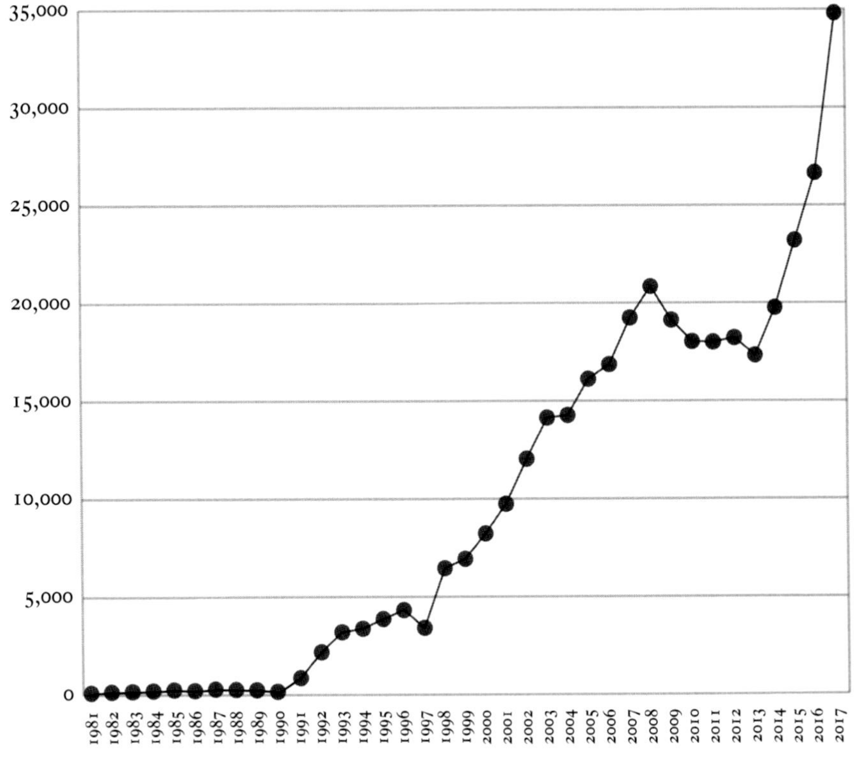

Source: DCU Finance Office.

4 The figure for 1981 incorporates other operating income accrued in 1980.

Fig. A6.5 Undergraduate population, 1980–2016[5]

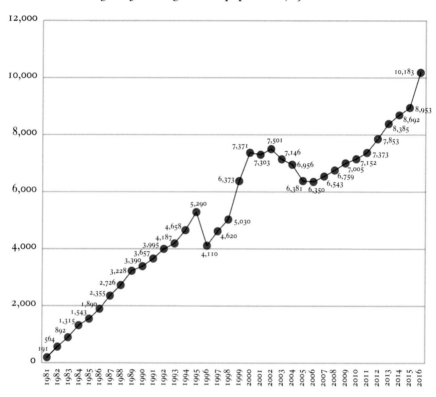

Source: DCU Quality Promotion Office.

5 Statistics show the year in which the academic year finished. E.g. the figure for 1981 shows the number of undergraduates enrolled for the 1980/1 academic year. See chapter 5, table 5.1 for postgraduate graduation statistics.

Fig. A6.6 Intake of new, full-time undergraduates per annum, 1980–2016[6]

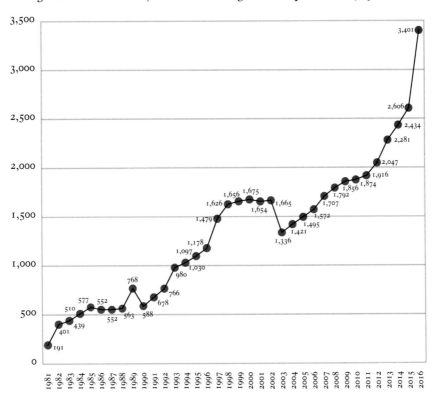

Source: DCU Quality Promotion Office.

6 Statistics show the year in which the academic year finished. E.g. the figure for 1982 shows the number of new enrolments for the 1981/2 academic year.

Fig. A6.7 Undergraduate enrolments by gender, 1980–2016

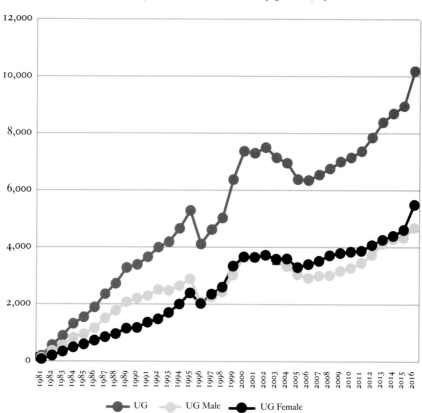

Source: DCU Quality Promotion Office.

Fig. A6.8 Combined postgraduate and undergraduate student population, 1980–2016[7]

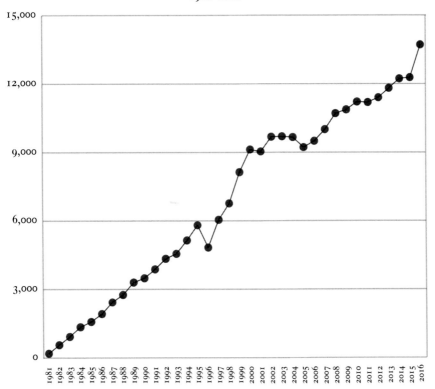

Source: DCU Quality Promotion Office.

7 Statistics show the year in which the academic year finished. E.g. the figure for 1982 shows the total number of students enrolled at the end of the 1981/2 academic year.

Bibliography

1. Manuscript material
2. Interviews
3. Reports, online sources and printed primary material
4. Secondary sources

1. MANUSCRIPT MATERIAL

Cornell University Library, Division of Rare and Manuscript Collections, Ithaca, New York
Atlantic Philanthropies Archive, no. 8540[1]

Dublin City University, Access Office
Unsorted collection of administrative documents

Dublin City University, Estates Office
Unsorted collection of building plans

Dublin City University, President's Office (DCUPO)[2]
AC80–AC2016: Academic council, minutes and papers
ACSC86–ACSC2006: Academic council standing committee, minutes and papers
ACUSC2006–16: Academic council university standards committee, minutes and papers
GB75–GB97: Governing body, minutes and papers
GA98–GA2018: Governing authority, minutes and papers

Dublin City University, Students' Union
Student publications (unsorted collection)

---

1 At the time the material in Atlantic Philanthropies Archive was consulted, documents relating to DCU were still in the process of being classified and catalogued. There are c.100 folders in the archive directly relating to the university, each folder associated with a particular grant application. The relevant grant ID (e.g. #7200) is recorded on each folder's cover, if funding was approved. All references in footnotes give this grant ID, and the folder number where more than one folder is associated with a grant (a sample reference would therefore read: APA, Grant #7032, 1/2). Eighteen grant applications were not approved – these are identified in footnotes by the titles on the relevant folder.   2 The records cited from the archive of the President's Office lack specific shelf marks. They are typically contained in folders housed in box files, organized along thematic lines. All references in footnotes give the title of the relevant document's enclosing box file. The exceptions to this are the minutes and papers of NIHED/DCU's governing body/authority, academic council and associated subcommittees.

National Archives of Ireland (NAI)
DFA, 444/5: Meeting of OECD at ministerial level, 1961–2
2005/7/352: Report of the HEA on university reorganization, 1973–4
2005/151/491: NIHE (non-statutory governing bodies), 1974–5
2006/133/307: NIHE (non-statutory governing bodies), 1976
2007/50/72: World Bank Loan: College of Commerce, Ballymun
2007/116/359: NIHE (non-statutory governing bodies), 1977
2008/148/523: NIHE Dublin, 1975–8
2009/135/242: NIHE (non-statutory governing bodies), 1978–81
2009/135/491: NIHE Limerick Act, 1980
2010/16/1: NIHE Limerick bill, 1979
2010/16/175: NIHE Dublin bill, 1980
2010/27/306: NIHE Limerick bill, 1979
2010/27/423: NIHE Limerick Act, 1980
2010/27/425: NIHE Dublin, 1980
2010/27/843: NIHE Dublin Act, 1980
2010/27/1142: NIHE Dublin bill, 1980
2010/53/413: NIHE Dublin Act, 1980
2010/53/462: NIHE Limerick Act, 1980
2010/66/72: NIHE Dublin Act, 1980
2011/16/127: NIHE Dublin Act, 1981 (form of consent), 1981
2011/17/626: NIHE Dublin Act, commencement order, 1981
2011/127/807: NIHE Dublin, appointment of chairman and members, 1981
2012/59/1057: EEC, grants to institutions of higher education, 1974–82
2012/90/660: NIHE Dublin, appointment of member of governing body, 1982
2013/100/554: NIHE Dublin, appointment of chairman and members, 1981
2014/23/390: National Institutes of Higher Education, fee concessions to staff, 1983–4
2014/67/93: Presentation of credentials to Emperor Hirohito by Ambassador Fogarty, 1973
2015/21/354: NIHE Dublin, licence to enable AIB to operate on campus, 1985
2017/4/1600: NIHE., Japan-Europe projects, 1987
2017/11/256: NIHE Dublin, appointment of chairman and members, 1987
2017/11/317: Question of Technological University, 1986
2017/11/807: Science parks, 1987
2018/69/508: Science parks, 1988

National Library of Ireland
MS 31,821: Documents re: inauguration of Dublin City University
MS 39,770/2–4: Records of the Irish Countrywomen's Association

National Library of Ireland, Genealogical Office
Genealogical Office (GO) Archive, arms and genealogy files

Private collections
Michael Burke Photographs

Eugene Kennedy Papers
Eunan O'Halpin Private Memoirs
Pat O'Mahony Papers
Brian Trench Papers

University College Dublin Archives (UCDA)
IE UCDA, P179: Gemma Hussey Papers
IE UCDA, AAC1: Records of the Albert Agricultural College

2. INTERVIEWS

Interviews recorded by author
Patricia Barker (20 September 2018)
Brian MacCraith (1 October 2018 and 16 May 2019)
Danny O'Hare (28 May 2018)
Albert Pratt (19 October 2018)
Ferdinand von Prondzynski (18 October 2018)
Brian Trench (9 May 2019)

Atlantic Philanthropies Oral History Project
Danny O'Hare (12 October 2005). Transcript kindly provided by Danny O'Hare.

DIT Voices Oral History Project
Paddy Donegan [1 Jan.] 2010
John Hayden [1 Jan.] 2010
https://arrow.tudublin.ie/ditaud/

Information also collated from informal discussions and correspondence with Chris Curran, Susan Folan, Anthony Glynn, John Horgan, Eugene Kennedy, Colum Kenny, Brigid McManus, Helena Sheehan, Frank Soughley, and Deirdre Wynter.

3. REPORTS, ONLINE SOURCES AND PRINTED PRIMARY MATERIAL

REPORTS

NIHED/DCU Reports and Strategic Plans
Arup, *Dublin City University: campus connectivity study* (Dublin, 2016).
DCU, *Annual reports* (Dublin, 1989–98).
—, *Library and Information Service: strategic plan, 1994–9* (Dublin, 1994).
—, *Strategy for the year 2000* (Dublin, 1995).
—, *Leading change: DCU strategic plan, 2001–5* (Dublin, 2001).
—, *President's reports* (Dublin, 2005–15). [No annual reports or president's reports were published for the periods 1999–2004, 2016 onwards].

—, *Leadership through foresight: DCU strategic plan, 2006–8* (Dublin, 2005).
—, *Quality assurance reports* (Dublin, 2006–12).
—, *Leading through challenge: university strategy, 2009–11* (Dublin, 2009).
—, *Celebrating success: 21 years of DCU Access service* (Dublin, 2011).
—, *Transforming lives and societies: DCU strategic plan, 2012–17* (Dublin, 2012).
—, *DCU in the Community: strategic plan, 2013–17* (Dublin, 2013).
—, *Capturing the economic and social value of higher education: a pilot study of Dublin City University* (Dublin, 2014).
—, *DCU Access impact reports* (Dublin, 2016–18).
—, *DCU Educational Trust supporter impact report, 2016–17* (Dublin, 2017).
—, *Talent, discovery, and transformation: DCU strategic plan, 2017–22* (Dublin, 2017).
NIHED, *An educational philosophy for the National Institute for Higher Education, Dublin* (Dublin, 1977).
—, *Plan for the future of the Institute* (Dublin, 1977).
—, *Annual reports* (Dublin, 1978–88).
—, *Plan for the physical development of the Institute* (Dublin, 1978).
—, *A general description of staff and facilities* (Dublin, Feb. 1981).
—, *Distance education: an international review and directions for development* (Dublin, 1982).
—, *Institutional review, 1980–86* (Dublin, Apr. 1986).
—, *Academic procedures* (Dublin, 1987).

Official papers and reports

Ballymun Regeneration Ltd, *Ballymun regeneration completion report* (Dublin, 2008).
Barlow, A.C., *The financing of third-level education* (Dublin, 1981).
CHIU (Conference of Heads of Irish Universities), *Universities Act, 1997, archive* (4 vols, Dublin, 2003).
CII (Confederation of Irish Industry), *Strategy for industrialisation: the role of third-level institutions* (Dublin, 1981).
Clancy, Patrick and Ciaran Benson, *Higher education in Dublin: a study of some emerging needs* (Dublin, 1979).
Combat Poverty Agency, *Submission on the National Programme of Community Interest for the greater Dublin area* (Dublin, 1988).
—, *Poverty – an agenda for the 90s: submission to the government on the 1990 budget* (Dublin, 1989).
Commission on Higher Education, *Presentation and summary* (Dublin, 1967).
Department of Education, *White paper on educational development* (Dublin, 1980).
—, *Programme for action in education, 1984–7* (Dublin, 1984).
—, *Technological education: report of the international study group to the minister for education* (Dublin, 1987).
—, *Charting our education future: white paper on education* (Dublin, 1995).
— and Children, *Report of the Commission on Nursing: a blueprint for the future* (Dublin, 1998).
— and Science, *Learning for life: white paper on adult education* (Dublin, 2000).
—, *Report of the action group on access to third level education* (Dublin, 2001).

— and Skills, *National strategy for higher education to 2030* (Dublin, 2011).

— and Skills, *Report of the international review panel on the structure of initial teacher education provision in Ireland* (Dublin, 2012).

— and Skills, *Investing in national ambition: a strategy for funding higher education* (Dublin, 2016).

Dublin arts report (Dublin, 1992)

Dublin City Council, *Dublin city development plan, 2011–17: record of protected structures* (Dublin, 2010).

European Commission, *COMETT: the training needs of staff in the Community's higher education sector engaged in cooperation with industry* (Luxembourg, 1988).

EUA (European University Association), *Institutional quality review of Dublin City University* (2005).

Government of Ireland, *Building on reality* (Dublin, 1984).

—, *Ireland: national development plan, 2000–6* (Dublin, 1999).

HEA (Higher Education Authority), *Report on the Ballymun project* (Dublin, 1972).

—, *Reports, accounts and student statistics, 1980–2004* (Dublin, 1980–2004).

—, *General report: 1974–84* (Dublin, 1985).

—, *Women academics in Ireland: report of the committee on the position of women academics in third level education in Ireland* (Dublin, 1987).

—, *Report of the high level group on university equality policies* (Dublin, 2004).

—, *The Programme for Research in Third Level Institutions [PRTLI] impact assessment* (2 vols, Dublin, 2004).

—, *Progressing the action plan: funding to achieve equity of access to higher education* (Dublin, 2005).

—, *Supporting investment in higher education: report of the working group* (Dublin, 2006).

—, *Review of student charge* (Dublin, 2010).

—, *Towards a future higher education landscape: DCU response* (Dublin, 2012).

— and Irish Universities Association, *Governance of Irish universities* (Dublin, 2012).

—, *How equal? Access to higher education in Ireland* (Dublin, 2013).

—, *Higher education system performance, 2014–16* (Dublin, 2016).

—, *Higher education institutional staff profiles by gender* (Dublin, 2018).

—, *The structure of teacher education in Ireland: review of progress in implementing reform* (Dublin, 2019).

ICSTI, *Technology foresight Ireland: an ICSTI overview* (Dublin, 1999).

IFUT, *Annual report 2017/18* (Dublin, 2018).

Irish Universities Quality Board, *IRIU report: institutional review of Dublin City University* (2010).

NBST (National Board for Science and Technology), *Education, innovation and entrepreneurship* (Dublin, 1983).

NorDubCo, *Consolidating north Dublin: an environmental investment strategy for north Dublin* (Dublin, 2001).

Northside Partnership and Dublin North West Area Partnership, *North Dublin Joint Partnership submission to DCU strategic plan, 2018–22* (Dublin, 2018).

Manpower Consultative Committee, *Review of links between industry and third-level education* (Dublin, 1985).

OECD, *Training of technicians in Ireland* (Paris, 1964).

Oireachtas Library and Research Service, *Higher education in Ireland: for economy and society?* (Dublin, 2014).

Oireachtas Parliamentary Budget Office, *An overview of tertiary education funding in Ireland* (Dublin, 2019).

QQI, *Institutional review report 2019: Dublin City University* (2019).

SIPTU, *A survey of academic staff on working conditions at DCU* (Dublin, 2015).

Society of College Lecturers, CDVEC, *Policy document on NIHE Dublin* (Dublin, 1975).

Steering committee on technical education report ... on regional technical colleges [1967] (Dublin, [1969]).

Technopolis Group and Department of Jobs, Enterprise and Innovation, *Ireland's future research infrastructure needs* (Dublin, 2015).

Trinity College Dublin, *Strategic plan 2014–19* (Dublin, 2014).

ONLINE SOURCES

Atlantic Philanthropies, *The Atlantic Philanthropies in the Republic of Ireland (1987–2014)* (http://www.atlanticphilanthropies.org/wp-content/uploads/2015/11/The-Atlantic-Philanthropies-Republic-of-Ireland.pdf, accessed 11 Apr. 2017).

DCU News (www.dcu.ie/news/archive).

Dictionary of Irish Biography (dib.cambridge.org).

Irish Statute Book (www.irishstatutebook.ie).

Oireachtas Debates and Proceedings (https:/www.oireachtas.ie/en/debates/).

PRINTED PRIMARY MATERIAL

Dublin City Council
Minutes of the Municipal Council of the City of Dublin, 1980–2016

Newspapers, newsletters and magazines
Ballymun Job Centre Newsletter
Dublin Tribune
Evening Herald
Inside Higher Ed
Irish Architect
Irish Business
Irish Examiner
Irish Independent
Irish Times
Northside People
Partnership News: Journal of the Irish American Partnership
Sunday Independent
Times Higher Education
UCD News
University Observer (UCD)
University Times (TCD)

NIHED/DCU newspapers, newsletters and magazines
Broadsheet: organ of the SUNIHE (NIHED SU newsletter)
By Degrees (NIHED staff newsletter, 1981–4)
The College View (DCU student newspaper)
DCU Bull Sheet/Bullsheet (DCU student newspaper)
DCU Connection
DCU Times, 25th-anniversary edition (2005)
DCU Voices
DCUSU Handbooks
Liblink (DCU library newsletter)
Newslink (Industrial Liaison Unit newsletter, 1984–99)
NIcHE (NIHED SU newspaper)
Nuacht (Staff newsletter, 1983–94)
The Sun: Student Union Newsletter (NIHED SU newspaper)
University View (DCU alumni magazine)

4. SECONDARY SOURCES

Adelman, Juliana, *Communities of science in nineteenth-century Ireland* (New York, 2009).
Atlantic Philanthropies, *Laying foundations for change: capital investments of the Atlantic Philanthropies* (2014).
Bartlett, Thomas (ed.), *The Cambridge history of Ireland*, iv: *1880 to the present* (4 vols, Cambridge, 2018).
Benum, Edgar, 'On the challenge of writing a university history: the University of Oslo', University of California Berkeley, Centre for Studies in Higher Education, Research and Occasional Paper Series, CSHE.5.99 (Berkeley, CA, 1999).
Boldt, Scott, *BITE: Ballymun Initiative for Third-Level Education, research evaluation* (Dublin, 2000).
Bonjean, Alain, William Angus and Maarten van Ginkel (eds), *The world wheat book: a history of wheat breeding* (London, 2011), vol. 2.
Boyle, Mark, 'Sartre's circular dialectic and the empires of abstract space: a history of space and place in Ballymun, Dublin', *Annals of the Association of American Geographers*, 95:1 (2005), pp 181–201.
Bradley, Tony, *'Twigs for an eagle's nest': a pictorial history of Dublin City University* (Dublin, 1999).
Breznitz, Dan, *Innovation and the state: political choice and strategies for growth in Israel, Taiwan and Ireland* (London, 2007).
Burke, Jim, John Spink and Richie Hackett, 'Wheat in the Republic of Ireland' in Alain Bonjean, William Angus and Maarten van Ginkel (eds), *The world wheat book: a history of wheat breeding* (London, 2011), pp 107–20.
Clancy, Patrick, 'The evolution of policy in third-level education' in D.G. Mulcahy and Denis O'Sullivan (eds), *Irish educational policy: process and substance* (Dublin, 1989), pp 99–132.
—, *Irish higher education: a comparative perspective* (Dublin, 2015).

Clarkson, L.A., *A university in troubled times: Queen's Belfast, 1945–2000* (Dublin, 2004).

Collins, Liam, *The Atlantic Philanthropies: Republic of Ireland* (New York, 2017).

Connolly, Lynn, *The Mun: growing up in Ballymun* (Dublin, 2006).

Coleman, Marie, *IFUT: a history, 1963–1999* (2nd ed., Dublin, 2010).

Coolahan, John, *Irish education: its history and structure* (Dublin, 1981).

—, 'The daring first decade of the Board of National Education, 1831–1841', *Irish Journal of Education*, 17 (1983), pp 35–54.

—, 'The Commission on Higher Education, 1967, and third-level policy in contemporary Ireland', *Irish Educational Studies*, 9:1 (1990), pp 1–12.

—, 'Higher education in Ireland, 1908–84' in J.R. Hill (ed.), *A new history of Ireland*, vii: *Ireland, 1921–84* (Oxford, 2003), pp 757–95.

—, 'The National University of Ireland and the changing structure of Irish higher education, 1967–2007' in Tom Dunne (ed.), *The National University of Ireland, 1908–2008: centenary essays* (Dublin, 2008), pp 261–79.

Cox, Gareth, *Seóirse Bodley*, Field Day Music 4 (Dublin, 2010).

Cullinan, John and Darragh Flannery, *Economic insights on higher education policy in Ireland: evidence from a public system* (London, 2017).

Curaj, Adrian, Luke Georghiou, Jennifer Cassingena Harper and Eva Egron-Polak (eds), *Mergers and alliances in higher education: international practice and emerging opportunities* (London, 2015).

Curran, Chris, 'Co-operative networks in higher distance teaching' in Urban Dahllof and Staffan Selander (eds), *New universities and regional context* (Uppsala, 1994), pp 161–76.

Dahllof, Urban and Staffan Selander (eds), *New universities and regional context* (Uppsala, 1994).

Daly, Mary, *The first department: a history of the Department of Agriculture* (Dublin, 2002).

Davies, Alun C., 'Ireland's Crystal Palace, 1853' in J.M. Goldstrom and L.A. Clarkson (eds), *Irish population, economy and society: essays in honour of the late K.H. Connell* (Oxford, 1981), pp 249–70.

Davis, Ruth and Mary Fenton, 'Partnership and collaboration in the new higher education landscape: the 3U Partnership experience', *All Ireland Journal of Teaching and Learning in Higher Education (AISHE–J)*, 7:1 (2015).

Delaney, Lorraine and Seamus Fox, 'The role of distance education in broadening access to Irish higher education' in HEA, *How equal? Access to higher education in Ireland* (Dublin, 2013), pp 21–9.

Dhondt, Pieter (ed.), *University jubilees and university history writing: a challenging relationship* (Leiden, 2015).

Doyle, Desmond, 'NIHE Dublin', *Irish Architect: The Bulletin of the Royal Institute of the Architects of Ireland*, 64 (Nov.–Jan. 1987/8), pp 13–15.

Duff, Thomas, Joe Hegarty and Matthew Hussey, *The story of Dublin Institute of Technology* (Dublin, 2000).

Dunne, Tom (ed.), *The National University of Ireland, 1908–2008: centenary essays* (Dublin, 2008).

—, 'Coming to terms with the 1997 act: the National University of Ireland Senate, 1997–2007' in idem (ed.), *National University of Ireland: centenary essays* (Dublin, 2008), pp 280–90.

Evans, Andrew and Stephen Martin, 'EC regional policy and the evolution of the structural funds' in Stephen Martin (ed.), *The construction of Europe: essays in honour of Emile Noël* (Florence, 1994), pp 41–70.

Fanning, Ronan, 'T.K. Whitaker, 1976–96' in Tom Dunne (ed.), *National University of Ireland: centenary essays* (Dublin, 2008), pp 146–62.

Fleming, Brian and Judith Hartford, 'Irish educational policy in the 1960s: a decade of transformation', *History of Education*, 43:5 (2014), pp 635–56.

Fleming, David, *The University of Limerick: a history* (Dublin, 2012).

Fleming, Ted and Fergal Finnegan, 'A critical journey towards lifelong learning: including non-traditional students in university' in Andrew Loxley, Aidan Seery and John Walsh (eds), *Higher education in Ireland: practices, policies and possibilities* (Basingstoke, 2014), pp 146–58.

Fleming, Ted and Anne Gallagher, 'Power, privilege and points: the choices and challenges of third level access in Dublin', Dublin Employment Pact Report (Dublin, 2003).

Fleming, Ted, Andrew Loxley and Fergal Finnegan, *Access and participation in Irish higher education* (London, 2017).

Flynn, Martin, Denis Staunton and Deirdre Creedon (eds), *Access: are we making the right connections? Proceedings from the pathways to education access conference* (Cork, 2011).

French, Nora, 'Journalism education in Ireland', *Irish Communications Review*, 10:1 (2007), pp 41–9.

Garvin, Tom, *Preventing the future: why was Ireland so poor for so long?* (Dublin, 2004).

Gaukroger, Alison and Leonard Schwarz, 'A university and its region: student recruitment to Birmingham, 1945–1975', *Oxford Review of Education*, 23:2 (1997), pp 185–202.

Gleeson, Jim, 'The European Credit Transfer System and curriculum design: product before process?', *Studies in Higher Education*, 38:6 (2013), pp 921–38.

Goldstrom, J.M. and L.A. Clarkson (eds), *Irish population, economy and society: essays in honour of the late K.H. Connell* (Oxford, 1981).

Harkin, Siobhan and Ellen Hazelkorn, 'Institutional mergers in Ireland' in Adrian Curaj, Luke Georghiou, Jennifer Cassingena Harper and Eva Egron-Polak (eds), *Mergers and alliances in higher education: international practice and emerging opportunities* (London, 2015), pp 105–23.

Hazelkorn, Ellen, Andrew Gibson and Soibhán Harkin, 'From massification to globalisation: reflections on the transformation of Irish higher education' in Kevin Rafter and Mark O'Brien (eds), *The state in transition: essays in honour of John Horgan* (Dublin, 2015), pp 235–60.

Hedley, Steve, 'Managerialism in Irish universities', *Irish Journal of Legal Studies*, 1:1 (2010), pp 117–41.

Hill, J.R. (ed.), *A new history of Ireland*, vii: *Ireland, 1921–1984* (Oxford, 2003).

Hoctor, Daniel, *The department's story: a history of the Department of Agriculture* (Dublin, 1971).

Hogan, John, 'Economic crises and the changing influence of the Irish Congress of Trade Unions on public policy' in John Hogan, Paul Donnelly and Brendan O'Rourke (eds), *Irish business and society: governing, participating and transforming in the 21st century* (Dublin, 2010), pp 253–76.

Hogan, John, Paul Donnelly and Brendan O'Rourke (eds), *Irish business and society: governing, participating and transforming in the 21st century* (Dublin, 2010).

Horgan, John, *Dublin City University: context and concept* (Dublin, 1989).

Houlihan, Barrie, *Sport, policy and politics: a comparative analysis* (London, 1997).

Howarth, Janet, 'Introduction' in *Writing University History*, special issue of *Oxford Review of Education*, 23:2 (1997), pp 147–50.

Hughes, Jean and Una Redmond, 'Learning from life: the Uaneen experience in Dublin City University' in Lorraine McIlrath, Alison Farrell, Jean Hughes, Seamus Lillis and Ann Lyons (eds), *Mapping civic engagement within higher education in Ireland* (2009), pp 116–23.

Hughes, Jean and Eloise Tan (eds), *The dynamic curriculum: shared experiences of ongoing curricular change in higher education* (Dublin, 2012).

Hughes, Jean and Morag Munro, 'Curriculum change: achieving institutional cohesion while maintaining individual autonomy' in Jean Hughes and Eloise Tan (eds), *The dynamic curriculum: shared experiences of ongoing curricular change in higher education* (Dublin, 2012), pp 19–36.

Hurley, Richard, 'Dublin City University master plan, 1991: critique' in *Irish Architect*, 85 (1991), pp 20–3.

Hussey, F.P., *Albert Agricultural College: centenary souvenir, 1838–1938* ([Dublin], 1938).

Hussey, Gemma, *At the cutting edge: cabinet diaries, 1982–1987* (Dublin, 1990).

Jarrell, Richard A., *Educating the neglected majority: the struggle for agricultural and technical education in nineteenth-century Ontario and Quebec* (Toronto, 2016).

Jones-Evans, Dylan, Magnus Klofsten, Ewa Andersson and Dipti Pandya, 'Creating a bridge between university and industry in small European countries: the role of the Industrial Liaison Office', *R&D Management*, 29:1 (1999), pp 47–56.

Keane, Elaine, 'Widening participation in higher education in the Republic of Ireland: report submitted to HEFCE and OFFA' (Bristol, 2013).

Kelleher, Patricia and Mary Whelan, *Dublin communities in action: a study of six projects* (Dublin, 1992).

Kelly, James (ed.), *St Patrick's College Drumcondra: a history* (Dublin, 2006).

—, 'Afterword' in idem (ed.), *St Patrick's College Drumcondra: a history* (Dublin, 2006), pp 267–74.

Kennedy, Michael and Eoin Kinsella, *Ireland and Japan, 1957–2017: diplomatic, economic and cultural connections* (Dublin, 2017).

Kintzer, 'The Regional Technical College System in Ireland', *Higher Education in Europe*, 6 (1981), pp 55–60.

Loxley, Andrew, Aidan Seery and John Walsh (eds), *Higher education in Ireland: practices, policies and possibilities* (Basingstoke, 2014).

Lynch, Brian, 'The first agricultural broadcasts on 2RN', *History Ireland*, 2:7 (1999).

MacCraith, Brian, 'Transforming our education system to deliver a new Ireland' in Joe Mulholland (ed.), *Transforming Ireland, 2011–2016: essays from the 2011 MacGill Summer School* (Dublin, 2011), pp 272–7.

—, 'DCU Institute of Education: the first Faculty of Education in an Irish university' in Brian Mooney (ed.), *Education Matters Yearbook, 2016–2017* (Castleisland, 2017), pp 25–30.

MacKeogh, Kay and Francesca Lorenzi, 'Preparing students for online learning: the Oscail experience' in Alan Tait and Anne Gaskell (eds), *Reflective practice in open and distance learning: how do we improve?* (Milton Keynes, 2005), pp 101–9.

Maegaard, Bente, 'Eurotra: the machine translation project of the European Communities', *Literary and Linguistic Computing*, 3:2 (1988), pp 61–5.

Manning, Maurice, 'Garret FitzGerald, 1997–' in Tom Dunne (ed.), *National University of Ireland: centenary essays* (Dublin, 2008), pp 163–76.

Martin, Stephen (ed.), *The construction of Europe: essays in honour of Emile Noël* (Florence, 1994).

Maxwell, Nicola and Claire Dorrity, 'Access to third level education: challenges for equality of opportunity in post Celtic-Tiger Ireland', *Irish Journal of Public Policy*, 2:1 (2009).

McCartney, Donal, 'University College Dublin' in Tom Dunne (ed.), *National University of Ireland: centenary essays* (Dublin, 2008), pp 87–99.

McCrea, Colin, 'The crucial role of philanthropy in the Republic of Ireland', https://www.atlanticphilanthropies.org/speeches/speech-dcu-leadership-circle-dinner, accessed 14 Jan. 2017.

Meenan, James, 'The university in Dublin', *Studies*, 57:3 (1968), pp 314–20.

Miller, Ian, *Reforming food in post-Famine Ireland: medicine, science and improvement, 1845–1922* (Manchester, 2014).

McIlrath, Lorraine, Alison Farrell, Jean Hughes, Seamus Lillis and Ann Lyons (eds), *Mapping civic engagement within higher education in Ireland* (2009).

McLoughlin, Cathy and Colette Keogh, 'From a localised Ballymun initiative to a national service – the Access service in DCU, 20 years on!' in Martin Flynn, Denis Staunton and Deirdre Creedon (eds), *Access: are we making the right connections? Proceedings from the pathways to education access conference* (Cork, 2011), pp 64–8.

McLoughlin, Cathy, 'The impact of gender, school status and geography on degree outcomes: a study on the academic performance of access students in Dublin City University, 2009/2010' in HEA, *How equal? Access to higher education in Ireland* (Dublin, 2013), pp 73–9.

McMillan, Norman and Martin Nevin (eds), 'Practical, business and physical education: perspectives from the early years – part 2 of a history of the RTC and IT Carlow', *Carloviana*, 53 (2004), pp 66–82.

Morgan, Mark, *Ballymun Initiative for Third Level Education (BITE) and Limerick Community-Based Educational Initiative (LCBEI): an evaluation of projects supported by the Irish American Partnership* (Dublin, 1995).

Mulcahy, D.G. and Denis O'Sullivan (eds), *Irish educational policy: process and substance* (Dublin, 1989).

Mulholland, Joe (ed.), *Transforming Ireland, 2011–2016: essays from the 2011 MacGill Summer School* (Dublin, 2011).

Munck, Ronaldo and Gordon McConnell, 'University strategic planning and the Foresight/Futures approach', *Planning for Higher Education*, 38:1 (2009), pp 31–40.

Munck, Ronaldo, 'Community-based research: genealogy and prospects' in Ronaldo Munck, Lorraine McIlrath, Budd Hall and Rajesh Tandon (eds), *Higher education and community-based research* (New York, 2014), pp 11–26.

Munck, Ronaldo, Lorraine McIlrath, Budd Hall and Rajesh Tandon (eds), *Higher education and community-based research* (New York, 2014).

Nelson, E.C., 'David Moore, Miles J. Berkeley and scientific studies of potato blight in Ireland, 1845–1847', *Archives of Natural History*, 11:2 (1983), pp 249–61.

Nic Pháidín, Caoilfhionn, 'University education through Irish: place or space?' in Caoilfhionn Nic Pháidín agus Donla uí Bhraonáin (eag.), *University education in Irish: challenges and perspectives* (Dublin, 2004), pp 77–96.

Nic Pháidín, Caoilfhionn agus Donla uí Bhraonáin (eag.), *University education in Irish: challenges and perspectives* (Dublin, 2004).

Nolan, Brian, and Christopher Whelan (eds), *Bust to boom? The Irish experience of growth and inequality* (Dublin, 2000).

Nolan, John, 'The recognised colleges' in Tom Dunne (ed.), *The National University of Ireland, 1908–2008: centenary essays* (Dublin, 2008), pp 192–227.

O'Clery, Conor, *The billionaire who wasn't: how Chuck Feeney secretly made and gave away a fortune* (New York, 2007).

O'Connor, John, *Memoir of a privileged time: a personal history of the development of the University of Limerick, 1972–2012, and pre-history, 1862–1972* (Limerick, 2016).

O'Connor, Muiris, 'Investment in edification: reflections on Irish education policy since independence', *Irish Education Studies*, 33:2 (2014), pp 193–212.

O'Donnell, Marie-Louise, 'The Helix', *Irish Arts Review*, 19:3 (2002), pp 90–7.

—, 'The Helix, Dublin City University: architect's account and review', *Irish Architect*, 183 (2003).

Ó hAilpín, Seán Óg, *The autobiography* (Dublin, 2013).

O'Hare, Daniel, 'The role of the National Institute for Higher Education Dublin in national development', *Science and Technology* (June–July 1981), pp 13–16.

—, 'Economic recession: restraint or opportunity for higher education?', *Irish Educational Studies*, 3:2 (1983), pp 228–37.

O'Rourke, Mary, *Just Mary: a memoir* (Dublin, 2012).

O'Sullivan, Denis, *Cultural politics and Irish education since the 1950s: policy, paradigms and power* (Dublin, 2005).

O'Reilly, Patricia, 'The evolution of university access programmes in Ireland', UCD Geary Institute Discussion Paper Series (Dublin, 2008), www.ucd.ie/geary/static/publications/workingpapers/gearywp200816.pdf, accessed 4 Feb. 2019.

Paletschek, Sylvia, 'The writing of university history and university jubilees: German examples', *Studium*, 5:3 (2012), pp 142–55.

Péchenart, Juliette, and Jenny Williams (eds), *School of Applied Languages and Intercultural Studies: celebrating 30 years, 1980–2010* (Dublin, 2012).

Pratt, John, *The polytechnic experiment, 1965–1992* (Buckingham, 1997).

Rafferty, Kevin, 'All Hallows: from a seminary to an institute for mission and ministry', *Colloque: Journal of the Irish Province of the Congregation of the Mission*, 32 (1995), pp 125–37.

Rafter, Kevin and Mark O'Brien (eds), *The state in transition: essays in honour of John Horgan* (Dublin, 2015).

Rothblatt, Sheldon, 'The writing of university history at the end of another century', *Oxford Review of Education*, 23:2 (1997), pp 151–67.

Rowley, Ellen (ed.), *More than concrete blocks: volume II, 1940–72: Dublin city's twentieth-century buildings and their stories* (Dublin, 2018).

Sheehan, Helena, *Navigating the zeitgeist: a story of the Cold War, the New Left, Irish republicanism, and International Communism* (New York, 2019).

Sheehan, Helena, *Living eons in decades: a story of history after the end of history* (forthcoming).

Sheehan, Paul, 'Dublin City University new library – a library for the information age', *Liber Quarterly*, 10:2 (2000), pp 84–93.

Smyth, Emer and Damian Hannan, 'Education and inequality' in Brian Nolan and Christopher Whelan (eds), *Bust to boom? The Irish experience of growth and inequality* (Dublin, 2000), pp 109–26.

Somerville-Woodward, Robert, *Ballymun, a history: volumes 1 and 2, c.1600–1997, synopsis* (Ballymun, 2002).

Sproule, John, *The Irish Industrial Exhibition of 1853* (Dublin, 1854).

Sugrue, Ciaran, 'Three decades of College life, 1973–99: the old order changeth?' in James Kelly (ed.), *St Patrick's College Drumcondra: a history* (Dublin, 2006), pp 225–66.

Sumner, Jennifer, 'Serving the system: a critical history of distance education', *Open Learning*, 15:3 (2000), pp 267–85.

Tanaka, Yasushi, *The economics of co-operative education* (New York, 2015).

Thelin, John and Richard Trollinger, *Philanthropy and American higher education* (New York, 2014).

Trench, Brian, Padraig Murphy and Declan Fahy (eds), *Little country, big talk: science communication in Ireland* (Dublin, 2017).

Trench, Brian, 'The rocky road of science communication in Ireland' in Brian Trench, Padraig Murphy and Declan Fahy (eds), *Little country, big talk: science communication in Ireland* (Dublin, 2017), pp 1–25.

Turner, Paul, *Campus: an American planning tradition* (Boston, 1984).

Walsh, Brendan (ed.), *Degrees of nonsense: the demise of the university in Ireland* (Dublin, 2012).

— (ed.), *Essays in the history of Irish education* (London, 2016).

Walsh, Ed, with Kieran Fagan, *Upstart: friends, foes and founding a university* (Cork, 2011).

Walsh, John, *The politics of expansion: the transformation of educational policy in the Republic of Ireland, 1957–72* (Manchester, 2009).

—, 'A quiet revolution: international influence, domestic elites and the transformation of higher technical education in Ireland, 1959–72', *Irish Educational Studies*, 30:3 (2011), pp 365–81.

—, 'The transformation of higher education in Ireland, 1945–80' in Andrew Loxley, Aidan Seery and John Walsh (eds), *Higher education in Ireland: practices, policies and possibilities* (Basingstoke, 2014), pp 5–32.

—, 'A contemporary history of Irish higher education, 1980–2011' in Andrew Loxley, Aidan Seery and John Walsh (eds), *Higher education in Ireland: practices, policies and possibilities* (Basingstoke, 2014), pp 33–54.

—, *Higher education in Ireland, 1922–2016: politics, policy and power* (London, 2018).

Walsh, John, Selina McCoy, Aidan Seery and Paul Conway (eds), *Investment in education and the intractability of inequality, Irish Educational Studies* special issue, 33:2 (2014).

Walsh, John, Selina McCoy, Aidan Seery and Paul Conway, 'Editorial: *Investment in education* and the intractability of inequality' in idem (eds), *Investment in education*, pp 119–22.

Walsh, Tom, 'The national system of education, 1831–2000' in Brendan Walsh (ed.), *Essays in the history of Irish education* (London, 2016), pp 7–43.

Walshe, John, *An education: how an outsider became an insider and learned what really goes on in Irish government* (Dublin, 2014).

Wejchert, Andrzej, *A&D Wejchert & Partners* (Kinsale, 2008).

White, Tony, 'Higher technological education in the 1970s', *Irish Educational Studies*, 1:1 (1981), pp 310–31.

—, *Investing in people: higher education in Ireland from 1960 to 2000* (Dublin, 2001).

Woodhall, Maureen, *Review of student support schemes in selected OECD countries* (Paris, 1978).

Theses

Leavy, M.G., 'Managing the nurse tutor transition: a case study of organisational socialisation' (MSc, DCU, 2003).

MacKeogh, Katherine M., 'Encouraging distance education? An analysis of EU policy on distance education, 1957–2004' (PhD, NUI Maynooth, 2005).

Index

Page numbers in italics refer to illustrations.